Mastering Resource Management

Using Microsoft® Project and Project Server 2010

Collin Quiring, *PMP, MCTS, MCT, MCP*
Tanya Foster, *PMP, MCTS, MCT*

ISBN-13: 978-1-60427-065-5

Printed and bound in the U.S.A. Printed on acid-free paper.

10 9 8 7 6 5 4 3 2 1

Library of Congress Cataloging-in-Publication Data

Quiring, Collin, 1970–
Mastering resource management using Microsoft Project and Project Server 2010 / by Collin Quiring and Tanya Foster.
p. cm.
Includes index.
ISBN 978-1-60427-065-5 (pbk. : alk. paper)
1. Microsoft Project. 2. Project management—Computer programs. I. Foster, Tanya. II. Title.
HD69.P75Q57 2011
658.4'04028553—dc23
2011025146

Direct all inquiries to J. Ross Publishing, Inc., 5765 N. Andrews Way, Fort Lauderdale, FL 33309.

Phone: (954) 727-9333
Fax: (561) 892-0700
Web: www.jrosspub.com

Contents

Acknowledgements v
About the Authors vii
Introduction ix

Chapter 1: Resource Management: What Is It Good For? 1

Different Perspectives of Resource Management 4
The Resource 5
The Resource Manager 5
The Project Manager 6
The Executive 6
What's New in Project 2010? 7
Standard and Professional Editions 7
Microsoft Project Versions 8
New Features in Project Server 2010 11

Chapter 2: Microsoft Project 2010: Why Use it? 17

Chapter 3: Things to Think About: Resource Calendars, Tasks, and Security 25

Project Calendars 25
Understanding Task Types 28
Task Type Examples 29
Security 31

Chapter 4: Who Can Work When: Project Calendars 35

Chapter 5: Resources in the Pool 51
Types of Resources 51
How to Use Resource Management in Project 2010 52
Resource Pool—PWA Initial Setup 53
Resource Pool—Stand-alone Setup 62
Using the Resource Pool 66

Chapter 6: Who Is Working When: Resource Calendars 73
Changing Working Time for One Resource 74

Chapter 7: Assigning a Resource 89
The Team Planner 104
Assigning Resources by Skill Set 113

Chapter 8: Update Cycle and Approvals 135
The Update Cycle 145
Automatic Approvals 162

Chapter 9: Timesheets 169
Timesheet Entry 170
Miscellaneous Items 186
Timesheet Setup 191

Chapter 10: Leveling Resource Assignments 209

Chapter 11: Utilizing Resources 219
The Resource Center 219
Stand-alone Resource Pool 225

Chapter 12: Information Is Everywhere 237
Views in Project Professional 238
Creating a New View 242
Editing an Existing View 244
Reports in Project Professional 249
Visual Reports 251
Views in Project Server 262
Reports in Project Server 268

Chapter 13: A Portfolio Perspective 279

Chapter 14: Questions and Answers 293

Chapter 15: Conclusion 301

Appendix A: Resource Planning 303

Appendix B: Resource Manager Guide 309

Index 321

Acknowledgements

Collin:

I would like to thank my family for their patience and understanding while I work on "that project management" thing. I would also like to thank George, Dennis, Tim, Tanya, and Bruce for keeping me on my toes and making sure that I keep enthusiastic and committed to resource and project management.

Tanya:

I would like to thank my family and friends for their support and encouragement. I would also like to thank Collin Quiring and Tim Gryder for sharing their knowledge of Microsoft Project and for encouraging me to jump in with both feet.

About the Authors

Collin Quiring

Collin Quiring has worked in the area of project management for over 15 years. He has implemented project management offices (PMOs) for two separate companies during that time and has worked with clients across industries and of various sizes. This includes Fortune 100, Global 100, mid-market and small-market organizations. His experience is in several industries and has concentrated on project management, resource management, product development, systems administration, and training.

During his career, he has developed a passion for helping organizations better understand their project and resource management needs and the methodologies to obtain and maintain that information. His focus is on aligning an organization's strategic objectives with the business and technology processes required to demonstrate effective results.

From a technical perspective, Collin is an expert in Microsoft Project Server. He has worked with all aspects of the tool from installation to configuration to daily administration. Due to his business perspective and insight, he has always worked with clients to have the software match the business needs as much as possible—rather than forcing the business to change everything they do to match a software setting.

Collin is a project manager, consultant, trainer and speaker for project management and Microsoft Project Server. He is the managing partner with PMP specialists and holds PMP, MCTS, MCT, MCP and CIRM certifications along with an MBA.

Read Collin's blog at www.PMPSpecialists.com/blog
Visit PMP Specialists at www.PMPSpecialists.com

Tanya Foster

Tanya Foster has over 10 years of experience in project management, scheduling administration, operations, customer service and training. She possesses strong communication and training skills which she has used to help organizations quickly bring their staff to a proficient level of use on new software tools or business processes. Her experiences have led her to interact with all levels of the organization and to customize her training material to emphasize what is important to each level of the organization.

During her career, Tanya has organized and consulted on project management offices and project management methodologies with specific industry accepted project management procedures. She has developed training programs for organizations for both Microsoft Project Server and PMOs. She has also created Microsoft Project training for computer based modules so that students could take the training when it was convenient to them. Along with teaching microsoft project, Tanya has trained students in the project management body of knowledge by the Project Management Institute.

She has also consulted with organizations to implement advanced scheduling techniques to best use Microsoft Project. Along with helping organizations with the tool, Tanya has assisted in the creation and implementation of the scheduling logic and project file creation. She has also actively administered Microsoft Project Server for organizations.

Tanya is a project manager, trainer and consultant for Microsoft Project Server and project management. She is a consultant with PMP Specialists and holds PMP, MCTS and MCT certifications.

Introduction

As we consult with different organizations in a myriad of industries and company sizes, we seem to continually encounter a need to better understand, utilize, and manage resources. There are other issues as well, but having the ability to understand and oversee resource capacity, utilization, and assignments assist organizations to gain better planning, scheduling, and awareness of their situation. This, in turn, helps in many areas of project management. Understanding resource management can allow an organization to better track costs as well as create a better plan. We wrote this book to help organizations with their resource management needs and ultimately their project management capabilities.

This book is broken into sections that cover the topics pertinent to resource management using Microsoft Project Server 2010 with Microsoft Project Professional and stand-alone Microsoft Project Professional. It is understood that the tool is complex and large; however it is not our goal to demonstrate every part of Microsoft Project Server 2010 or Microsoft Project Professional. The purpose of this book is to cover the parts of the tool that directly affect resources and scheduling. For example, in this book we discuss resource calendars, which directly affect when a resource can work. This, in turn, affects how tasks are scheduled, start dates, finish dates, costs, and other variables. While we cover the calendars and the effects on the resource and the schedule, we do not attempt to include every possible side effect to the overall schedule—we demonstrate only how a calendar will change a tasks' date when assigned to a resource.

Where applicable, each chapter is broken into sections that include a bit of the philosophy or the "why" part of how Project Server works. It is our experience with clients that understanding "why" the tool does something is as important as understanding how to set it up.

Microsoft Project is based upon the Project Management Institute's standards for project management and as such uses similar terminology. It also has a philosophy behind how it is designed. One example of this is that it accounts for a project manager, resource manager, and resource as three separate individuals. They have three separate functions (explained in more detail in Chapter 1 and throughout this book) and at some companies there are separate individuals performing each of these roles. However, at some organizations one person is the project manager, resource manager and even sometimes a resource on their own schedule. So while we talk about these as separate individuals, please note that in some cases they are one person.

There is more than one version of Microsoft Project 2010 on the market so it is important to note that all discussions and examples are with Project Professional 2010. Due to the fact that many customers have Microsoft Project Professional without Microsoft Project Server, this book is about Project Server and stand-alone project professional. That said, each chapter will first cover how server and/or professional work and then how professional works in stand-alone mode. Normally, server will have more capabilities and functions than the stand-alone version and we will highlight those as we go through each chapter.

This book has free material available for download from the Web Added Value™ resource center at *www.jrosspub.com*

At J. Ross Publishing we are committed to providing today's professional with practical, hands-on tools that enhance the learning experience and give readers an opportunity to apply what they have learned. That is why we offer free ancillary materials available for download on this book and all participating Web Added Value™ publications. These online resources may include interactive versions of material that appears in the book or supplemental templates, worksheets, models, plans, case studies, proposals, spreadsheets and assessment tools, among other things. Whenever you see the WAV™ symbol in any of our publications, it means bonus materials accompany the book and are available from the Web Added Value Download Resource Center at www.jrosspub.com.

Downloads available for *Mastering Resource Management Using Microsoft® Project and Project Server 2010* consist of:

Tips On:

- How the project server administrator can forcibly check in a project when it incorrectly appears to be checked out
- Options that affect schedule date movement
- Differences in the Save, Save As and Publish options and how they affect the project managers and team members that are using the schedule
- The three task types to calculate the time of a task and how this works in Microsoft Project

Templates:

- A quick guide to some of the latest modifications found in Microsoft Project
- A new detailed feature's guide for Project 2010

Presentation:

- Making a Case for Implementing Microsoft Project, Project Server and Project Management Concepts—'The Value of Project Management'

1

Resource Management: What Is It Good For?

Resource management is an area of project management that is often overlooked. However, it is a critical part of the process of providing value to customers. Whether your projects are for internal or external customers, the ability to understand resource needs is critical.

Consider this example, when a manufacturing company gets a one million dollar sale for 1000 widgets, they should know the costs, how long it will take to produce the widgets, what the profit margins will be, and numerous other variables. This is because they know the costing variables, the machine production rates, the capacity of each machine in the plant, the number of other jobs in the queue, and they have tracked these variables over time to gain a perspective of what the numbers should be for a normal production run. However, this is not always the case when an organization gets a one million dollar sale that involves human resources. Most organizations that rely on their human resources to produce an end product usually do not have a great tracking method, and therefore do not have a historical perspective of the timelines and costs involved in producing the deliverables for a new sale.

In the manufacturing example, a key variable that is usually known is what effect a new job will have on existing jobs if it is given a higher priority. This is not the case when dealing with work that involves people. For some reason, there seems to be an assumption that capacity is always available and that all work gets done on the original timeline, even as new work is added or as priorities shift.

While there is a myriad of reasons why some projects fail, it is our experience that resource management is a key factor. Failing to realize the effects of changing priorities on existing work or on additional work will almost always result in a failed project, whether by missing the deadline, in costing more than estimated, or through poorer results.

This book is about human resources and how Microsoft Project helps to better manage and understand an organization's ability to utilize them. This book does not assume that people and their productivity are just as easily quantified as a machine that makes widgets. In fact, it is this very distinction of people vs. machines that makes resource management so difficult.

When executives or other stakeholders need to know the capacity of the workforce, they should be able to easily obtain an answer. In fact, they should be able to ask a number of questions and get answers very quickly. For example, they should be able to ask:

- What is the resource capacity?
- What is the capacity for a given skill set?
- What are our available skill sets?
- What is the existing utilization of our capacity?
- What is the utilization of our specific skill sets?
- How long does it normally take to do this type of project?
- What is the existing portfolio of our projects?
- How does the portfolio of projects affect our resources?
- What types of skill sets do we need for proposed projects?
- How will existing projects be affected by a new project?
- If we take on a new project, when can we realistically tell the customer we can complete it?
- What will our resource costs be for a new project?
- What are the costs for our existing projects?
- What existing projects are on track?
- What projects are late or costing us more due to lack of resources?
- How can we resolve resource issues?
- Does the resource know what work they are expected to do this week?
- Does the resource know what work they are expected to do next week, or next month?

- Does the project manager know how much capacity and utilization a resource has to help on their project?

Resource management is a valuable tool that can answer these questions, and in the level of detail that you want in order to track and understand the answers. In other words, it is possible to know what every resource in your organization is doing every minute of the day. Although, you would have to be willing to track at a level that would be burdensome on resources and make reporting so voluminous as to be meaningless. However, it is possible to track at a level that gives the detailed information desired without being burdensome.

It isn't that difficult to track detailed information, but it does require a level of discipline and a desire to use the information. At this point, saying "it isn't that difficult" doesn't always agree with experience. And, that statement is not taken lightly.

Think of it this way: starting a project with any new tactic can be difficult, but the authors contend that you are already doing this at one level or another. Let's start at the end. How do you know when a project is complete? There is a deliverable or task that is completed, and then the original intent of the project is done; however, how do you know that the work is done? Does the resource manager or project manager ask the resource responsible regarding when the work is done? Does the resource tell you it is done? There is *some* method that you know to call the project complete when the work is done. So start there, and build on that foundation.

When a task is assigned, how do you know how long it will take? Does the resource give you the number of days it will take? Great, we have some information with which to start. As we track durations over time, the ability (and that of the resource) will get better and at some point we will *know* how long it takes to do a job. That new knowledge will give us a better ability to assign resources and understand their capacity and utilization.

There are lots of opportunities to set up Microsoft Project Server and Microsoft Project Professional to gain better information about resources so that managers can be better schedulers. Like many programs produced by Microsoft, there are numerous configurations and options available. The authors do not advocate using every option and feature on the first day, but, rather, developing the ability to set up more and more of the options, so that information is available that provides real value.

Resource management should be about making information available to those that need it in a timely manner, so that better business decisions can be made. Better decisions can become a competitive advantage over other businesses or can become a center of excellence within an organization. This ability can also avert lots of frustration.

When a customer is told that their organization will receive a product or service from you on a certain date, he or she will expect it on that date. If you can't deliver it on time, the customer may not have a choice but to stay with you this time. However, if a competitor can explain to the customer how long it will take them and give some sort of data to back it up, then the competitor will probably get the business next time. How many times can a project be late before the market in general takes notice and stops dealing with your organization? There are some customers that have other commitments that are based upon yours, and the cost to them of your being late can be huge. Resource management alone is not the sole cause for being late, nor is it the sole answer to being on time, but it does seem to be a substantial cause. There seems to be an assumption that human capacity is unlimited in our organizations, and another sale is always a good thing or another internal project is acceptable. Generally, this leads to issues if relying on resource skill sets in short supply.

We have seen numerous lawsuits that have roots in poor resource management. One involved bidding against another company for some work that involved a large number of people over a period of a few years. We produced a few reports based on experience and also showed the customer a schedule in Microsoft Project. Our competitor promised the same deliverables at a slightly higher cost within a significantly reduced time period. We explained to the customer that we had no understanding of how they could do it in that time period without a lot more resources and more cost. Our competitor also didn't produce a schedule or other reports for the customer. Well, the customer went with the competitor. After a couple years, the project was cancelled because it was drastically over budget and was behind on deliverables. The customer is suing our competitor and now has wasted two years and millions of dollars and still has nothing to show for it.

Different Perspectives of Resource Management

Let's take a moment to view resource management from a few different perspectives. Resource management is not just for the benefit of a project management office or to be able to create a set of reports. It is to benefit all persons and organizations involved.

The Resource

First, take the perspective of a resource. Put yourself in the place of the resource. You have project work to do; you always have project work to do! But, is there a comprehensive list of that work somewhere, and, how does that project work coordinate with all of the other things you have to do—like going to company meetings, required training, administrative duties, and other time consuming items that aren't accounted for on the project list? Do the project managers and resource managers know about all the things you have to do that aren't on the one project? Do they know about the vacation that you are taking next month? How do you let all the project and resource managers know about your upcoming vacation when none of them are in your corporate chain of command?

In addition to similar things to worry about, do you have a way to demonstrate your workload to the project and resource managers? Do you have a way to show your supervisor that work? It is one thing to claim that you are busy, but it is another to demonstrate how busy you are. Also, how do you go about updating your tasks to show what work you are doing, what you have done, and what might be late? If you are overcapacity and supposed to be working on two separate projects at the same time, which one is the priority?

The Resource Manager

Now, put yourself in the place of the resource manager. This is the person responsible for a group of resources. For this case, let's say you are the resource manager of 25 people, all of whom have different capabilities. You will want to know:

- Who is available, and when?
- Who has what skill set?
- When each of them is going on vacation?
- Can they be assigned work by other resource or project managers, and are they being requested for other projects?
- What is the capacity of each resource, and what is their utilization?

- What hours and days do resources work, and what time zone are they in?

From a functional viewpoint as the resource manager, you want to also make sure that the resources are updating their tasks in a timely manner. How are they updating them? Are all the resources doing it the same way? Are they updating tasks to show which ones they will be on time with or late in completing?

The Project Manager

Switch perspectives to the view of the project manager. The focus is on resource management, so thinking about how resources are affecting the project schedule as a project manager will lead you to having the same questions as the resource manager. You will also be thinking about how a resource's updating affects your master schedule. Assuming a waterfall schedule format, if a resource isn't updating at all, it can affect your schedule since you have to assume that the work isn't done and you can't move on to the next task. Or, if a resource is updating a task and states that he or she will be two weeks late, how does that affect your schedule? What if you are expecting a task to be completed on a certain date, but don't know if that is the time period when a resource is on vacation? How are your projects and that of other project managers interrelated, and being affected by a particular resource?

The Executive

Now, put yourself in the place of an executive in charge of the portfolio selection process. You will want to know:

- How many resources with a certain skill set are needed next month? What about next year?
- What schedules are sliding because you don't understand current resource issues?
- How are resources being utilized?
- How much time is being spent on certain projects?
- How much cost is associated with those projects?
- Which projects have the same resource promised to them?
- How do you communicate the priority level of each project to every resource (not just to project managers or other executives)?

- Which of the proposed projects can you do now and which should you wait on due to resource constraints?

Proper resource management helps a resource, resource manager, project manager, and executive answer all of those questions, and more. As long as managers assume that there is unlimited human capacity, the practice will continue of over-promising and under-delivering to customers. Or, will surprise events drive "all hands on deck" situations where everybody stops what they are doing on multiple projects to concentrate their work on one project—all because the resource situation was not managed well from the beginning!

Now, let us review what is new about Microsoft Project 2010 as it pertains to resource management.

What's New in Project 2010?

Standard and Professional Editions

Throughout this book we demonstrate and discuss the features and functionality of Microsoft Project Professional 2010 and Microsoft Project Server 2010 as they relate to resources and resource management. The authors do not always indicate when an item is new, modified, enhanced, or a previous feature or function. However, the authors wanted to provide an indication of what is new in the latest version in regard to resource management. Before discussing what is new, we want to explain the Project 2010 editions on the market.

To clarify, there are two editions of Project 2010. This is the software that is installed on the client machine (the project manager or resource manager's computer). There are the Project 2010 Standard and Professional editions. The only edition that can connect to Project Server is the Professional edition. The Professional edition has more functions and features. If you are in the market for this software, you can purchase the Professional edition even if you don't currently have Project Server. This edition may be more useful because you would have to upgrade to Professional if you want to use Project Server later, and because it has some more capabilities that you may wish to use as project needs change.

Microsoft provides documentation from a high-level view about differences in the Standard and Professional editions. A summary chart of edition differences can be found on Microsoft's website. The part of this chart that is most pertinent to resource management is "At-a-Glance Resource Management."

This refers to the new Team Planner view and other capabilities of Project Professional 2010. We cover the Team Planner in detail in Chapter 7, Assigning a Resource. The chart appears in Figure 1–1.

Microsoft Project Versions

Now that we have clarified some differences between the Standard and Professional editions, we want to show some differences in the versions of Microsoft Project. Again, Microsoft has provided a document to review all of this information, which can be downloaded as a PDF file from the Microsoft website.

Which Edition Of Project Is Right For You ?

	Microsoft Project Standard 2010	Microsoft Project Professional 2010
Simplified Navigation New graphical menus and a more intuitive experience make every action easier.	★	★
New Timeline With a clearer view of tasks, milestones, and phases, your timelines are easier to see and share.	★	★
Flexible Scheduling Reduce complexity with the ability to choose the level of detail that's right for your project.	★	★
At-A-Glance Resource Management Visually create the right mix of resources—it's as easy as drag-and-drop.		★
Easier Collaboration Connect your teams with Microsoft SharePoint Foundation 2010 synchronization or Microsoft Project Server 2010.		★

Figure 1–1

We have copied the part of that chart that most directly applies to the resource management aspects of Microsoft Project. To help understand the symbols in the chart, the key is in Figure 1–2.

Feature Key:

included	improved	new

Figure 1–2

When the word PRO appears (next to Team Resources and Team Planner), it represents capabilities that are available in Professional 2010 but not Standard 2010, as shown in Figure 1–3.

Resource Planning and Management	2003	2007	Project Standard 2010/Project Professional 2010
Work, Generic and Material Resources Define and assign named work (person or equipment) resources, generic (skill-based, for example, DBA) resources, or consumable material resources such as lumber or concrete.	●	●	●
Cost Resources Support accounting system integration and definition of multiple time-phased fixed costs on each task.		✪	●
Team Resources PRO Associate enterprise resources with a team to show team allocation, assignment and status and to allow resources within the team to assign themselves to team tasks.*		✪	●
Team Planner PRO Visually drag and drop resources in an interactive resource view to simplify complex resource scenarios.			✪
Resource Sheet and Usage Views Use variety of views to change resource information and review work and allocation details.	●	●	●
Resource Leveling Recognize and correct resource overload scenarios using various resource leveling techniques.	●	●	●
Resource Substitution Easily locate qualified resources to substitute for scarce or unavailable resources.	●	●	●

Figure 1–3

New Features in Project Server 2010

Microsoft Project Server 2010 has new features and functions. Microsoft has produced a document for this as well on its website. The key is the same as in the Project Professional versions documentation shown in Figure 1–4.

Feature Key:
included improved new

Figure 1–4

This document covers many items. The pieces of this document that are most pertinent to resource management are given in Figures 1–5, 1–6, 1–7, and 1–8.

Capacity Planning (Skill level)	EPM 2003		EPM 2007		EPM 2010
	Project Server 2003 & Project Professional 2003	Project Portfolio Server 2006	Project Server 2007 & Project Professional 2007	Project Portfolio Server 2007	Project Server 2010 & Project Professional 2010
Understand Resource Capacity Proactively identify resource (by skill) surplus and deficit across a planning horizon.	○		○		●
Reschedule Projects to Maximize Resource Utilization Improve utilization and fully staff projects by adjusting schedules within the planning horizon.					✪
Model Headcount Decisions Model headcount decisions by hiring full-time or contract resources and understand impact on the project portfolio.					✪
Easily Compare Capacity Planning Scenarios Compare and contrast capacity analyses side by side.					✪
Automate Portfolio Selection Commit selected portfolio scenario and automatically update project workflow.					✪

Figure 1–5

Resource Management	EPM 2003		EPM 2007		EPM 2010
	Project Server 2003 & Project Professional 2003	Project Portfolio Server 2006	Project Server 2007 & Project Professional 2007	Project Portfolio Server 2007	Project Server 2010 & Project Professional 2010
Enterprise-wide Resource Pool Create and manage an enterprise resource pool containing all resources and skills.	○	○	○	○	●
Filter Resources by Business Units Establish and manage resources at the business unit level.					✪
Automate Resource Pool Creation Automate resource pool creation by syncing with Active Directory or integrating with ERP or line-of business systems.	○		○		●
Define Material Resources Add consumable material resources such as lumber or concrete and assign them to tasks.	○		○		○
Resource Calendars Define resource calendars to reflect resource-specific working times, availability and non-working exceptions (e.g., vacations, sick days, etc.)	○		●		○
Multiple-skill Resources Assign multiple skills and cost rates to an individual resource.	○		○		○
Match Resources Based on Multiple Dimensions Easily find resources with availability to work on the project using multiple criteria (e.g., skills, location, availability, department etc.)	○		○		○
Capture Resource Demand Plan resource demand prior to assigning resources to tasks.		○	✪	○	○
Proposed vs. Committed Bookings Differentiate between proposed and committed resource assignments.	○		○		○
Support Team Assignments Assign work to teams and allow a member of the team to take ownership of the assignment.			✪		○

Figure 1–6

	EPM 2003		EPM 2007		EPM 2010
	Project Server 2003 & Project Professional 2003	Project Portfolio Server 2006	Project Server 2007 & Project Professional 2007	Project Portfolio Server 2007	Project Server 2010 & Project Professional 2010
Resource Management					
Effectively Manage Resources Intuitively and effectively manage assignments by resource and quickly visualize over allocation.	○		○		●
Easily Substitute Resources Effectively substitute resources.	○		○		●
Communicate and Delegate Tasks Communicate resource assignments and allow individuals to accept and delegate tasks.	○		●		●
Balance Resource Workloads Use resource leveling features to overcome over-allocation.	○		○		●
Time and Task Management					
Web-based Timesheet System Easy to use time entry for timesheet (including working and non-working time, e.g., vacation, sick leave, etc.) and task updates.	○		●		●
Consolidated Progress and Time Tracking Submit project status and timesheet entries from a single interface.					★
Integrate Time Reporting with Financial Systems Report actual hours for project, administrative, and non-working time to financial systems (e.g., for payroll, costing, chargeback, etc.)			★		●
Create New Tasks for Time Reporting Allow users to add tasks to projects and timesheets for complete time reporting.	○		●		●
Use Outlook to View and Update Tasks Maximize user productivity by managing tasks in Outlook.	○		●		●
Communicate on Task Assignments Receive task notification and updates via PC and Web.	○		○		●

Figure 1–7

Time and Task Management	EPM 2003		EPM 2007		EPM 2010
	Project Server 2003 & Project Professional 2003	Project Portfolio Server 2006	Project Server 2007 & Project Professional 2007	Project Portfolio Server 2007	Project Server 2010 & Project Professional 2010
Timesheet Approvals Project and functional managers approve progress and timesheet updates.	○		●		●
Multi-Level Timesheet Routing Perform multi-step timesheet reviews and approvals.					✪
Approval Preview Preview changes online before accepting them into your schedule.			✪		●
Control Timesheet Entry Allow time entry within approved and open date ranges.			✪		○
Submit and Approve Time on Behalf of Others Take on a role of another user to perform time entry and task approvals when needed.			✪		●
Extensible Timesheets Flexible and extensible timesheet design.			✪		●

Figure 1–8

As can be seen by the starred items in the figures above, many new capabilities have been added to Microsoft Project Server 2010. Also, as shown by the darkened circles, there have been a lot of improvements. These modifications have made the information flow faster and easier between the resources and the resource manager. The new modifications have also allowed resource information to be seen from multiple viewpoints.

2

Microsoft Project 2010: Why Use It?

As stated in the Introduction, some of the philosophical background behind Microsoft Project will be provided to help understand the "why" of each chapter. The authors' goal is to help you understand not just "check box 4, on screen 3" but *why* that box should be checked. This chapter is an introduction to Microsoft Project Server and Microsoft Project Professional, and how they interact, to provide a foundation for understanding the following chapters. As such, while this chapter is an introduction of a technical, software "tool," it is important to understand that this tool is there to help with project management, resource management, and portfolio management.

While Project 2010 is constructed to include as many variables and customer types as possible, and designed to be a viable product on the market, it should be used to best match your organization's needs. The options and capabilities should be used according to your business and to customer and stakeholder needs. We will discuss how to match needs and software options in more detail in the following chapters.

Microsoft spent considerable time and effort aligning Project Professional and Project Server to the standards of the Project Management Institute's Project Management Body of Knowledge (*PMBOK® Guide*). This coordinated effort helps organizations that align their business processes to the *PMBOK® Guide* to more easily use Microsoft Project. Use of the guide has helped in the area of vocabulary since many terms in the *PMBOK® Guide* and in Microsoft Project are the same and have the same definitions. At the same time, Project is flexible enough that those organizations that do not adhere as tightly to the principles in the *PMBOK® Guide* can still use the software in their own manner. It all comes down to which options you set, and your business procedures, on how to best use this tool.

Since this chapter is the introduction to the tools that are used for resource management, it is beneficial to know the philosophy that Microsoft has placed behind their product. It sometimes helps to have an understanding of what the tools' goals are, and the philosophy of the developers, to better understand how to configure settings for your needs. Therefore, we have added some of Microsoft's philosophy about these tools as they relate to resource management:

> In today's competitive and changing markets, organizations are looking to maximize return on investment (ROI) and drive efficiencies to sustain the business and support future growth. Resources are arguably an organization's most valuable asset and potentially its biggest expense. Proper management and optimal use of resources is key for an organization to realize its business strategy. With intelligent resource management, an organization can develop and retain a world-class workforce.

Adopting best-practice resource management techniques helps organizations accomplish the following:

> **Gain visibility and control using an enterprise resource pool.** With a large number of employees and globally dispersed teams, it can become difficult to keep track of who is available, what they are capable of doing, and where they are located. Centralizing resources and standardizing metadata about the enterprise resource pool is the first step to gaining visibility and control.
>
> **Proactively compare capacity to demand to maximize resource utilization.** Resource capacity often will determine whether organizations are able to complete strategic projects in a specific planning horizon. Capturing resource requirements early in the project life cycle helps analysts anticipate future demand and proactively schedule projects to maximize resource utilization.

Find the right people for the project. Projects often include globally dispersed teams and require a diverse set of skills. Finding the right people with availability for each project significantly increases the chance of successfully completing the initiative and realizing ROI. Managers need to be able to effectively tap the resource pool to find potential candidates and then quickly see if they are available to join the team.

Intuitively manage resource assignments and overcome conflicts. Managers improve project success rates by effectively managing resource assignments. This means quickly resolving over-allocation and reacting to resource conflicts. Managers require tools that help them assess and manage assignments through the project life cycle and easily communicate with team members about assignments. (*Microsoft Enterprise Project Management, Microsoft EPM Solution Guide*, Microsoft Corporation, 2010, p. 48)

Many customers have Project Professional without Project Server and this book is about Microsoft Project Server *and* stand-alone Microsoft Project Professional which acknowledges those customers. Some books are just about how Project Professional and Project Server interact without consideration of how Professional is used by organizations without Project Server. Therefore, when applicable, each chapter will first cover how Project Server and/or Project Professional work together, and then how Project Professional works in stand-alone mode. Normally, Project Server will have more capabilities and functions than the stand-alone version of Project Professional, and we will highlight some differences in each chapter.

The first step in using the Project Server capabilities is to be able to connect to Project Professional. In order to connect, you need to have Microsoft Project Professional 2010. The Microsoft Project 2010 Standard edition does not connect to Project Server. Also, note that Project Professional 2007 can connect to Project Server 2010 if the Server has the compatibility option selected.

Since this book is only about the resource management portions of Project Server and not about its installation or configuration, it is assumed that you already have a fully functional connection to an installed Project Server 2010 installed with your client copy of Project Professional 2010. However, we also understand that this might be your starting point and you may not have connected to Project Server. Therefore, here are the steps to connect Project Server 2010:

1. Open Project Professional.
2. Go to File, Info, Manage Accounts (Figure 2–1).

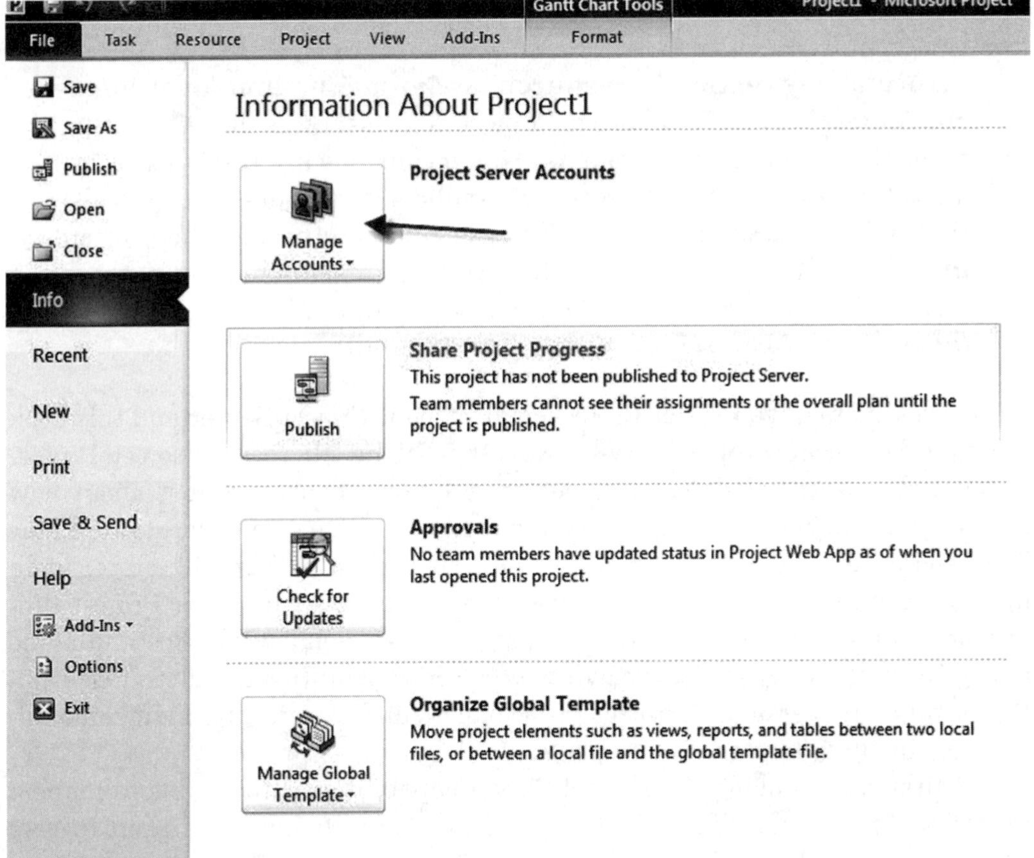

Figure 2–1

A pop-up box, Project Server Accounts, appears (Figure 2–2).

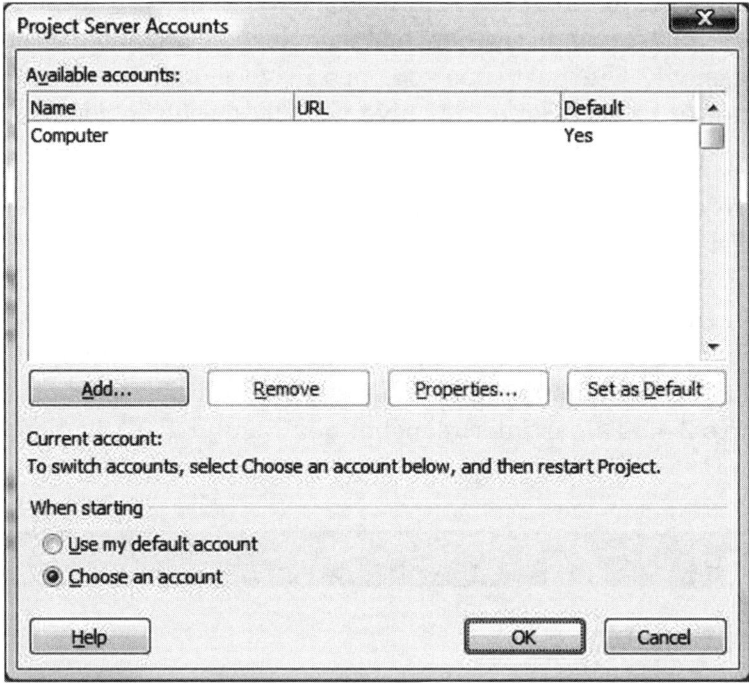

Figure 2–2

3. Click Add.
4. Enter something you will remember in the *Account Name* field.
5. Enter the URL in the *Project Server URL* field (Figure 2–3).

Account Properties

Account Name:

My PWA Site Name

Project Server URL:

http://servername.com/instance

Set as default account

OK Cancel

Figure 2–3

6. If this is the URL that you use most often, then select the *Set as default account* checkbox.

7. After clicking OK, you are back at the *Project Server Accounts* box.
8. Select *Choose an Account*, in case you add more instances or often go off-line.
9. Close Professional. The next time you open Professional, it will automatically connect to Project Server (or give you the option to connect if you chose the Manual option).

As a note of clarification, when this book refers to Project Server, it is really referring to Project Web App (PWA), not the actual hardware where the Project Server software is residing. The PWA homepage may look different for different users based upon the security settings and organizational design of the page. Since it is SharePoint Server based, web parts can be easily modified, added, or removed, resulting in some instances of PWA looking different than others. As an example, Figure 2–4 is a partial screenshot of a regular PWA homepage for an Administrator.

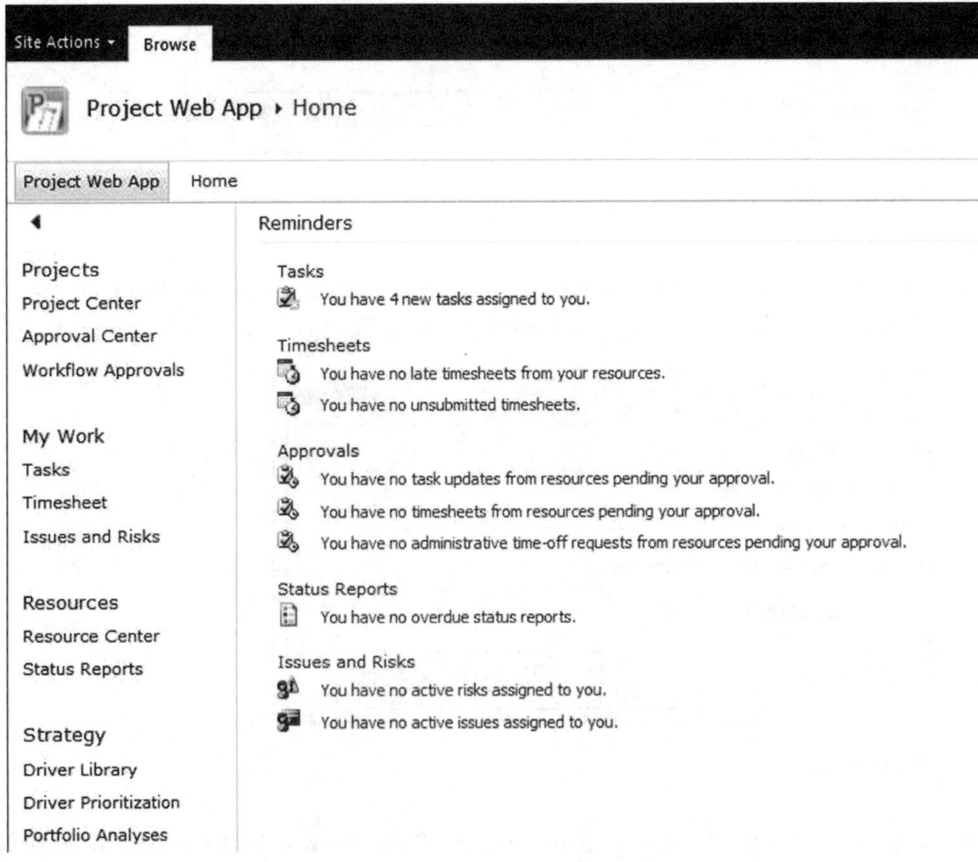

Figure 2–4

Figure 2–5 is an example of that same page for a user with more limited permissions.

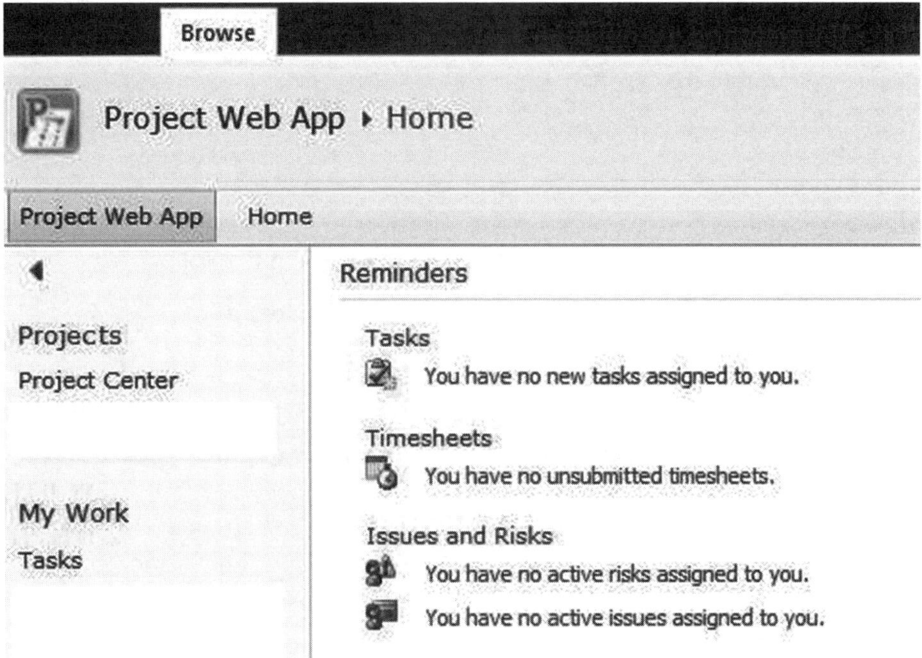

Figure 2–5

The screenshots and images used in this book are based upon the "out of the box" Project Server 2010 and Project Professional 2010 software. There are no third-party software additions to the examples. Understanding how Project Server and Project Professional work in a normal environment help the organization gain more value from the software. Understanding how the existing software works is key to being able to understand when it might be beneficial to purchase third-party software to add functionality.

It is the authors' goal that you and your organization will benefit from Project Professional and Project Server by gaining a better understanding of how a feature or function works *and* some of the reasoning as to why it works the way that it does. Learning resource management and Project is a bit like putting together the pieces of a puzzle and in some cases it takes an awareness of many of the pieces before a more comprehensive understanding is obtained. The authors' intention is to help you put those pieces together.

Things to Think About: Resource Calendars, Tasks, and Security

While this book concentrates on resources, there are many decisions about how to set up Microsoft Project 2010 that affect the way a schedule interacts with resources. The settings for task movement, task types, and the general way in which a schedule is constructed all affect how resources interact with the schedule. The security for what a resource can and can't do in PWA or Project Professional is determined by the Administrator and can be either restrictive or permissive. Security settings and many scheduling options are outside the scope of this book, so we will not be covering them in-depth. However, the general hierarchy of security is discussed at the end of this chapter.

It is important to note there are some scheduling options that are not necessarily specific to resources that will affect the resource or affect how a resource assignment can modify the schedule. An argument could be made that "everything affects everything" in Project Professional (whether stand-alone or with Project Server). In this chapter, we highlight some items that directly affect resources or affect how a resource will alter the schedule.

Project Calendars

One setting that is often forgotten is the project calendar. This is the calendar that affects when tasks in the schedule *can* be worked on. This is a key setting that has a default that might not match when you and your organization actually perform work. The default working time is Monday through Friday, 8:00 AM to 5:00 PM, with 8 hours of work per day. For many organizations, these time settings are fine and might even be the level at which work is tracked and how work is assigned. The more detailed the level that you wish to track assignments, the more precise this setting needs to be accurate.

What if a person doesn't work within those default hours? Perhaps there are staggered shifts, the organization has a 24-hour schedule, or there are resources in other time zones. Options for using Microsoft Project 2010 might be best explained by looking at a few different scenarios where time settings will vary from the default.

Scenario One: Night Shift Let's start with a simple scenario. Your project calendar is set to the default settings and a resource works the night shift (11:00 PM to 8:00 AM the next day, with a one-hour break). If you try to assign the resource to that task, you will get an error message warning you about the fact that there is no overlapping time. In other words, you have told the system that the work can only be done from 8:00 AM to 5:00 PM, but you have also told the system that the resource works different hours. Therefore, you have a conflict—the resource and the project calendar do not have overlapping time. In this situation, a message will appear letting you know that what you are trying to do is not possible. This is illustrated in Figure 3–1.

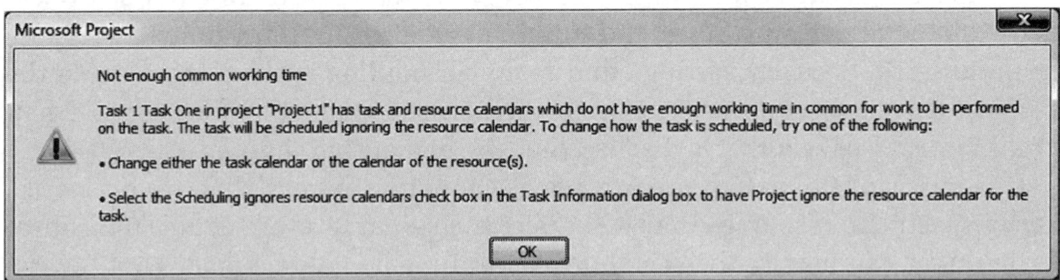

Figure 3–1

Scenario Two: Time Zones This scenario is a bit tougher because it is less obvious in what is displayed. Again, you will use the default settings for the project calendar. This time, the resource is in a different time zone. The Project Server is set to the Eastern Standard Time Zone (EST), but the resource works in the Pacific Standard Time Zone (PST). The resource works 8:00 AM to 5:00 PM, Monday through Friday, but in *their* time zone.

This means that when you assign a task to this resource, he or she is working an eight-hour day, but the software will only see the hours that overlap between the resource calendar and the project calendar. In this scenario, that is about 4 hours (11:00 AM to 5:00 PM EST, and then reduced by an hour break for *each* calendar). Therefore, when you assign this resource, the scheduled task will move automatically to represent the overlapping time.

To better understand this example, we changed the Start and Finish date columns to display the time. Notice what happens to Task One. In Figure 3–2, the task is originally scheduled to start on Monday, July 26, 2010, at 8:00 AM, and finish on Tuesday, July 27, 2010, at 5:00 PM, as a two-day duration task. As shown in Figure 3–3, when we assign the resource from the Pacific Standard Time Zone, the scheduled task stretches to Thursday, July 29, 2010, at 9:00 AM. Notice how this moves the next linked task as well. (It is outside the scope of this book to explain every reason why, but the duration did not change from two days, even though the Finish date moved.)

Figure 3–2 shows the tasks before the resource is added.

Task Name	Duration	Start	Finish
Task One	2 days	July 26, 2010 8:00 AM	July 27, 2010 5:00 PM
Task Two	2 days	July 28, 2010 8:00 AM	July 29, 2010 5:00 PM

Figure 3–2

Figure 3–3 shows the tasks after the resource is added.

Task Name	Duration	Start	Finish
Task One	2 days	July 26, 2010 8:00 AM	July 29, 2010 9:00 AM
Task Two	2 days	July 29, 2010 9:00 AM	August 2, 2010 9:00 AM

Figure 3–3

We won't dive into more scenarios, but the more you think about the question of "when can people work?" the more complex this topic becomes. Think about the times where you have people working a 4/10 shift (four days per week, 10 hours per day), or if you have resources who work in other countries. As seen in these scenarios, it is important to have your project calendar set to the times when work can be done on that project. It is recommended that the project calendar is set to time frames that match when the resources are going to actually do the work.

How to create and modify a project calendar is discussed in the next chapter. In addition to the project calendar, using a resource calendar allows for the work to be scheduled based on when each resource does the work. How to add a resource to a specific calendar, and how to adjust the resource calendar, is covered in a separate chapter.

Understanding Task Types

Another item that significantly affects how resource assignments can modify the schedule is Task Types. The Task Types being used can dramatically affect how a schedule is modified when resources are added or removed. There are three types of Task Types: Fixed Units, Fixed Work, and Fixed Duration. The definitions of the Task Types are:

Fixed Units—the percentage of a resource's capacity being used to complete the task (assumed to be 100%).

Fixed Work—the amount of actual working time (usually measured in hours) that it takes for a task to be completed.

Fixed Duration—the amount of time during which the task can be done (usually measured in days).

In our experience, most people think about work in terms of Fixed Duration. This is a natural way to discuss the timing of work and is commonly used in most conversations. For example, when asking a contractor how long it will take to build a new house, he or she will probably give you a number of days, weeks, or months, but not give you a number of hours. Or, when asking somebody when they can get a task done at work, the most common response seems to be provided as a number of days. Even if the task will take a person two hours of actual work, they will probably answer in terms of days (and they will probably add other work in their calculation). You would probably get an answer of "one day" or "two days" if you asked somebody when they can complete their task. These are Fixed Duration answers.

To clarify further, here is another example. If I tell you that I will work one normal work day, all day, devoted solely to a task, then I am saying that I have duration of 1 day, work of 8 hours, and 100% of my units. If I tell you that I will accomplish a task in one day, but I will only spend half my time on it, then I am saying that duration is 1 day, work is 4 hours, and you are only getting 50% of my units during that 1 day duration.

Task Type Examples

The following section provides the definition and an example for each Task Type.

DEFINITION

Fixed Units—the percentage of a resource's capacity being used to complete the task (assumed to be 100%). **Note:** The duration of the task changes when you add (or reduce) resources.

EXAMPLE

One painter (100% units) is assigned to paint a room in 4 days; the work is 32 hours.

The painter becomes available at half time or 50% units, so the duration becomes 8 days with work of 32 hours.

OR

If you change the duration to 2 days with work at 32 hours, the resource is now at 200%.

DEFINITION

Fixed Work—the amount of actual working time (usually measured in hours) that it takes for a task to be completed. **Note:** Work does NOT change as you change duration or units. Units can be at, under, or over 100%.

EXAMPLE

One painter (100% units) is assigned to paint a room in 4 days; the work is 32 hours.

A second painter (100%) is assigned, and the work stays at 32 hours; the duration is reduced to 2 days.

100 painters = 32 hours and about 20 minutes duration.

DEFINITION

Fixed Duration—the amount of time during which the task can be done (usually measured in days). **Note:** The duration of the task does *not* change when you add (or reduce) resources. The units of the resource can be at, under, or over 100%.

EXAMPLE

One painter (100% units) is assigned to paint a room in 4 days; the work is 32 hours.

A second painter (100%) is assigned, the days stay the same (4), and the work jumps to 64 hours.

100 painters = 4 days duration and 3200 hours work.

The system calculates the two variables (or one) that you do not enter. The system uses the formula of Duration = Work/Units. It is also important to understand that the system does this automatically and in the background. When the system uses this formula, it might modify the dates of your schedule in a manner that you don't expect.

It is also critical to note that the system uses Fixed Units as the default setting. While this is probably the best way to schedule resources and the most precise from a project and resource management perspective, it is our experience that it is also the least common method being used by most organizations. Most organizations actually think of, and have business practices, that are designed around Fixed Duration. This is a setting that should be considered before starting to assign resources to tasks.

Also, it is important to know if the type of task that is chosen is reflected in the resource's assignments, and therefore if that choice affects his or her capacity and utilization. Understanding how this works is important for being able to maintain effective and meaningful reports. Microsoft Project uses the Duration = Work/Units formula to calculate the dates and resource information.

An example of how the system will use the formula to calculate the other information about Task Types is explained in Table 3–1.

IN A...	IF YOU REVISE UNITS...	IF YOU REVISE DURATION...	IF YOU REVISE WORK...
Fixed-units task	Duration is recalculated.	Work is recalculated.	Duration is recalculated.
Fixed-work task	Duration is recalculated.	Units are recalculated.	Duration is recalculated.
Fixed-duration task	Work is recalculated.	Work is recalculated.	Units are recalculated.

Table 3–1

An example of how this formula will affect reporting can be shown with Fixed Duration. If we use Fixed Duration task types and assign a resource to a two-day task, the system will assume 100% units. If we are using the default calendar, the system will assume 8 hours per day, Monday through Friday. Therefore, when we look at a report, the resource will appear to be fully booked for two full days. But, what if the task is really a task that takes only two hours of work? If that is the situation, we will be showing 14 hours more work for the resource than is actually being done.

It may be beneficial to start out this way because at least you are now starting to get reports on utilization. We cover similar utilization and capacity issues in later chapters.

Security

Setting up full security for users and resources is outside the scope of this book. There are numerous books and articles created by Microsoft and others on the setup and configuration of Project Server, where security settings are explained in detail. Therefore, we will only briefly explain security from a high level to help with general understanding of how the set up process works.

It is important to understand that there is a difference between a user and a resource. A resource can be assigned to a task, while a user is someone that can sign onto the Server. Resources are typically users, but not all users are resources. For example, a senior executive might be a user that can sign onto Project Server, but isn't a person who is ever assigned to tasks as a resource. Therefore, from a Project Server perspective, security settings apply to a user.

User security is based upon the user settings, groups, categories, and views. The best practice, when a user is added to the Project Server, is that one or more groups are assigned to the user. The group is where the global permissions are granted, and one or more categories are assigned. The categories determine which projects, resources, and views can be accessed. There is also a level of security above the user level where you can turn off a feature entirely—in Project Web App permissions.

Project Server comes with a pre-defined set of permission templates based upon normal organizational roles. For example, there is a project manager and a team member template, with the team member being "just" a resource that is assigned tasks, while the project manager has more authorization to use features and functions on the Server. Security settings can become quite extensive—to the point of limiting an individual to only see a specific view for a specific project. Or, they can be more open with "everybody doing everything" on the Project Server. It is recommended that you start out by using the security templates provided with Project Server, and that you read the security documentation provided by Microsoft to determine how to set up your security.

In Figure 3–4, we give a high level flowchart of how the views, categories, groups, and user settings tie together.

The security for the stand-alone version of Project is much easier. If a person has Project Professional installed on their computer and access to the network share or other file location where the schedules reside, they can almost always do anything they want to any schedule.

Project Web App – Permission Settings

PWA Access Permissions (Server Permissions)

Can the feature be done at all on this server?

No

Nobody Can do it

Yes

Category
(Which views can which users or groups see on which projects)

Is this User in this Group?

Is this Group in this category?

No

Is this view in this category?

Is this Project in this category?

No

The user can not access this category

No

No

The view is not available for this category

Yes

Yes

The group can not access this category

The Project is not available for this category

Yes

Yes

Is this User in this category?

No

Yes

Note:
A user may or may not be in a group

Users

Groups

Views

Does the User or Group have permission for this functionality?

No

Yes

The User or Group can Not perform the function in this category for this project in this view.

The User or Group can perform the function in this category for this project in this view.

Figure 3–4

This book has free material available for download from the Web Added Value™ resource center at *www.jrosspub.com*

4

Who Can Work When: Project Calendars

In the previous chapter, we discussed some of the items that affect how a resource assignment can modify a schedule due to defaults, setup, or behind-the-scenes settings. We also discussed how a project calendar can affect the scheduling of a project. A project calendar can be set for a specific schedule as a one-use calendar, but if you are using Project Server, it is best to create an Enterprise Calendar that can be used by any project and by any resource.

There are actually three types of calendars in Microsoft Project. These are the task calendar, project calendar, and resource calendar. In this chapter, we discuss the project calendar, although any calendar that is created can be assigned at the project, task, or resource level.

As an example of a project calendar, we will set up an enterprise calendar for a 4/10 shift (four days per week, 10 hours per day). In this case, "4/10" represents a shift that works Monday through Thursday, ten hours per day, with a one hour break during the day. In Project Server, it is recommended that only the Administrator has the ability to create and modify enterprise calendars. Therefore, it is assumed that the person making these changes has the correct permissions and knowledge about who might use this calendar and in what situations.

The first step, shown in Figure 4–1, is to open the Project Web App and click on Server Settings.

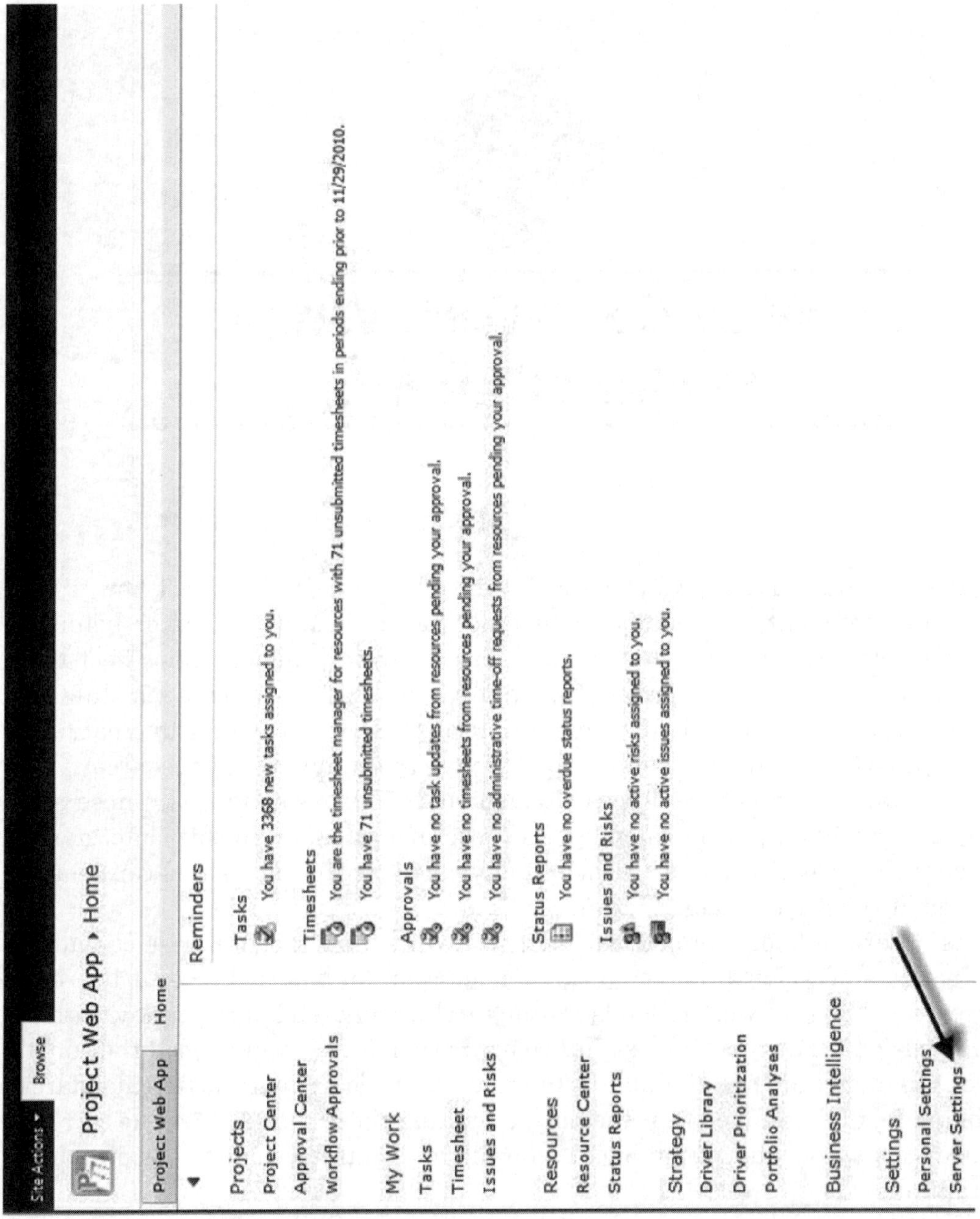

Site Actions ▾ Browse

Project Web App ▸ Home

Project Web App | Home

Projects
Project Center
Approval Center
Workflow Approvals

My Work
Tasks
Timesheet
Issues and Risks

Resources
Resource Center
Status Reports

Strategy
Driver Library
Driver Prioritization
Portfolio Analyses

Business Intelligence

Settings
Personal Settings
Server Settings

Reminders

Tasks
You have 3368 new tasks assigned to you.

Timesheets
You are the timesheet manager for resources with 71 unsubmitted timesheets in periods ending prior to 11/29/2010.
You have 71 unsubmitted timesheets.

Approvals
You have no task updates from resources pending your approval.
You have no timesheets from resources pending your approval.
You have no administrative time-off requests from resources pending your approval.

Status Reports
You have no overdue status reports.

Issues and Risks
You have no active risks assigned to you.
You have no active issues assigned to you.

Figure 4–1

Once the Server settings screen opens, select Enterprise Calendars under Enterprise Data, as shown in Figure 4–2.

Once in the Enterprise Calendars screen, you will see the existing list of calendars that are already available to the enterprise. As demonstrated in Figure 4–3, three calendars already exist. They are named Calendar 1, Standard, and Process Calendar. **Note:** If you are creating a new calendar based upon an existing calendar, select the row of the calendar you want to copy, and then select the *Copy Calendar* option. This is particularly useful when you have a calendar that is created with your organization's nonworking days. (There is more information about this later in the chapter.)

To create the new calendar, select the *New Calendar* option.

After the *Change Working Time* box opens, enter the title of the new calendar in the text area at the top of the box. In this case, we will call our schedule "Four Ten Hours" so that it is easy to determine the working hours that are represented in this calendar.

We recommend using easy-to-remember and descriptive names, even if it seems simple.

Since we want to modify the working hours, select the Work Weeks tab, making sure that Default is highlighted, and then click on the Details button, as shown in Figure 4–4.

Selecting the Details button will open the Details for '[Default]' box, shown in Figure 4–5, for the highlighted row of Default. Once in the Details for '[Default]' box, highlight the days to be changed. In this case, we want to change the days Monday through Thursday. After highlighting those days, select *Set day(s) to these specific working times*. This allows us to change the working time from the system's default hours to the four, ten-hour days that we want. In the *From* and *To* fields, change the times to represent a ten-hour day. In this case, the hours are from 7:00 AM to 6:00 PM.

At this point, we have changed the working hours for Monday through Thursday. However, the system default still has working time for Friday and we want to make Friday a nonworking day. To do this, highlight *Friday* and select the *Set days to nonworking time* option. Click the OK button to return to the *Change Working Time* box, shown in Figure 4–6.

The nonworking days in our calendar are indicated by the gray highlight. The legend for what each color represents is on the left hand side of the *Change Working Time* box. In Figure 4–7, notice that the Change Working Time box now shows Friday, Saturday, and Sunday as nonworking days. Also, when selecting

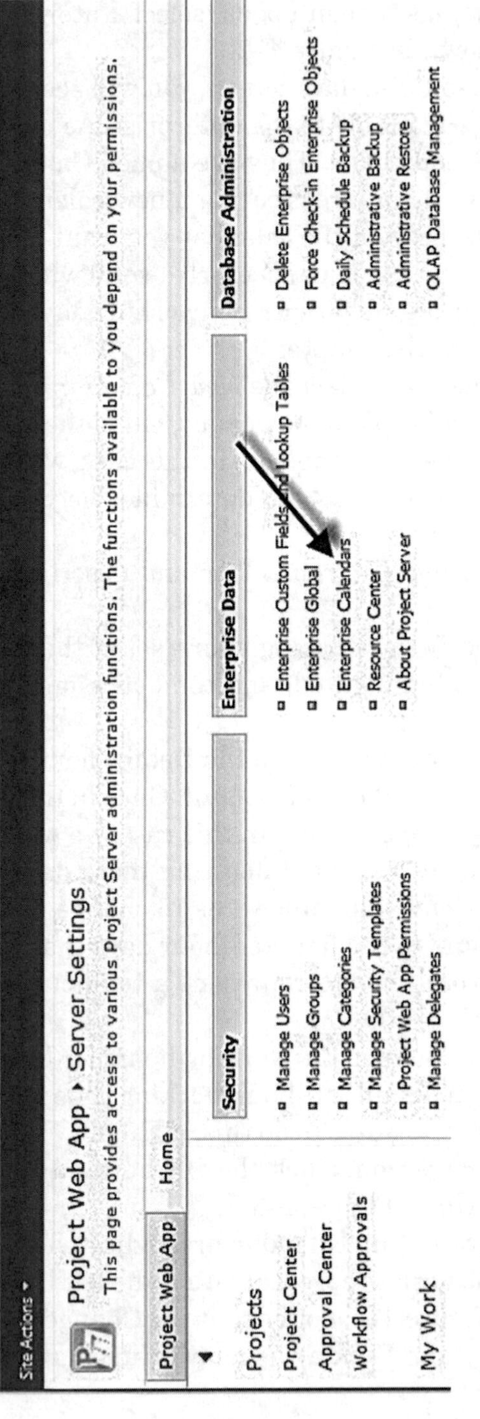
Site Actions
Project Web App ▸ Server Settings
This page provides access to various Project Server administration functions. The functions available to you depend on your permissions.
Project Web App
Home
Projects
Project Center
Approval Center
Workflow Approvals
My Work
Security
Manage Users
Manage Groups
Manage Categories
Manage Security Templates
Project Web App Permissions
Manage Delegates
Enterprise Data
Enterprise Custom Fields and Lookup Tables
Enterprise Global
Enterprise Calendars
Resource Center
About Project Server
Database Administration
Delete Enterprise Objects
Force Check-in Enterprise Objects
Daily Schedule Backup
Administrative Backup
Administrative Restore
OLAP Database Management

Figure 4–2

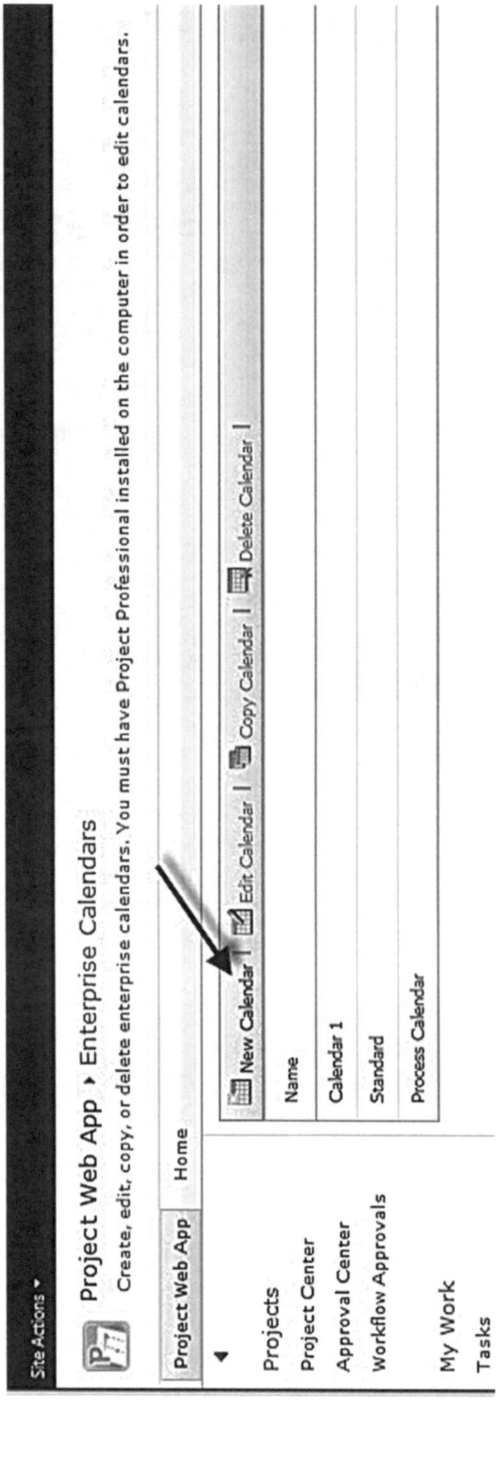

Site Actions ▾

Project Web App ▸ Enterprise Calendars

Create, edit, copy, or delete enterprise calendars. You must have Project Professional installed on the computer in order to edit calendars.

Project Web App | Home

Projects
Project Center
Approval Center
Workflow Approvals

My Work
Tasks

New Calendar | Edit Calendar | Copy Calendar | Delete Calendar |

Name
Calendar 1
Standard
Process Calendar

Figure 4–3

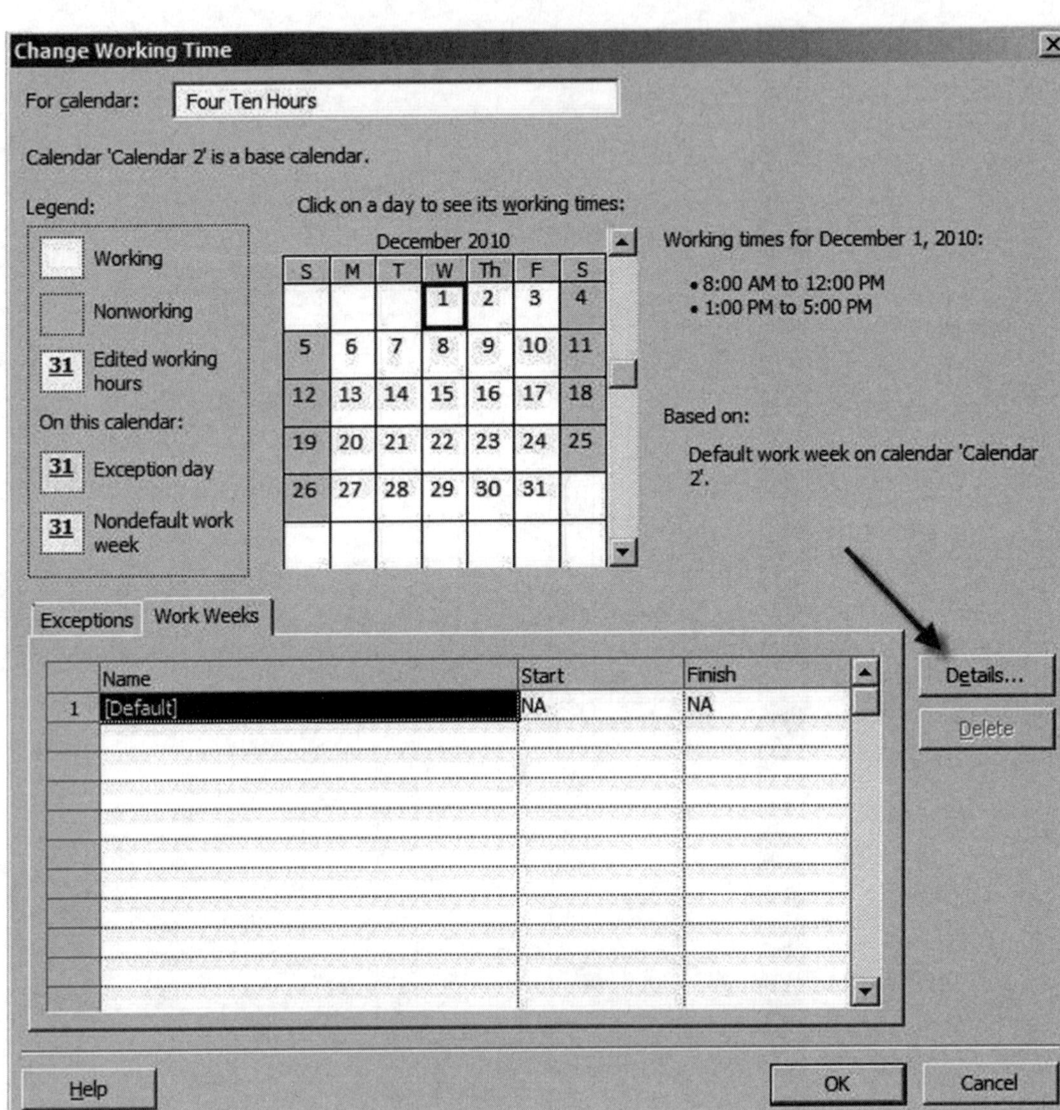
Change Working Time
For calendar: Four Ten Hours
Calendar 'Calendar 2' is a base calendar.
Legend:
Working
Nonworking
Edited working hours
On this calendar:
Exception day
Nondefault work week
Click on a day to see its working times:
December 2010
Working times for December 1, 2010:
• 8:00 AM to 12:00 PM
• 1:00 PM to 5:00 PM
Based on:
Default work week on calendar 'Calendar 2'.
Exceptions
Work Weeks
Name
Start
Finish
[Default]
NA
NA
Details...
Delete
Help
OK
Cancel

Figure 4–4

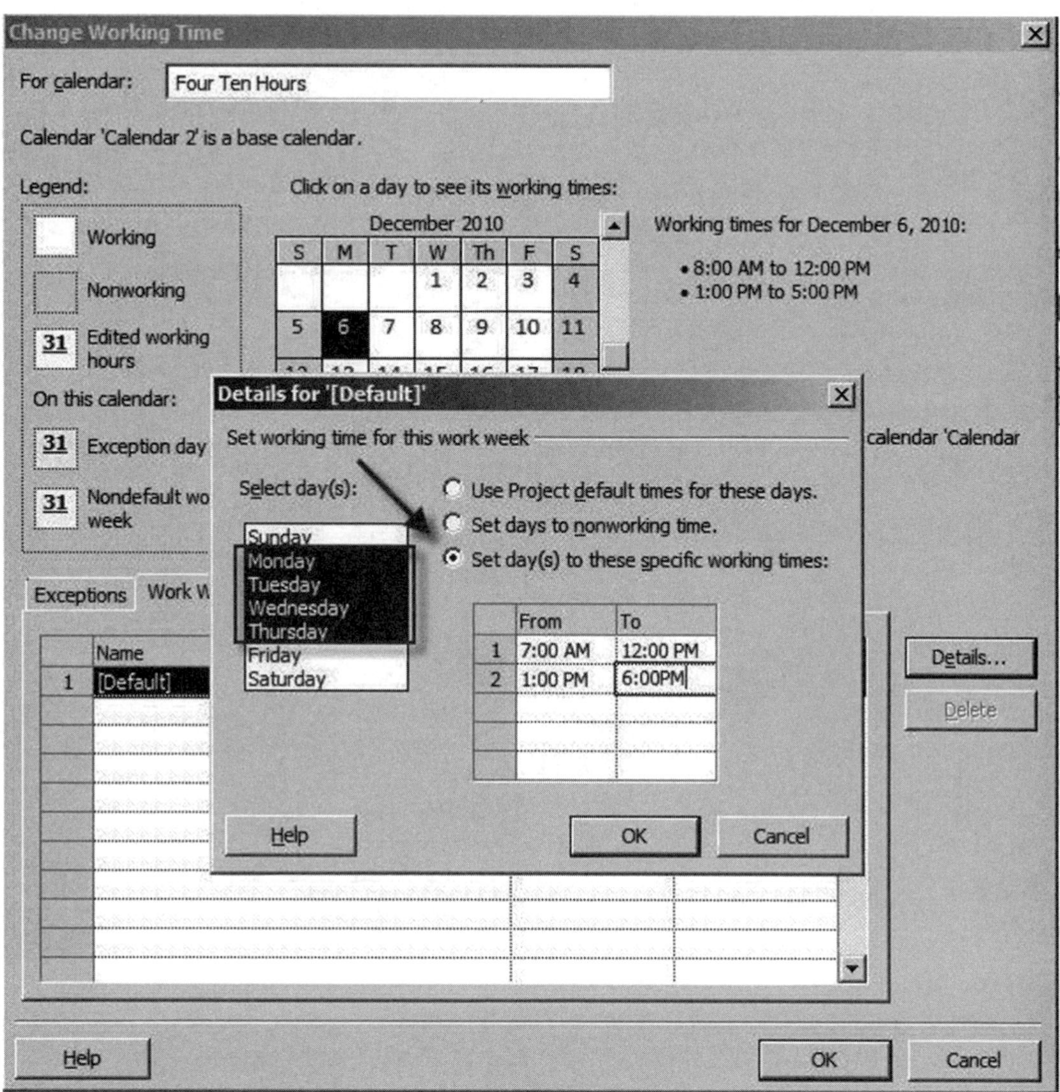
Change Working Time
For calendar: Four Ten Hours
Calendar 'Calendar 2' is a base calendar.
Legend:
Working
Nonworking
Edited working hours
On this calendar:
Exception day
Nondefault work week
Click on a day to see its working times:
December 2010
Working times for December 6, 2010:
• 8:00 AM to 12:00 PM
• 1:00 PM to 5:00 PM
calendar 'Calendar
Exceptions
Name
[Default]
Details...
Delete
Help
OK
Cancel
Details for '[Default]'
Set working time for this work week
Select day(s):
Sunday
Monday
Tuesday
Wednesday
Thursday
Friday
Saturday
Use Project default times for these days.
Set days to nonworking time.
Set day(s) to these specific working times:
From
To
7:00 AM
12:00 PM
1:00 PM
6:00PM
Help
OK
Cancel

Figure 4–5

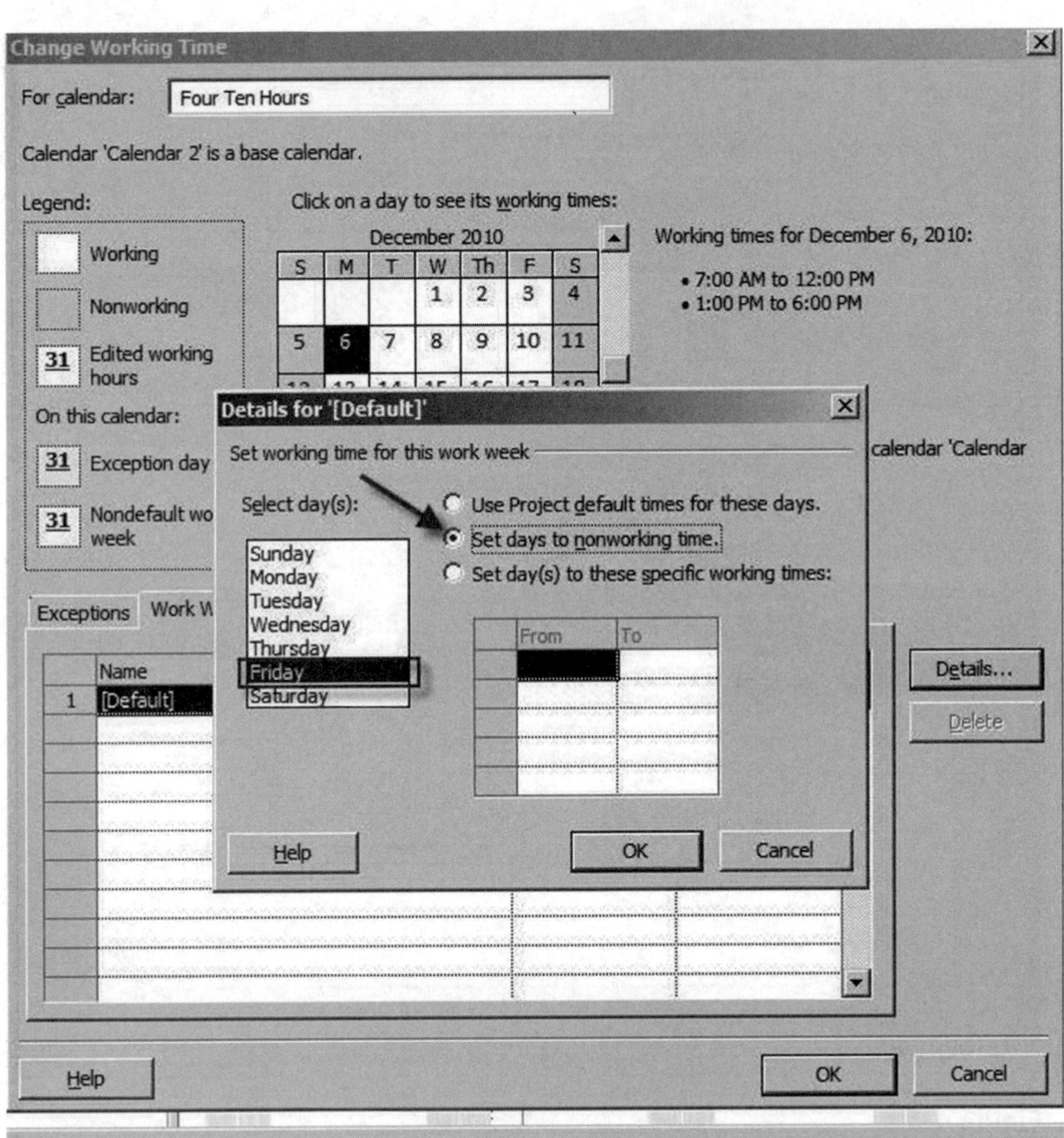
Change Working Time
For calendar: Four Ten Hours
Calendar 'Calendar 2' is a base calendar.
Legend:
Working
Nonworking
31 Edited working hours
On this calendar:
31 Exception day
31 Nondefault wo week
Click on a day to see its working times:
December 2010
S M T W Th F S
Working times for December 6, 2010:
• 7:00 AM to 12:00 PM
• 1:00 PM to 6:00 PM
calendar 'Calendar
Exceptions
Work W
Name
1 [Default]
Details...
Delete
Help
OK
Cancel
Details for '[Default]'
Set working time for this work week
Select day(s):
Sunday
Monday
Tuesday
Wednesday
Thursday
Friday
Saturday
Use Project default times for these days.
Set days to nonworking time.
Set day(s) to these specific working times:
From
To
Help
OK
Cancel

Figure 4–6

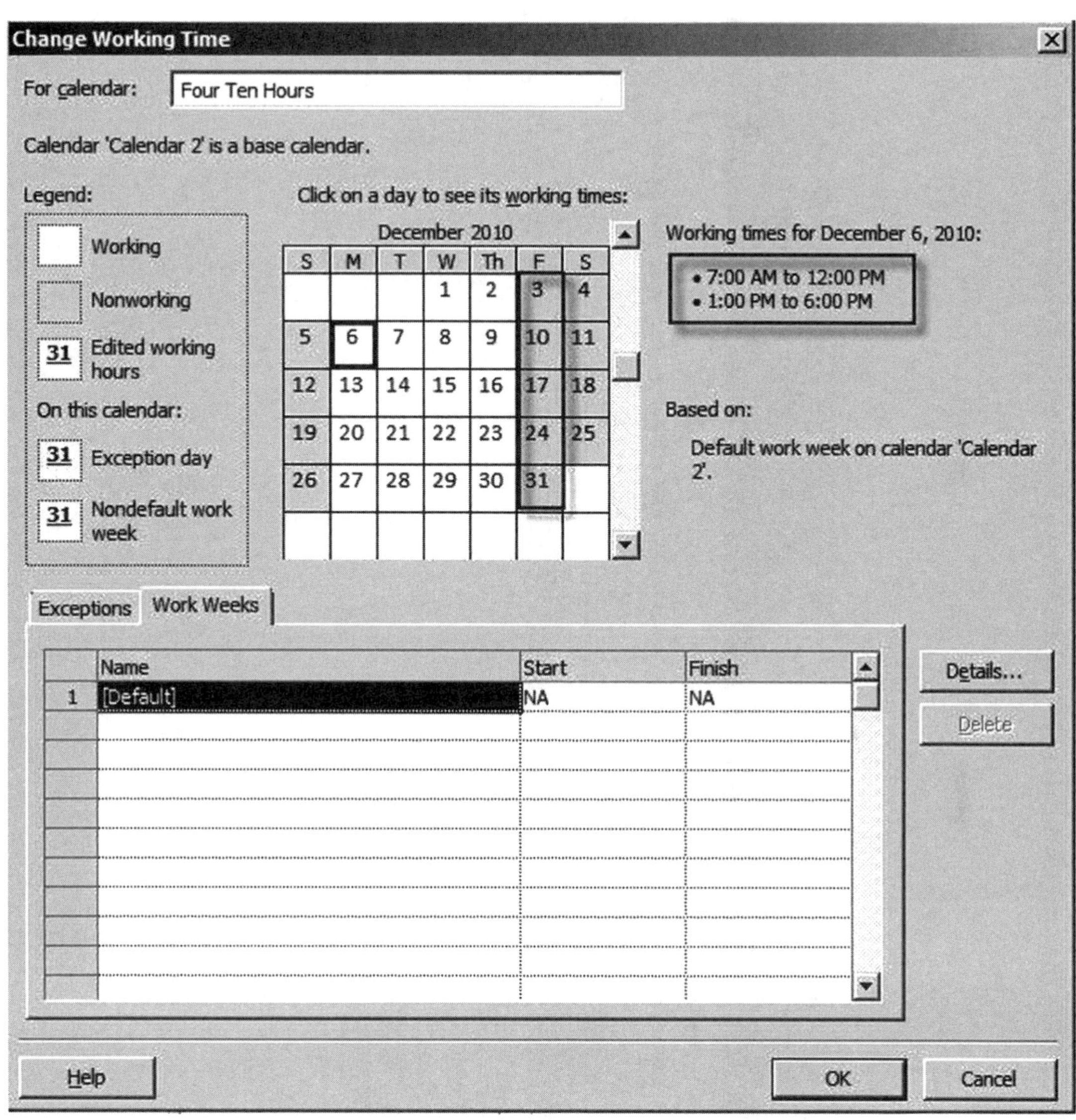
Change Working Time
For calendar: Four Ten Hours
Calendar 'Calendar 2' is a base calendar.
Legend:
Working
Nonworking
Edited working hours
On this calendar:
Exception day
Nondefault work week
Click on a day to see its working times:
December 2010
Working times for December 6, 2010:
• 7:00 AM to 12:00 PM
• 1:00 PM to 6:00 PM
Based on:
Default work week on calendar 'Calendar 2'.
Exceptions
Work Weeks
Name
Start
Finish
[Default]
NA
NA
Details...
Delete
Help
OK
Cancel

Figure 4–7

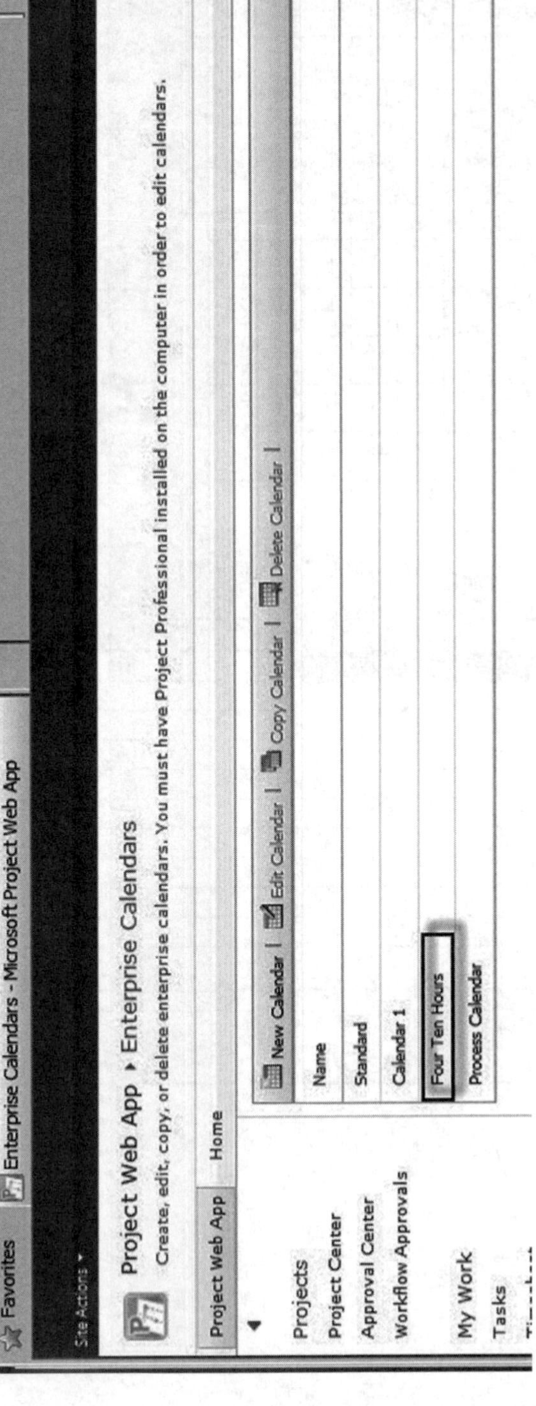
Favorites
Enterprise Calendars - Microsoft Project Web App
Site Actions
Project Web App › Enterprise Calendars
Create, edit, copy, or delete enterprise calendars. You must have Project Professional installed on the computer in order to edit calendars.
Project Web App
Home
Projects
Project Center
Approval Center
Workflow Approvals
My Work
Tasks
New Calendar
Edit Calendar
Copy Calendar
Delete Calendar
Name
Standard
Calendar 1
Four Ten Hours
Process Calendar

Figure 4–8

one of the working days, the working hours will be displayed on the right hand side of the box.

After selecting OK, we see that we have a new Enterprise Calendar in the list of available calendars, as shown in Figure 4–8. Later, we will demonstrate how to select this calendar for resources to use.

To use this new Enterprise Calendar for our project, we need to go to the Project tab and select the Project Information icon, shown in Figure 4–9.

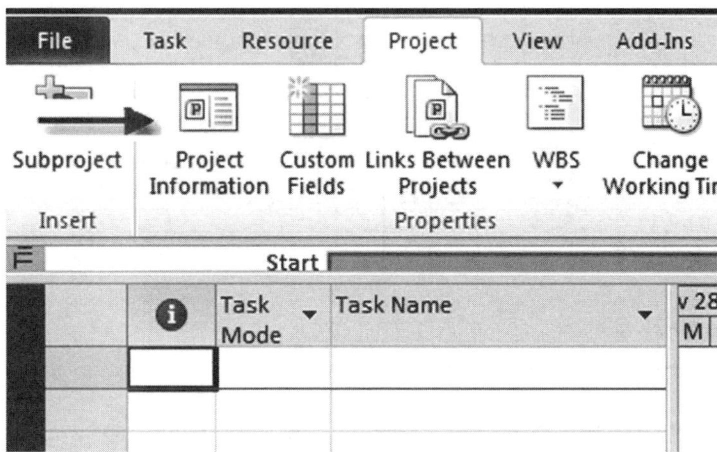

Figure 4–9

In the Project Information box, on the right hand side, is the Calendar drop-down box. This is shown in Figure 4–10. Select the new calendar that we just created called Four Ten Hours, and select OK. The project calendar has been changed to Four Ten Hours.

Project Information for 'Project1'
Start date:
Current date:
Finish date:
Status date: NA
Schedule from: Project Start Date
Calendar: Standard
Four Ten Hours
Standard
All tasks begin as soon as possible.
Priority:
Enterprise Custom Fields
Department:

Figure 4–10

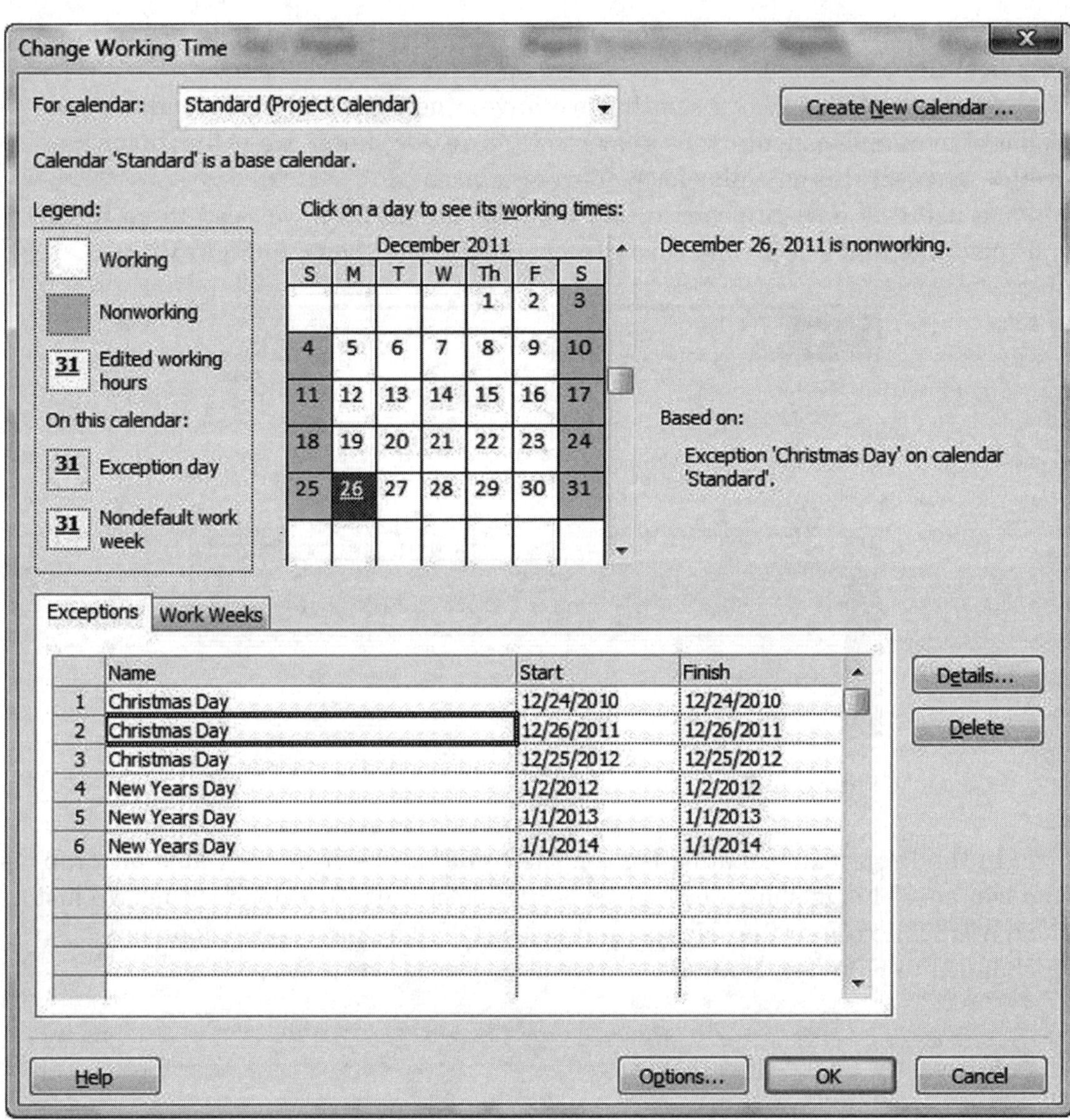

	Name	Start	Finish
1	Christmas Day	12/24/2010	12/24/2010
2	Christmas Day	12/26/2011	12/26/2011
3	Christmas Day	12/25/2012	12/25/2012
4	New Years Day	1/2/2012	1/2/2012
5	New Years Day	1/1/2013	1/1/2013
6	New Years Day	1/1/2014	1/1/2014

Figure 4–11

Earlier in this chapter, we suggested making sure that the calendar has your organization's nonworking days listed. To do this, you will need to add those nonworking days to the Exceptions tab. In the previous example, we showed how to modify the working time by adjusting the hours for the default row in Work Week tab. The Exceptions tab settings are meant to override the Work Week settings.

For example, if your organization gives Christmas Day and New Year's Day off (or the nearest working day), you could use an existing calendar, or create a new one and select the Exceptions tab. In the Exceptions tab, we have entered Christmas Day and New Year's Day for the next three years. This means that anytime a resource is assigned a task that falls on one of those dates, Project will not allow this specific day to be assigned without giving you a warning message.

Figure 4–11 shows what the Exceptions tab looks like when filled out for Christmas Day and New Year's Day, as in the example. Note that the calendar image for Monday, December 26, 2011, is highlighted as an Exception day for this calendar.

We recommend that your standard project calendar have your organization's nonworking days listed. Whenever you need to create a new calendar, use your standard project calendar as the basis, and that way your organizations non-working days will already be set.

For organizations that are not using Project Server, the method to change the working time is exactly the same, but the technique to make changes is a little different. In Project Professional, the first step to create a new calendar is to select the *Change Working Time* option from the Project tab, as shown in Figure 4–12.

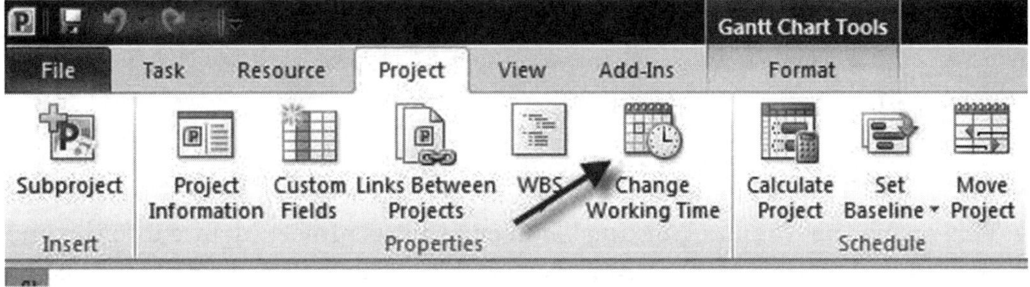

Figure 4–12

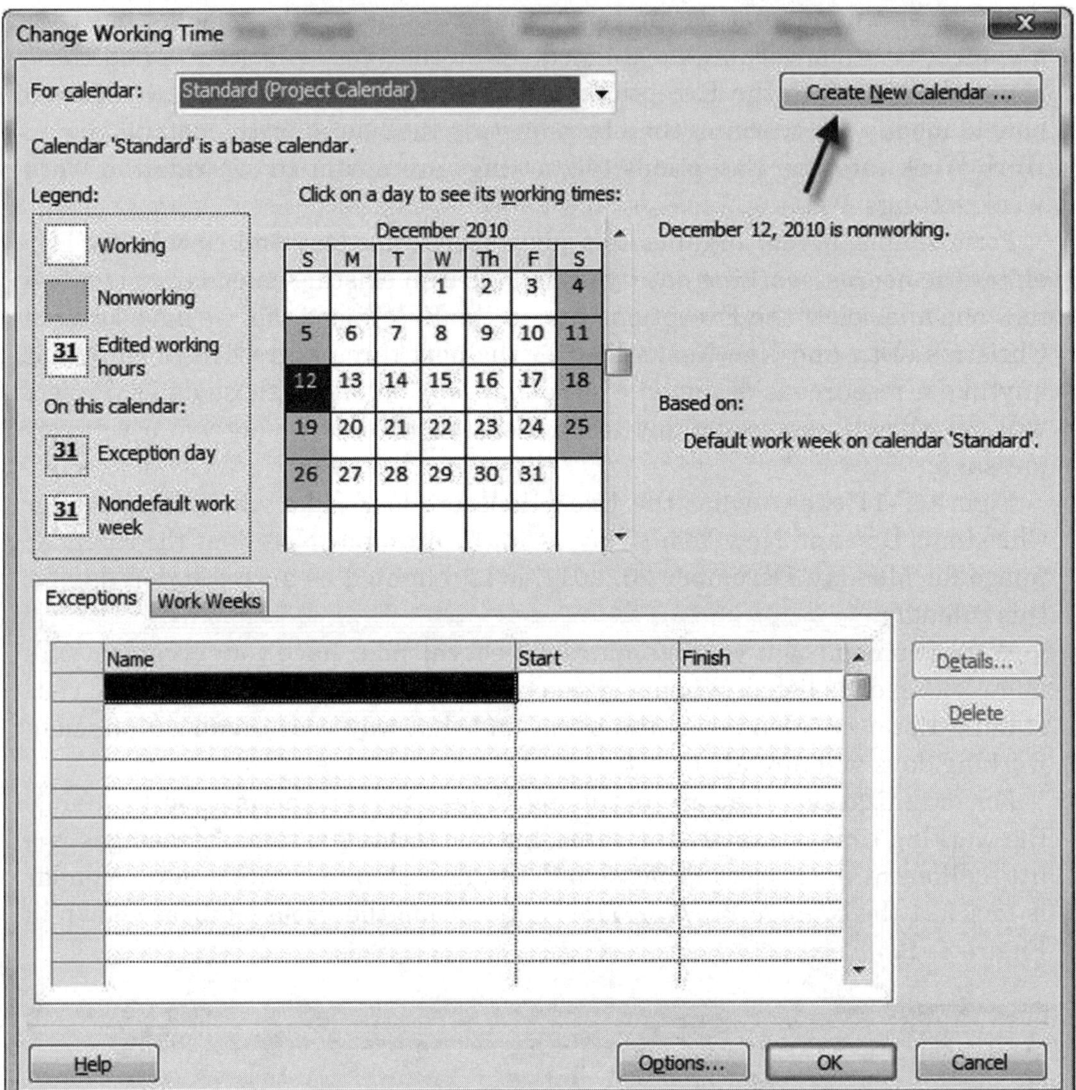

Figure 4–13

This opens the Change Working Time box that is almost identical to the one opened in Project Server. The difference is that in the top right corner of the box is the Create New Calendar button. This is shown in Figure 4–13.

In the *Name* field, enter the new calendar's name and select either the *Create new base calendar* or *Make a copy of ________ calendar* option, where you can select a calendar from a drop-down list. This is shown in Figure 4–14.

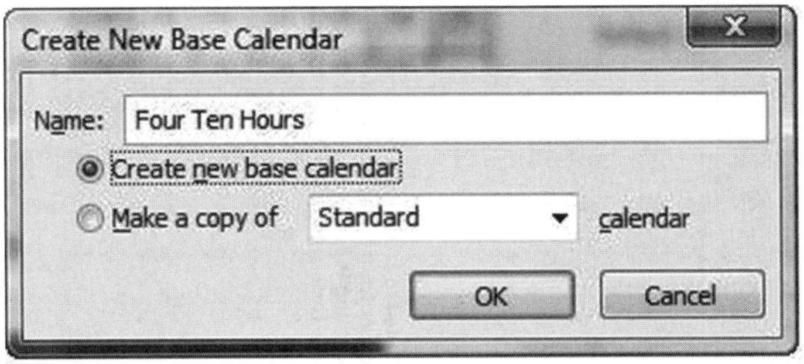

Create New Base Calendar

Name: Four Ten Hours

Create new base calendar

Make a copy of Standard calendar

OK Cancel

Figure 4–14

Additionally, we want to demonstrate that there is another way to change the working time on a specific schedule without using a project calendar. This isn't the recommended method; changing working time after a schedule has already had information added to it can create significant scheduling issues. However, it is a technique to change the working time for a stand-alone schedule. For a specific project, you can change the working time by going to File, Options, and then selecting the Schedule option. The default start and end times can be selected here, as shown in Figure 4–15.

Once an enterprise calendar has been created for Project Server, or a calendar has been created for Project Professional, it can be used by resources as well.

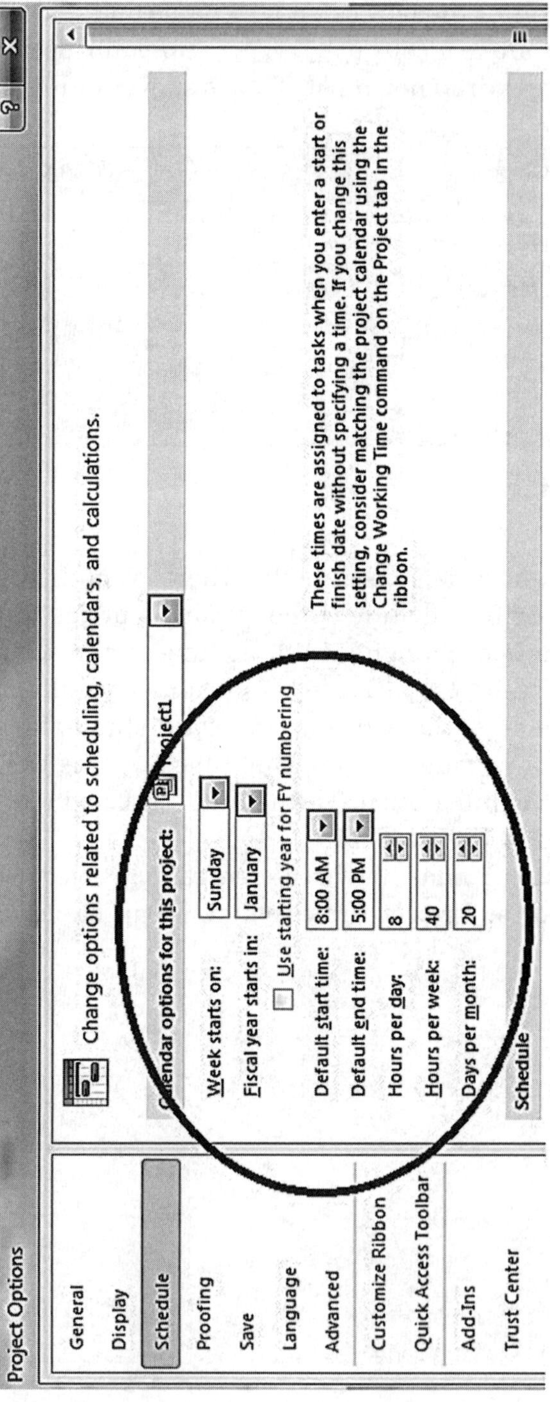
Project Options
General
Display
Schedule
Proofing
Save
Language
Advanced
Customize Ribbon
Quick Access Toolbar
Add-Ins
Trust Center
Change options related to scheduling, calendars, and calculations.
Calendar options for this project:
Project1
Week starts on:
Sunday
Fiscal year starts in:
January
Use starting year for FY numbering
Default start time:
8:00 AM
Default end time:
5:00 PM
Hours per day:
8
Hours per week:
40
Days per month:
20
These times are assigned to tasks when you enter a start or finish date without specifying a time. If you change this setting, consider matching the project calendar using the Change Working Time command on the Project tab in the ribbon.
Schedule

Figure 4–15

5

Resources in the Pool

While the term *resource* is most often used when talking about people, there are three types of resources available in Microsoft Project Server and Microsoft Project Professional.

Types of Resources

A resource can be defined as work, material, or cost type. Material resources are consumable items like concrete or paint. Cost type resources are meant for controlling or reporting costs such as airfare or lodging. Work resources are people or equipment, and can be generic or actual (sometimes called *Named*). A generic resource is a skill set or type of resource, and an actual resource is a person.

For example, a generic resource might be called something like carpenter, painter, system administrator, DBA, or project manager. The generic resource is then replaced by an actual resource with the appropriate skill set at a later time. We will discuss how to replace generic resources in more detail later in this book.

As mentioned in Chapter 3, there is a difference between a user and a resource. A resource can be assigned to a task while a user is somebody who can sign onto the Server. Resources are customarily users, but not all users are also a resource. For example, a senior executive might be a user who can sign onto Project Server, but isn't ever assigned to tasks as a resource. At this point, we concentrate on how to add resources, which may or may not be users as well.

How to Use Resource Management in Project 2010

In Chapter 2, we discussed some of the philosophy of resource management from Microsoft's perspective. Now that we have that understanding of the philosophy behind the tool, and how to connect Professional to Server, we need to discuss how we get our resources into the system. Microsoft Project is very specific about how it reads a name. This is great for reporting purposes and for a way to separate people from each other. But, let's reiterate that sentence again, with a different emphasis: Project is *specific* about how it reads a name. For example, John Doe is not the same person as "john doe." In fact, here is a sample list of John Doe names that are considered totally different people by Project:

John Doe
John doe
john doe
John Doe (two spaces between John and Doe)
 John Doe (a space before John)
Johnn Doe

And, on and on the list can go.

So, what's the point? Let's say your manager wants a report of how busy John Doe is next week. You might respond with "which one?" Or, you might provide information that underreports the amount of work assigned to John Doe because you chose the wrong person. Or, if you understand that a name issue is a possibility, you might create a report that finds all similar names and then combines them into one report. None of these options are efficient or effective (or fast)!

This is where the concept of having a single source of information about a resource originates. If every resource manager uses the same single source for selecting and assigning resources, then we will be able to run a report for John Doe in a matter of seconds—without any reporting gymnastics to get the "right" one. This is one of the key places where the business philosophy, business procedures, and the tool work in tandem. The software tool allows us to create a single place where all the resource information is stored. But, to be effective, the tool needs to be used by resource managers as they add resources to their schedules.

The single source of information about all resources is called the Resource Pool. By using the Resource Pool, reports can be created easily and quickly. The pool allows for changes to be made in one place, rather than having each project manager or resource manager modify every individual schedule. For example, if you have a resource whose e-mail address changes, the administrator of the Resource Pool can make the change, and it will be changed for all users from that moment on. However, if the administrator does not use a Resource Pool, every schedule that has the resource in it will have to be opened and modified.

The Resource Pool works for both the stand-alone and Server editions. Whether on Microsoft Project Server or in Microsoft Project Professional, you need to first enter the resources individually to create the Resource Pool. In Microsoft Project Server, when you enter the resources, they automatically become part of the Resource Pool. The stand-alone method with Microsoft Project Professional has a few more steps to set up a Resource Pool and those steps are outlined later in this chapter.

Resource Pool—PWA Initial Setup

On Project Server, the resources entered into the Resource Pool are called *Enterprise Resources*. To add resources to Project Server 2010, you must have the appropriate security permissions. This is usually limited to only a few people, or perhaps only the project server administrator. It is recommended that you do not have very many people who can change users or resources since the ramifications affect the entire Resource Pool and its associated permissions.

To set up Enterprise Resources, go to PWA in Microsoft Project Server. Look on the left hand side of the page to the Settings section. As shown in Figure 5–1, click on Server Settings.

The Server Settings area will open. Under the Security section, you will see a link called *Manage Users*. This link will take you to the area where you can add new users or edit existing users, as shown in Figure 5–2.

To add a new user, simply click on the *New User* link, shown in Figure 5–3. This will open up the page for you to fill in the fields for a new user. You must create a new user one at a time.

The New User is an important screen with a number of important settings, including the RBS. *RBS* is the acronym for the resource breakdown structure. The RBS is an important part of security settings for Project Server and can be

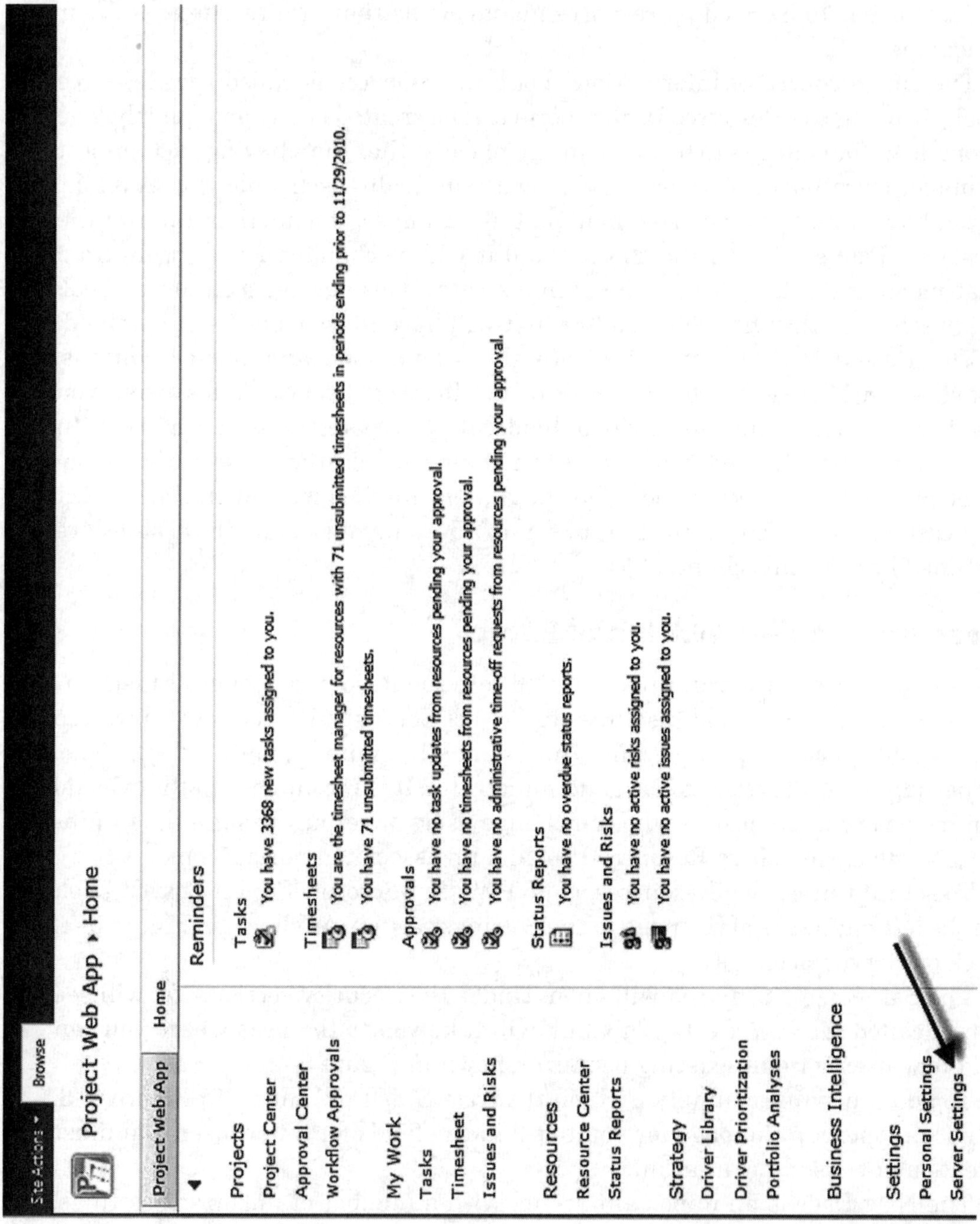

Site Actions ▾ Browse

Project Web App ▸ Home

Project Web App | Home

Projects
Project Center
Approval Center
Workflow Approvals

My Work
Tasks
Timesheet
Issues and Risks

Resources
Resource Center
Status Reports

Strategy
Driver Library
Driver Prioritization
Portfolio Analyses

Business Intelligence

Settings
Personal Settings
Server Settings

Reminders

Tasks
You have 3368 new tasks assigned to you.

Timesheets
You are the timesheet manager for resources with 71 unsubmitted timesheets in periods ending prior to 11/29/2010.
You have 71 unsubmitted timesheets.

Approvals
You have no task updates from resources pending your approval.
You have no timesheets from resources pending your approval.
You have no administrative time-off requests from resources pending your approval.

Status Reports
You have no overdue status reports.

Issues and Risks
You have no active risks assigned to you.
You have no active issues assigned to you.

Figure 5–1

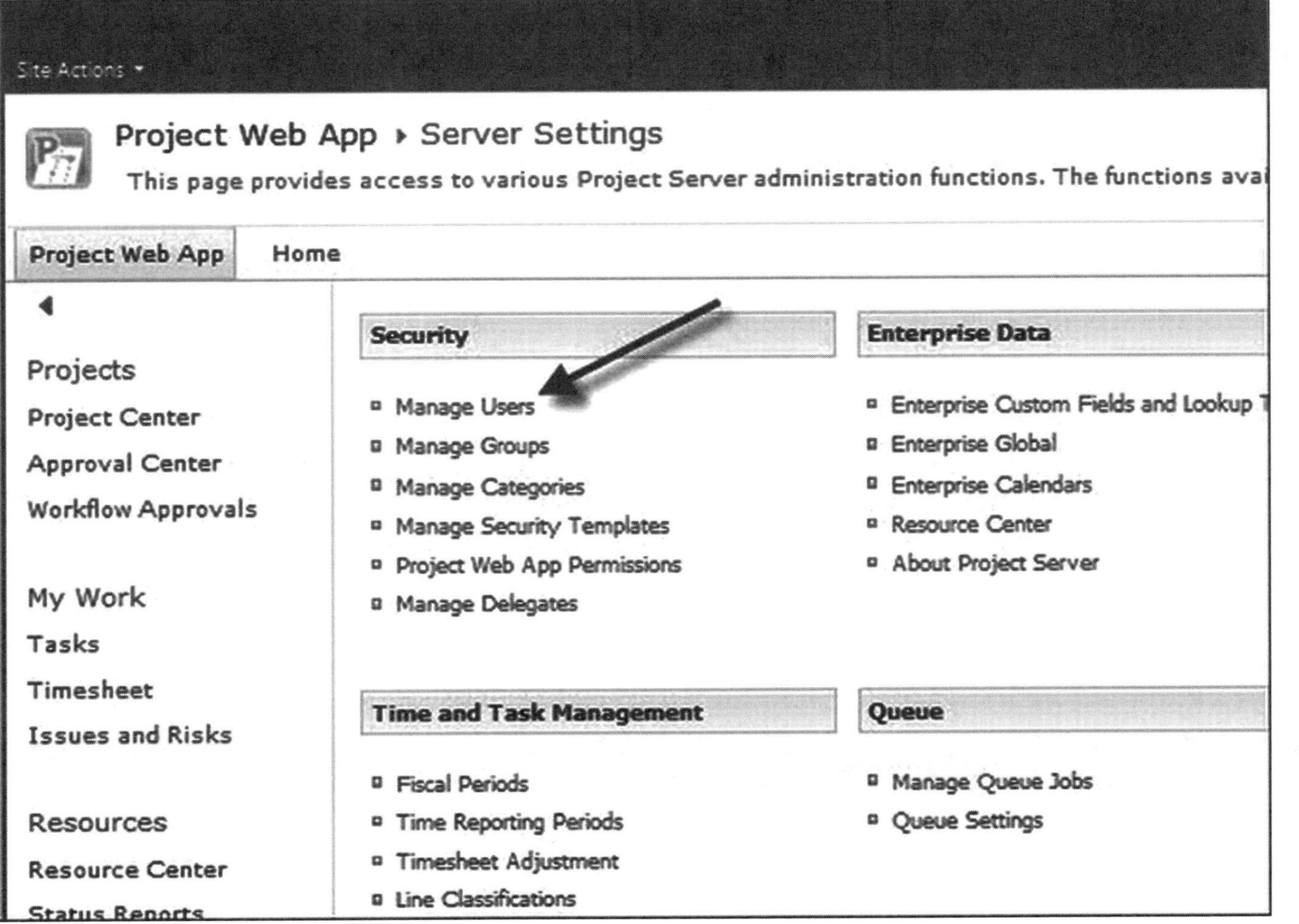
Site Actions
Project Web App ▸ Server Settings
This page provides access to various Project Server administration functions. The functions avai
Project Web App
Home
Projects
Project Center
Approval Center
Workflow Approvals
My Work
Tasks
Timesheet
Issues and Risks
Resources
Resource Center
Security
Manage Users
Manage Groups
Manage Categories
Manage Security Templates
Project Web App Permissions
Manage Delegates
Enterprise Data
Enterprise Global
Enterprise Calendars
Resource Center
About Project Server
Time and Task Management
Fiscal Periods
Time Reporting Periods
Timesheet Adjustment
Line Classifications
Queue
Manage Queue Jobs
Queue Settings

Figure 5–2

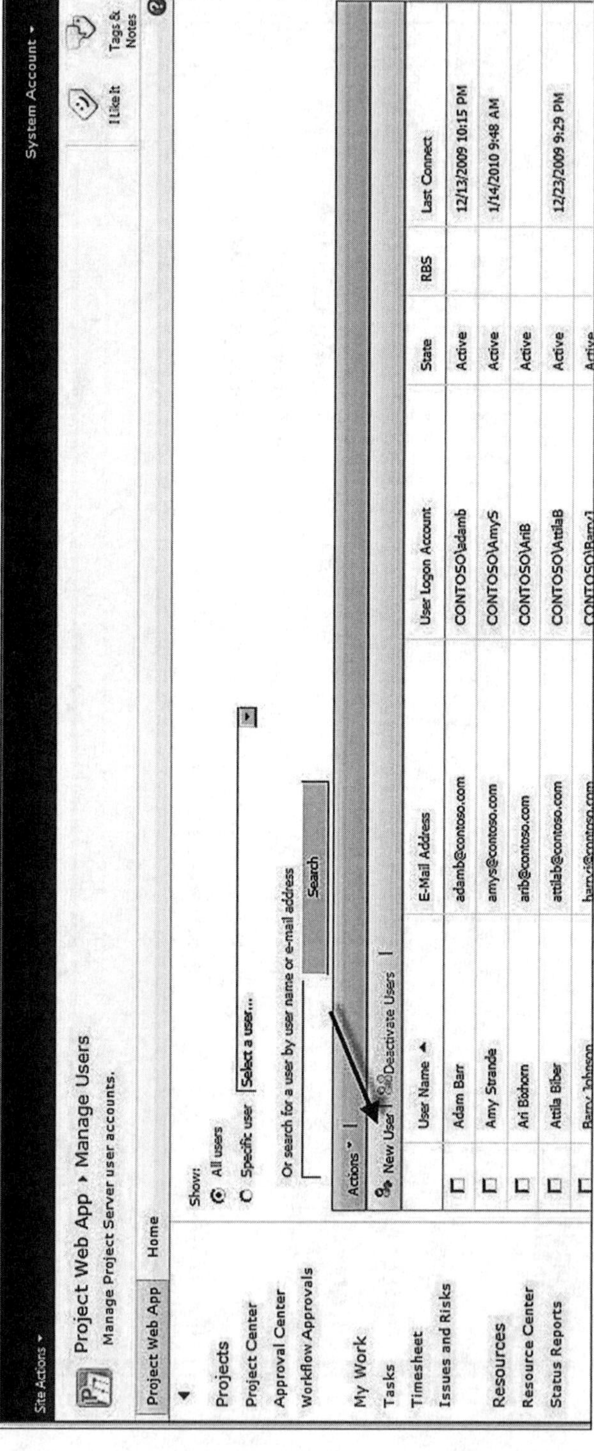

Site Actions
System Account
Project Web App › Manage Users
Manage Project Server user accounts.
I Like It
Tags & Notes
Project Web App
Home
Projects
Project Center
Approval Center
Workflow Approvals
My Work
Tasks
Timesheet
Issues and Risks
Resources
Resource Center
Status Reports
Show:
All users
Specific user
Select a user...
Or search for a user by user name or e-mail address
Search
Actions
New User
Deactivate Users
User Name
E-Mail Address
User Logon Account
State
RBS
Last Connect
Adam Barr
adamb@contoso.com
CONTOSO\adamb
Active
12/13/2009 10:15 PM
Amy Strande
amys@contoso.com
CONTOSO\AmyS
Active
1/14/2010 9:48 AM
Ari Bixhorn
arib@contoso.com
CONTOSO\AriB
Active
Attila Biber
attilab@contoso.com
CONTOSO\AttilaB
Active
12/23/2009 9:29 PM

Figure 5–3

valuable information for reporting in both Project Server and Project Professional. It can be used to determine what views and information can be seen by a resource.

The RBS is a custom field based upon a custom Lookup table. The Lookup table is populated by you, and often closely resembles an organizational chart. This is an optional field that should be set for either all the resources or none of the resources, due to its security implications.

The more aligned to a resource manager hierarchy the organization is, the more important the RBS setup is to how effectively Project works and matches the organization's needs. For highly matrixed organizations with resources being pulled from "everywhere," the RBS is less important.

On the authors' website, http://www.pmpspecialists.com/WhitePapers.html, there is a sample RBS file. You are encouraged to take a look at this document as an illustration of what an RBS might look like. All required RBS fields are indicated by an asterisk (*) symbol. By default, there are only two required fields, but you can make other fields required, or create extra custom fields for resources and determine if you want those to be required as well.

The first option in the New User screen is actually a check box. This check box is very important. If you leave it unchecked, the user that you are adding will not show up as a resource. You won't be able to assign him or her to tasks, or see the resource in the Resource Center.

The *Display Name* field is not what the user uses to sign in with. It's the name that shows up in the Enterprise Resource Center. If you have users who are known throughout the company by a different name than their given name, then you will probably want to use that name here. Some examples would be Bob instead of Robert, or Pat instead of Patricia, or someone who goes by a middle name instead of their first name.

The E-mail Address field is for the e-mail address where the resource will receive notifications about assignments (if that option is on). Unless your organization has restrictions otherwise, the e-mail address can be any valid e-mail address, not just an internal address that belongs to the organization. For example, you could put in a __________*@yahoo.com* or __________*@gmail.com* address.

The Initials, Hyperlink Name, and Hyperlink URL can be completed based on whatever criteria your organization would like to use. The hyperlink information can be used for team or organizational websites or a hyperlink to that person's own website, whether internal or external.

The User Logon Account is a critical piece of information as well. This is what the user will sign into PWA with when they log onto the system. If your organization uses Active Directory Synchronization, do not select the check box below this field. If using Forms Authentication, you can allow users who are not part of your organization. Figure 5–4 shows these fields from the default New User screen.

Figure 5–5 shows the next section of the default New User screen. The Assignment Attributes section shows options specific to the resource and does not need to be completed if this is just a user.

If the resource can be leveled within schedules, select the check box. Choose the default calendar for the resource by selecting from the Base Calendar drop-down menu. *Booking Type* refers to whether or not the default assignment type will be Committed or Proposed. A Committed Booking Type is most common and allocates the resource to the assignment when you make an assignment in a schedule. The Proposed Booking Type means that the resource's availability isn't reduced by an assignment. This is normally used when assigning a resource that you aren't sure will be the resource that does the work, or if a schedule is just a proposal and not a definite, approved schedule.

If you are using the timesheet functionality of Project Server, you need to enter the individual who approves the timesheet entries. This is done by using the Timesheet Manager option. The Default Assignment Owner is the individual who is responsible for entering time into the timesheet or entering task updates for this resource.

The Earliest and Latest Available options indicate when a resource is available to be assigned to tasks. In most cases, these are left blank to indicate that there is no restriction. The Standard Rate and Overtime Rate options are for entering default rates for the resource. The Current Max Units box can be used to limit the percentage of time the resource is available for assignments. The Cost/Use box is for a per-use cost for every time the resource is used. This is normally used for work or material resources.

If your organization has set up Exchange Server Integration, you can select the Synchronize Tasks check box for the resource.

The Departments, Resource Custom Fields, Security Groups, and Categories sections of the default New User screen are shown in Figure 5–6. The *Resource Departments* field is used to filter out information in Views and other areas of PWA and Microsoft Project Professional. Resource Custom fields are used to aid in reporting and classifying information. Custom fields can be set up

Site Actions ▾

System Account ▾

* Indicates a required field

Save | Cancel

Identification Information

The Display Name cannot contain square brackets or the server list separator.

☑ User can be assigned as a resource

* Display Name:

E-mail address:

RBS:

Initials:

Hyperlink Name:

Hyperlink URL:

User Authentication

Enter the user account that the resource will need to logon.

* User logon account:

☐ Prevent Active Directory synchronization for this user

Figure 5–4

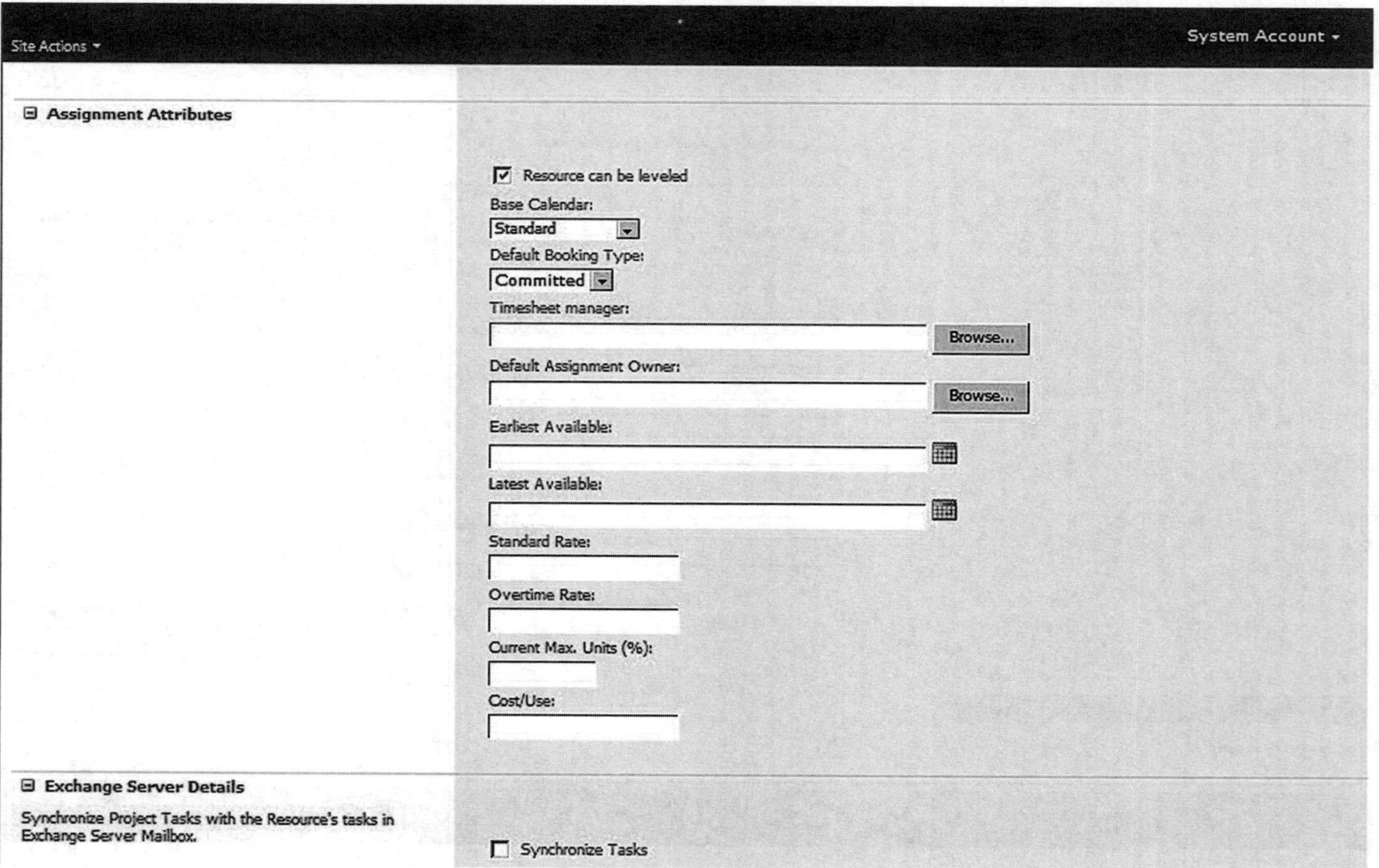

Site Actions
System Account
Assignment Attributes
Resource can be leveled
Base Calendar:
Standard
Default Booking Type:
Committed
Timesheet manager:
Browse...
Default Assignment Owner:
Browse...
Earliest Available:
Latest Available:
Standard Rate:
Overtime Rate:
Current Max. Units (%):
Cost/Use:
Exchange Server Details
Synchronize Project Tasks with the Resource's tasks in Exchange Server Mailbox.
Synchronize Tasks

Figure 5–5

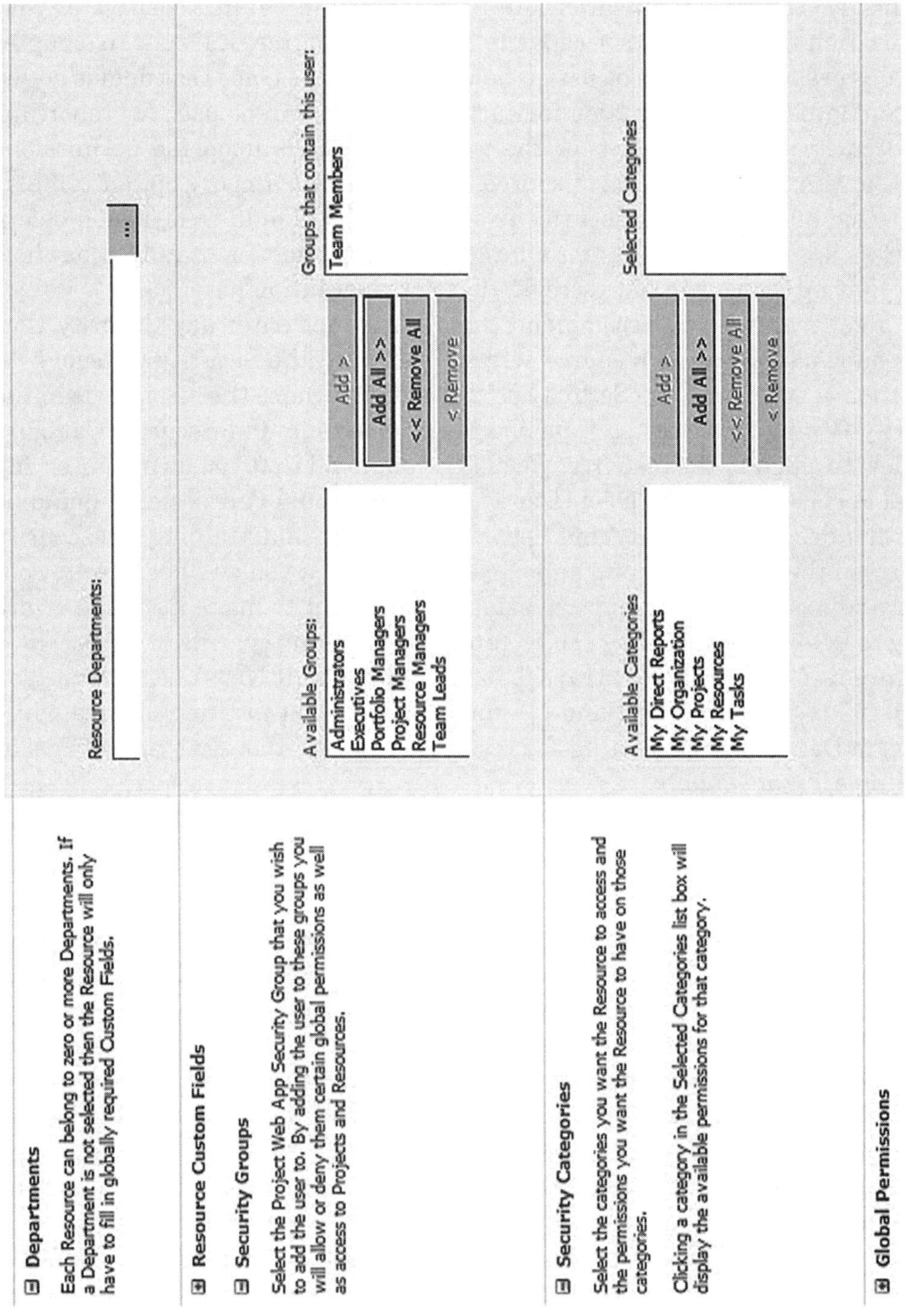

Departments

Each Resource can belong to zero or more Departments. If a Department is not selected then the Resource will only have to fill in globally required Custom Fields.

Resource Departments:

...

Resource Custom Fields

Security Groups

Select the Project Web App Security Group that you wish to add the user to. By adding the user to these groups you will allow or deny them certain global permissions as well as access to Projects and Resources.

Available Groups:

Administrators
Executives
Portfolio Managers
Project Managers
Resource Managers
Team Leads

Add >
Add All >>
<< Remove All
< Remove

Groups that contain this user:

Team Members

Security Categories

Select the categories you want the Resource to access and the permissions you want the Resource to have on those categories.

Clicking a category in the Selected Categories list box will display the available permissions for that category.

Available Categories

My Direct Reports
My Organization
My Projects
My Resources
My Tasks

Add >
Add All >>
<< Remove All
< Remove

Selected Categories

Global Permissions

Figure 5–6

specifically for your organization. An example would be an executive of your organization who wants to see capacity based on resource skill sets. In Chapter 7, we discuss how to create a custom field for resources. Once that field is added and populated with information for each resource, it can be used for reporting. The Security Group to select for the resource depends upon the permissions that you want to grant to the resource. The Security Category option can also be selected along with the Security Group. Security should be designed before resources are added, and there is a large quantity of documentation about how to set that up, so we will not recreate that documentation here.

As a general rule, we recommend that you do not enter any Security Category information in the resource screen. Normally, the Security Category information is entered in the Security Group settings. Since the resource is in the Security Group, the settings from the Security Group and Security Category will flow through to the resource. We also recommend that you do not enter any Global Permissions in the New User screen. The Global Permissions should be set in the Security Category and Security Group. By maintaining the security settings in the Security Group and Security Category, you will not have to constantly adjust the resource's permissions if you want to make a change or are trying to determine why they can or can't do something specific in PWA.

Figure 5–7 shows the last two sections of the default New User screen. The Group fields are for costing and grouping information for the resource while the Team Details are for putting the resource into either an Assignment Pool or selecting a Team Name.

Once you are finished adding a new user, click on the Save button.

Resource Pool—Stand-alone Setup

The method for creating a Resource Pool in Microsoft Project Professional requires creating a new project that all of the other projects will access. The first step is to create a blank project. By this, we mean a project that has no tasks or other information in it. The blank project will only contain a list of resources. Whenever a new project is created, this blank Resource Pool project can be opened and the resources assigned from there. This will create a way to look at the resources in the Resource Pool and see all of the work assigned across the board, not just a specific project. Be sure to include all of the resources into the Resource Pool project and not just resources for one specific project.

When creating the Resource Pool, go to the Resource View that you want to use to enter the information. Normally, the Resource Sheet is used, but any

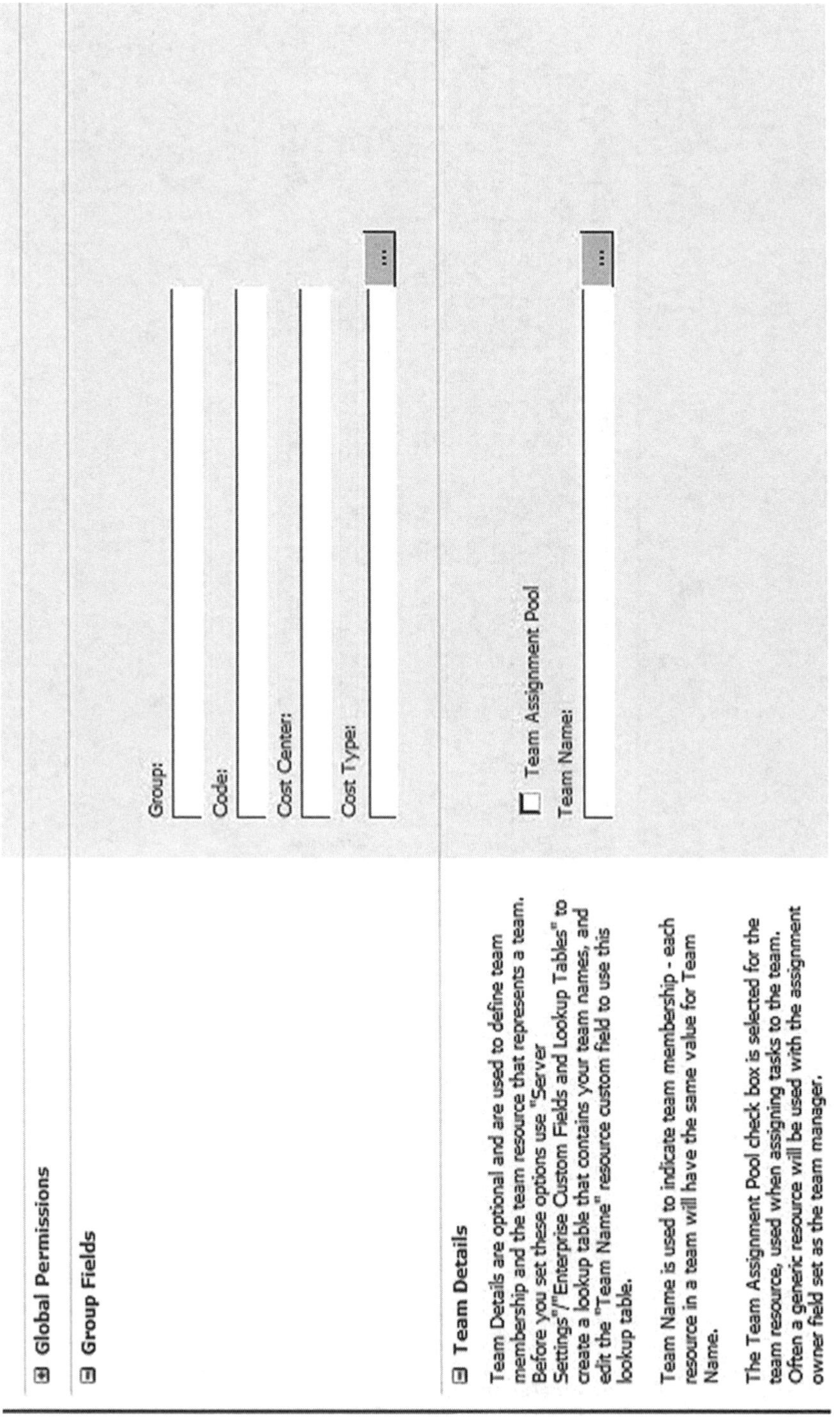

⊞ **Global Permissions**

⊟ **Group Fields**

Group:

Code:

Cost Center:

Cost Type:

⊟ **Team Details**

Team Details are optional and are used to define team membership and the team resource that represents a team. Before you set these options use "Server Settings"/"Enterprise Custom Fields and Lookup Tables" to create a lookup table that contains your team names, and edit the "Team Name" resource custom field to use this lookup table.

Team Name is used to indicate team membership - each resource in a team will have the same value for Team Name.

The Team Assignment Pool check box is selected for the team resource, used when assigning tasks to the team. Often a generic resource will be used with the assignment owner field set as the team manager.

☐ Team Assignment Pool

Team Name:

Figure 5–7

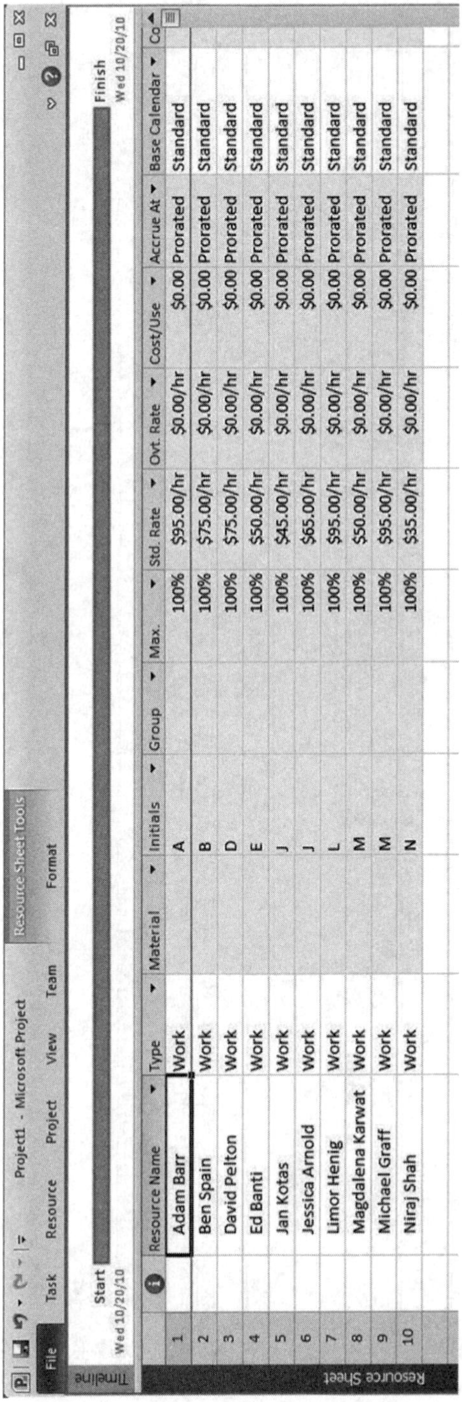

Project1 - Microsoft Project

File | Task | Resource | Project | View | Team | Format

Resource Sheet Tools

Timeline: Start Wed 10/20/10 — Finish Wed 10/20/10

	Resource Name	Type	Material	Initials	Group	Max.	Std. Rate	Ovt. Rate	Cost/Use	Accrue At	Base Calendar
1	Adam Barr	Work		A		100%	$95.00/hr	$0.00/hr	$0.00	Prorated	Standard
2	Ben Spain	Work		B		100%	$75.00/hr	$0.00/hr	$0.00	Prorated	Standard
3	David Pelton	Work		D		100%	$75.00/hr	$0.00/hr	$0.00	Prorated	Standard
4	Ed Banti	Work		E		100%	$50.00/hr	$0.00/hr	$0.00	Prorated	Standard
5	Jan Kotas	Work		J		100%	$45.00/hr	$0.00/hr	$0.00	Prorated	Standard
6	Jessica Arnold	Work		J		100%	$65.00/hr	$0.00/hr	$0.00	Prorated	Standard
7	Limor Henig	Work		L		100%	$95.00/hr	$0.00/hr	$0.00	Prorated	Standard
8	Magdalena Karwat	Work		M		100%	$50.00/hr	$0.00/hr	$0.00	Prorated	Standard
9	Michael Graff	Work		M		100%	$95.00/hr	$0.00/hr	$0.00	Prorated	Standard
10	Niraj Shah	Work		N		100%	$35.00/hr	$0.00/hr	$0.00	Prorated	Standard

Resource Sheet

Figure 5–8

view that provides the columns that you want to complete can be used. Figure 5–8 is a sample screenshot of what the new Resource Pool project will look like. In this case, there are ten resources added. As in the PWA New User screen, there are default fields that can be completed. If a particular field isn't shown in the default view, you can right click on any column and select *Insert Column.* After selecting Insert Column, that column will be available for selection. It is common to add the E-mail Address column to this view.

After you have entered the resource information into the project, you will need to save this project to a commonly accessible location, like a network share. Using *Save as*, save the Resource Pool, as shown in Figure 5–9.

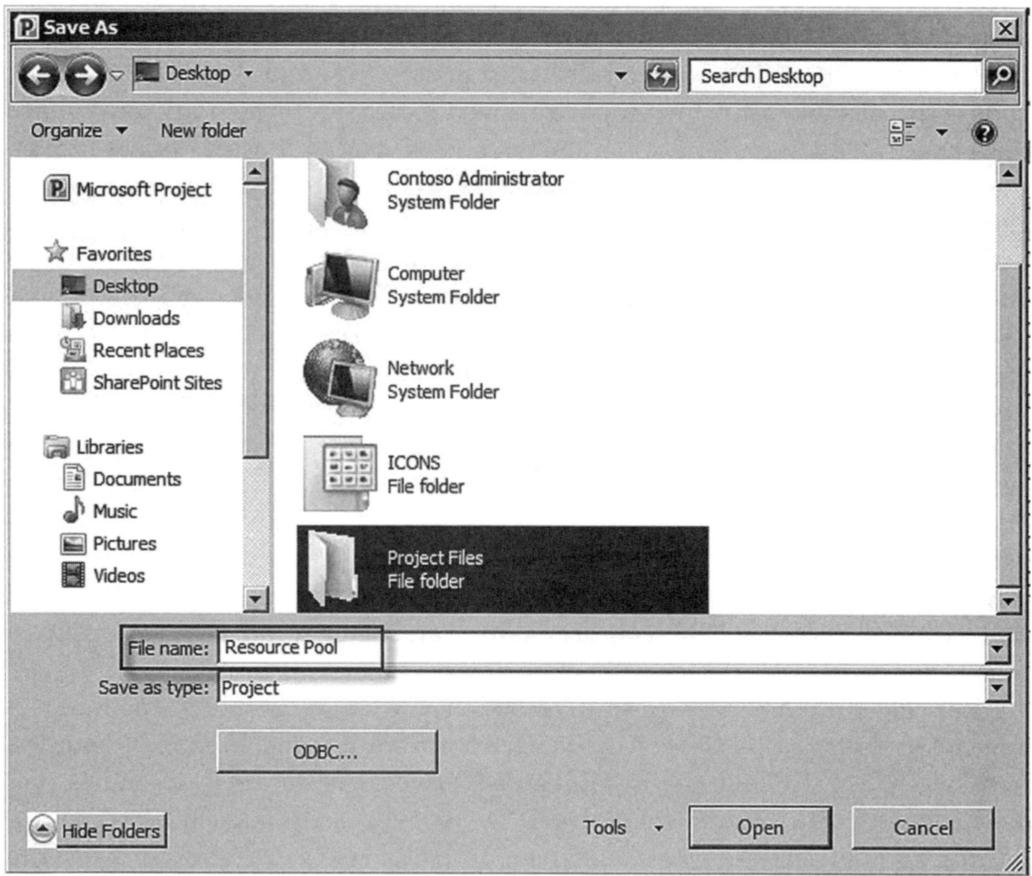

Figure 5–9

That is all you have to do to create a Resource Pool for the stand-alone version. However, the trick is in using the Resource Pool. The next section of this chapter is an example of how to do that.

Using the Resource Pool

The first step in using the Resource Pool is to create or open a project. For an example, we will create a new project, as shown in Figure 5–10. After entering Task Names, we will add resources—from the Resource Pool, rather than typing them into this specific project.

To use the Resource Pool in setting up a new project, we need to have the Resource Pool project open as well. It is imperative to have both files open at the same time or this feature will not work correctly. You can open the Resource Pool from the Recently Used project list, shown in Figure 5–11.

As a tip, you can tell which files are saved locally and which are saved onto the server by the icon. Since we are using a version of Microsoft Project Professional that can connect to Project Server but are demonstrating how the stand-alone version works, we have both server and local files available to us. In a true stand-alone environment, the server files would not appear. However, the authors think it important to understand the distinction between server and local files since it is possible to use Professional to create local-only files, even when it can connect to Project Server. To help distinguish between server and local files, the icons are different as demonstrated in Figure 5–12.

Figure 5–13 shows that we have both files open—the Resource Pool and the new project file. But, we have no resources entered in the project file and no tasks in the Resource Pool.

Now that both files are open, make sure you're in the new project file where you want to assign resources. If you have the default Ribbon, click the Resource tab, click the Resource Pool icon drop-down, and then select *Share Resources*. This is demonstrated in Figure 5–14.

After selecting the Share Resources option, the Share Resources pop-up box appears so that you can select the file where you want to use to share resources. In this case, you will use the Resource Pool project. As Figure 5–15 shows, you have two sets of options to select from. The first set is to determine which resources you will use. You can select the option to use the resources from the schedule itself, but that would defeat the purpose of using a Resource Pool. Therefore, select the second option, which is *Use Resources from another file*. In the drop-down menu, select the Resource Pool project.

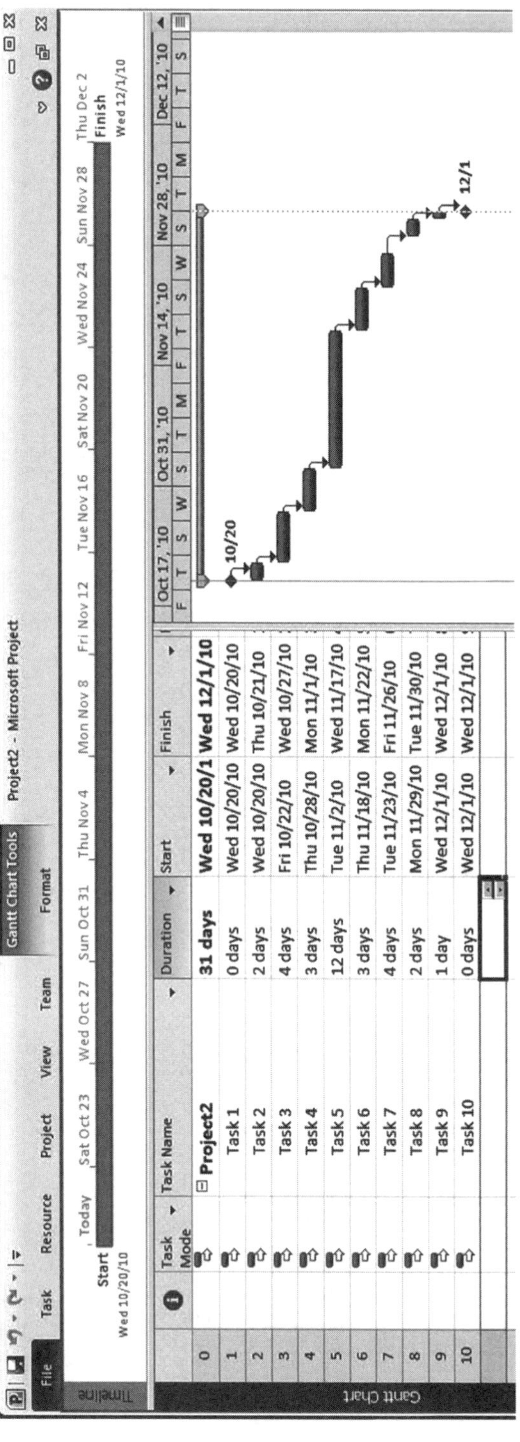
Project2 - Microsoft Project
Gantt Chart Tools
File
Task
Resource
Project
View
Team
Format
Timeline
Start
Wed 10/20/10
Today
Sat Oct 23
Wed Oct 27
Sun Oct 31
Thu Nov 4
Mon Nov 8
Fri Nov 12
Tue Nov 16
Sat Nov 20
Wed Nov 24
Sun Nov 28
Thu Dec 2
Finish
Wed 12/1/10
Task Mode
Task Name
Duration
Start
Finish
0 Project2 31 days Wed 10/20/1 Wed 12/1/10
1 Task 1 0 days Wed 10/20/10 Wed 10/20/10
2 Task 2 2 days Wed 10/20/10 Thu 10/21/10
3 Task 3 4 days Fri 10/22/10 Wed 10/27/10
4 Task 4 3 days Thu 10/28/10 Mon 11/1/10
5 Task 5 12 days Tue 11/2/10 Wed 11/17/10
6 Task 6 3 days Thu 11/18/10 Mon 11/22/10
7 Task 7 4 days Tue 11/23/10 Fri 11/26/10
8 Task 8 2 days Mon 11/29/10 Tue 11/30/10
9 Task 9 1 day Wed 12/1/10 Wed 12/1/10
10 Task 10 0 days Wed 12/1/10 Wed 12/1/10
Oct 17, '10
Oct 31, '10
Nov 14, '10
Nov 28, '10
Dec 12, '10
10/20
12/1
Gantt Chart

Figure 5–10

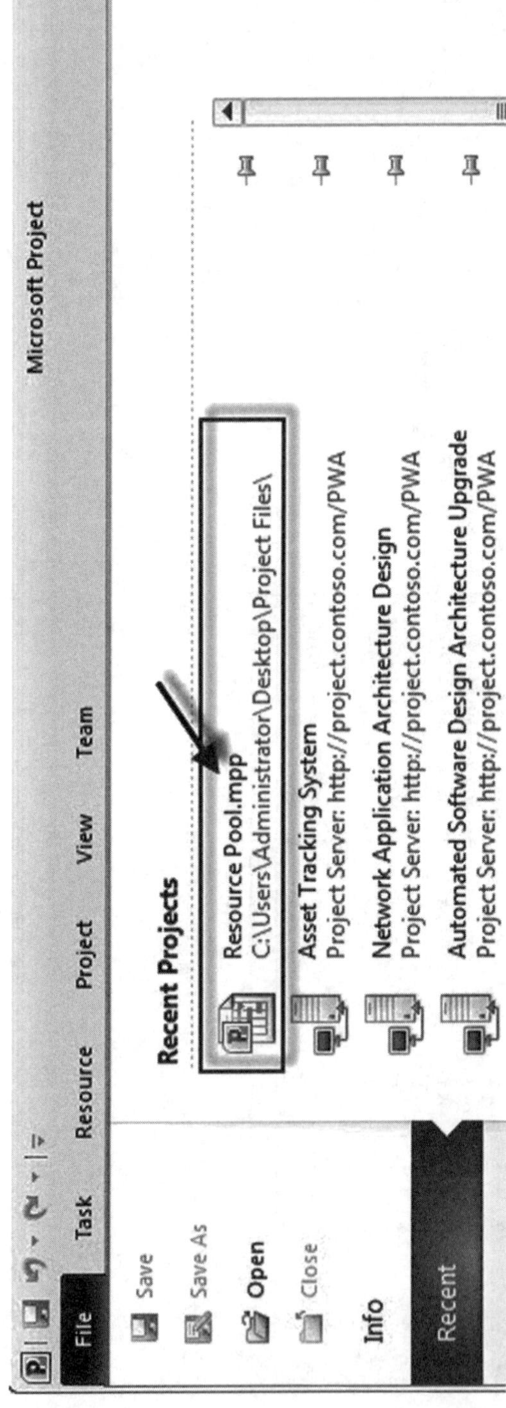

Figure 5–11

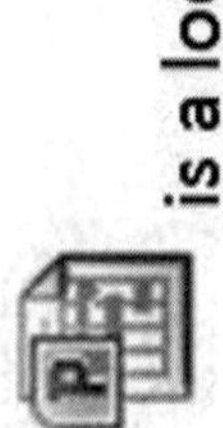

Figure 5–12

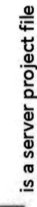

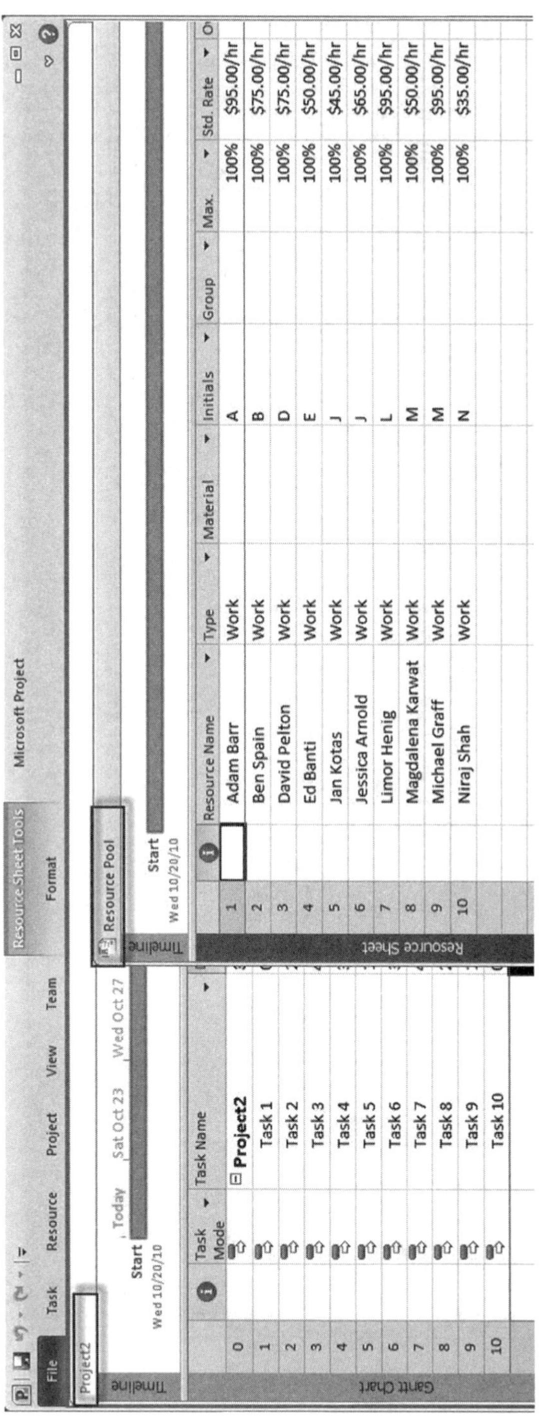
Microsoft Project
Resource Sheet Tools
File
Task
Resource
Project
View
Team
Format
Project2
Timeline
Start
Wed 10/20/10
Today
Sat Oct 23
Wed Oct 27
Task Mode
Task Name
Project2
Task 1
Task 2
Task 3
Task 4
Task 5
Task 6
Task 7
Task 8
Task 9
Task 10
Gantt Chart
Resource Pool
Resource Name
Type
Material
Initials
Group
Max.
Std. Rate
Adam Barr Work A 100% $95.00/hr
Ben Spain Work B 100% $75.00/hr
David Pelton Work D 100% $75.00/hr
Ed Banti Work E 100% $50.00/hr
Jan Kotas Work J 100% $45.00/hr
Jessica Arnold Work J 100% $65.00/hr
Limor Henig Work L 100% $95.00/hr
Magdalena Karwat Work M 100% $50.00/hr
Michael Graff Work M 100% $95.00/hr
Niraj Shah Work N 100% $35.00/hr
Resource Sheet

Figure 5–13

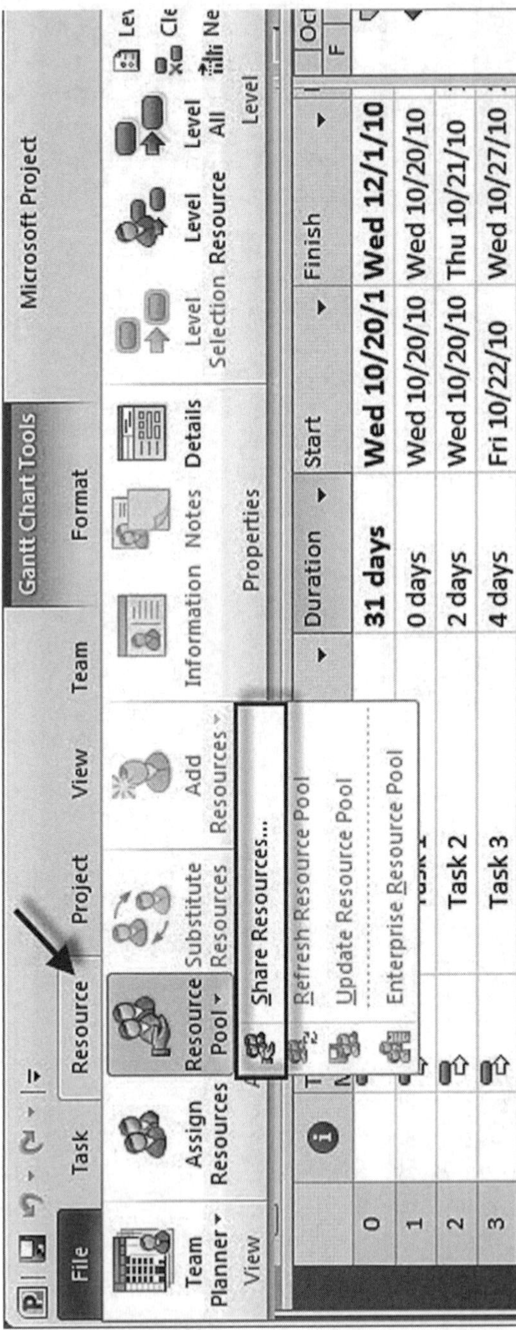
Gantt Chart Tools
Microsoft Project
File
Task
Resource
Project
View
Team
Format
Team Planner
View
Assign Resources
Resource Pool
Substitute Resources
Add Resources
Information
Notes
Details
Properties
Level Selection
Level Resource
Level All
Level
Share Resources...
Refresh Resource Pool
Update Resource Pool
Enterprise Resource Pool
Duration
Start
Finish
31 days
Wed 10/20/1
Wed 12/1/10
0 days
Wed 10/20/10
Wed 10/20/10
Task 2
2 days
Wed 10/20/10
Thu 10/21/10
Task 3
4 days
Fri 10/22/10
Wed 10/27/10

Figure 5–14

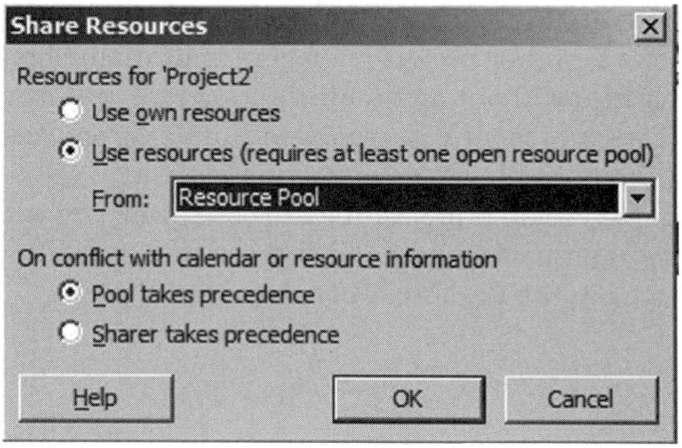

Share Resources

Resources for 'Project2'

Use own resources

Use resources (requires at least one open resource pool)

From: Resource Pool

On conflict with calendar or resource information

Pool takes precedence

Sharer takes precedence

Help OK Cancel

Figure 5–15

The second set of options determines whether the Resource Pool or the new project file (the Sharer) takes precedence whenever there is a calendar or resource conflict. Since it is important to have the Resource Pool regulate the resources, you should select the *Pool takes precedence* option.

Once this has been completed, all resources from the Resource Pool are available to the new project file. And, every other project file that is linked to this Resource Pool will use the same resources.

In the future, whenever you open a project file that is linked to the Resource Pool file, you will get the pop-up box shown in Figure 5–16. There are three

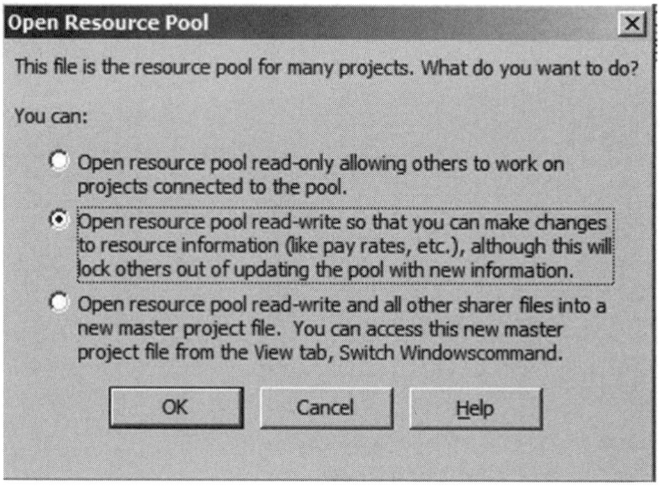

Open Resource Pool

This file is the resource pool for many projects. What do you want to do?

You can:

Open resource pool read-only allowing others to work on projects connected to the pool.

Open resource pool read-write so that you can make changes to resource information (like pay rates, etc.), although this will lock others out of updating the pool with new information.

Open resource pool read-write and all other sharer files into a new master project file. You can access this new master project file from the View tab, Switch Windowscommand.

OK Cancel Help

Figure 5–16

options that appear in the pop-up box. Typically, you will select the first option because that allows for other project managers and resource managers to also open their project files without any conflicts. However, you can select the second option if you want to modify resources in the Resource Pool file. The third option is if you want to create a new master project file.

Once the Resource Pool and project file are both open, you will be able to use the Resource Pool information, and any changes you make to the project file will also be reflected in the Resource Pool views and reports.

6

Who Is Working When: Resource Calendars

An organization usually starts "small" and works its way through the more complex functions of Project Professional and Project Server. Creating a resource and a Resource Pool are important first steps in using resource management. Creating a standard calendar is another important step to having consistent working times. A third step is to customize a resource's calendar to match his or her specific schedule.

Once a resource is assigned to a calendar, whether a standard or customized one (like the Four Ten Hours calendar built in Chapter 4), you can adjust the working times for that resource. This allows for better information and more realistic scheduling for the resource. Following the philosophy of starting small, we don't recommend trying to enter every possible event that is an exception to the resource's normal working times. For example, if a resource is taking a two-week vacation, it would be good to enter that into their calendar. However, if they are leaving work a half hour early tomorrow, you shouldn't worry about trying to get that into their calendar.

The goal of resource management is to accurately predict working times, availability, scheduling, and other factors. It is up to you and your organizational structure to determine the depth and level of detail that you want to use to manage those items. Updating a resource's calendar for a two-week vacation is probably more important than trying to modify their calendar for the "timetable of life." If a resource is out of the office for two straight weeks, that could significantly affect one or more schedules, but if he or she has to leave a little early one day, there may be a plan to make that time up, so any adjustments to calendars would only be extra administrative work.

The authors have worked with clients who have certain schedules that are literally designed to report down to the minute. In those situations, and for the resources assigned to those schedules, it may be very important to account for every minute of their time. This is an example to illustrate that you should plan to manage resource calendars to the depth and level of detail that your organization needs.

Changing Working Time for One Resource

Once you have all of your organization's enterprise resources set up, you can begin to update their individual resource calendars. There are some important things to understand about calendars before we just jump in here. As discussed in Chapter 4, Microsoft Project has three types of calendars: task calendars, resource calendars, and project calendars. In this case, we will adjust the working time in the resource calendar for a specific resource. Therefore, it is important to note that we are modifying the working time for the resource only and not for everybody assigned to this specific resource calendar.

We will walk through this process step-by-step. This is one case where the Project Server and Project Professional stand-alone versions overlap, so we won't need to demonstrate this example in two separate ways. The Project Server method involves a few more steps than directly changing the working time in the stand-alone version. For Project Server, shown in Figure 6–1, you need to go to PWA and click on Resource Center on the left-hand side of the page.

The Resource Center in Microsoft Project Server is now open. Since we are adjusting an existing resource, we are going to take a resource that's already been created, and then modify the working time for this resource's resource calendar. First, you need to click in the check box next to the resource name. As shown in Figure 6–2, we have selected the resource *Adam Barr*. You can select more than one resource at a time to open in the Enterprise Resource Global file by selecting more than one check box. Once you have the resource(s) selected, click on the Open icon near the top left of the default resources tab on the Resource Center screen. This will open Microsoft Project Professional and the Enterprise Resource Global file.

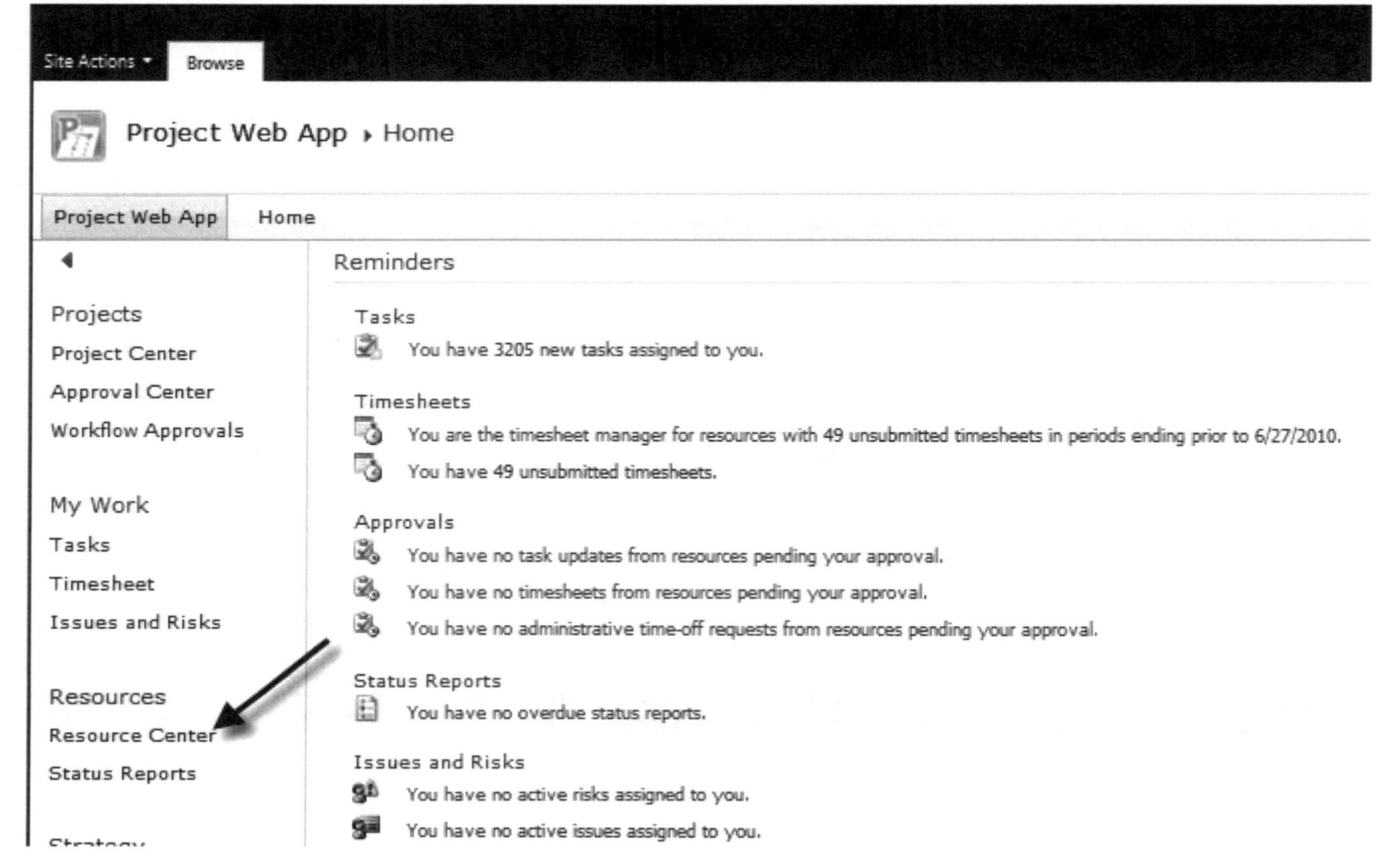

Site Actions
Browse
Project Web App ▸ Home
Project Web App
Home
Projects
Project Center
Approval Center
Workflow Approvals
My Work
Tasks
Timesheet
Issues and Risks
Resources
Resource Center
Status Reports
Reminders
Tasks
You have 3205 new tasks assigned to you.
Timesheets
You are the timesheet manager for resources with 49 unsubmitted timesheets in periods ending prior to 6/27/2010.
You have 49 unsubmitted timesheets.
Approvals
You have no task updates from resources pending your approval.
You have no timesheets from resources pending your approval.
You have no administrative time-off requests from resources pending your approval.
Status Reports
You have no overdue status reports.
Issues and Risks
You have no active risks assigned to you.
You have no active issues assigned to you.

Figure 6–1

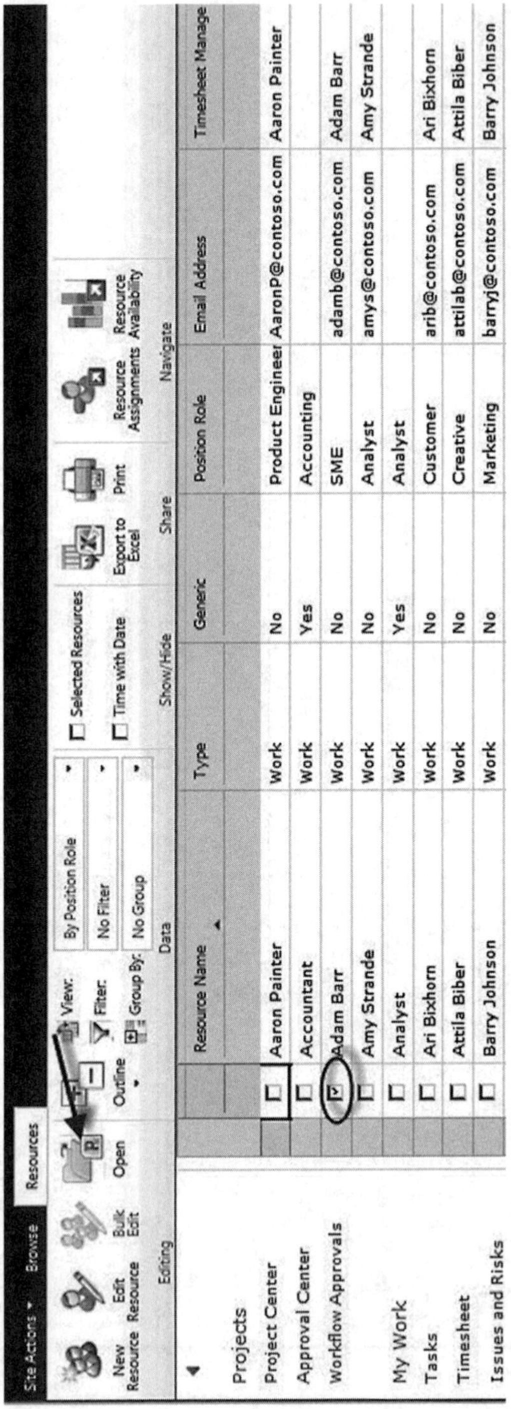

Resource Name	Type	Generic	Position Role	Email Address	Timesheet Manage
Aaron Painter	Work	No	Product Engineer	AaronP@contoso.com	Aaron Painter
Accountant	Work	Yes	Accounting		
Adam Barr	Work	No	SME	adamb@contoso.com	Adam Barr
Amy Strande	Work	No	Analyst	amys@contoso.com	Amy Strande
Analyst	Work	Yes	Analyst		
Ari Bixhorn	Work	No	Customer	arib@contoso.com	Ari Bixhorn
Attila Biber	Work	No	Creative	attilab@contoso.com	Attila Biber
Barry Johnson	Work	No	Marketing	barryj@contoso.com	Barry Johnson

Figure 6–2

As shown in Figure 6–3, the Enterprise Resource sheet in Microsoft Project Professional looks just like the regular resource sheet except it clearly states enterprise resources at the top of the screen. In order to get to the resource calendar, find the name of the resource whose calendar you want to modify and simply double click on their name. This will open the Resource Information box.

It is at this point where the stand-alone and Server versions are similar. In the stand-alone version, you will need to select your resource from the Resource Pool directly. However, once you have selected the resource and double clicked on the name, the Resource Information box will open. As shown in Figure 6–4, this box looks the same whether in the Server or stand-alone version.

The Resource Information box contains several pieces of information. This is the information that was completed when the resource was set up. The main thing to look for at this time is the Change Working Time button. Once you click on that button, the Change Working Time box appears.

The Change Working Time box is where you will actually change the working time for the particular resource. Let's say that Adam is going to be on vacation the first full week in July. In order to denote that on Adam's calendar, you need to get to July. It is important to make sure that you are in the correct month since the box may open to a different date than you expect. There are two common methods to get to the correct date. You could simply either scroll up or down using the arrows, or type in the dates, using the Start and Finish columns. Both of these options are shown in Figure 6–5.

You can select consecutive days by holding down the Shift key and highlighting the dates, or you can go to the Start and Finish columns and click on dates from the drop-down calendars. Once the dates are selected, or if you are going to type in the dates, you must give it an applicable description. As you can see in Figure 6–6, we've titled Adam's week off as *Vacation*.

Once you have modified the dates in the Change Working Time box, the days you set up in the vacation week are noted as being "nonworking" days. This is shown in Figure 6–7 on the right side of the box. Also, the dates are highlighted visually in the calendar to show that an exception has been made. The lower right hand side of the box states the exception that we called "Vacation" is now on the calendar for Adam.

Again, it is important to note that we are adjusting the calendar only for Adam Barr and not the entire calendar for everybody. If you look in the Change Working Time box, you will see that it states the information in the Standard

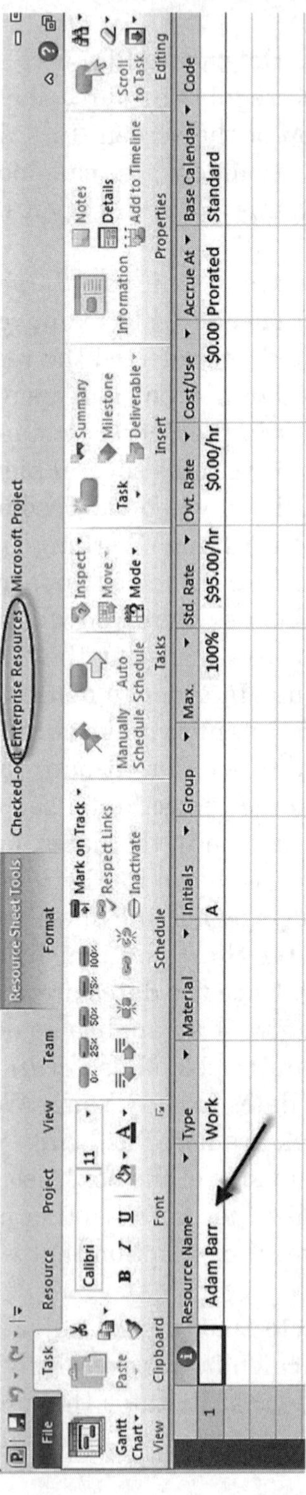
File
Task
Resource
Project
View
Team
Resource Sheet Tools
Format
Checked-out Enterprise Resources
Microsoft Project
Gantt Chart
Paste
Calibri
11
Mark on Track
Respect Links
Inactivate
Manually Schedule
Auto Schedule
Inspect
Move
Mode
Task
Summary
Milestone
Deliverable
Information
Notes
Details
Add to Timeline
Scroll to Task
View
Clipboard
Font
Schedule
Tasks
Insert
Properties
Editing
Resource Name
Type
Material
Initials
Group
Max.
Std. Rate
Ovt. Rate
Cost/Use
Accrue At
Base Calendar
Code
1
Adam Barr
Work
A
100%
$95.00/hr
$0.00/hr
$0.00
Prorated
Standard

Figure 6–3

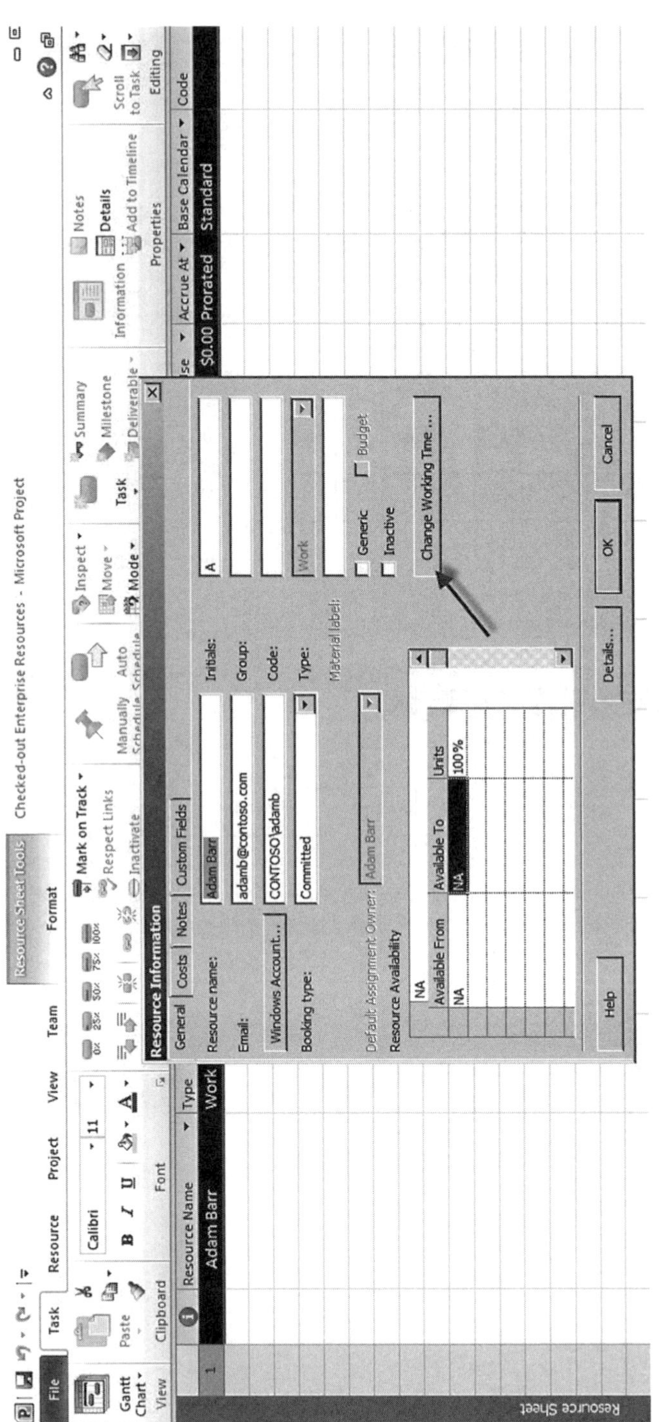
Checked-out Enterprise Resources - Microsoft Project
Resource Sheet Tools
File
Task
Resource
Project
View
Team
Format
Resource Information
General
Costs
Notes
Custom Fields
Resource name:
Adam Barr
Initials:
A
Email:
adamb@contoso.com
Group:
Windows Account...
CONTOSO\adamb
Code:
Booking type:
Committed
Type:
Work
Material label:
Default Assignment Owner:
Adam Barr
Generic
Budget
Inactive
Resource Availability
Available From
Available To
Units
NA
100%
Change Working Time ...
Help
Details...
OK
Cancel
Resource Name
Adam Barr
Accrue At
$0.00 Prorated
Base Calendar
Standard
Code
Resource Sheet

Figure 6–4

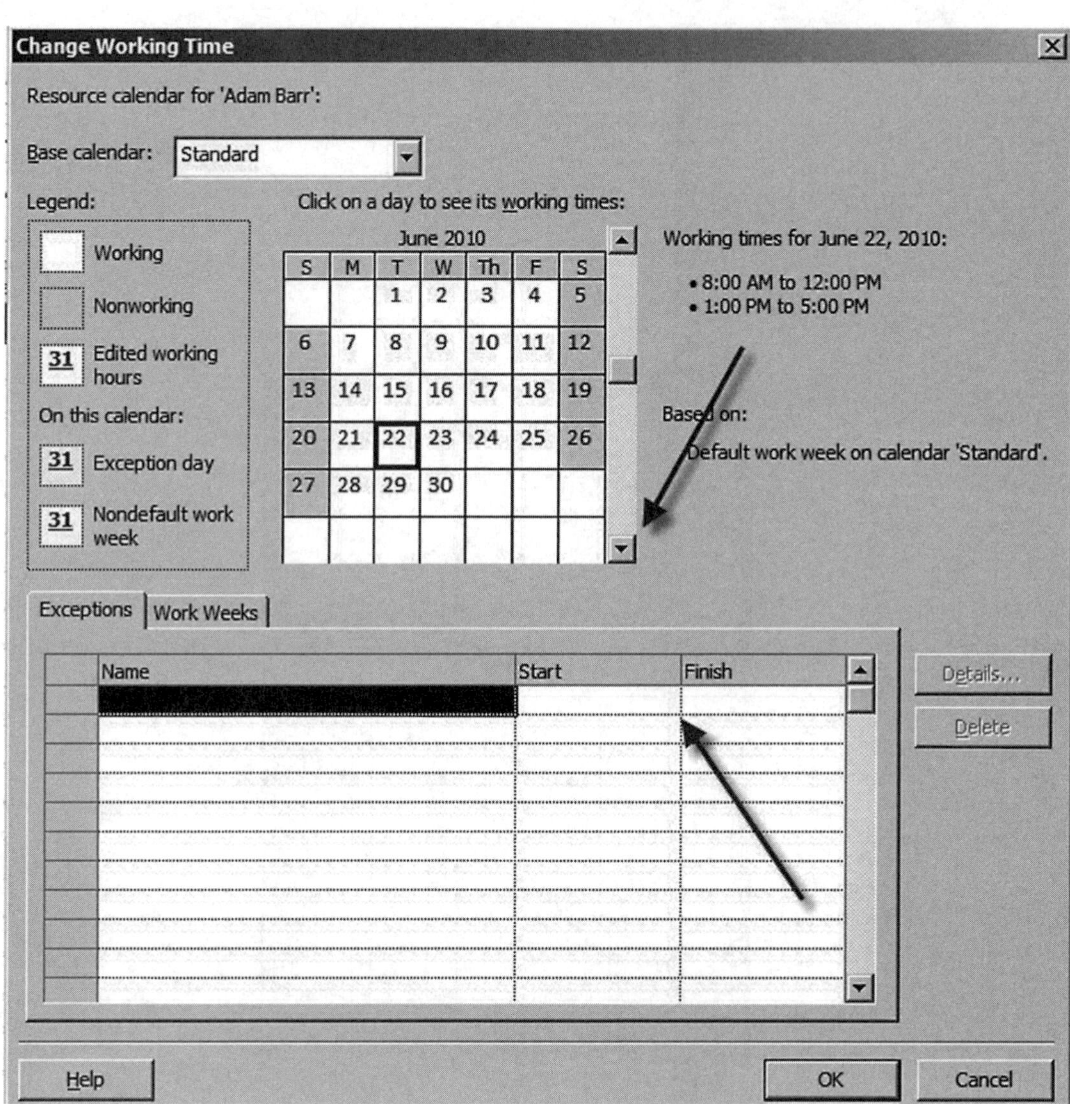
Change Working Time
Resource calendar for 'Adam Barr':
Base calendar: Standard
Legend:
Working
Nonworking
31 Edited working hours
On this calendar:
31 Exception day
31 Nondefault work week
Click on a day to see its working times:
June 2010
S M T W Th F S
Working times for June 22, 2010:
• 8:00 AM to 12:00 PM
• 1:00 PM to 5:00 PM
Based on:
Default work week on calendar 'Standard'.
Exceptions
Work Weeks
Name
Start
Finish
Details...
Delete
Help
OK
Cancel

Figure 6–5

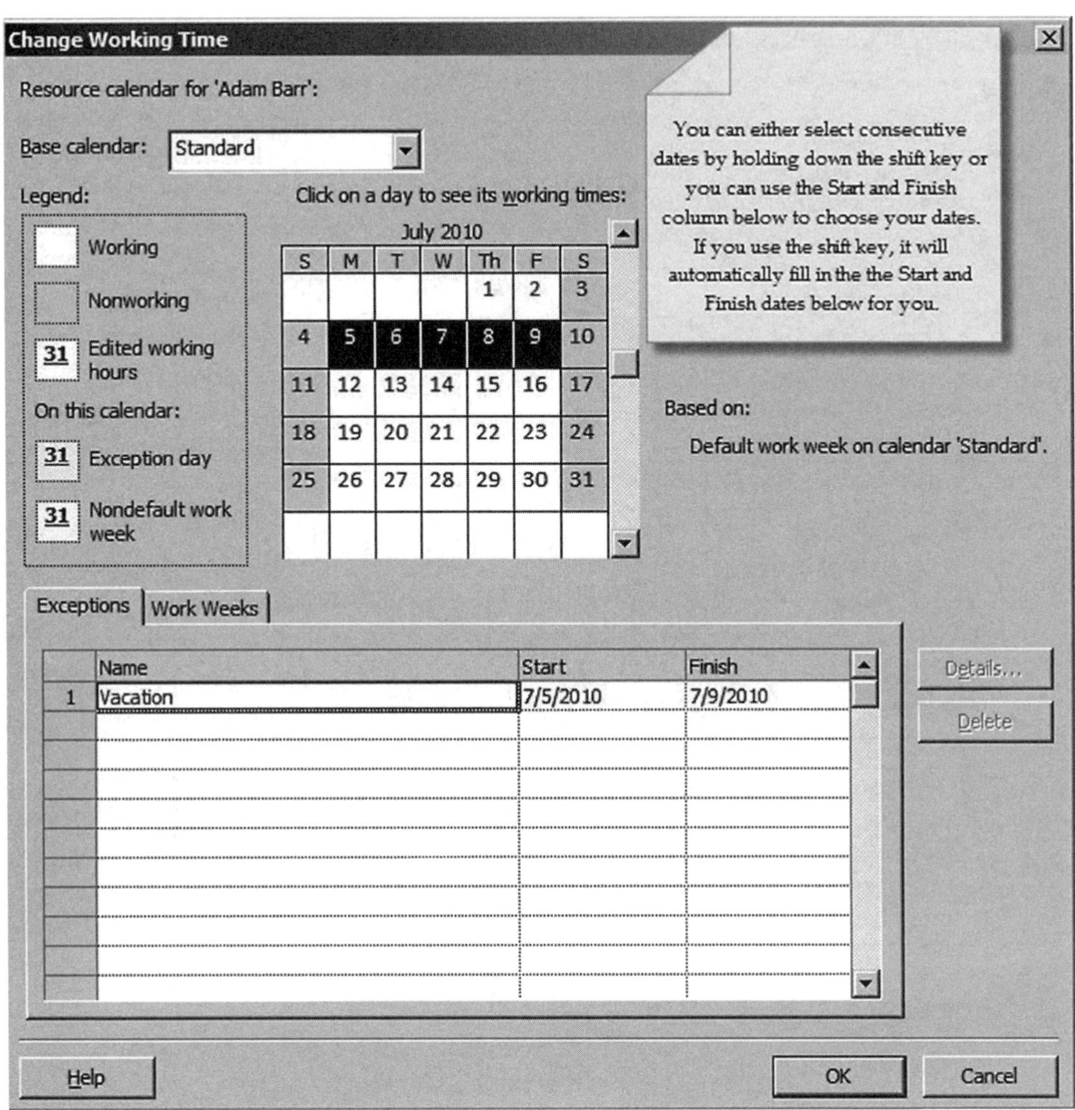
Change Working Time
Resource calendar for 'Adam Barr':
Base calendar: Standard
Legend:
Working
Nonworking
Edited working hours
On this calendar:
Exception day
Nondefault work week
Click on a day to see its working times:
July 2010
You can either select consecutive dates by holding down the shift key or you can use the Start and Finish column below to choose your dates. If you use the shift key, it will automatically fill in the the Start and Finish dates below for you.
Based on:
Default work week on calendar 'Standard'.
Exceptions
Work Weeks
Name
Start
Finish
Vacation
7/5/2010
7/9/2010
Details...
Delete
Help
OK
Cancel

Figure 6–6

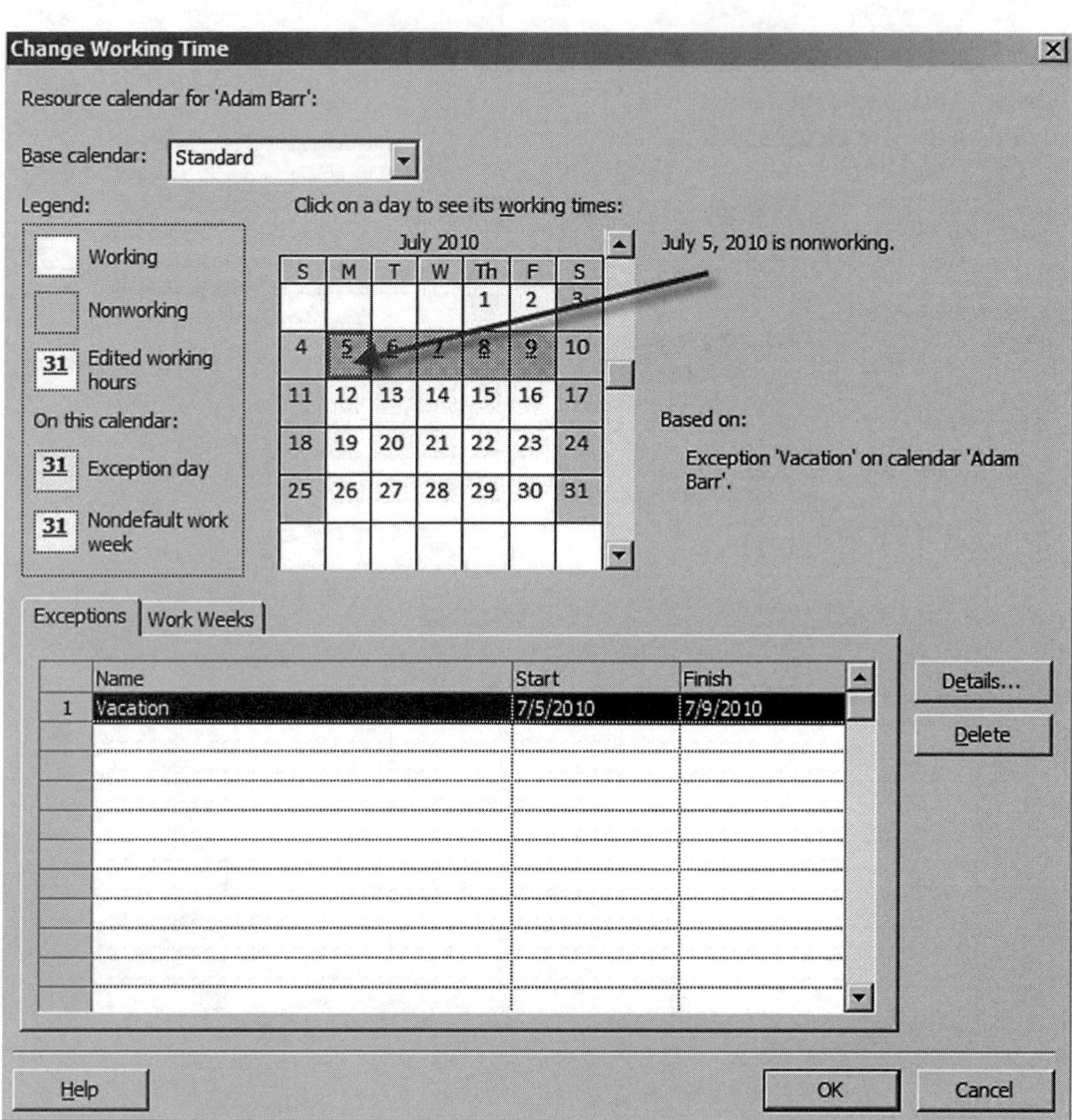
Change Working Time
Resource calendar for 'Adam Barr':
Base calendar: Standard
Legend:
Working
Nonworking
31 Edited working hours
On this calendar:
31 Exception day
31 Nondefault work week
Click on a day to see its working times:
July 2010
S M T W Th F S
July 5, 2010 is nonworking.
Based on:
Exception 'Vacation' on calendar 'Adam Barr'.
Exceptions
Work Weeks
Name Start Finish
1 Vacation 7/5/2010 7/9/2010
Details...
Delete
Help
OK
Cancel

Figure 6–7

calendar on the top of the screen, but just above that it also states that it is in the resource calendar for Adam.

You could do this exact same scenario for only one day off. If Adam knows he's going to be gone for his son's birthday, then you can mark that off on his resource calendar.

You can also change working time, not just days. Let's say Adam had a week where he was only working four hours per day for that entire week. We could enter that on the calendar as well.

To change the working time for Adam, we will have steps very similar to those used to change the working time for the project calendar called Four Ten Hours. For this example, we selected the week of August 16th and called the Exception "Half Time." Adam is only going to work half time, or four hours, each day that week. Since we've typed in our exception name and selected the days, now all you need to do is to indicate to the system that Adam's hours are only going to be four hours per day. To do this, click on the Details button, as shown in Figure 6–8.

Clicking on the Details button brings up the Exceptions Details box. As demonstrated in Figure 6–9, select the Working Times option. After selecting this option, delete the 1:00 PM to 5:00 PM entry in the Times area (this will probably be line 2). This will change Adam's working times for that week from 8:00 AM to 12:00 PM. In the bottom of the box, in the Range of Recurrence section, you can see the range starts on 8/16 and ends after five occurrences. This automatically filled in once the dates were selected in the other screen. Click on the OK button to go back to the Change Working Time box.

Just as when we modified the calendar for vacation time, we can now see that Adam's working times for those particular days are highlighted as an exception, as shown in Figure 6–10.

After clicking on OK from the Change Working Time box, you will be back to the Resource sheet. When you're finished in the Enterprise Resource sheet, it's very important to Save and Close the sheet. This is where the stand-alone and Server versions differ. For the stand-alone version, when you have saved the Resource Pool and closed the project, you are done.

For the Server version, you need to Save, Close, and check back in the resources that you have checked out. As shown in Figure 6–11, you will need to

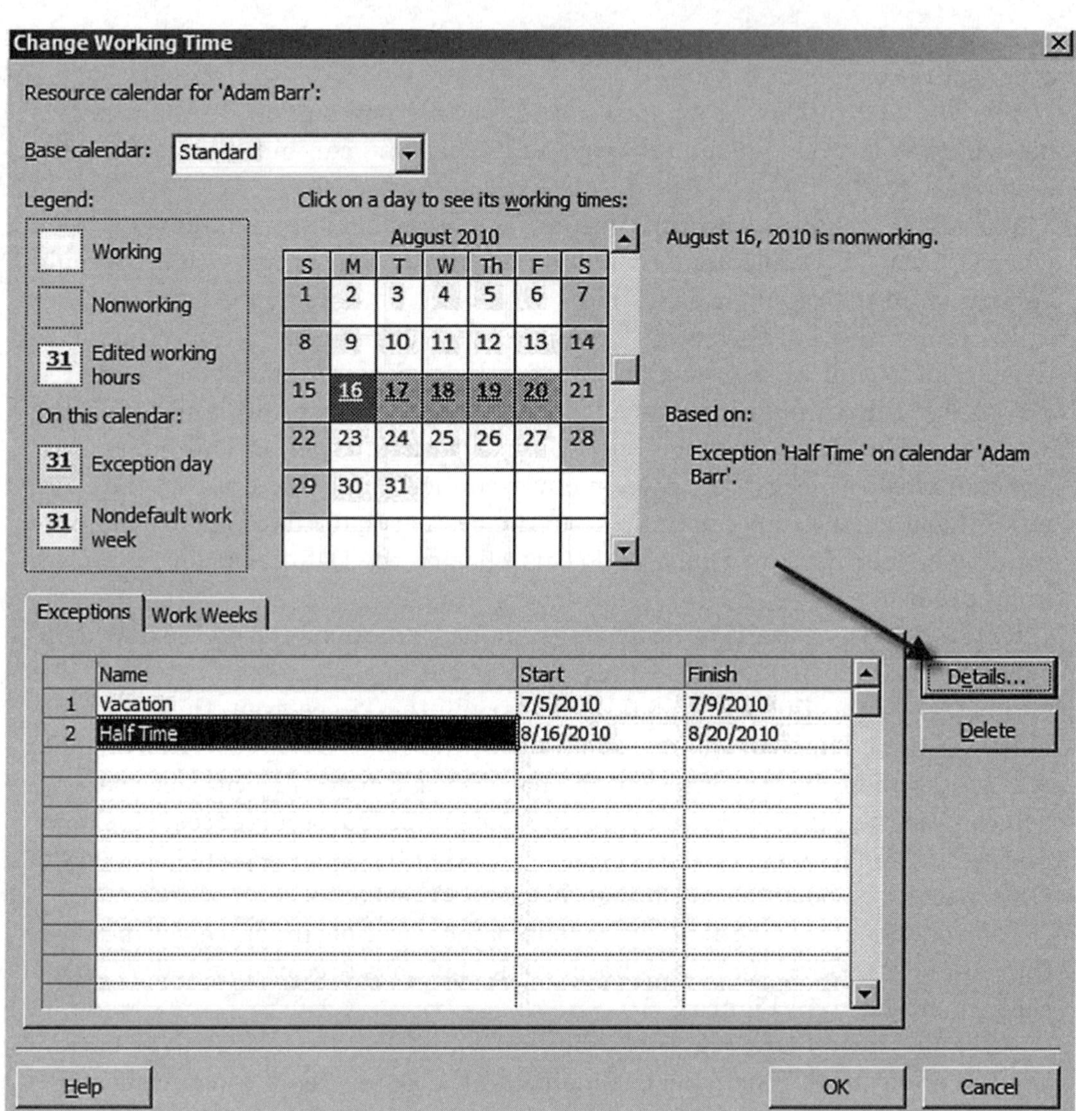
Change Working Time
Resource calendar for 'Adam Barr':
Base calendar: Standard
Legend:
Working
Nonworking
31 Edited working hours
On this calendar:
31 Exception day
31 Nondefault work week
Click on a day to see its working times:
August 2010
S M T W Th F S
1 2 3 4 5 6 7
8 9 10 11 12 13 14
15 16 17 18 19 20 21
22 23 24 25 26 27 28
29 30 31
August 16, 2010 is nonworking.
Based on:
Exception 'Half Time' on calendar 'Adam Barr'.
Exceptions
Work Weeks
Name
Start
Finish
1 Vacation 7/5/2010 7/9/2010
2 Half Time 8/16/2010 8/20/2010
Details...
Delete
Help
OK
Cancel

Figure 6–8

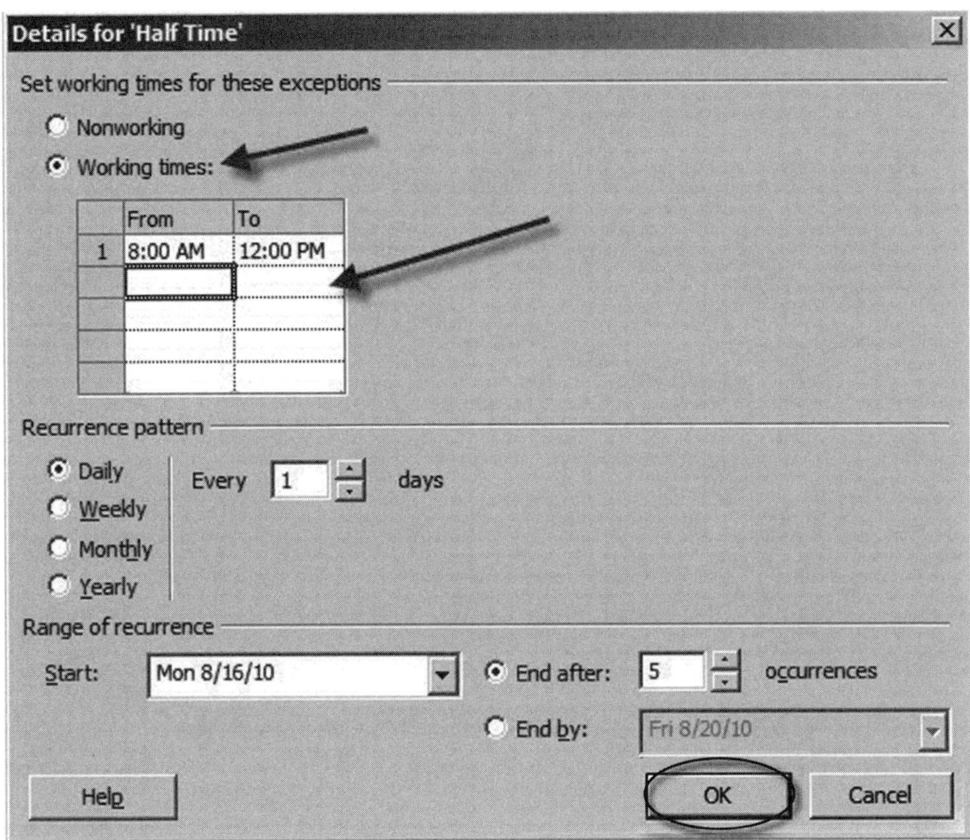

Figure 6–9

click on File at the top left corner of the screen in Project Professional, and then choose Close.

To have the best information about resources, their availability, and how that affects your schedules requires a minimal amount of setup. The level of setup required is determined by the amount of information and the level of detail about that information that your organization desires. It is recommended to start out with less information and work your way up to having more details over time. By starting with a Resource Pool and then adding a standard calendar for your organization you begin to gain some understanding of your resource capacity and utilization.

Once a standard calendar is built, one or more calendars that better matches the working hours of groups of resources can be built to give even more clarity

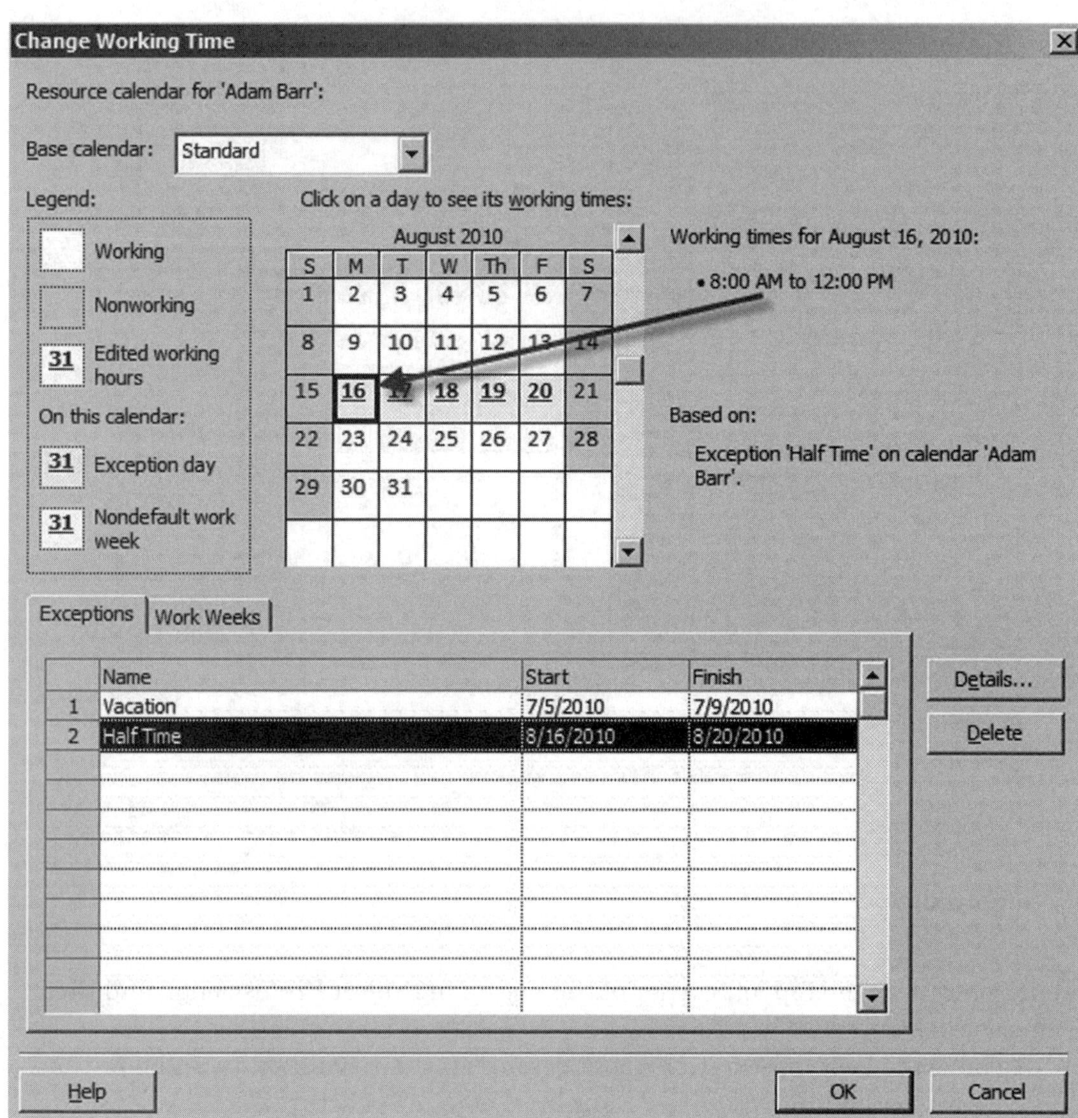
Change Working Time
Resource calendar for 'Adam Barr':
Base calendar: Standard
Legend:
Working
Nonworking
31 Edited working hours
On this calendar:
31 Exception day
31 Nondefault work week
Click on a day to see its working times:
August 2010
S M T W Th F S
1 2 3 4 5 6 7
8 9 10 11 12 13 14
15 16 17 18 19 20 21
22 23 24 25 26 27 28
29 30 31
Working times for August 16, 2010:
• 8:00 AM to 12:00 PM
Based on:
Exception 'Half Time' on calendar 'Adam Barr'.
Exceptions
Work Weeks
Name
Start
Finish
1 Vacation 7/5/2010 7/9/2010
2 Half Time 8/16/2010 8/20/2010
Details...
Delete
Help
OK
Cancel

Figure 6–10

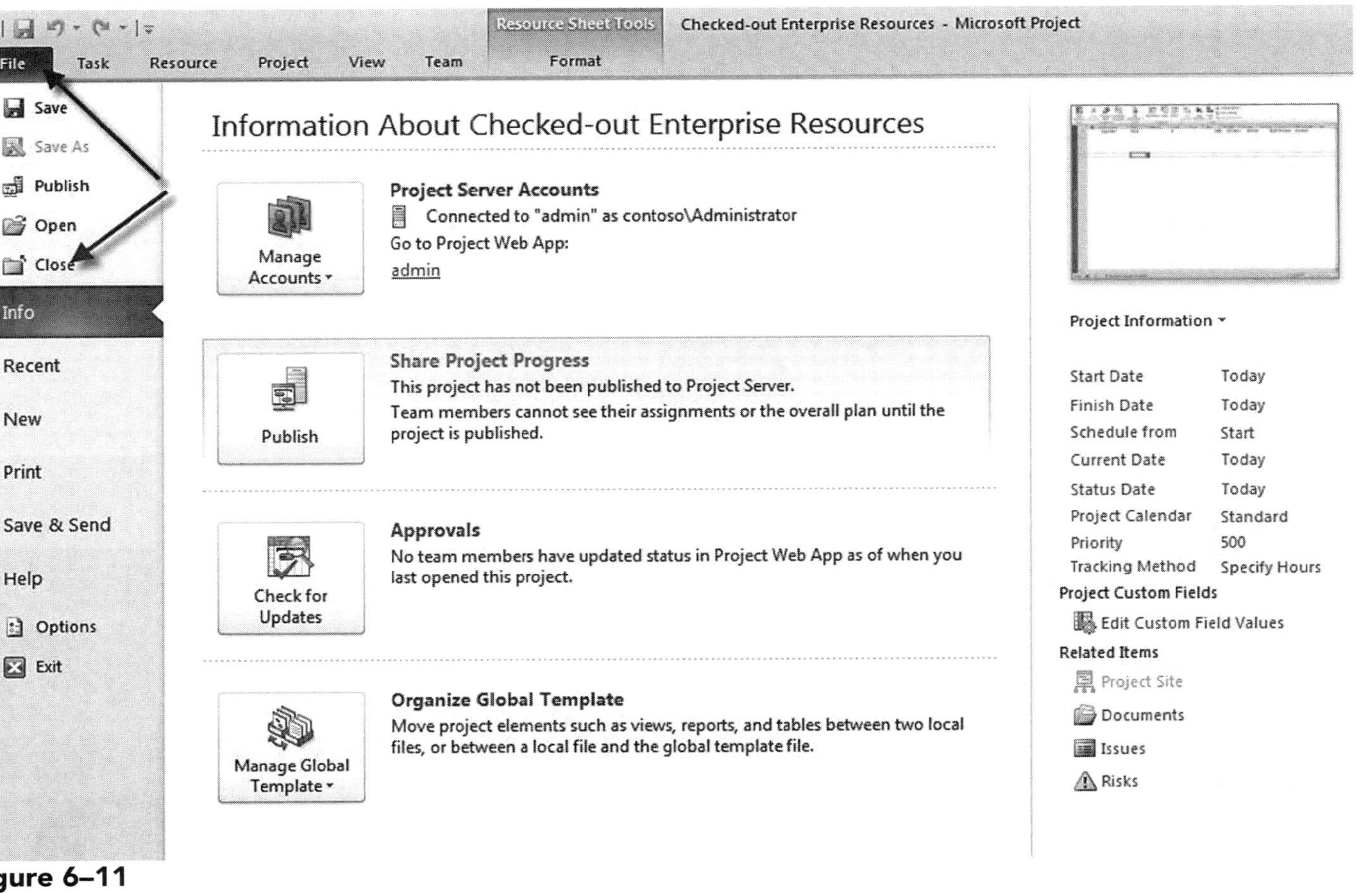
Checked-out Enterprise Resources - Microsoft Project
Resource Sheet Tools
File
Task
Resource
Project
View
Team
Format
Save
Save As
Publish
Open
Close
Info
Recent
New
Print
Save & Send
Help
Options
Exit
Information About Checked-out Enterprise Resources
Manage Accounts
Project Server Accounts
Connected to "admin" as contoso\Administrator
Go to Project Web App:
admin
Publish
Share Project Progress
This project has not been published to Project Server.
Team members cannot see their assignments or the overall plan until the project is published.
Check for Updates
Approvals
No team members have updated status in Project Web App as of when you last opened this project.
Manage Global Template
Organize Global Template
Move project elements such as views, reports, and tables between two local files, or between a local file and the global template file.
Project Information
Start Date Today
Finish Date Today
Schedule from Start
Current Date Today
Status Date Today
Project Calendar Standard
Priority 500
Tracking Method Specify Hours
Project Custom Fields
Edit Custom Field Values
Related Items
Project Site
Documents
Issues
Risks

Figure 6–11

concerning your resource's capacity and utilization. Then, over time, your organization can begin to add individual resource information to those calendars to even further define specific capacity and utilization. Along with giving more information about resources and their working times, your organization can also gain valuable information that will affect the timing of your project file.

7

Assigning a Resource

This chapter covers a large quantity of information about assigning a resource to a task. There are a few different ways to assign a resource to a task, and we will demonstrate the most common methods. There are a few assumptions being made, though. It is assumed that you are using a Resource Pool, whether on Server or in stand-alone mode. It is also assumed that most, if not all, of the resource managers are using the same Resource Pool and are assigning tasks.

While there are several ways to assign resources to a task, it's good practice to get into the habit of assigning, removing, replacing, and matching resources in the Assign Resources dialog box. If you use shortcuts, it's easy to leave some hours assigned to a deleted task or to accidentally remove a resource without removing the hours first, which could result in some lingering data still showing up for that specific resource, whether it be in a report or on his or her task page. This may not sound like much of an issue, but if you're the person that this happens to, it's no fun to see the same phantom task over and over on your task page every day if no one can tell you what it is, how it got there, or how to make it go away!

The first thing that you want to do is to select the resources that you will be using on a project. This is called "building the team" and the drop-down item is titled as such. This will allow you to go through and select as many resources as you think you'll use, and then add them to your team.

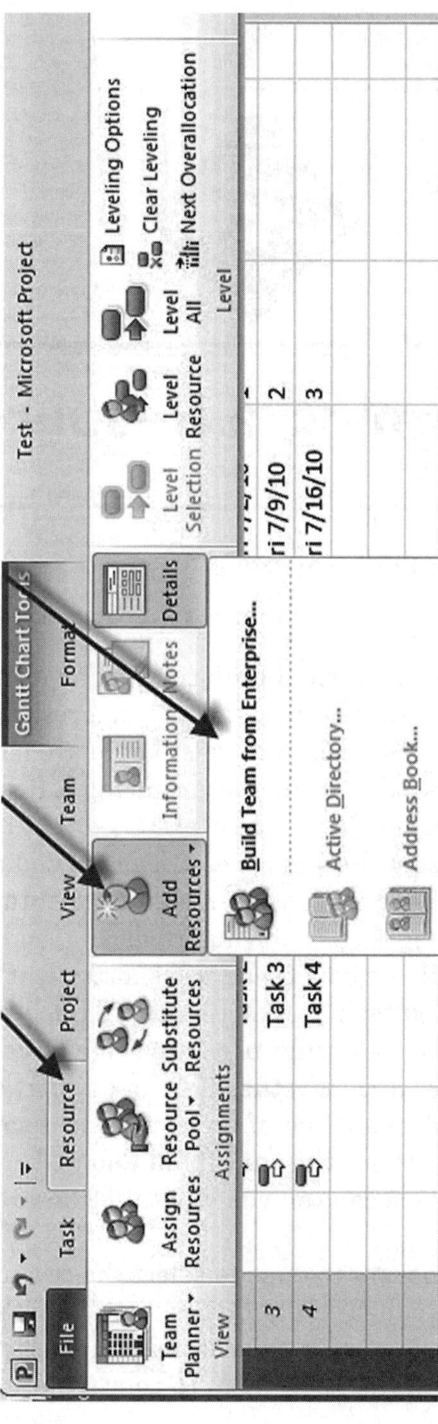
Test - Microsoft Project
File
Task
Resource
Project
View
Team
Gantt Chart Tools
Format
Team Planner ▾
View
Assign Resources
Resource Pool ▾
Substitute Resources
Assignments
Add Resources ▾
Information
Notes
Details
Level Selection
Level Resource
Level All
Leveling Options
Clear Leveling
Next Overallocation
Level
Build Team from Enterprise...
Active Directory...
Address Book...
3
4
Task 3
Task 4
ri 7/9/10
ri 7/16/10
2
3

Figure 7–1

For those using Project Server, once in Project Professional, on the default Resource menu bar, click Add Resources and select Build Team from Enterprise in the drop-down, as shown in Figure 7–1.

The Build Team dialog box will open, as shown in Figure 7–2. Let's take a look at the Build Team dialog box and see some of its capabilities. The Build Team dialog box can be a very useful tool if you know how to use it.

The top portion will help you set up filters so that you don't have to scroll down through all of the enterprise resources to find the particular ones that you want. In this list, we have 127 resources available so it would not really take too long to scroll through the list to find the resources that you're looking for. However, if you had 500, that would be a different story! But, if you only need one or two resources, even 127 might be a lengthy number of resources to scroll through.

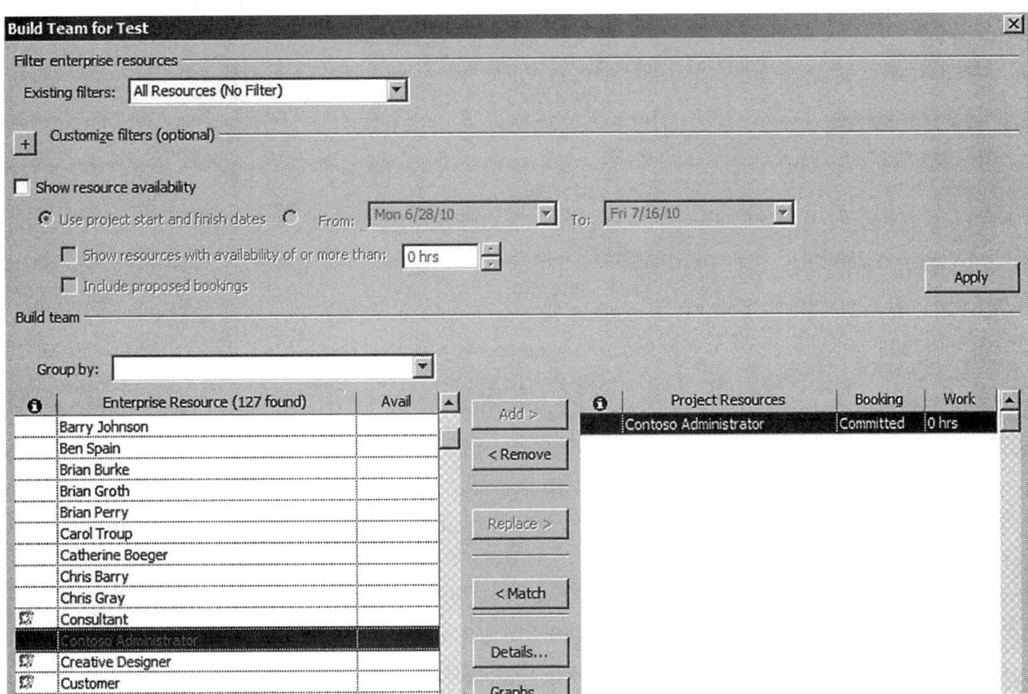

Figure 7–2

One time-saving tip is to type in the first few letters of the resource name that you are looking for in the resource list. This will cause the list box to jump to the resource name that you are looking for.

In the Build Team box, you will see the name of the project in the top bar. In the example, the project name is Test, and so the box states *Build Team for Test.* The left, lower portion of the box is the list of available resources. The right side is the list of already selected resources. In this case, we are using Microsoft's demonstration site user; it shows that we have already selected the resource named Contoso Administrator, which is the resource that we are using to sign into the project.

To set up a filter, you can click on the drop-down box next to Existing filters, and filter the resource list by using any of the pre-defined filters. This is demonstrated in Figure 7–3.

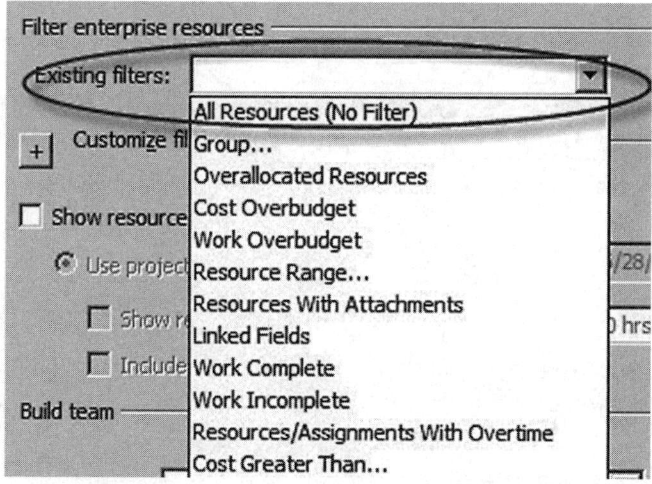

Figure 7–3

Clicking the plus sign next to *Customize Filters (optional)* opens a section where you can create custom filters and save them. We have created one just to give you an idea of what you can create, but you have a lot of different options to choose from. You can select a single value or multiple values to create a custom filter. In the example shown in Figure 7–4, we want to filter out all of the generic resources so that only the named resources are shown in the available list. We have chosen Generic from the Field Name drop-down, and *does not equal* from the Test drop-down. The Value(s) drop-down is Yes. We are telling this custom filter that we want to see all of the resources where the generic field name does not equal Yes. A generic resource is noted in the icon field by the two heads icon. When this filter is applied, those resources disappear from the list. Figure 7–4 shows the creation of the filter; the arrow shows the Generic Resource icon with the *Apply button to filter the list* not chosen.

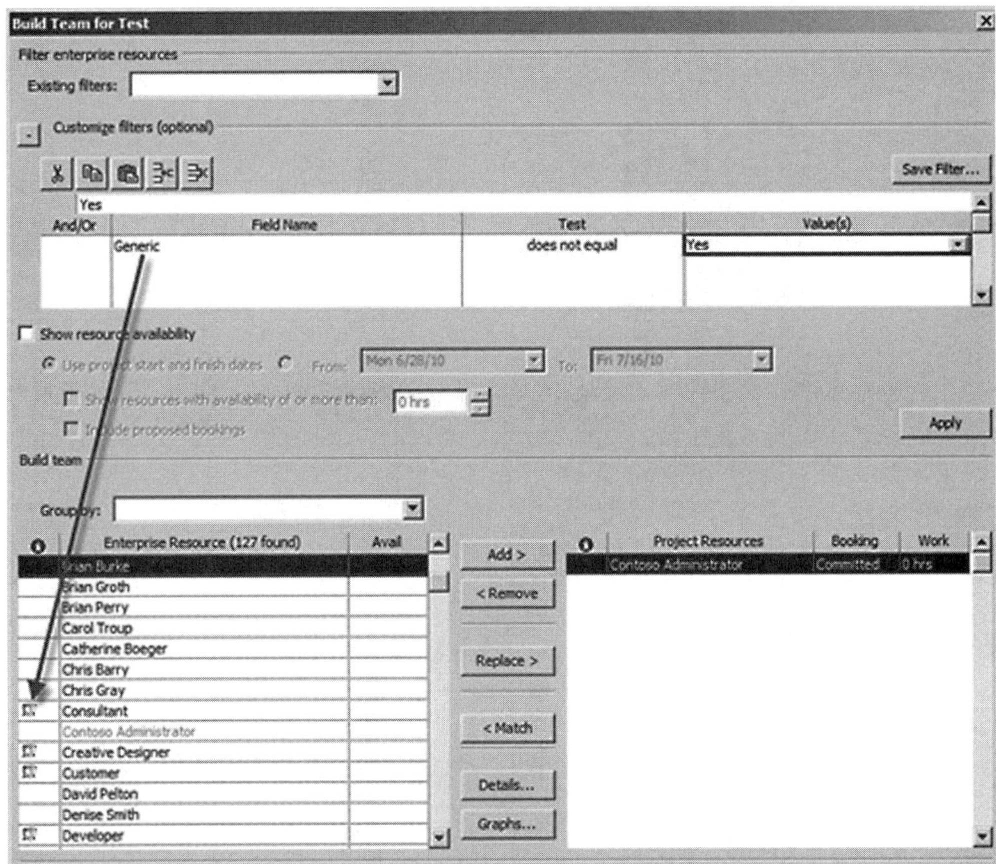

Figure 7–4

Figure 7–5 shows the bottom half of the Build Team box after the filter has been applied. Now you can see that the resources list went from 127 to 104. Choosing the Generic Resource filter should mean that we don't see any of the two head icons in our resource list. Since we don't see those in the indicator column, we can conclude that the custom filter worked. If you create a custom

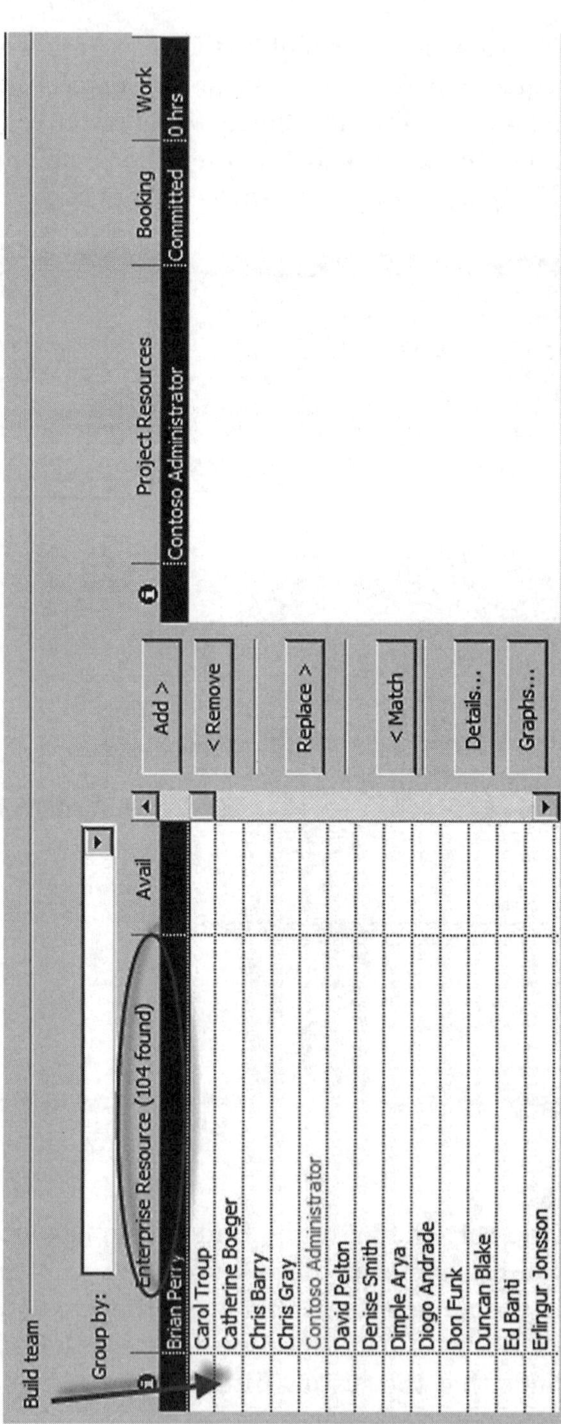
Build team
Group by:
Enterprise Resource (104 found)
Avail
Brian Perry
Carol Troup
Catherine Boeger
Chris Barry
Chris Gray
Contoso Administrator
David Pelton
Denise Smith
Dimple Arya
Diogo Andrade
Don Funk
Duncan Blake
Ed Banti
Erlingur Jonsson
Add >
< Remove
Replace >
< Match
Details...
Graphs...
Project Resources
Booking
Work
Contoso Administrator
Committed
0 hrs

Figure 7–5

filter that you like, and you know that you will use again, there is a Save Filter... button located at the right side of the Customize Filters section. Simply name the filter and it will show up in the Existing Filters drop-down box; the filter will be available to select the next time you come back to the Build Team option.

The next section of the box contains the Show Resource Availability checkbox. Clicking this checkbox tells Microsoft Project 2010 that it needs to look at how much time the resource has available to work on this project. You will need to tell Microsoft Project what variables to consider by using the radio buttons, check boxes, and drop-down boxes located within this section.

This option will use the Resource Pool information, so this is only an effective tool if the resources are being assigned in other projects as well. This is demonstrated in Figure 7–6.

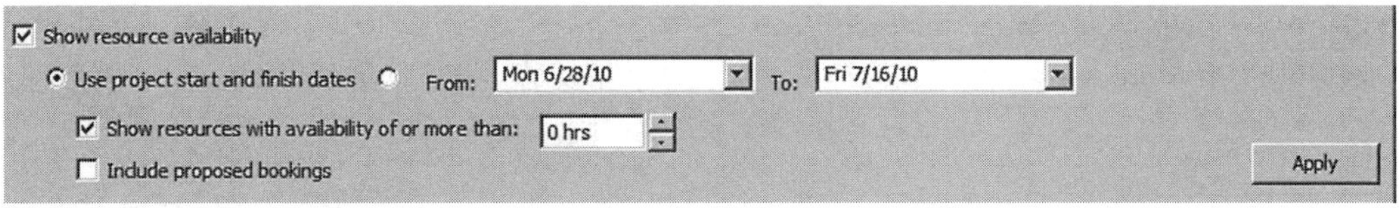

Figure 7–6

You can use the *Use project start and finish dates* radio button to let Microsoft Project use the current project's start and finish dates to weed out any resources that aren't available during that time. You can also click the radio button next to the From drop-down box and select a specific From and To date range for Microsoft Project to use. Microsoft Project will look at each resource's resource calendar to make sure that they are available during the time frames that you have chosen. If they are not, then the resources will not be available in the list once you click the Apply button.

You can also filter out specific resources by placing a check in the *Show resources with availability of or more than:* check box and then providing a number in the hours box. For example, you could place the number 15 in the hours box and Microsoft Project will filter out all of the resources that do not have at least 15 hours of available time that could be assigned to them. You could also include proposed bookings so as not to overallocate a resource that has potential work assigned to them.

The last section of the Build Team box allows you to select the resources that you want to add to the project's team. You can add as many resources as you'll need by simply clicking on them and then clicking the Add button. Once a resource has been selected, it will be displayed in a list on the right side of Project Resources. Figure 7–7 shows the resource list with no resources selected.

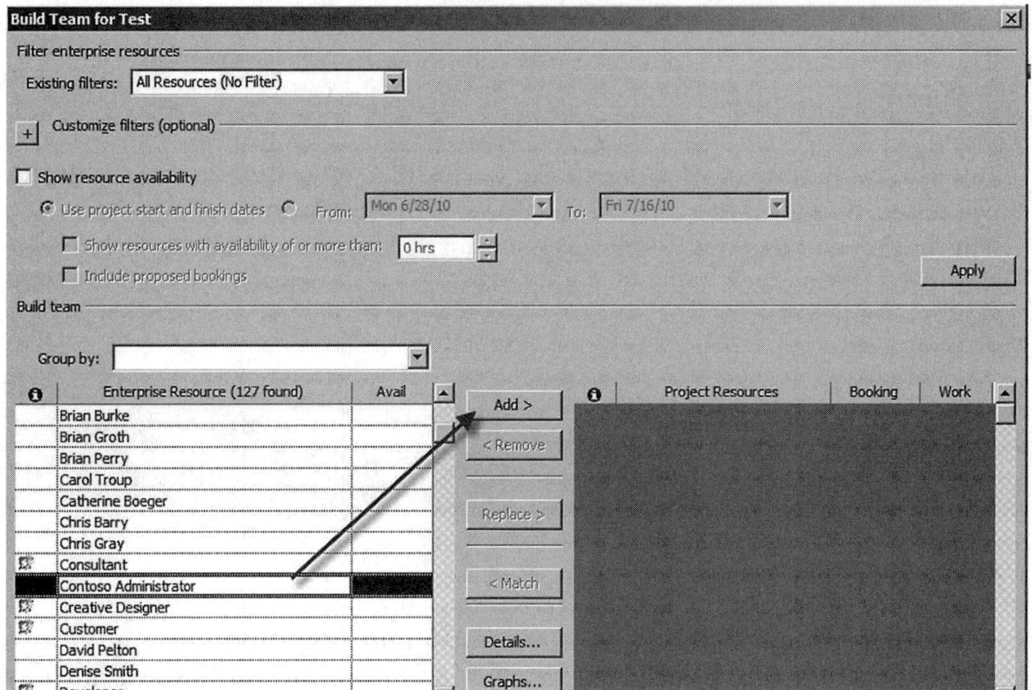

Figure 7–7

You can select multiple resources in the Enterprise Resource box by hitting Shift and selecting a list of consecutive resources, demonstrated in Figure 7–8. Once you click on Add, they will be added to the list on the right.

You can also hold down Ctrl and select multiple resources that are not consecutive, as shown in Figure 7–9.

Only one resource was added this time and it's the Contoso Administrator resource, as shown in Figure 7–10. Once you've added the selected resources to the right side, the Add button is grayed out when you highlight the name on the left side. It will also display as grayed out in the left-hand list if they are already selected. This is helpful when you have made numerous selections, and it isn't easy to just visually look at each side and know the names selected.

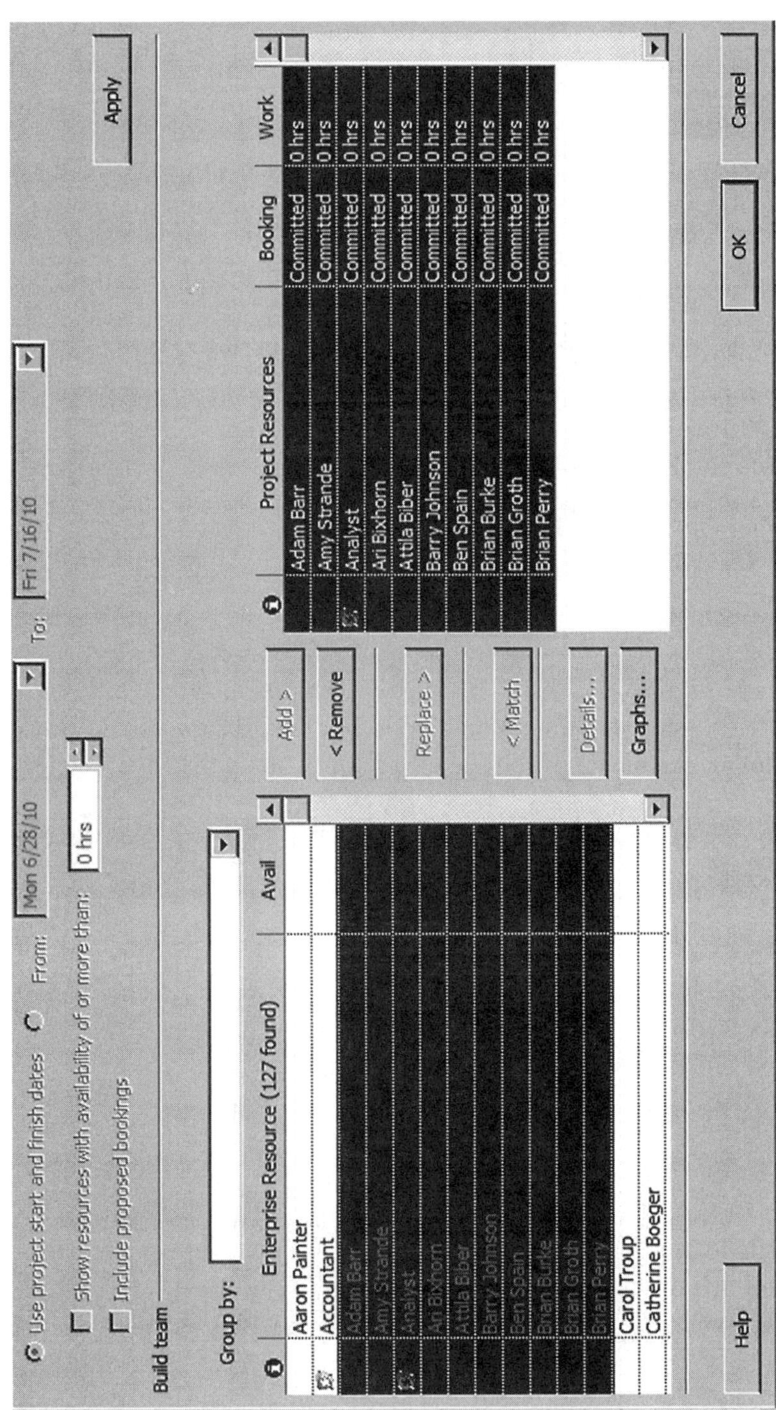
Use project start and finish dates
From:
Mon 6/28/10
To:
Fri 7/16/10
Show resources with availability of or more than:
0 hrs
Include proposed bookings
Apply
Build team
Group by:
Enterprise Resource (127 found)
Avail
Aaron Painter
Accountant
Adam Barr
Amy Strande
Analyst
Ari Bixhorn
Attila Biber
Barry Johnson
Ben Spain
Brian Burke
Brian Groth
Brian Perry
Carol Troup
Catherine Boeger
Add >
< Remove
Replace >
< Match
Details...
Graphs...
Project Resources
Booking
Work
Adam Barr
Amy Strande
Analyst
Ari Bixhorn
Attila Biber
Barry Johnson
Ben Spain
Brian Burke
Brian Groth
Brian Perry
Committed
0 hrs
Help
OK
Cancel

Figure 7–8

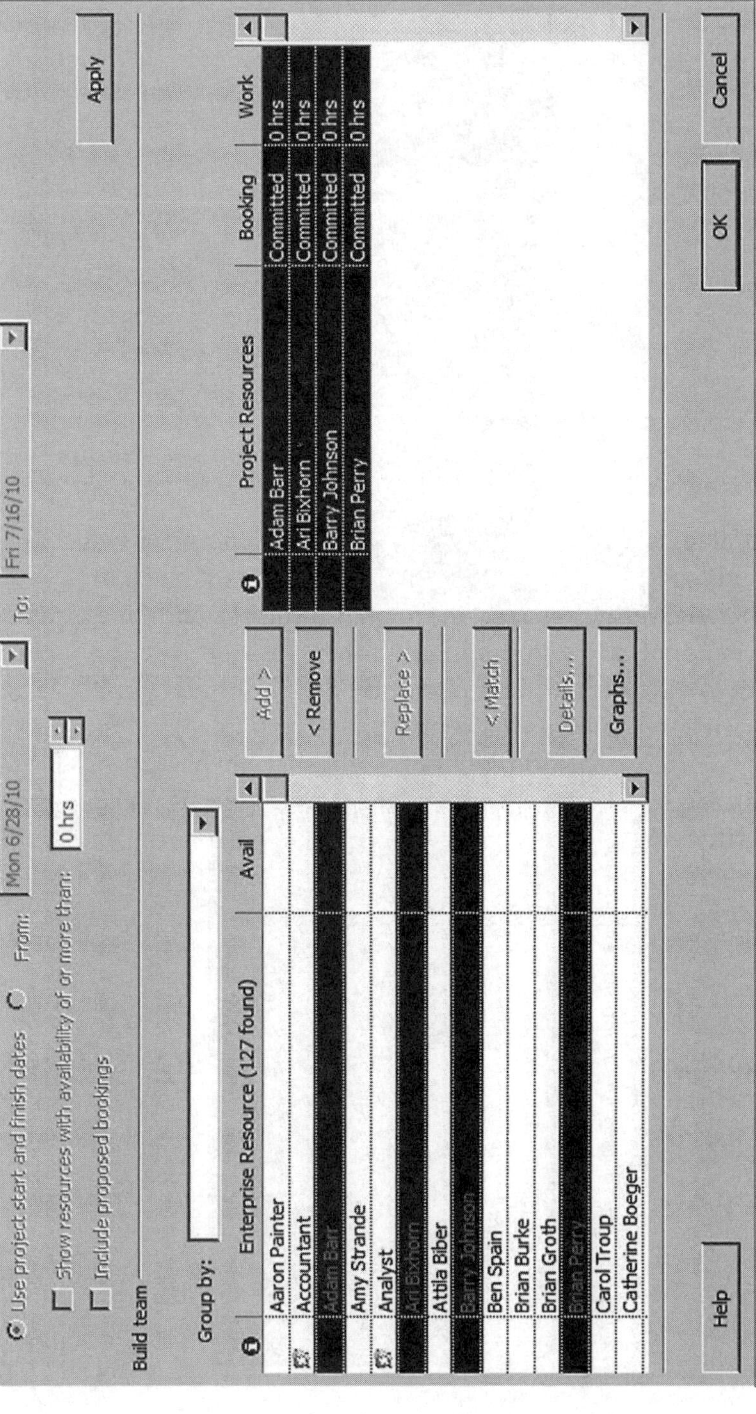
Use project start and finish dates
From: Mon 6/28/10
To: Fri 7/16/10
Show resources with availability of or more than: 0 hrs
Include proposed bookings
Apply
Build team
Group by:
Enterprise Resource (127 found)
Avail
Aaron Painter
Accountant
Adam Barr
Amy Strande
Analyst
Ari Bixhorn
Attila Biber
Barry Johnson
Ben Spain
Brian Burke
Brian Groth
Brian Perry
Carol Troup
Catherine Boeger
Add >
< Remove
Replace >
< Match
Details...
Graphs...
Project Resources
Booking
Work
Adam Barr
Committed
0 hrs
Ari Bixhorn
Committed
0 hrs
Barry Johnson
Committed
0 hrs
Brian Perry
Committed
0 hrs
Help
OK
Cancel

Figure 7–9

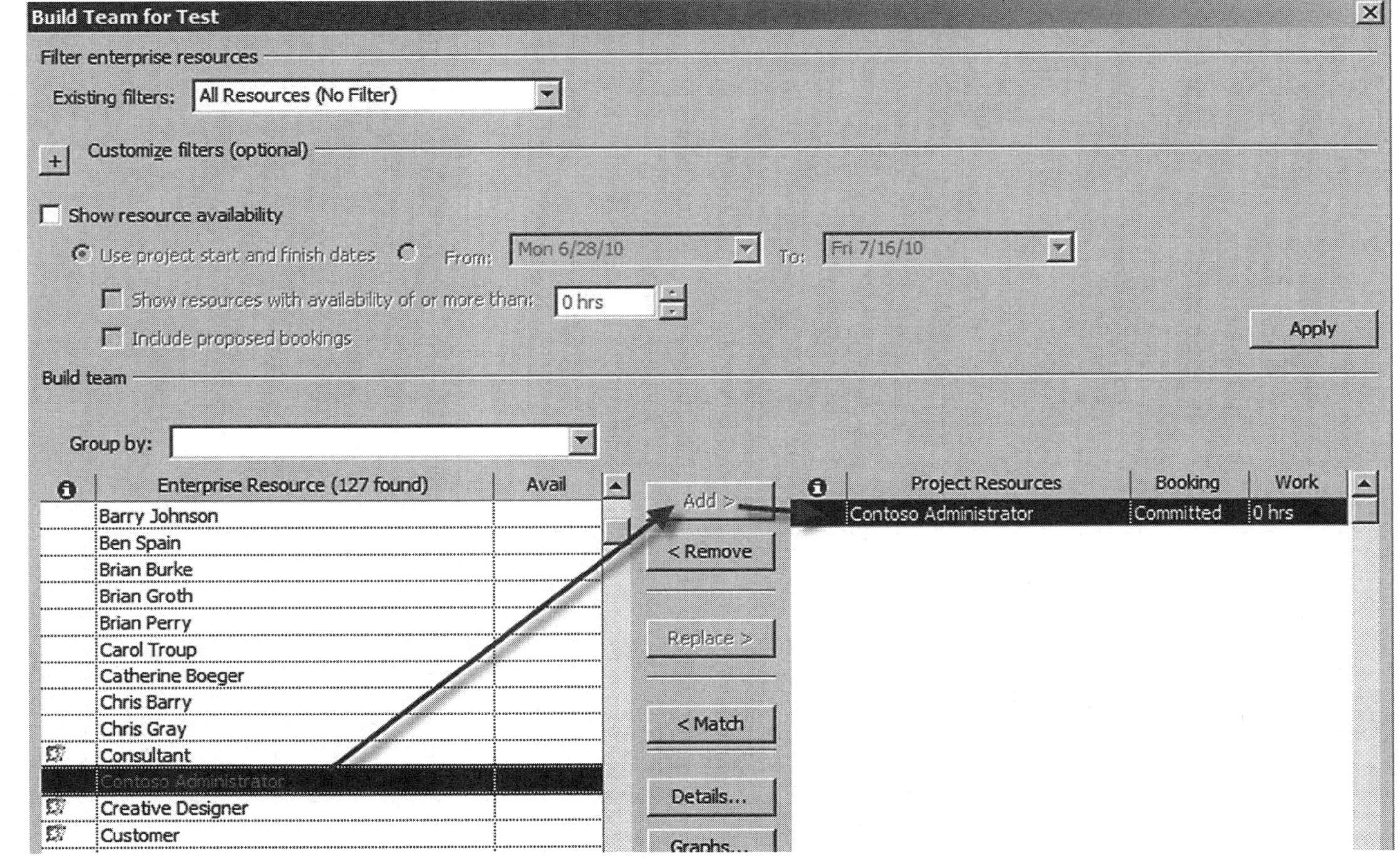
Build Team for Test
Filter enterprise resources
Existing filters:
All Resources (No Filter)
Customize filters (optional)
Show resource availability
Use project start and finish dates
From:
Mon 6/28/10
To:
Fri 7/16/10
Show resources with availability of or more than:
0 hrs
Include proposed bookings
Apply
Build team
Group by:
Enterprise Resource (127 found)
Avail
Barry Johnson
Ben Spain
Brian Burke
Brian Groth
Brian Perry
Carol Troup
Catherine Boeger
Chris Barry
Chris Gray
Consultant
Contoso Administrator
Creative Designer
Customer
Add >
< Remove
Replace >
< Match
Details...
Project Resources
Booking
Work
Contoso Administrator
Committed
0 hrs

Figure 7–10

Once you have the resources selected and added, simply click on OK to exit out of the Build Team dialog box. Then, you'll be back in the main screen where you can assign your resource(s) to tasks! Simply click the arrow in the drop-down box under the Resource Names column and click in the check box next to the resource(s) you want to assign to that specific task. Figure 7–11 shows how the resources you selected in the Build Team box are now available to the project.

To select a resource in Project Professional from the drop-down, just click in the check box beside the name. You can select multiple names from the available resource list. In this example, we have only the one resource available and so the drop-down only includes one name.

As Figure 7–12 shows, after you have selected the resource check box and then move to another field in Project Professional, you will see that the resource is now assigned to that task. You can also see in the Work column that there are now hours assigned to that task. Along with the hours being assigned to the task, there are now hours assigned to that resource.

The previous example concerned how to assign a resource from a Project Professional application that was using Project Server. Figure 7–13 shows how to use the Resource Pool from the stand-alone version of Project Professional. When you open a project file in the Project Professional stand-alone edition that is linked with a Resource Pool, the *Open Resource Pool* option box will appear. If you are going to just assign resources from the Resource Pool, the first option should be selected. If you are going to modify the resource in the Resource Pool, then the second option should be selected. Normally, selecting the first option will be sufficient.

Now that we've designated the Resource Pool as shared, we can assign tasks different ways. Figure 7–14 shows the drop-down method. This may be the easiest way to assign a resource to a task because all you need to do is to click in the Resource Names column next to the task and select the resources from the drop-down. Simply click the check box to select a resource. More than one resource can be assigned to a task by checking multiple check boxes.

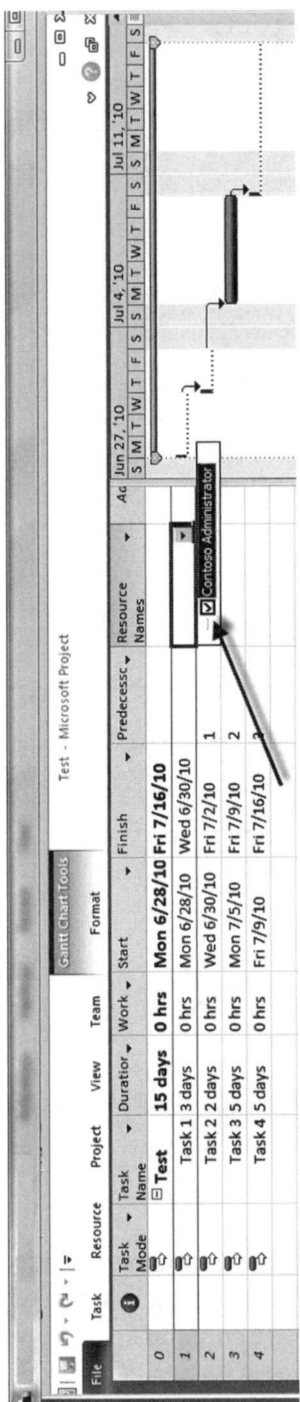

Figure 7–11

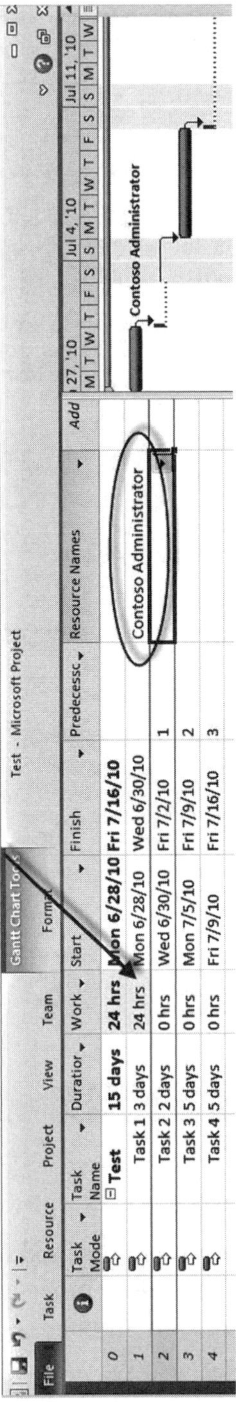

Figure 7–12

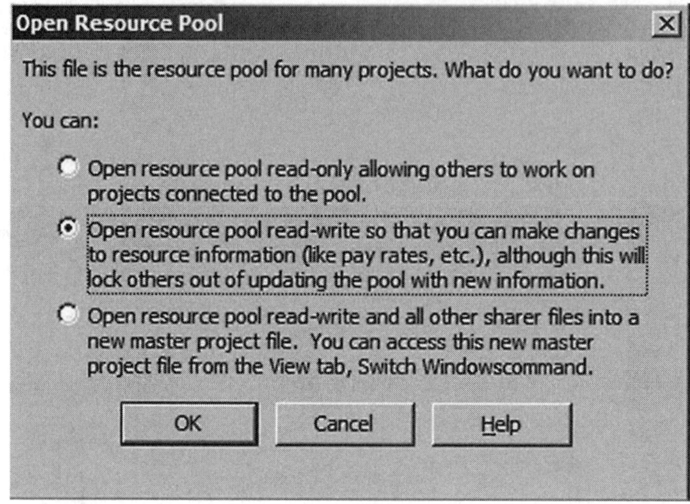

Figure 7–13

Figure 7–14

The recommended method for assigning a resource is shown in Figure 7–15. While this might seem more cumbersome when assigning the resources, it can save significant amounts of energy and frustration when making changes, deletions, or replacements. When you are used to using the Assign Resources box, it becomes second nature to use it for all resource needs. This method is the way

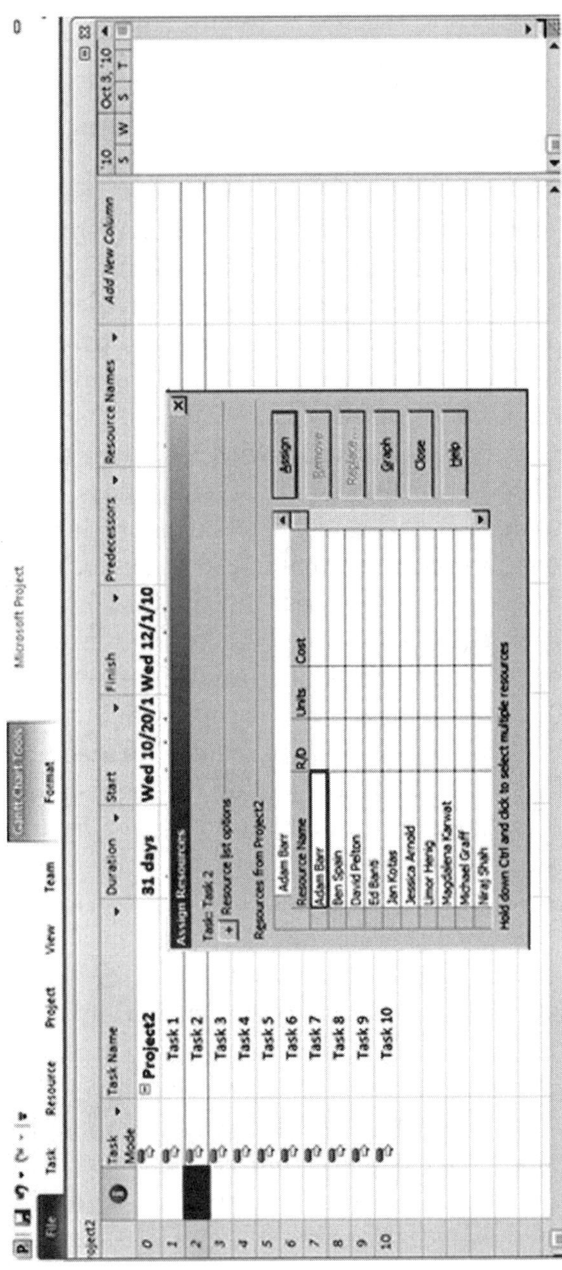
Microsoft Project
Gantt Chart Tools
File
Task
Resource
Project
View
Team
Format
Task Mode
Task Name
Duration
Start
Finish
Predecessors
Resource Names
Add New Column
Project2
31 days
Wed 10/20/1
Wed 12/1/10
Task 1
Task 2
Task 3
Task 4
Task 5
Task 6
Task 7
Task 8
Task 9
Task 10
Assign Resources
Task: Task 2
Resource list options
Resources from Project2
Resource Name
R/D
Units
Cost
Adam Barr
Ben Spain
David Pelton
Ed Banti
Jan Kotas
Jessica Arnold
Limor Henig
Magdalena Karwat
Michael Graff
Niraj Shah
Assign
Remove
Replace...
Graph
Close
Help
Hold down Ctrl and click to select multiple resources

Figure 7–15

to use the pop-up box to assign resources. In this case, you select the resource name and then click on the Assign button.

The Team Planner

Project Professional 2010 has a new feature called the Team Planner. This feature is available in stand-alone and Server versions. Once you have the resources selected from the Resource Pool, you can go the Team Planner view. As with many Microsoft products, there are numerous methods to get to that view. In Figure 7–16 we get there by using the View tab and then selecting the Team Planner view.

The Team Planner is a view created to allow you to visually see some of the assignments already made, and to interact with resources and tasks together. It is a powerful new method to see, and modify, assignments. The next few figures are presented to acquaint you with some of the capabilities of this new view.

As Figure 7–17 shows, a resource name in red indicates the resource is overallocated. A task outlined in red indicates that the task is also overallocated.

A task will show up in the Unscheduled Tasks column when it doesn't have enough information to be scheduled. As Figure 7–18 shows, a task will appear in the Unscheduled Tasks when a resource is assigned, but the task isn't scheduled. The task in this example, Obtain approval to proceed, has a Start Date, but no Finish Date. Therefore, it can't be put on the right-hand side of the view. Once the Finish Date is added to the task, it will move from the Unscheduled Tasks column to the scheduling grid on the right.

Hovering over a task will display a pop-up box with the task details, as shown in Figure 7–19. This allows you to see information about the task without having to go back to a task or assignment view.

Figure 7–20 shows that tasks listed at the bottom of the screen are Unassigned Tasks. The number listed beside the words *Unassigned Tasks* is the number of unassigned tasks. The task itself will be displayed on the grid on the right side of the screen to show its current Start and Finish Dates.

The unassigned task can be assigned from this view by clicking and dragging it to the correct date in the row of the resource to assign. Figure 7–21 shows that we have dragged the task that was in the Unassigned Tasks section to resource Jim Kim's row. This means that we have now assigned Jim Kim this task.

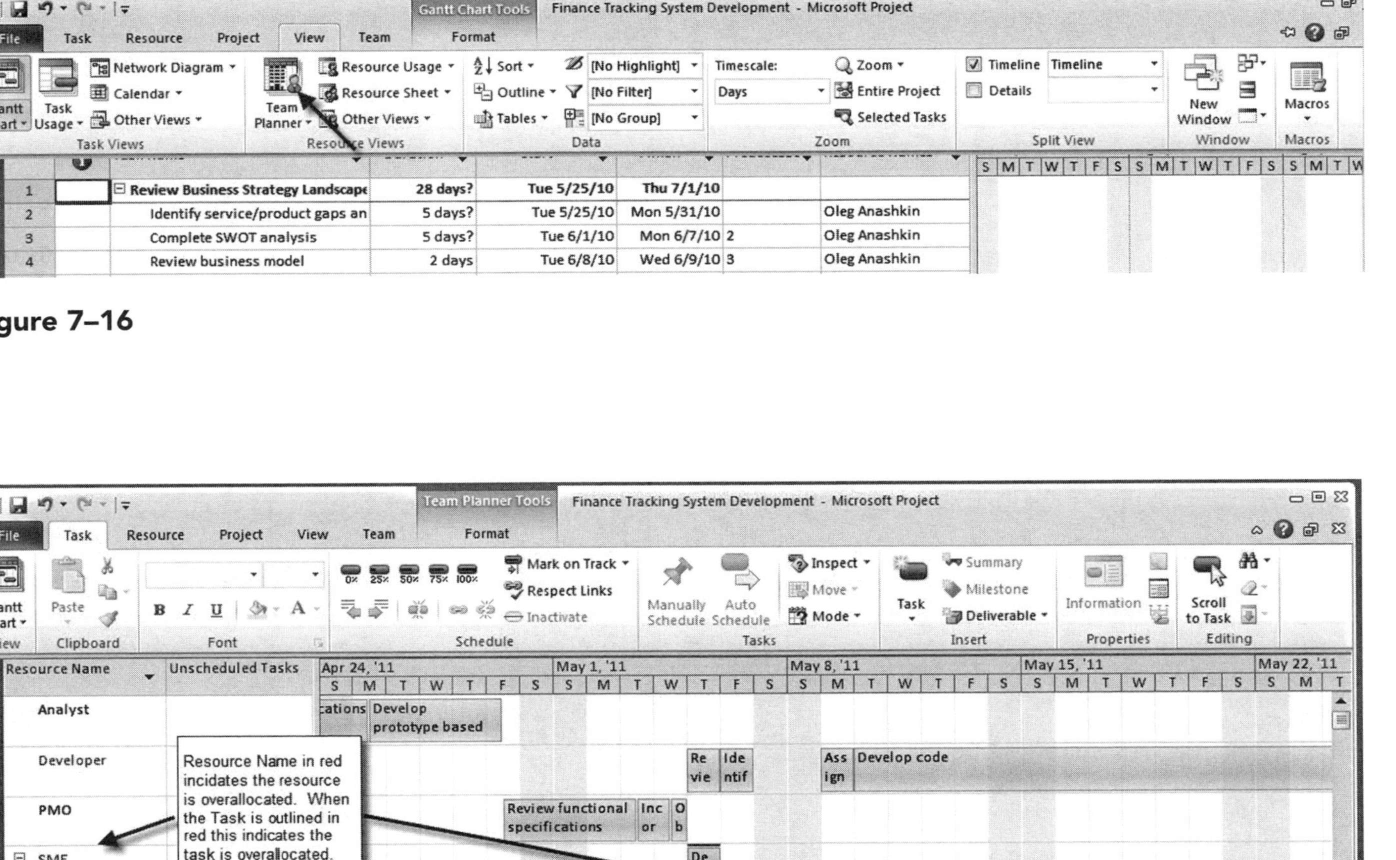

Figure 7–16

Figure 7–17

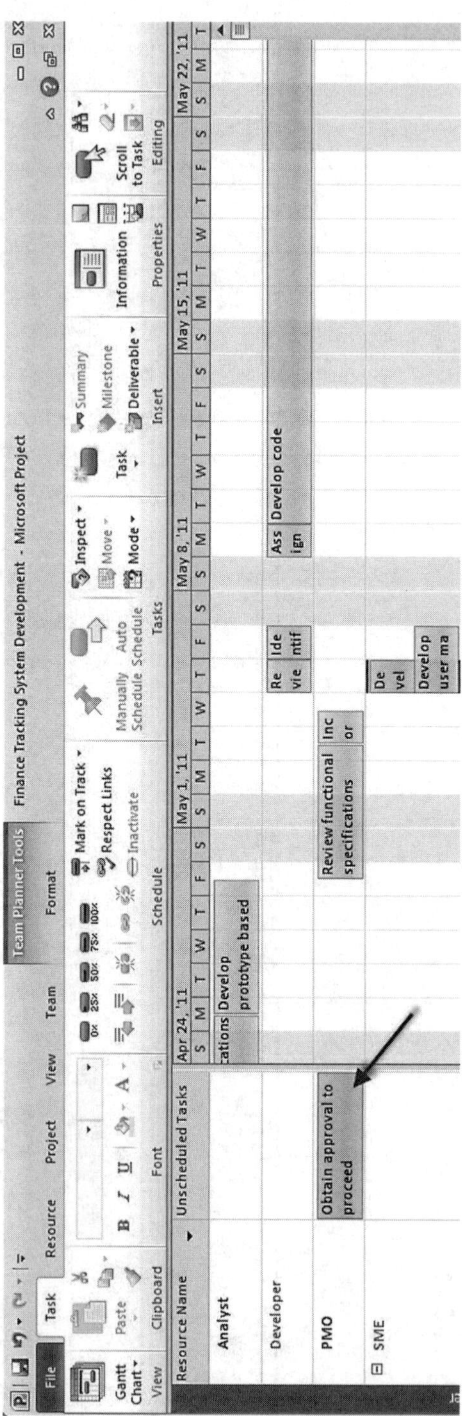
Finance Tracking System Development - Microsoft Project
Team Planner Tools
File
Task
Resource
Project
View
Team
Format
Gantt Chart
Paste
Clipboard
Font
Mark on Track
Respect Links
Inactivate
Schedule
Manually Schedule
Auto Schedule
Inspect
Move
Mode
Tasks
Task
Summary
Milestone
Deliverable
Insert
Information
Properties
Scroll to Task
Editing
Resource Name
Unscheduled Tasks
Apr 24, '11
May 1, '11
May 8, '11
May 15, '11
May 22, '11
Analyst
Developer
PMO
SME
Develop prototype based
Obtain approval to proceed
Review functional specifications
Develop code
Develop user ma

Figure 7–18

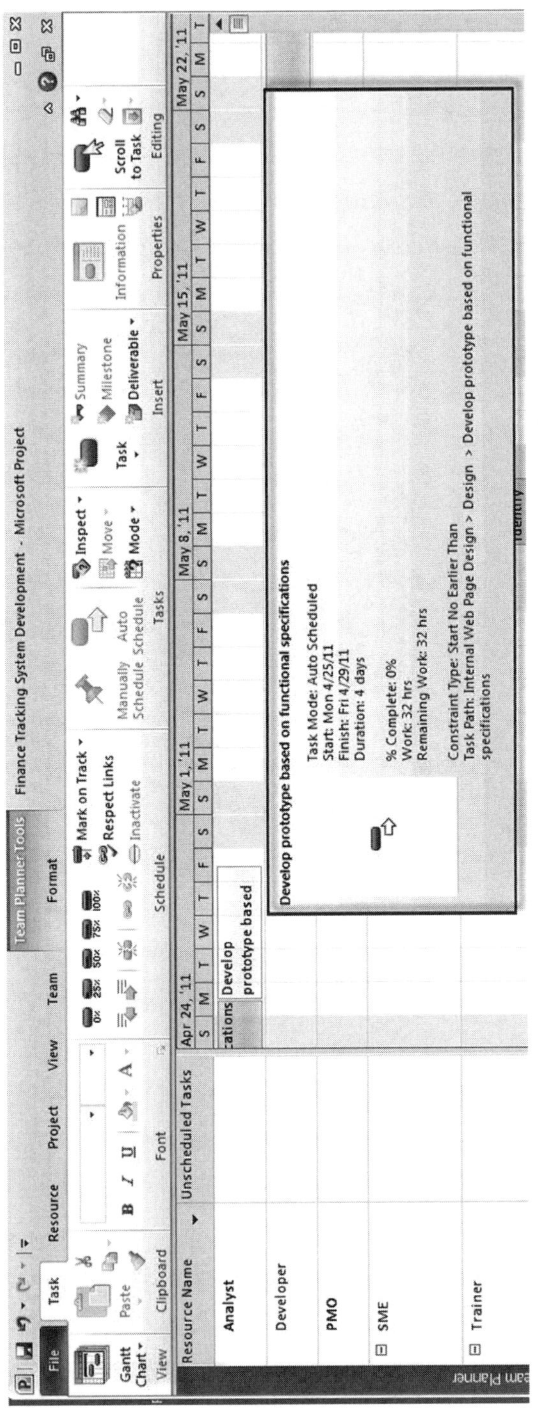
Finance Tracking System Development - Microsoft Project
Team Planner Tools
File
Task
Resource
Project
View
Team
Format
Gantt Chart
Paste
Clipboard
Font
Mark on Track
Respect Links
Inactivate
Schedule
Manually Schedule
Auto Schedule
Inspect
Move
Mode
Tasks
Task
Summary
Milestone
Deliverable
Insert
Information
Properties
Scroll to Task
Editing
Resource Name
Unscheduled Tasks
Analyst
Developer
PMO
SME
Trainer
Apr 24, '11
May 1, '11
May 8, '11
May 15, '11
May 22, '11
Develop prototype based
Develop prototype based on functional specifications
Task Mode: Auto Scheduled
Start: Mon 4/25/11
Finish: Fri 4/29/11
Duration: 4 days
% Complete: 0%
Work: 32 hrs
Remaining Work: 32 hrs
Constraint Type: Start No Earlier Than
Task Path: Internal Web Page Design > Design > Develop prototype based on functional specifications

Figure 7–19

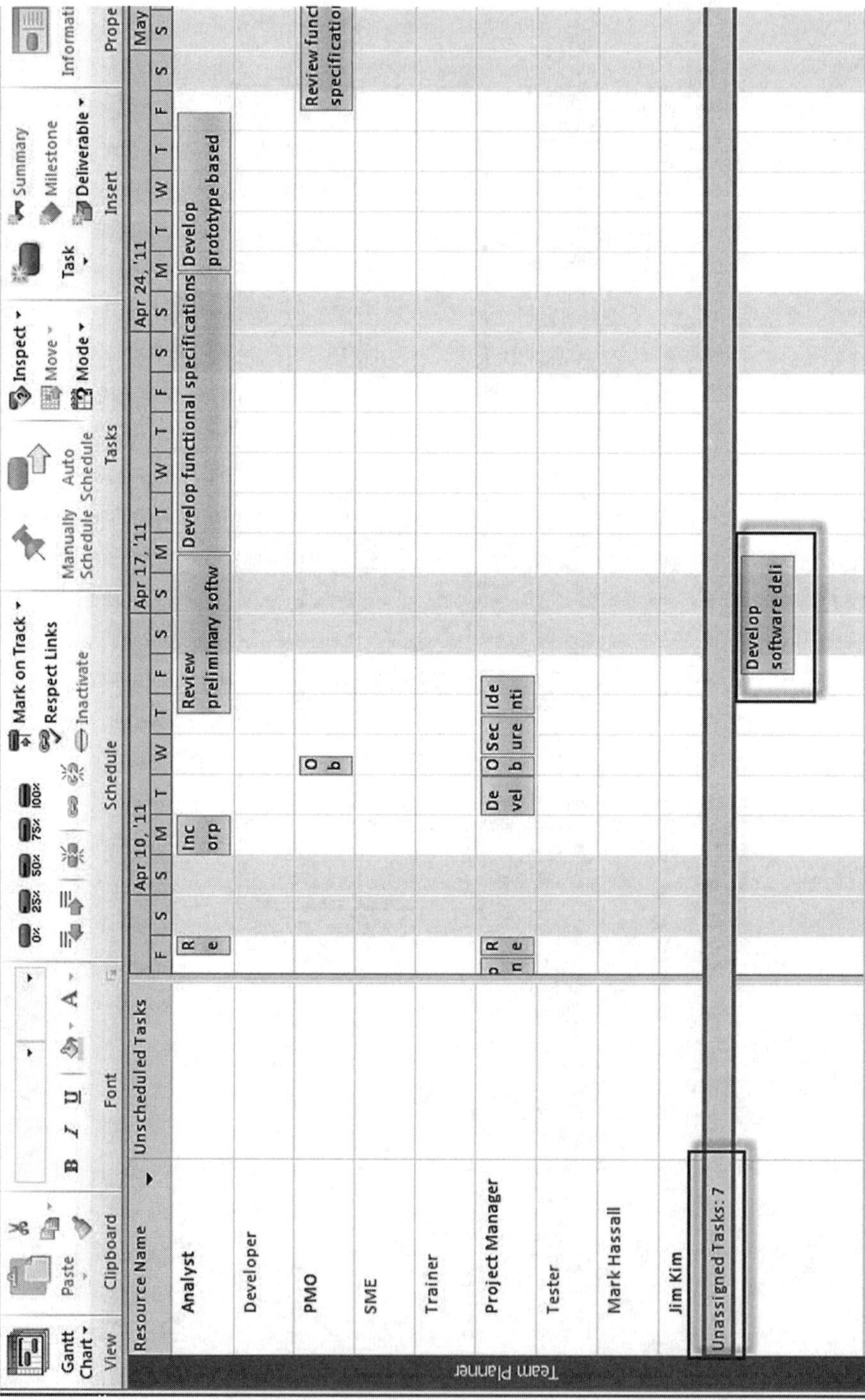
Gantt Chart
View
Paste
Clipboard
Font
Mark on Track
Respect Links
Inactivate
Schedule
Manually Schedule
Auto Schedule
Inspect
Move
Mode
Tasks
Task
Summary
Milestone
Deliverable
Insert
Informati
Prope
Team Planner
Resource Name
Unscheduled Tasks
Apr 10, '11
Apr 17, '11
Apr 24, '11
May
Analyst
Developer
PMO
SME
Trainer
Project Manager
Tester
Mark Hassall
Jim Kim
Unassigned Tasks: 7
Review preliminary softw
Develop functional specifications
Develop prototype based
Review func specificatio
Develop software deli

Figure 7–20

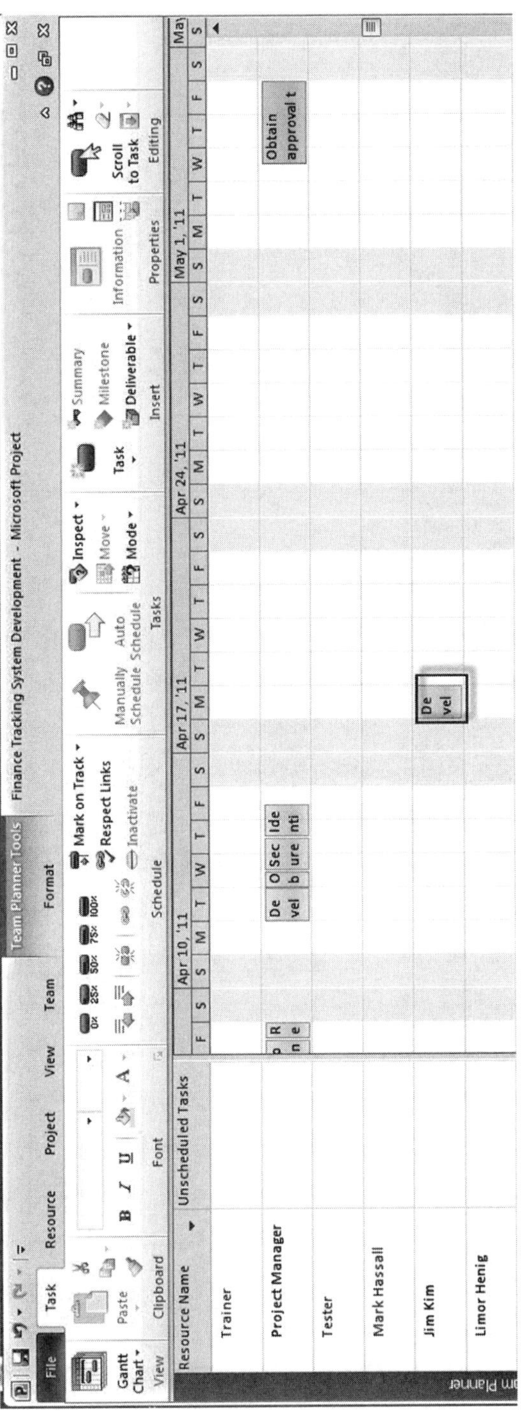
Finance Tracking System Development - Microsoft Project
Team Planner Tools
File
Task
Resource
Project
View
Team
Format
Gantt Chart
Paste
Clipboard
Font
Mark on Track
Respect Links
Inactivate
Schedule
Manually Schedule
Auto Schedule
Inspect
Move
Mode
Tasks
Task
Summary
Milestone
Deliverable
Insert
Information
Properties
Scroll to Task
Editing
Resource Name
Unscheduled Tasks
Apr 10, '11
Apr 17, '11
Apr 24, '11
May 1, '11
Trainer
Project Manager
Tester
Mark Hassall
Jim Kim
Limor Henig
Obtain approval t

Figure 7–21

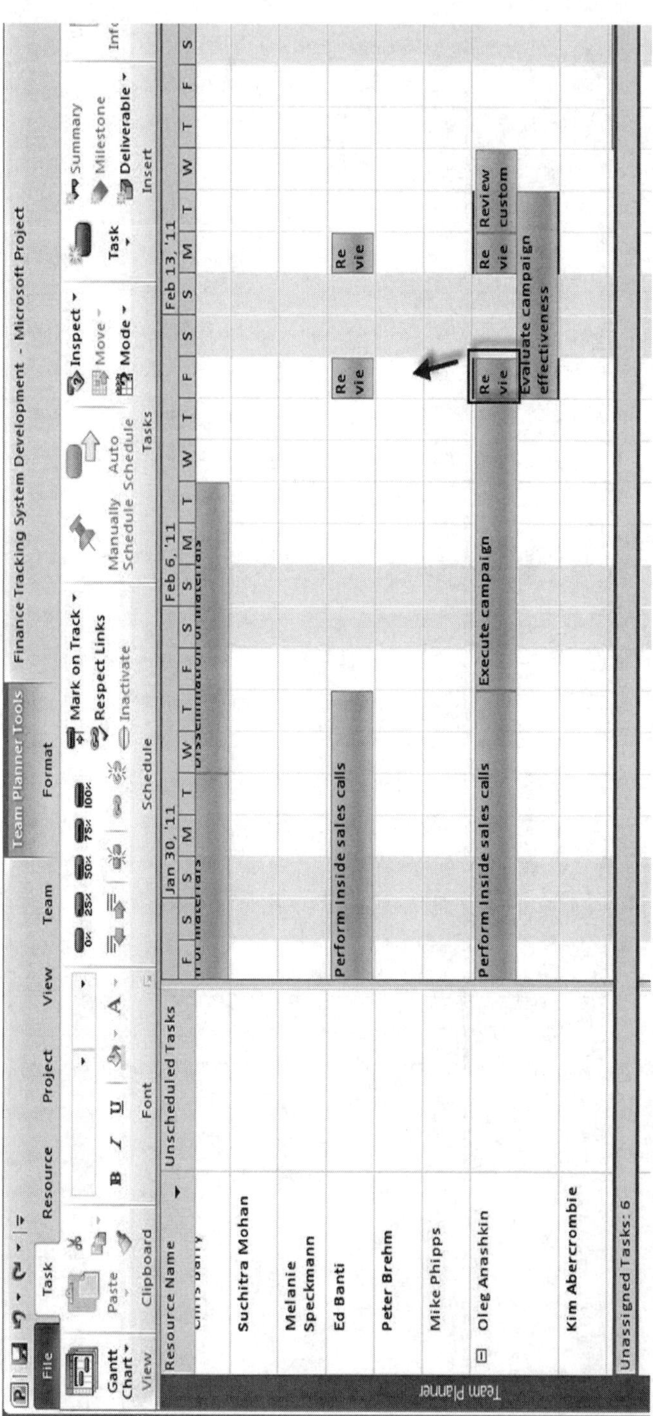
Team Planner Tools
Finance Tracking System Development - Microsoft Project
File
Task
Resource
Project
View
Team
Format
Gantt Chart
Paste
Clipboard
Font
Schedule
Mark on Track
Respect Links
Inactivate
Manually Schedule
Auto Schedule
Inspect
Move
Mode
Tasks
Task
Summary
Milestone
Deliverable
Insert
Resource Name
Unscheduled Tasks
Jan 30, '11
Feb 6, '11
Feb 13, '11
Suchitra Mohan
Melanie Speckmann
Ed Banti
Peter Brehm
Mike Phipps
Oleg Anashkin
Kim Abercrombie
Perform Inside sales calls
Execute campaign
Evaluate campaign effectiveness
Review custom
Unassigned Tasks: 6
Team Planner

Figure 7–22

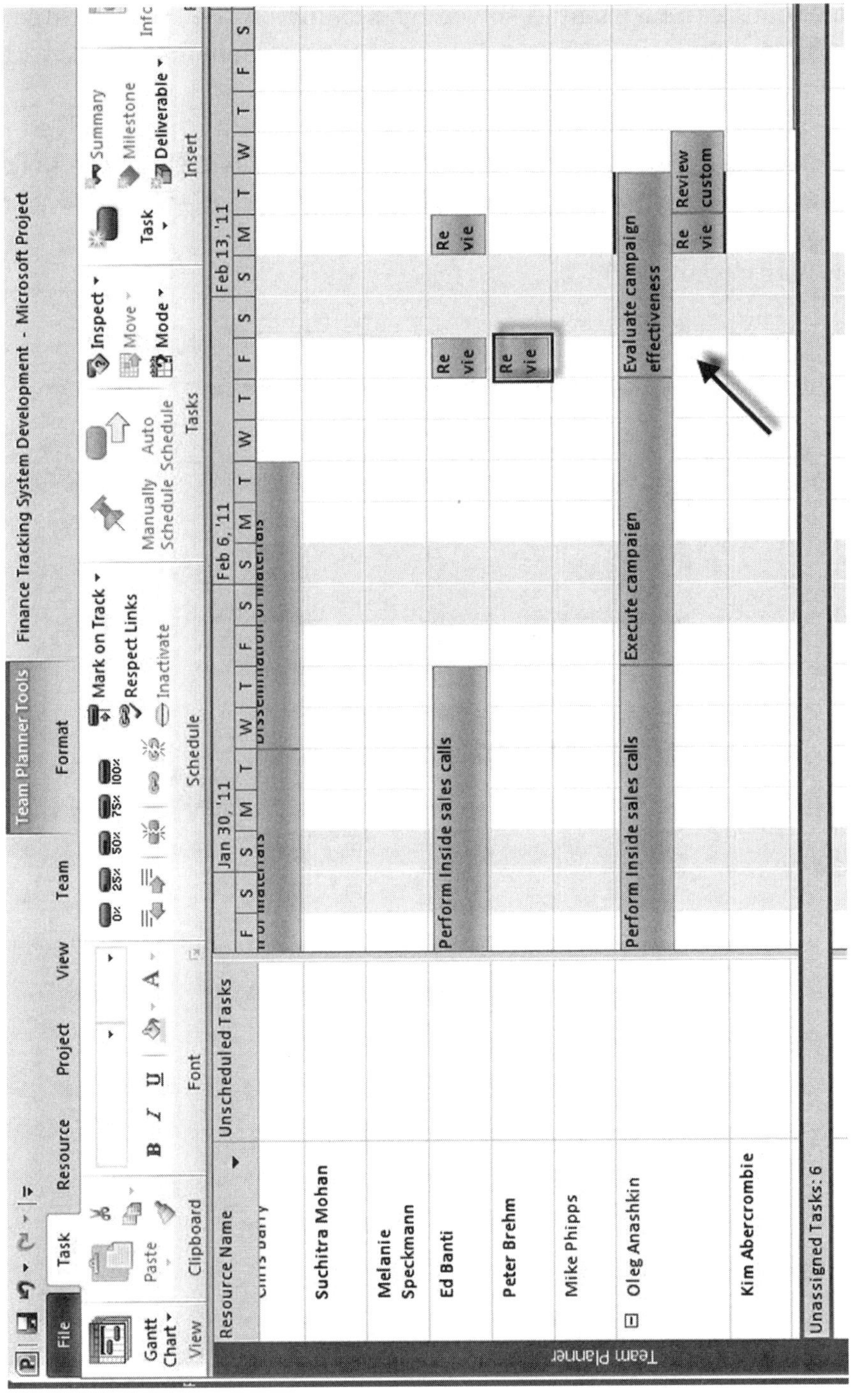
Team Planner Tools
Finance Tracking System Development - Microsoft Project
File
Task
Resource
Project
View
Team
Format
Gantt Chart
Paste
Clipboard
Font
Mark on Track
Respect Links
Inactivate
Schedule
Manually Schedule
Auto Schedule
Inspect
Move
Mode
Tasks
Task
Summary
Milestone
Deliverable
Insert
Resource Name
Unscheduled Tasks
Jan 30, '11
Feb 6, '11
Feb 13, '11
Suchitra Mohan
Melanie Speckmann
Ed Banti
Peter Brehm
Mike Phipps
Oleg Anashkin
Kim Abercrombie
Perform Inside sales calls
Execute campaign
Evaluate campaign effectiveness
Review custom
Unassigned Tasks: 6
Team Planner

Figure 7–23

Overallocations can be easily resolved by clicking on the overallocated task and dragging and dropping it to another resource, as demonstrated in Figure 7–22.

Figure 7–23 shows the overallocation from Figure 7–22 being resolved.

You can also resolve overallocations by moving the task. Click the task and drag it to the new date and drop the task in place. Figures 7–24 and 7–25 demonstrate the "before and after" of this overallocation.

Before it is resolved:

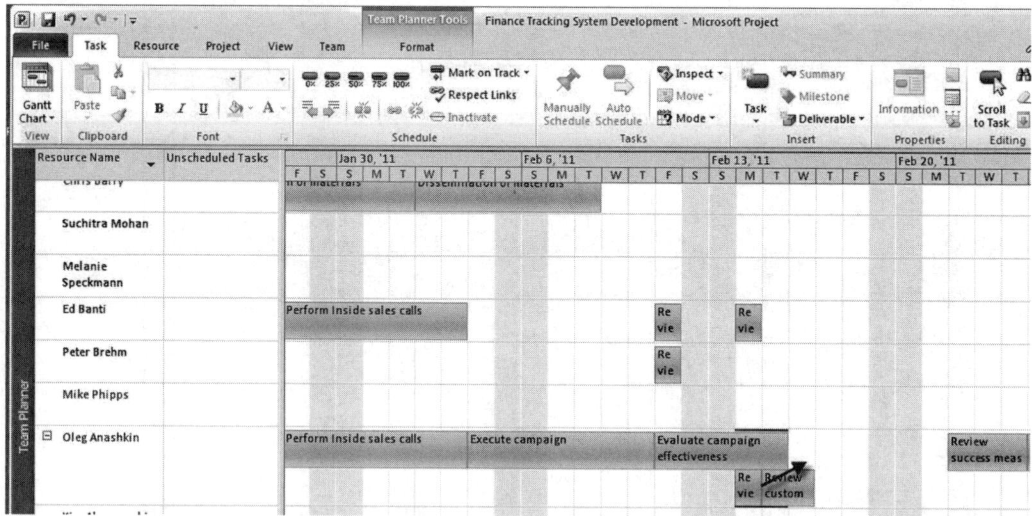

Figure 7–24

After it is resolved:

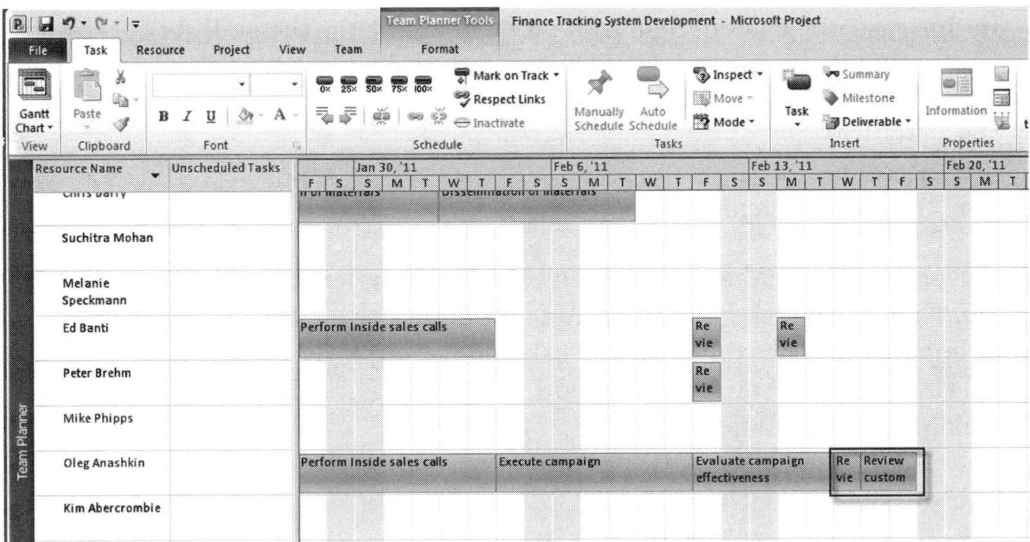

Figure 7–25

Assigning Resources by Skill Set

Let's say you wanted to add a resource, but didn't really know who the specific resource was going to be when you originally created the project file. The common method is to assign a generic resource based on a certain skill set, and then to replace the generic resource with a named resource when you know who the resource is going to be. In this case, you know that the resource you need is an analyst, but until you have a little more information about this particular task or until it gets closer to time for the project to start, you don't know which analyst to assign. Microsoft Project 2010 allows you to assign a generic resource to a task and replace it later with a specific resource. Please note that before you can add a generic resource to the schedule, the generic resource has to be set up in the Enterprise Resource Global file or the Resource Pool.

The function that we will be using is the Match function. However, before you can use the Match function in Microsoft Project 2010, enterprise resources have to be set up and they have to have at least one custom field that contains the skill set information. A custom field can be created with multiple levels of skills, or many custom fields can be created to be used in conjunction with each other.

In this case, the custom field that you will create for the skill set will be singular. By that, we mean only one level to the field, such as:

- Analyst
- Accountant
- Project manager

However, you can make a custom field with many levels in the Lookup table setup. This is beneficial when trying to differentiate a skill set. For example, if your organization has an IT Help Desk and its employees are differentiated as Level One Support, Level Two Support, and Level Three Support, you can build a Lookup table like this:

- Help Desk: Level One
- Help Desk: Level Two
- Help Desk: Level Three

Let's walk through the Custom field information so you will have an understanding of it. The project administrator will be the one to actually set it up on the Project Server. But, whoever is in charge of the stand-alone Resource Pool can create the Custom field for the stand-alone version. For example, assume that a skill set custom field has not yet been created. Figure 7–26 shows that to set up the Custom field, you should open the Enterprise Resource Global file, right click on a column, and select *Custom Fields*.

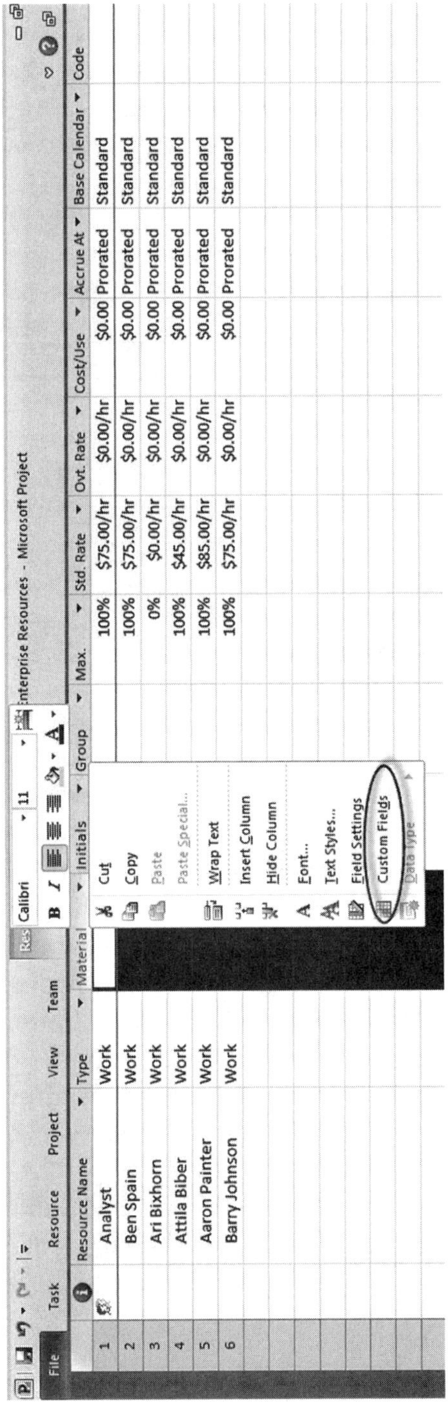
Enterprise Resources - Microsoft Project
File
Task
Resource
Project
View
Team
Resource Name
Type
Material
Initials
Group
Max.
Std. Rate
Ovt. Rate
Cost/Use
Accrue At
Base Calendar
Code
Analyst
Ben Spain
Ari Bixhorn
Attila Biber
Aaron Painter
Barry Johnson
Work
100%
0%
$75.00/hr
$0.00/hr
$45.00/hr
$85.00/hr
$0.00
Prorated
Standard
Calibri
11
Cut
Copy
Paste
Paste Special...
Wrap Text
Insert Column
Hide Column
Font...
Text Styles...
Field Settings
Custom Fields
Data Type

Figure 7–26

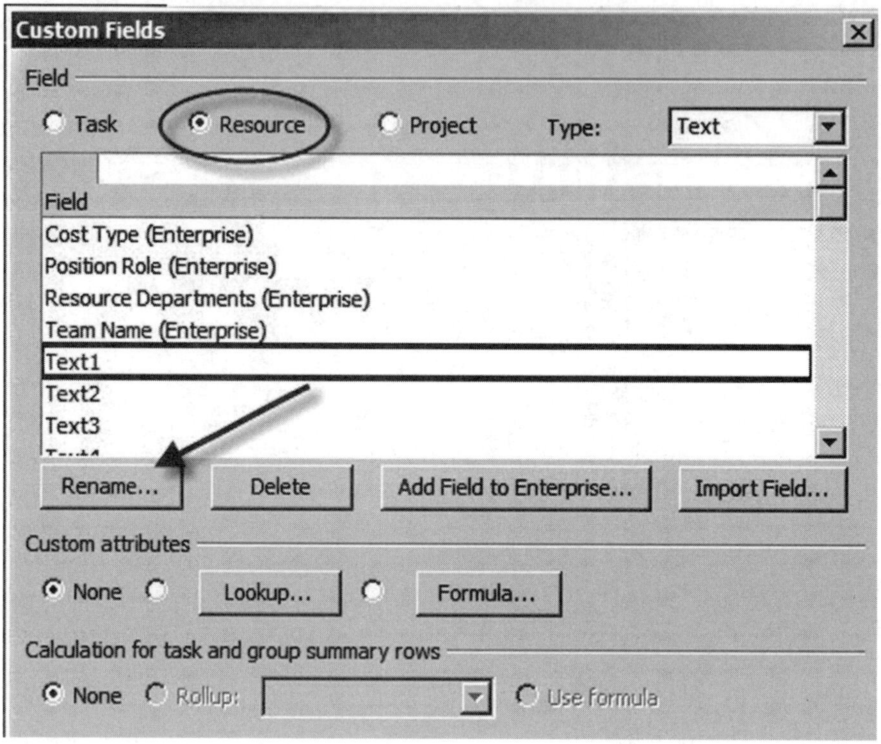

Figure 7–27

For the Custom field, you will use the term *Position*. Since you are going to create a field where you will be entering text (alphanumeric), you will need to make sure that you're using a Text field. As shown in Figure 7–27, make sure that the Text1 field is highlighted. Since we are going to be assigning the information in this field to resources, make sure the radio button for Resource is selected. Click the Rename button to rename the field to something more meaningful. After clicking on the Rename button, a pop-up box will appear with a text box to enter the field name we are going to use. In this case, type *Position* in the field.

In Figure 7–28, you can see that the new field was added as a text field. This field can now be searched in the future by looking for either *Text1* or *Position*. As shown, the fields that are on the Server are indicated by the word (Enterprise),

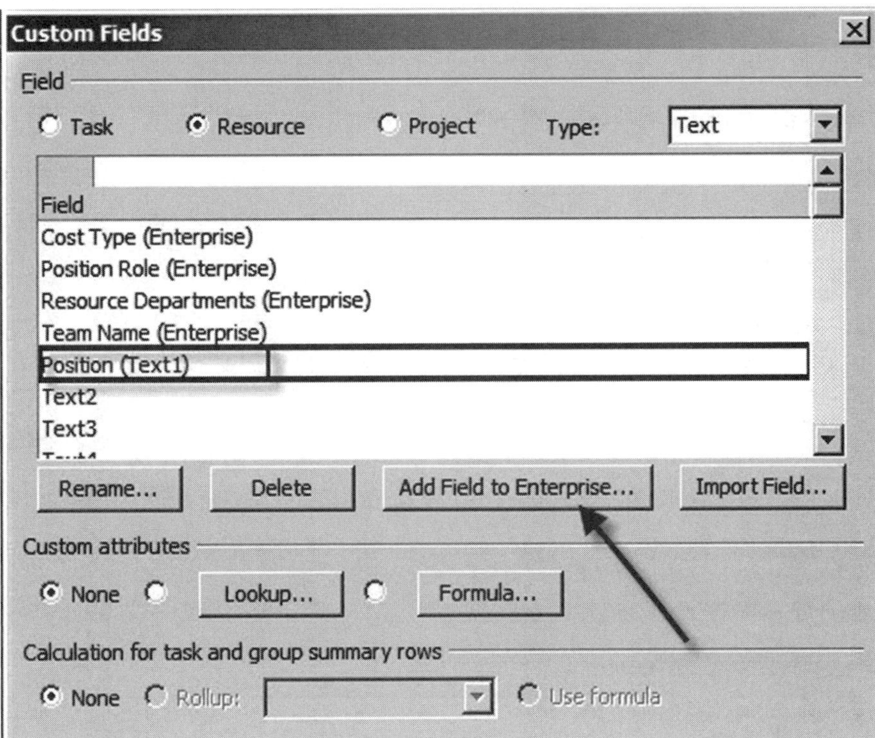

Figure 7–28

in parenthesis. In this example, four fields are Enterprise fields, and the field *Position* that we just created is still just local to this schedule. For the Server option, click the Add Field to Enterprise button to add this field to the Enterprise and make it available to any schedule. For the stand-alone version, the Add Field to Enterprise button will be unavailable (it will be grayed out).

When you click on the Add Field to Enterprise button, a box will pop up, requesting the name that you want to call this field. If there is a Lookup Table that you will associate with the Custom field, you can enter that here as well. In this case, you can call the Lookup Table the same name as the Custom field: Position.

You can set up the Lookup table next. You will want to make sure that the name of the Lookup table is going to be something that you'll associate with this particular field. Figure 7–29 shows the field being added to the Enterprise.

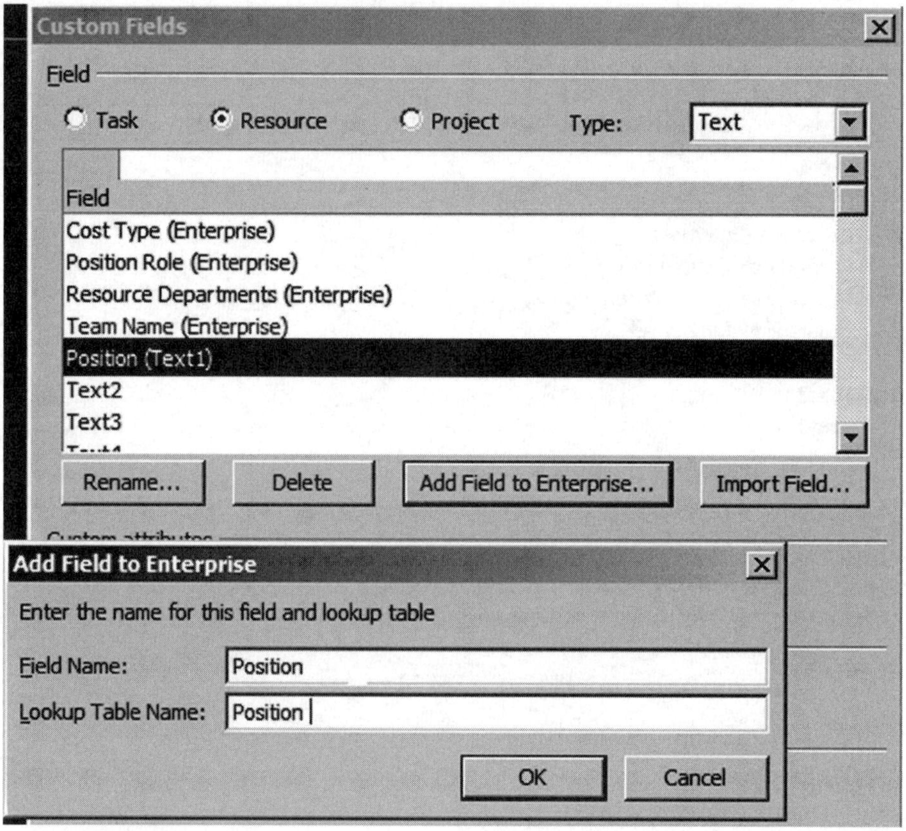

Figure 7–29

Now we need to define the Lookup table associated with the Position field. As shown in Figure 7–30, click on *Lookup* under the *Custom attributes* section. You can also see that *Position* is now an Enterprise field.

Since it's a Position field, you will want to list the department positions within the organization. We will use the three options of Analyst, Accountant, and Project Manager, as shown in Figure 7–31. You also have the option for Lookup table items to be in display order by ascending, descending, or row number. In the Data Entry Options section, you can also allow others to enter new values, which will then be added to the Lookup table. Once all of the Lookup table values and the other options are entered, click Close to exit the Lookup Table box.

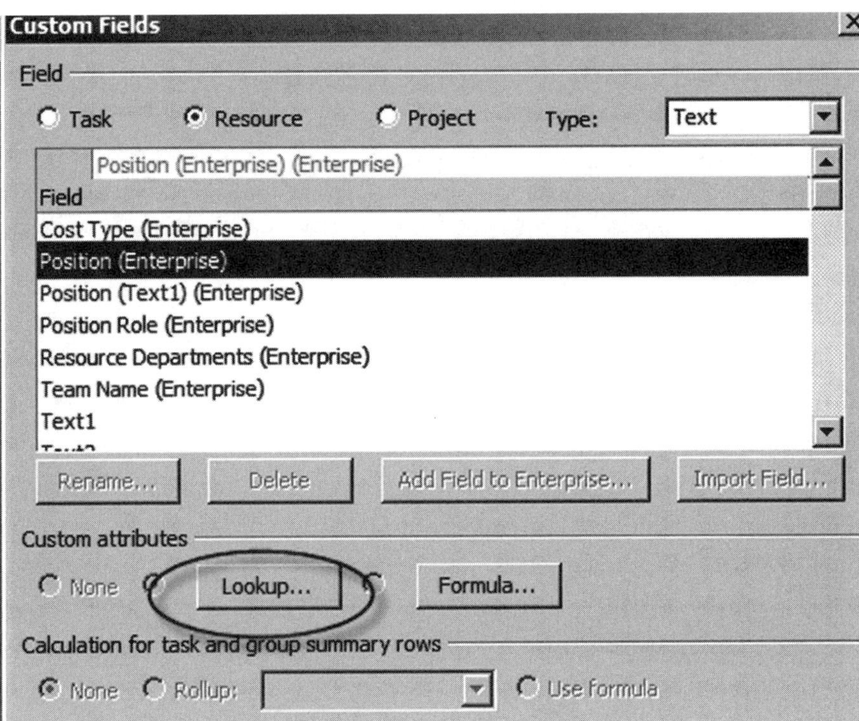

Figure 7–30

After clicking Close, a pop-up box appears, stating that the field was added and Project Professional will need to be restarted in order for the field to be visible. Figure 7–32 is an example of that pop-up box. Project Professional needs to be closed and reopened because it needs to have the global settings reset to include the new field.

Once Project Professional has been closed and restarted, find where you want to insert the new column, and right click on column header, then select Insert. Type the letter *P* for Position and the name of the new custom field, and then select it once you find it. Figure 7–33 demonstrates how to insert and name the new Custom field.

In the case of Project Server, this addition creates a new field in the Enterprise Resource Global file. From there, use the drop-down arrow to add the position for each resource. See Figure 7–34 for an example. Once finished, save Enterprise Resource Global file, and Close. For stand-alone versions, this field

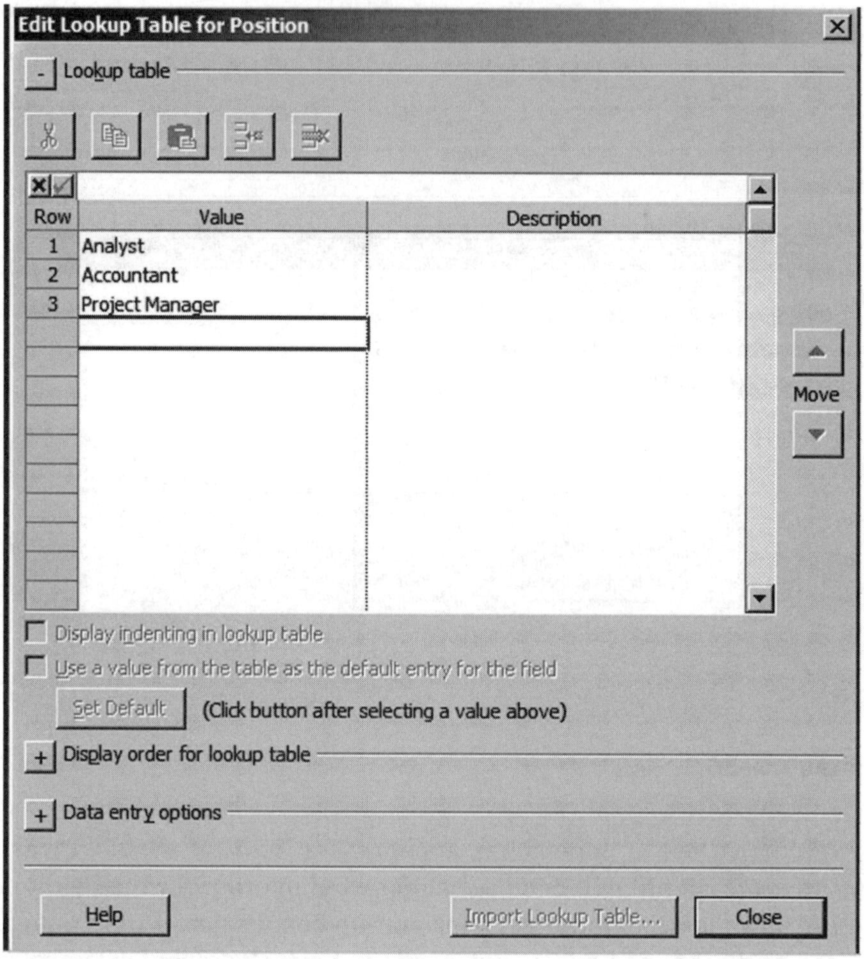

Figure 7–31

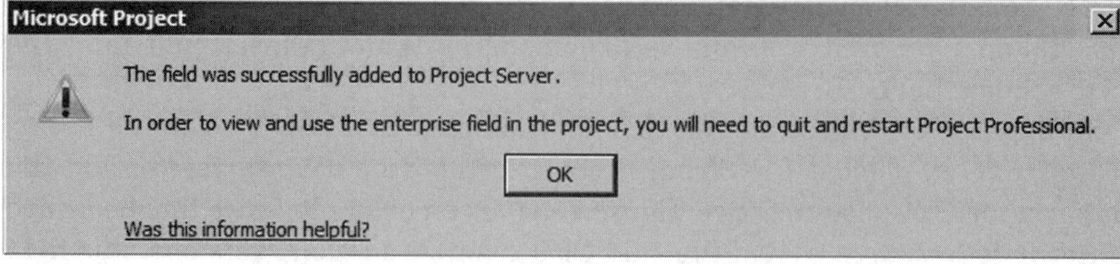

Figure 7–32

		Resource Name	Type	peak	Position (Text1)	Material Label	Initials
1		Analyst	Work	Peak			A
2		Ben Spain	Work	Phonetics			B
3		Ari Bixhorn	Work	Position (Enterprise)			A
4		Attila Biber	Work	Position (Text1) (Enterprise)			A
5		Aaron Painter	Work	Position Role (Enterprise)			A
6		Barry Johnson	Work	Project			B

Figure 7–33

		Resource Name	Type	Position (Enterprise)	Material	Initials
1		Analyst	Work			A
2		Ben Spain	Work	Analyst		B
3		Ari Bixhorn	Work	Accountant		A
4		Attila Biber	Work	Analyst		A
5		Aaron Painter	Work	Project Manager		A
6		Barry Johnson	Work	Analyst		B

Figure 7–34

will need to be added either in a standard template or through the Organizer, so that everybody will have this same field available to them.

Now that you have added the new field and have assigned a skill set to each resource, you'll need to add the resources to the project by using the *Build Team from Enterprise* option from the menu bar as shown in Figure 7–35. This will open the Build Team dialog box.

As a reminder, generic resources are easy to find in the Build Team box because of their icon located in the indicator column. The icon shows two heads. Once you find the generic resource that you want to use, click Add to add the

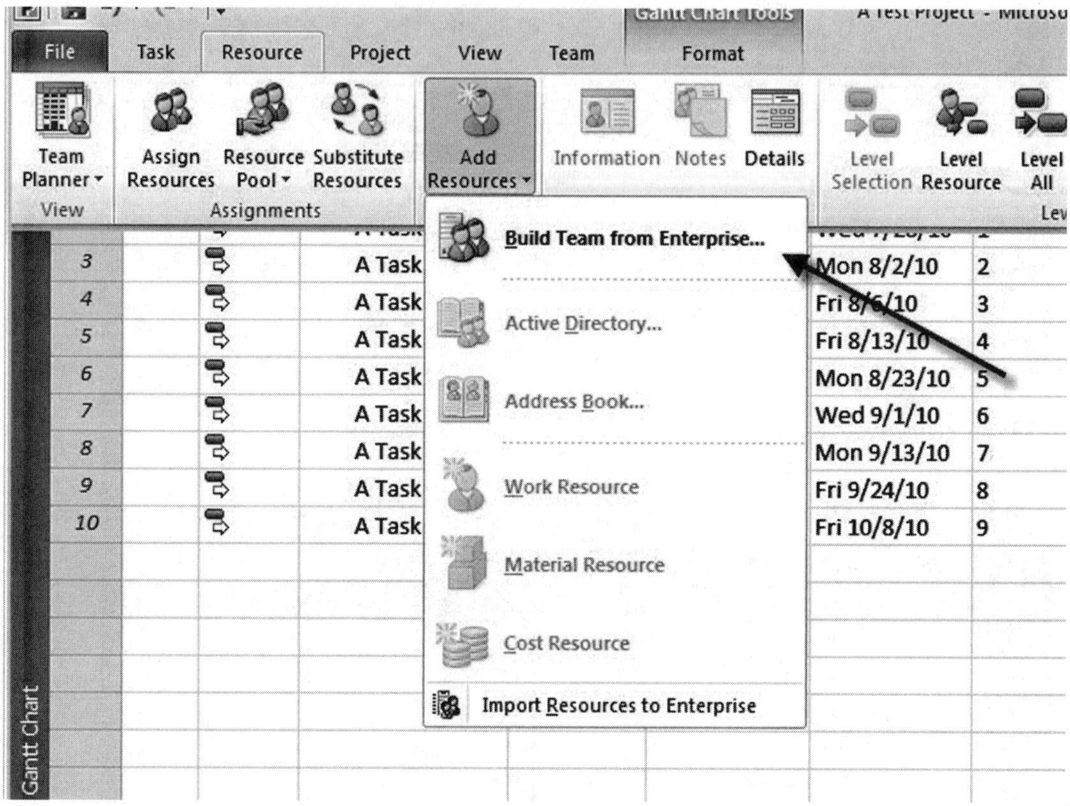

Figure 7–35

resource to the Resource Pool, as demonstrated in Figure 7–36. Click OK once you've added all of the resources to the Resource Pool. You can add multiple generic resources and/or regular enterprise resources to the Resource Pool.

After selecting the resource and getting back into the schedule, click on the drop-down arrow in the Resource Names column and select *Analyst*, just like you would a regular resource. As you can see in Figure 7–37, the analyst is assigned to several tasks.

Remember, our goal is to demonstrate how to replace a generic resource with a named resource, based upon a common skill set. So, let's replace our analyst resource with a named resource. Open the Build Team dialog box by clicking on Resource, Add Resources, Build a Team from Enterprise.

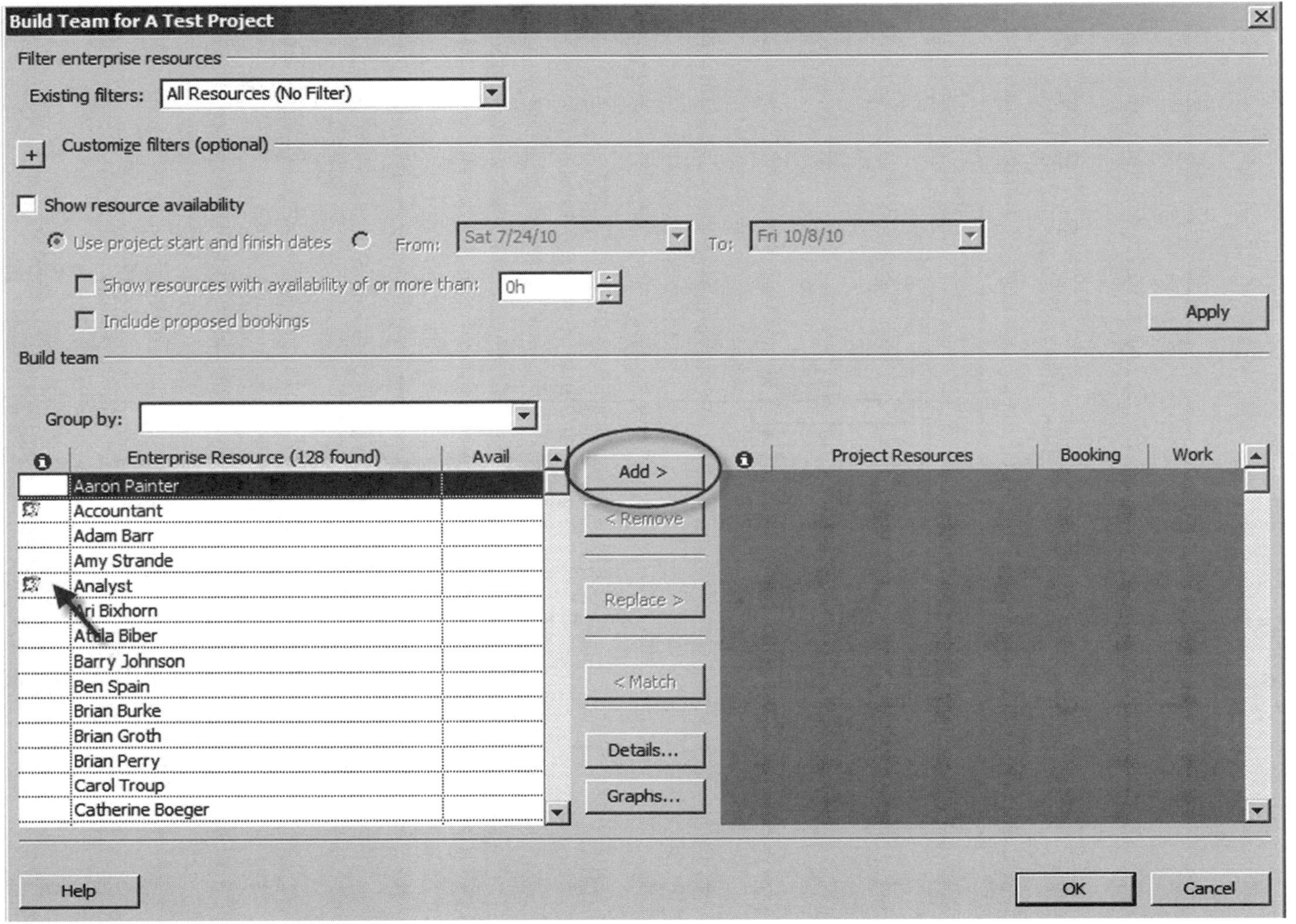
Build Team for A Test Project
Filter enterprise resources
Existing filters:
All Resources (No Filter)
Customize filters (optional)
Show resource availability
Use project start and finish dates
From:
Sat 7/24/10
To:
Fri 10/8/10
Show resources with availability of or more than:
0h
Include proposed bookings
Apply
Build team
Group by:
Enterprise Resource (128 found)
Avail
Aaron Painter
Accountant
Adam Barr
Amy Strande
Analyst
Ari Bixhorn
Attila Biber
Barry Johnson
Ben Spain
Brian Burke
Brian Groth
Brian Perry
Carol Troup
Catherine Boeger
Add >
< Remove
Replace >
< Match
Details...
Graphs...
Project Resources
Booking
Work
Help
OK
Cancel

Figure 7–36

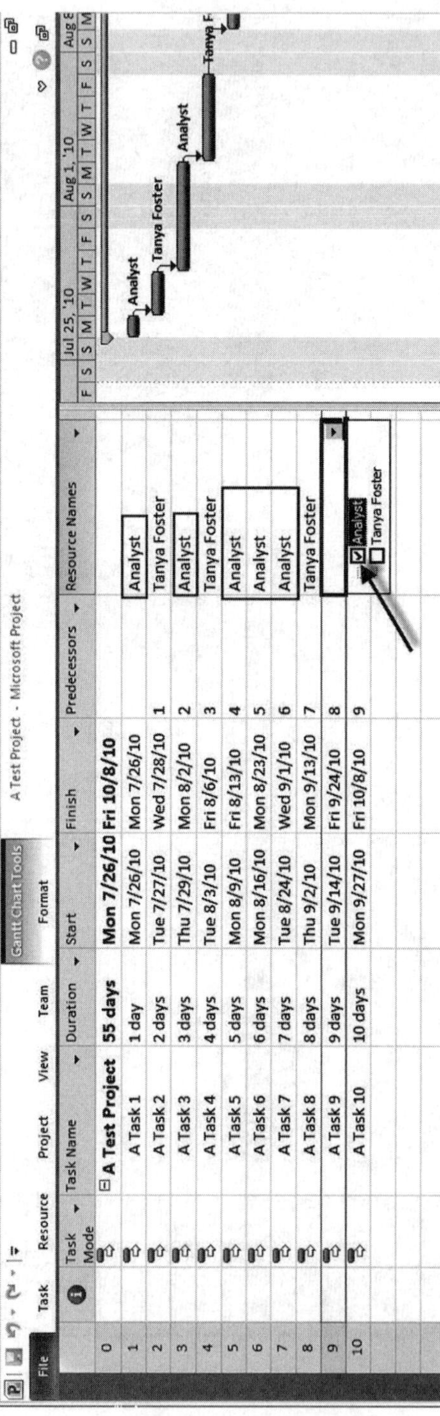
File
Task
Resource
Project
View
Team
Gantt Chart Tools
Format
A Test Project - Microsoft Project
Task Mode
Task Name
Duration
Start
Finish
Predecessors
Resource Names
0 A Test Project 55 days Mon 7/26/10 Fri 10/8/10
1 A Task 1 1 day Mon 7/26/10 Mon 7/26/10 Analyst
2 A Task 2 2 days Tue 7/27/10 Wed 7/28/10 1 Tanya Foster
3 A Task 3 3 days Thu 7/29/10 Mon 8/2/10 2 Analyst
4 A Task 4 4 days Tue 8/3/10 Fri 8/6/10 3 Tanya Foster
5 A Task 5 5 days Mon 8/9/10 Fri 8/13/10 4 Analyst
6 A Task 6 6 days Mon 8/16/10 Mon 8/23/10 5 Analyst
7 A Task 7 7 days Tue 8/24/10 Wed 9/1/10 6 Analyst
8 A Task 8 8 days Thu 9/2/10 Mon 9/13/10 7 Tanya Foster
9 A Task 9 9 days Tue 9/14/10 Fri 9/24/10 8
10 A Task 10 10 days Mon 9/27/10 Fri 10/8/10 9
Analyst
Tanya Foster
Jul 25, '10
Aug 1, '10
F S S M T W T F S S M T W T F S S M
Analyst
Tanya Foster
Analyst
Figure 7–37

Make sure that *Analyst* is highlighted in the list on the right side by clicking on it once, as shown in Figure 7–38. Then click the Match button once.

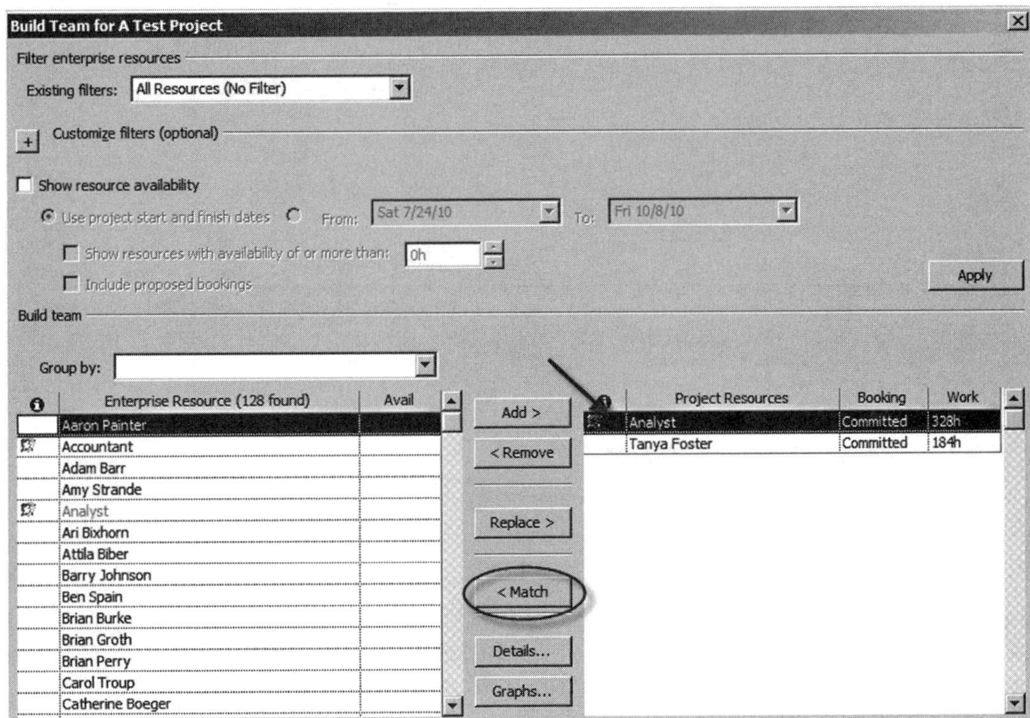

Figure 7–38

In Figure 7–39, you can see how Microsoft Project 2010 filters the resources that have the skill set of Position as Analyst, and displays those in the list on the left-hand side.

To double check the resource information, simply click on a resource in the list, and click the Details button, as shown in Figure 7–40. Notice that the Custom Field Name of Position and the Value of Analyst are in the Resource Information box. When you clicked on Match in the Build Team box, Microsoft Project searched for and filtered all of the resources that had the value of Analyst in this field. Click OK when finished to go back to the Build Team box. In this case, we clicked on the user named "ProjUser."

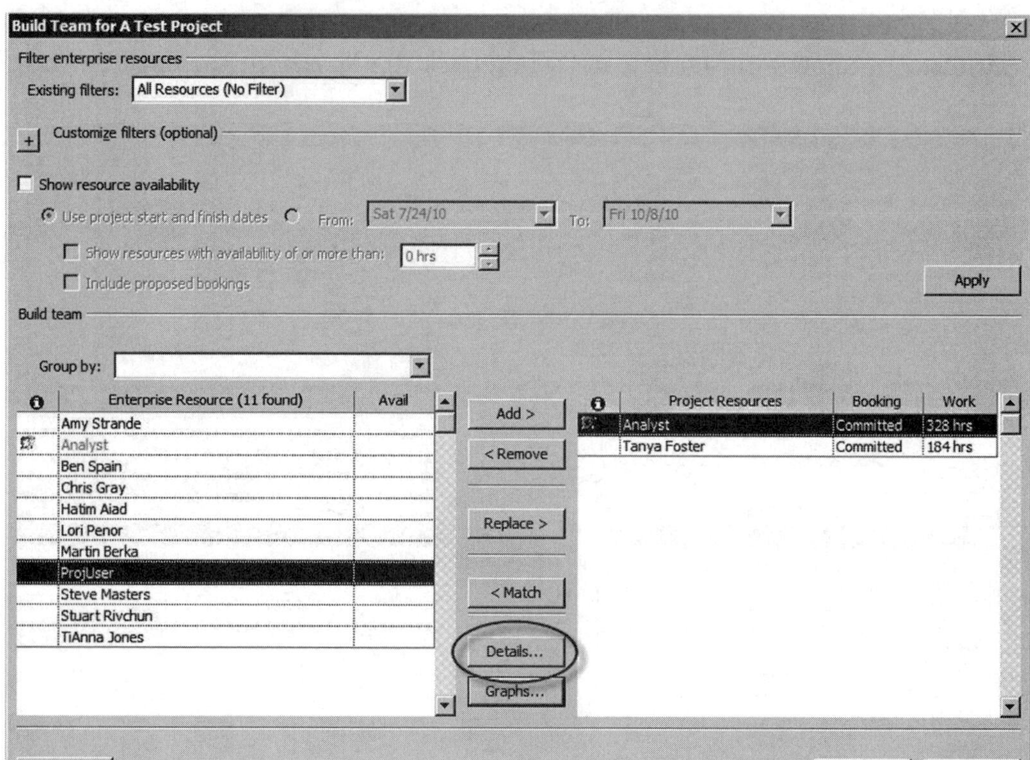

Figure 7–39

Now the big question is how to know which analyst to assign. How do you know who is available and who isn't, who has too much work assigned, who has too little work, etc.? Microsoft Project 2010 can help you in that area too! Click on the Graphs button in the Build a Team box while a resource is highlighted to see a series of graphs to help you determine which resource best fits within the schedule. The Graphs button is shown in Figure 7–41.

You can see the Assignment Work by Resource graph as it is displayed in Project Server and shown in Figure 7–42. The stand-alone version graph looks different in that it will open a view in Project Professional, usually in a split-screen view, that shows each resources' capacity, assignments, and overallocations. We will cover views and reports in detail later, but this is a quick summary of the Project Server view. Look at the View Options in the lower right corner that is circled. Within the View Options, you can select a date range, view the units in days, weeks, months, quarters, or years, and choose whether

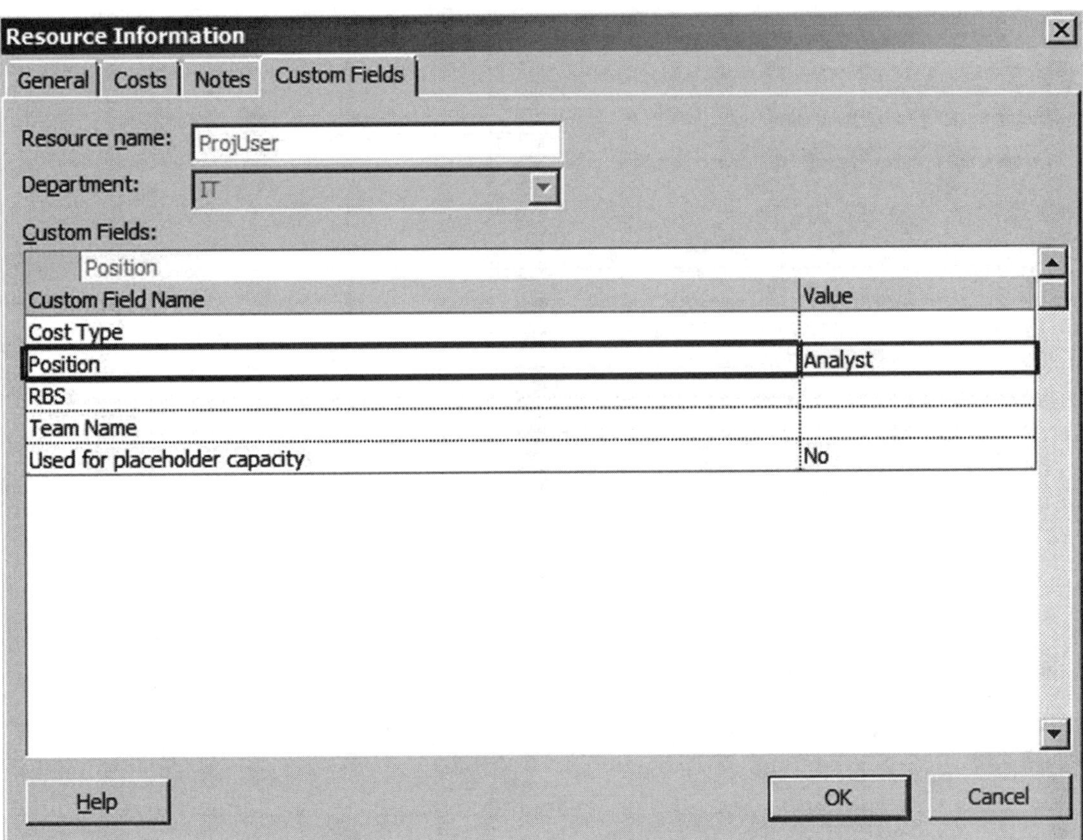

Figure 7–40

or not to include proposed bookings. The current view contains a date range of 7/25/10 to 8/30/10; we're looking at it in days and we've included the proposed bookings. The top right corner, the Legend, is also circled and shows the colors represented in the graph for each resource listed. The solid black line in the graph indicates the capacity line for ALL the resources selected in the top right. Looking at our graph below you can see that Analyst is very much over capacity and ProjUser has nothing assigned to them yet. Let's make some assignments and take another look at this graph. In the example, ProjUser is a named resource and represents an individual.

Since the graph shows that the named resource ProjUser has lots of available capacity, we will use that name to replace the generic resource called Analyst.

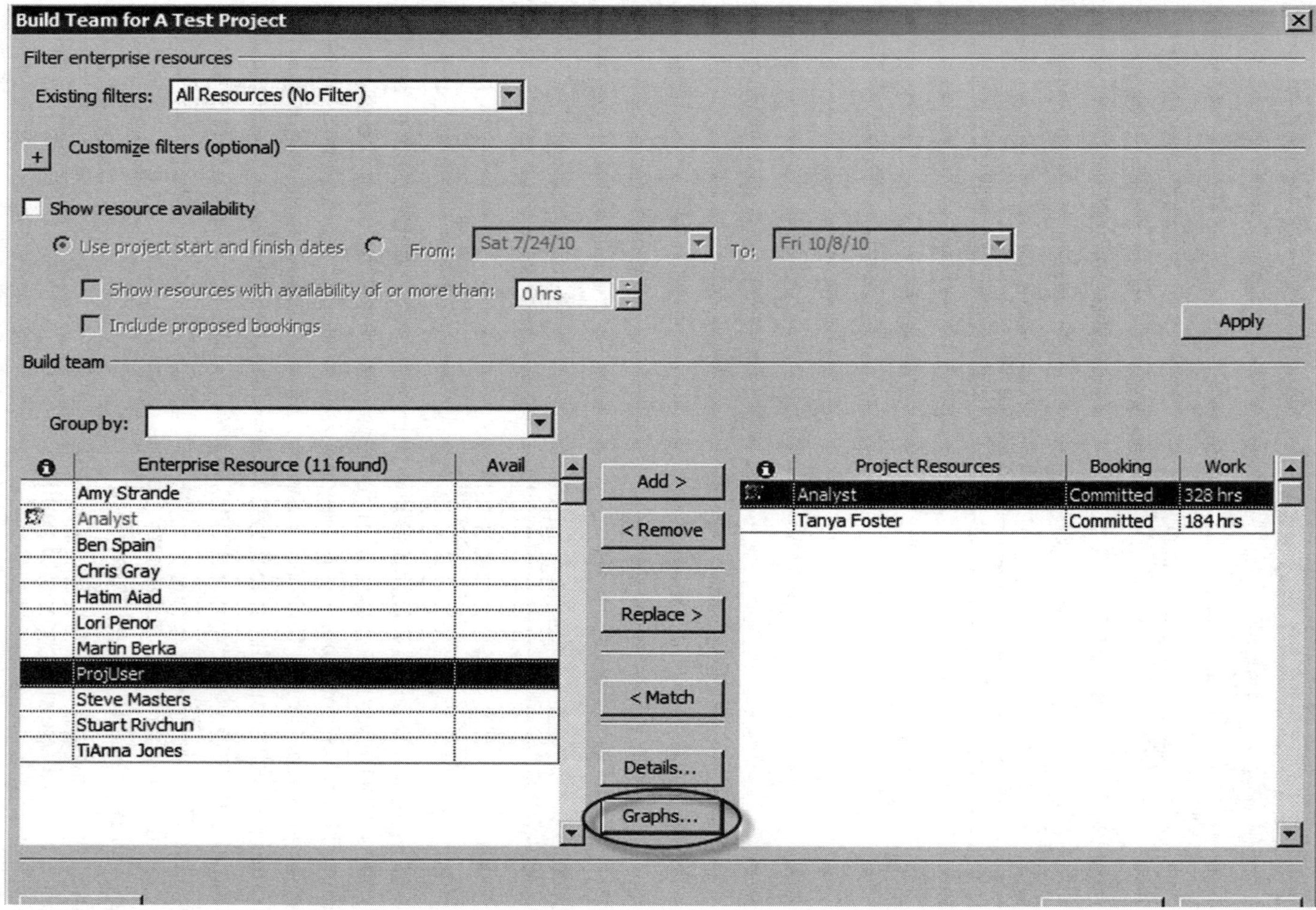
Build Team for A Test Project
Filter enterprise resources
Existing filters:
All Resources (No Filter)
Customize filters (optional)
Show resource availability
Use project start and finish dates
From:
Sat 7/24/10
To:
Fri 10/8/10
Show resources with availability of or more than:
0 hrs
Include proposed bookings
Apply
Build team
Group by:
Enterprise Resource (11 found)
Avail
Amy Strande
Analyst
Ben Spain
Chris Gray
Hatim Aiad
Lori Penor
Martin Berka
ProjUser
Steve Masters
Stuart Rivchun
TiAnna Jones
Add >
< Remove
Replace >
< Match
Details...
Graphs...
Project Resources
Booking
Work
Analyst
Committed
328 hrs
Tanya Foster
Committed
184 hrs

Figure 7–41

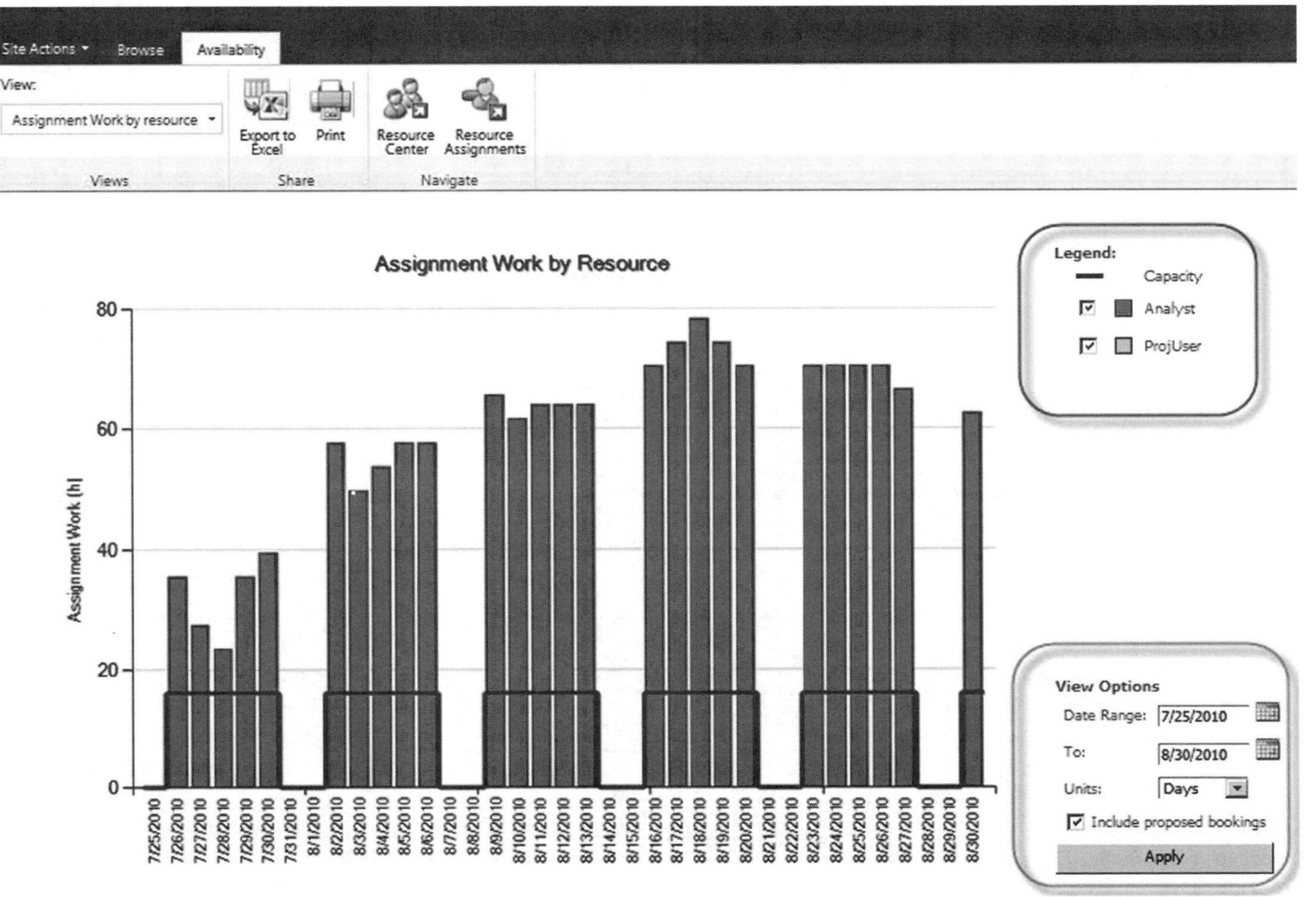
Site Actions
Browse
Availability
View:
Assignment Work by resource
Export to Excel
Print
Resource Center
Resource Assignments
Views
Share
Navigate
Assignment Work by Resource
Assignment Work (h)
80
60
40
20
0
7/25/2010
7/26/2010
7/27/2010
7/28/2010
7/29/2010
7/30/2010
7/31/2010
8/1/2010
8/2/2010
8/3/2010
8/4/2010
8/5/2010
8/6/2010
8/7/2010
8/8/2010
8/9/2010
8/10/2010
8/11/2010
8/12/2010
8/13/2010
8/14/2010
8/15/2010
8/16/2010
8/17/2010
8/18/2010
8/19/2010
8/20/2010
8/21/2010
8/22/2010
8/23/2010
8/24/2010
8/25/2010
8/26/2010
8/27/2010
8/28/2010
8/29/2010
8/30/2010
Legend:
Capacity
Analyst
ProjUser
View Options
Date Range: 7/25/2010
To: 8/30/2010
Units: Days
Include proposed bookings
Apply

Figure 7–42

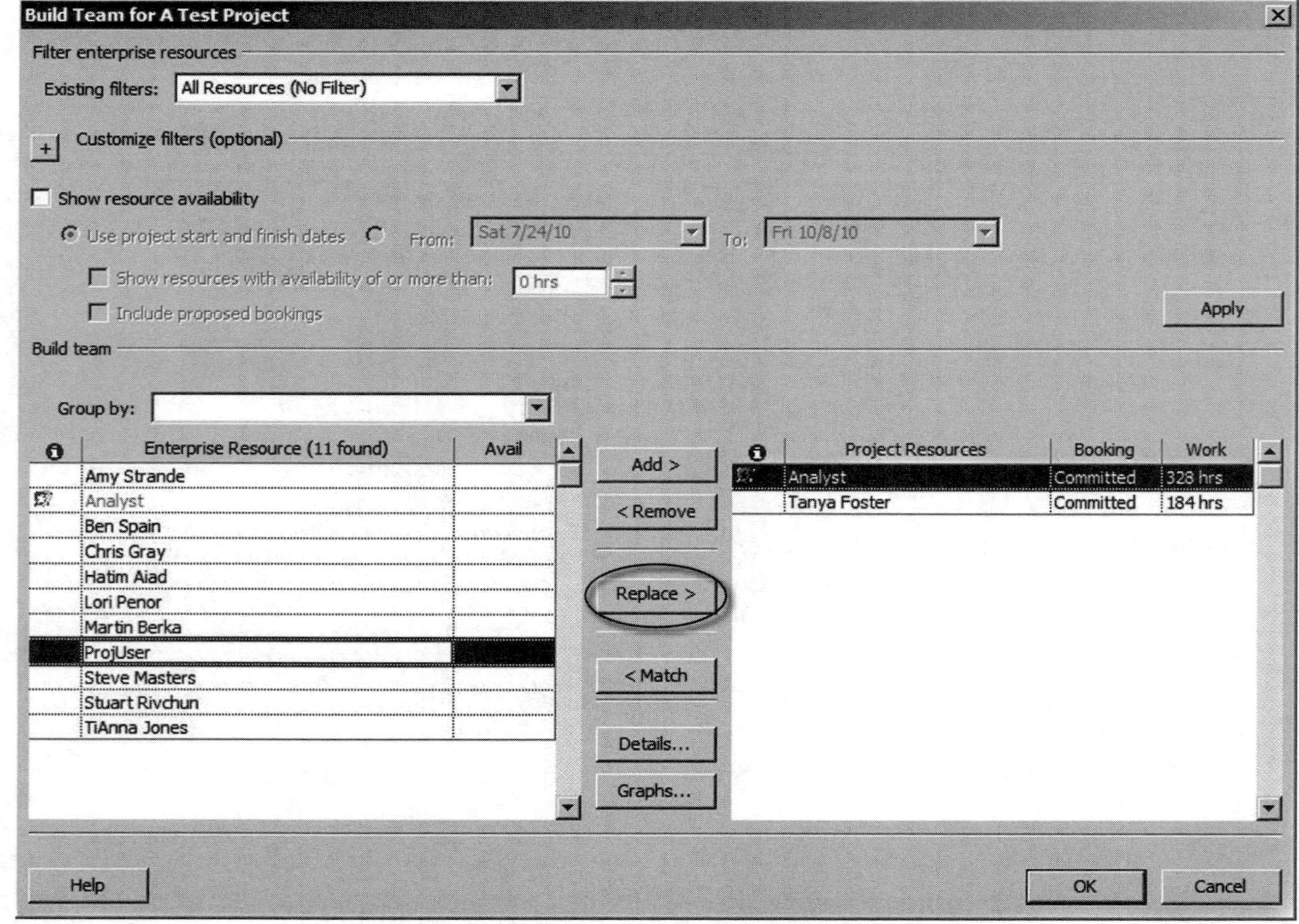
Build Team for A Test Project
Filter enterprise resources
Existing filters: All Resources (No Filter)
Customize filters (optional)
Show resource availability
Use project start and finish dates
From: Sat 7/24/10
To: Fri 10/8/10
Show resources with availability of or more than: 0 hrs
Include proposed bookings
Apply
Build team
Group by:
Enterprise Resource (11 found)
Avail
Amy Strande
Analyst
Ben Spain
Chris Gray
Hatim Aiad
Lori Penor
Martin Berka
ProjUser
Steve Masters
Stuart Rivchun
TiAnna Jones
Add >
< Remove
Replace >
< Match
Details...
Graphs...
Project Resources
Booking
Work
Analyst
Committed
328 hrs
Tanya Foster
Committed
184 hrs
Help
OK
Cancel

Figure 7–43

To replace the generic resource with the real Analyst, we will choose a resource from the left side, and click the Replace button, as shown in Figure 7–43. This will replace the generic resource with a regular resource. Click OK when finished.

Now the schedule has the new resource in place of the generic one, as shown in Figure 7–44. Once the schedule is published, ProjUser would be able to see these tasks on their Task page in Project Server.

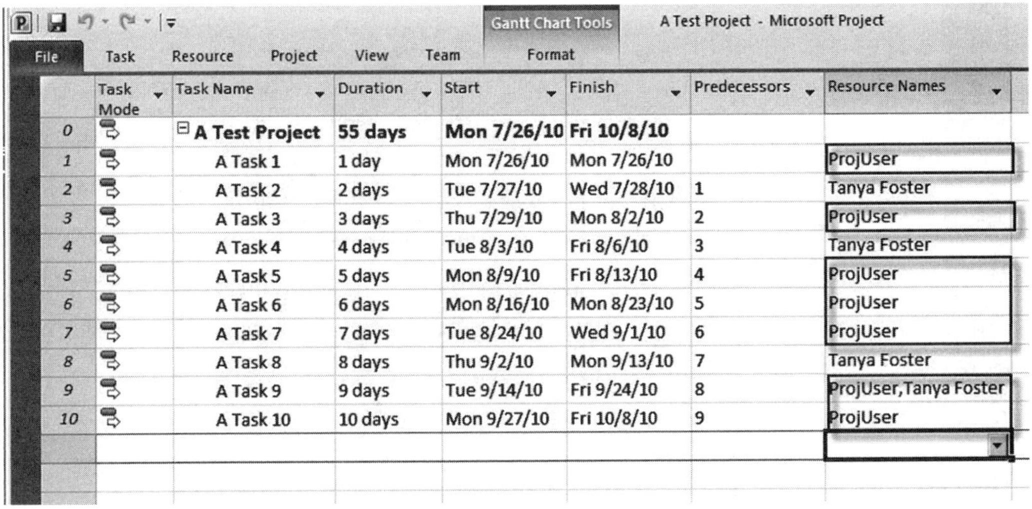

Gantt Chart Tools A Test Project - Microsoft Project

File Task Resource Project View Team Format

	Task Mode	Task Name	Duration	Start	Finish	Predecessors	Resource Names
0		⊟ **A Test Project**	**55 days**	**Mon 7/26/10**	**Fri 10/8/10**		
1		A Task 1	1 day	Mon 7/26/10	Mon 7/26/10		ProjUser
2		A Task 2	2 days	Tue 7/27/10	Wed 7/28/10	1	Tanya Foster
3		A Task 3	3 days	Thu 7/29/10	Mon 8/2/10	2	ProjUser
4		A Task 4	4 days	Tue 8/3/10	Fri 8/6/10	3	Tanya Foster
5		A Task 5	5 days	Mon 8/9/10	Fri 8/13/10	4	ProjUser
6		A Task 6	6 days	Mon 8/16/10	Mon 8/23/10	5	ProjUser
7		A Task 7	7 days	Tue 8/24/10	Wed 9/1/10	6	ProjUser
8		A Task 8	8 days	Thu 9/2/10	Mon 9/13/10	7	Tanya Foster
9		A Task 9	9 days	Tue 9/14/10	Fri 9/24/10	8	ProjUser,Tanya Foster
10		A Task 10	10 days	Mon 9/27/10	Fri 10/8/10	9	ProjUser

Figure 7–44

If we go back and look at the Assignment Work by Resource graph, we will see that the graph looks different now. Figure 7–45 shows that by looking at our new assigned resource, we can see that ProjUser is not over capacity for those days and also has a few days, 7/27 being one of them, where they have nothing assigned.

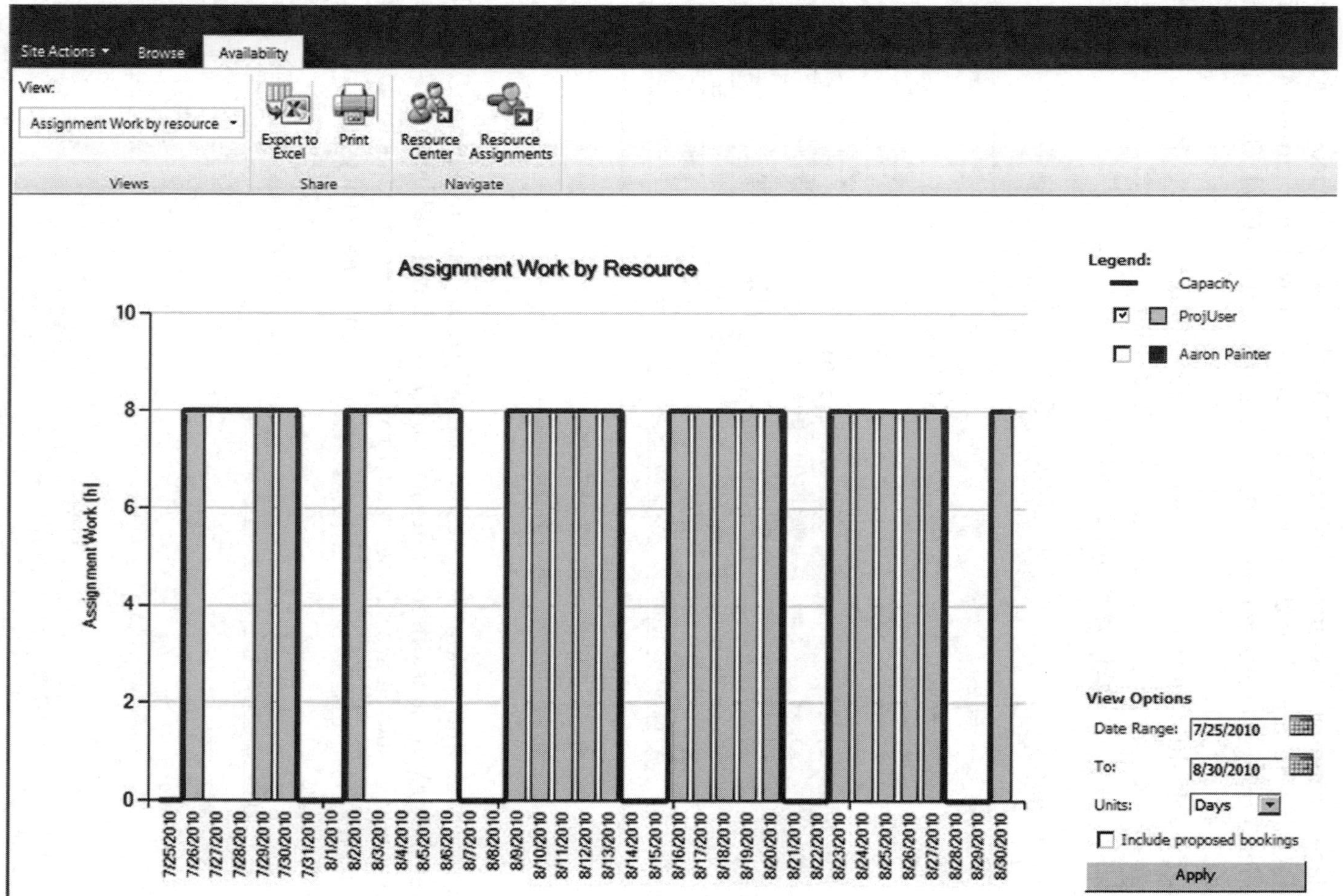
Site Actions
Browse
Availability
View:
Assignment Work by resource
Views
Export to Excel
Print
Share
Resource Center
Resource Assignments
Navigate
Assignment Work by Resource
Assignment Work (h)
10
8
6
4
2
0
7/25/2010
7/26/2010
7/27/2010
7/28/2010
7/29/2010
7/30/2010
7/31/2010
8/1/2010
8/2/2010
8/3/2010
8/4/2010
8/5/2010
8/6/2010
8/7/2010
8/8/2010
8/9/2010
8/10/2010
8/11/2010
8/12/2010
8/13/2010
8/14/2010
8/15/2010
8/16/2010
8/17/2010
8/18/2010
8/19/2010
8/20/2010
8/21/2010
8/22/2010
8/23/2010
8/24/2010
8/25/2010
8/26/2010
8/27/2010
8/28/2010
8/29/2010
8/30/2010
Legend:
Capacity
ProjUser
Aaron Painter
View Options
Date Range: 7/25/2010
To: 8/30/2010
Units: Days
Include proposed bookings
Apply

Figure 7–45

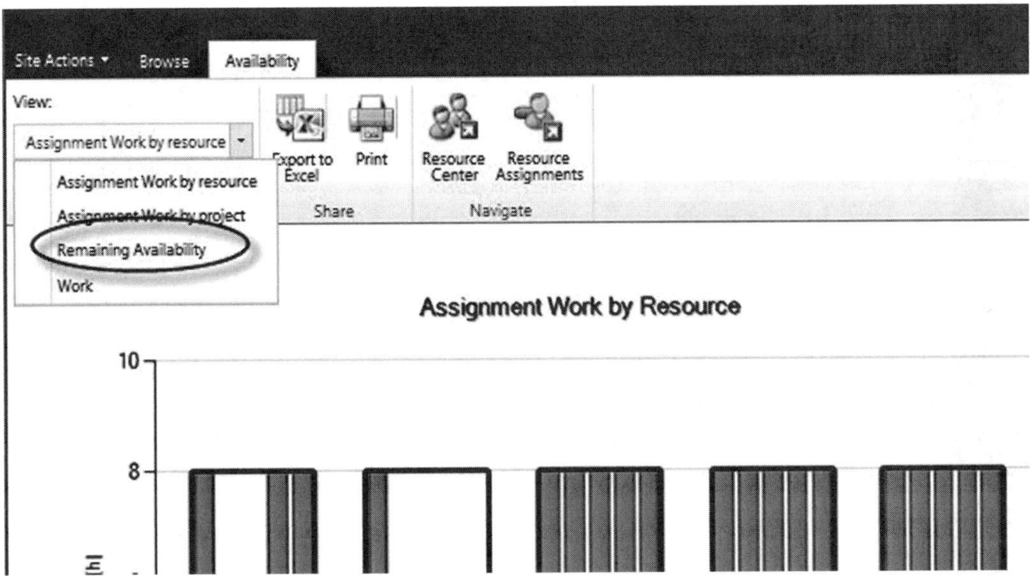

Figure 7–46

Let's take a look at another graph for a different way to view the information.

Figure 7–46 shows that if you click on the drop-down arrow next to the report name at the top left, you will see the list of available reports. Let's look at the Remaining Availability report.

Figure 7–47 shows the Remaining Availability graph. This graph tells us how much available time a resource has that they can still be scheduled for. You can see that ProjUser has six available days at 8 hours each day that they can still be scheduled for.

Assigning by skill set and using these graphs can be very useful tools in Microsoft Project 2010. We cover how to find some of this information in more detail in the Chapter 12—Information Is Everywhere.

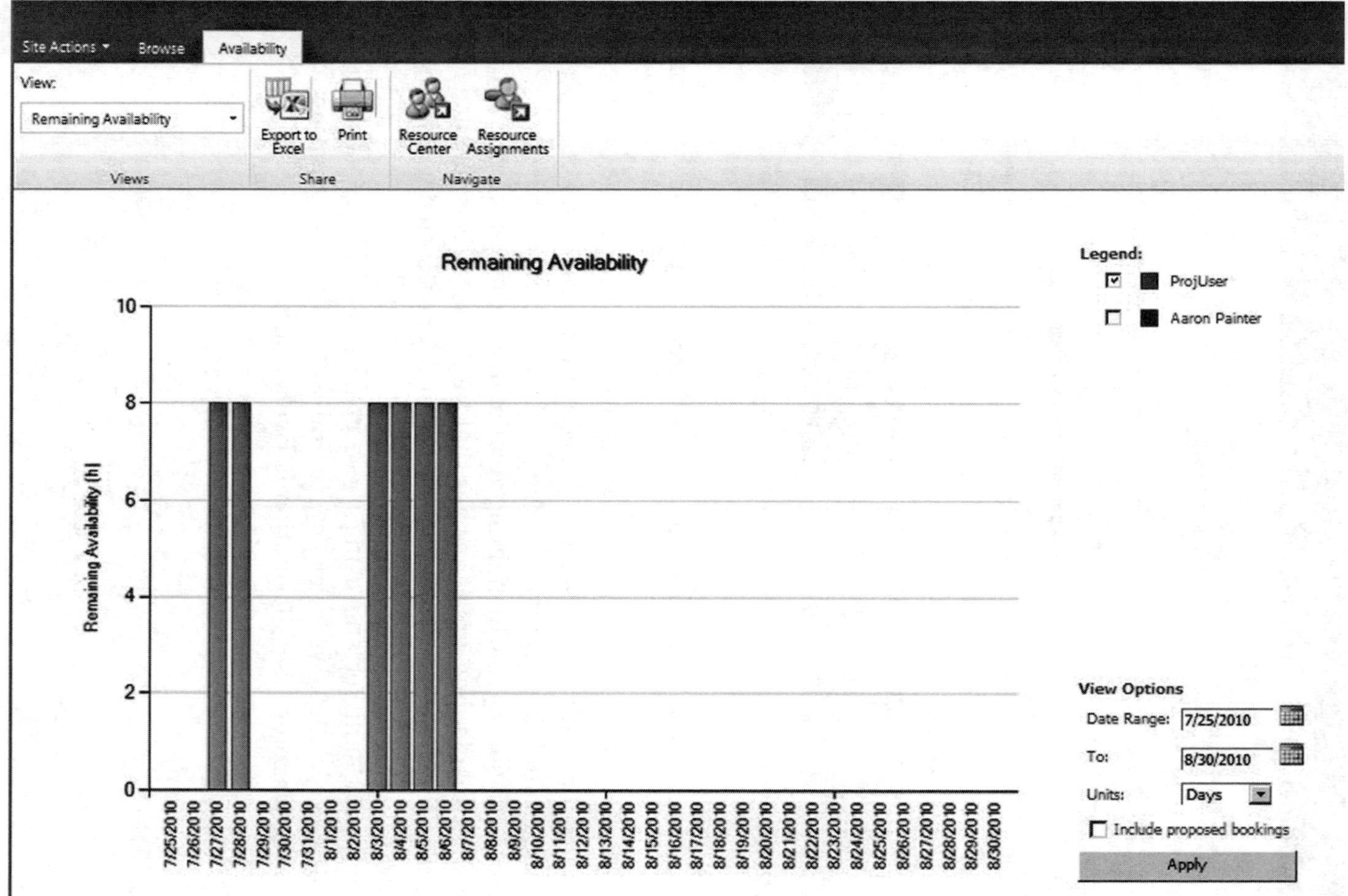
Site Actions
Browse
Availability
View:
Remaining Availability
Views
Export to Excel
Print
Share
Resource Center
Resource Assignments
Navigate
Remaining Availability
Remaining Availability (h)
10
8
6
4
2
0
7/25/2010
7/26/2010
7/27/2010
7/28/2010
7/29/2010
7/30/2010
7/31/2010
8/1/2010
8/2/2010
8/3/2010
8/4/2010
8/5/2010
8/6/2010
8/7/2010
8/8/2010
8/9/2010
8/10/2010
8/11/2010
8/12/2010
8/13/2010
8/14/2010
8/15/2010
8/16/2010
8/17/2010
8/18/2010
8/19/2010
8/20/2010
8/21/2010
8/22/2010
8/23/2010
8/24/2010
8/25/2010
8/26/2010
8/27/2010
8/28/2010
8/29/2010
8/30/2010
Legend:
ProjUser
Aaron Painter
View Options
Date Range: 7/25/2010
To: 8/30/2010
Units: Days
Include proposed bookings
Apply

Figure 7–47

8

Update Cycle and Approvals

While this book concentrates on the resource management portions of Microsoft Project Server and Microsoft Project Professional, it is beneficial to know how a resource will see his or her task information. While security settings determine what views from which specific projects a resource can see, the resource can't see assignments on Project Server until a project file is published. There is a difference between saving a file to Project Server and publishing a file.

A project file that is *saved* to Project Server can be viewed, edited, and modified. However, while the saved project file can be modified by the project manager and resource manager, the resource won't get any notifications or see the project file's assignments in his or her task views. This allows for a project file to be modified repeatedly until the resource manager and project manager are ready for it to "go live." When the managers are ready for the project file to become part of the resource's task list, they have to *publish* the file.

To publish a project file, click on the File tab and select Publish, as shown in Figure 8–1.

If this is the first time that you are publishing the project file, or if the project file does not have a corresponding SharePoint site created, you will see the Publish Project box. The corresponding SharePoint site is called the Project Site or Workspace, since it is unique to the project file. The Publish Project box

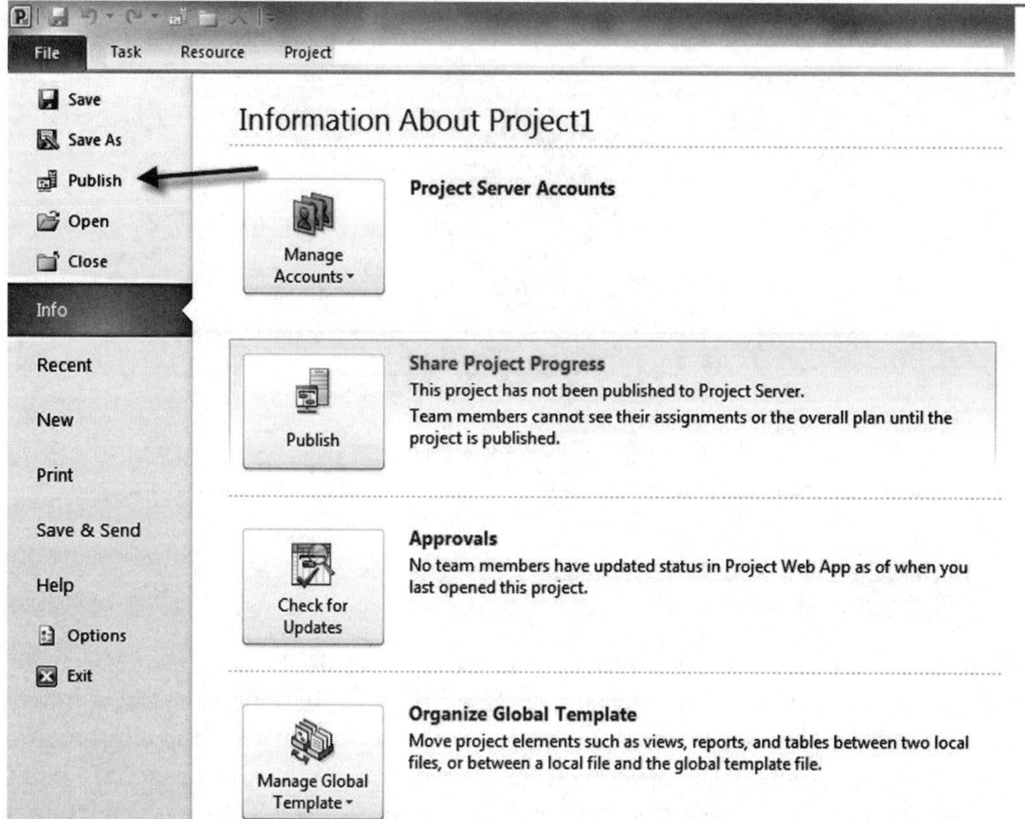

Figure 8–1

will ask you to publish the project, and to choose whether or not you are going to create the Project Site.

Notice the radio button next to *Create a site for this project* is selected by default. There is a check box to set up this new site as a subsite to an existing project. Since we don't want to make this a subsite of another project, we have left that box unchecked. The Web Application, Site URL, and Target URL are set up by the project server administrator and will be listed automatically in the appropriate fields when the Publish Project box opens.

The Target URL line is displayed to help you see exactly where this site will be located. In Figure 8–2, you can see that this project file, named Test, will be saved to pmpspecialists.com in the Project Server instance, called PWA, which will display in the URL as pmpspecialists.com/PWA. Your organization may have more than one instance, for example, they may have a development instance titled something like "DEV" and the URL would then be pmpspecialists.com/DEV. The term "PWA" can be a bit confusing as most organizations use the letters P, W, and A to designate the normal instance that most users will use. Also, the home page that the user opens when they go to the instance is called the Project Web App, or, PWA for short. Because of this potential confusion, some organizations call their normal instance something other than PWA, such as "Live". In that case, the instance would be pmpspecialists.com/Live. Once you have selected a site for this project file, click the Publish button to publish the project file to the Project Server.

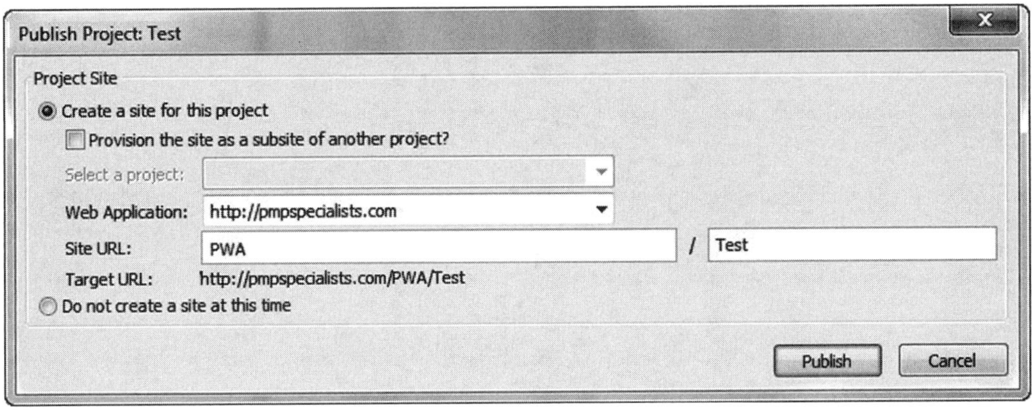

Figure 8–2

Once you have successfully published the project file, the resource will be able to see his or her tasks. Figure 8–3 shows the project file Test that was just published. You can see that the schedule has four tasks, and that they are assigned to David Pelton or Tanya Foster, or to both of them.

Tanya has work assigned to her on tasks 2 through 4. When she signs into the Project Web App, if the security settings allow her to, she will see those tasks. It is important to note that your project server administrator can modify the views in almost an innumerable amount of methods. Therefore, it is entirely possible that the views in the example look different than your views. In the example, Tanya has the appropriate security permissions to see her tasks.

When Tanya Foster logs into the Project Web App, her homepage will show any new tasks that have been assigned to her. To show the new tasks, Tanya can click on the link that explains how many new tasks are assigned to her,

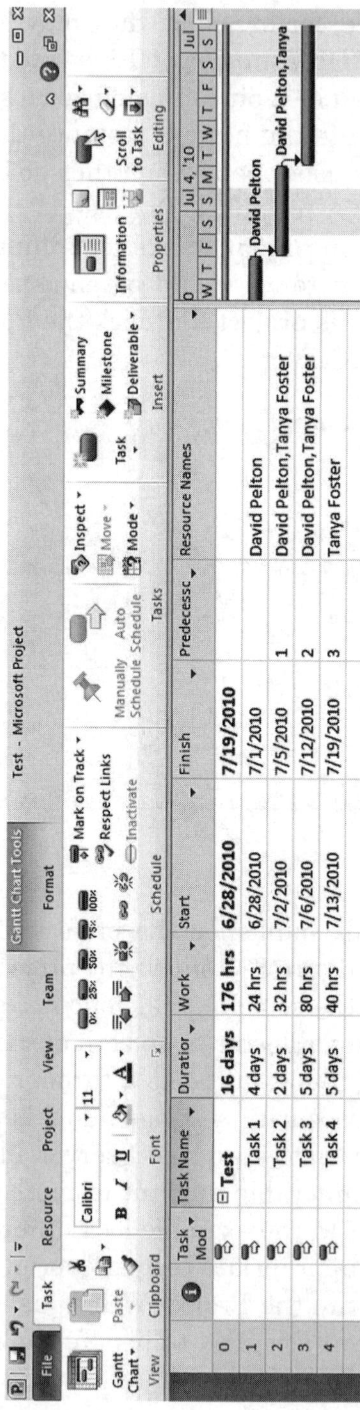

	Task Mode	Task Name	Duration	Work	Start	Finish	Predecessors	Resource Names
0		**Test**	**16 days**	**176 hrs**	**6/28/2010**	**7/19/2010**		
1		Task 1	4 days	24 hrs	6/28/2010	7/1/2010		David Pelton
2		Task 2	2 days	32 hrs	7/2/2010	7/5/2010	1	David Pelton,Tanya Foster
3		Task 3	5 days	80 hrs	7/6/2010	7/12/2010	2	David Pelton,Tanya Foster
4		Task 4	5 days	40 hrs	7/13/2010	7/19/2010	3	Tanya Foster

Figure 8–3

the Tasks header, or the Tasks link under the My Work grouping in the Quick Launch area. These three locations are shown in Figure 8–4.

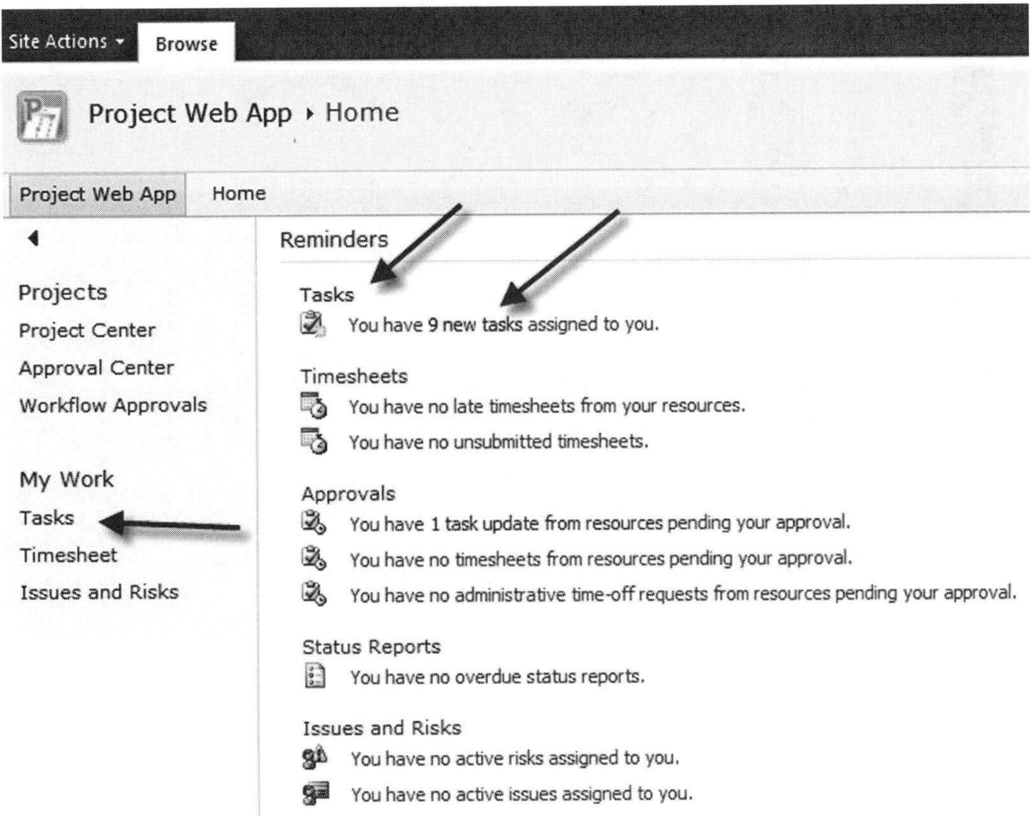

Figure 8–4

Any of these three links will bring Tanya to her tasks screen. The view in this example is the My Assignments view with no Filter and no Group By option selected. The *Custom Group By* displayed in the Group By drop-down is because we have set each grouping to None. This view shows the tasks assigned, shown in Figure 8–5, but doesn't easily help to distinguish which task applies to which project file. Just like the example, you may have tasks that are similarly named in different projects, and that makes it even harder to know which task belongs to which project file.

There are a few methods to help resources understand which tasks go with which project files. One way is to add fields (whether custom or standard) to the

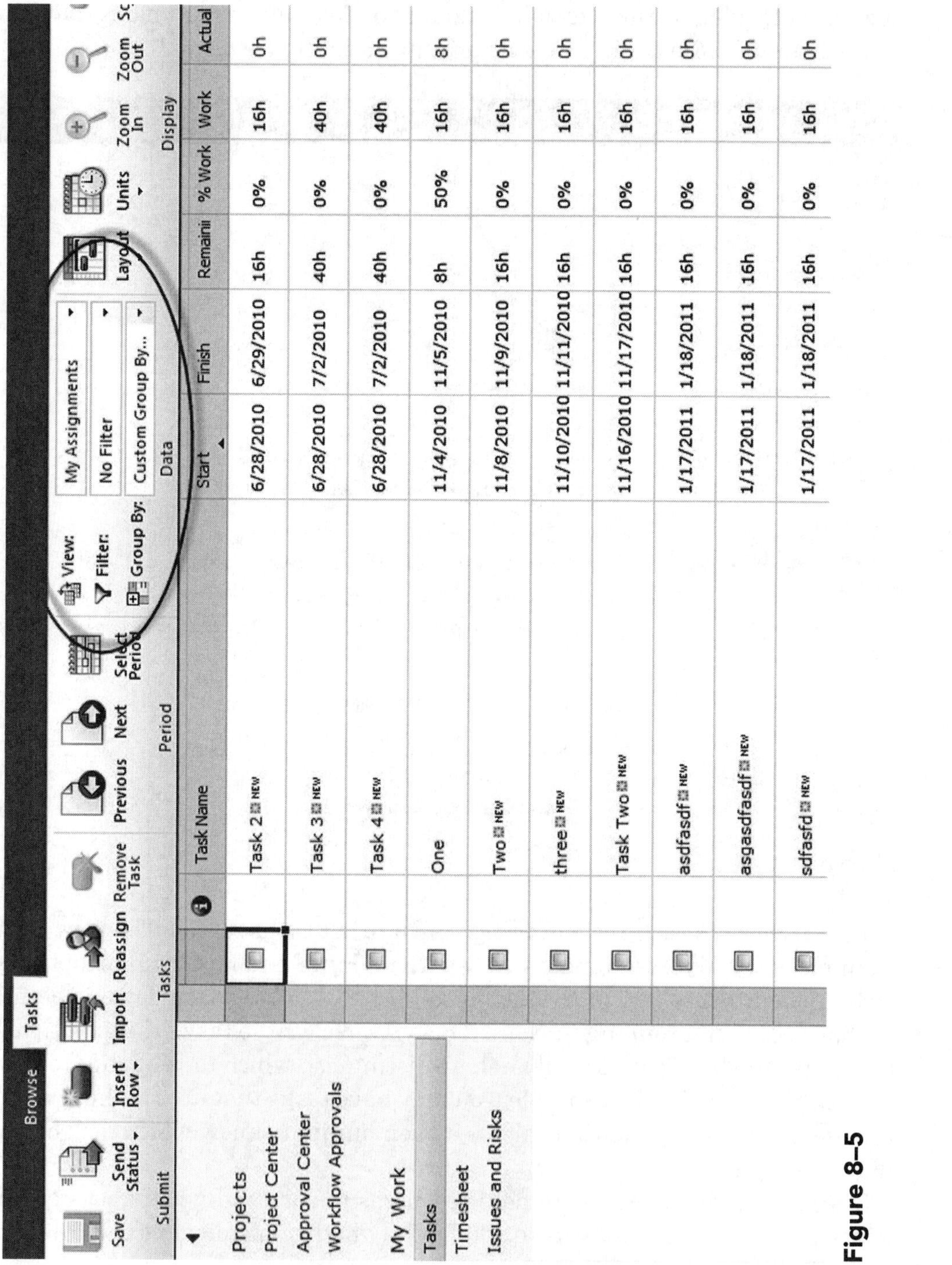
Browse
Tasks
Save
Send Status
Insert Row
Import
Reassign
Remove Task
Previous
Next
Select Period
View: My Assignments
Filter: No Filter
Group By: Custom Group By...
Layout
Units
Zoom In
Zoom Out
Submit
Tasks
Period
Data
Display
Projects
Project Center
Approval Center
Workflow Approvals
My Work
Tasks
Timesheet
Issues and Risks
Task Name
Start
Finish
Remaini
% Work
Work
Actual
Task 2 NEW 6/28/2010 6/29/2010 16h 0% 16h 0h
Task 3 NEW 6/28/2010 7/2/2010 40h 0% 40h 0h
Task 4 NEW 6/28/2010 7/2/2010 40h 0% 40h 0h
One 11/4/2010 11/5/2010 8h 50% 16h 8h
Two NEW 11/8/2010 11/9/2010 16h 0% 16h 0h
three NEW 11/10/2010 11/11/2010 16h 0% 16h 0h
Task Two NEW 11/16/2010 11/17/2010 16h 0% 16h 0h
asdfasdf NEW 1/17/2011 1/18/2011 16h 0% 16h 0h
asgasdfasdf NEW 1/17/2011 1/18/2011 16h 0% 16h 0h
sdfasfd NEW 1/17/2011 1/18/2011 16h 0% 16h 0h

Figure 8–5

view. Another way is to use the built-in Filter and Group By options. The same information in Figure 8–5 can be seen in an easier to read format by changing the Group By option to sort by the name of the project file. By using the project file grouping, Tanya can now more easily navigate through her tasks, as seen in Figure 8–6.

To see more information about a task, the resource can drill down into more detail on any particular task. In the example shown in Figure 8–7, we will click on Task 3 and drill down to see more information about this task. The first section of the Task details screen provides General Details. Depending on the permission settings for the resource and what items he or she can update, the items in the General Details may be grayed out. In this example, the resource can update the Start Date, Finish Date, and Remaining Work.

If there has been any history of task changes, updates, or approvals, they will be listed in the Recent Task Changes section. In the Update Cycle section of this chapter, we will use this screen again. If there are any attachments to this task, they will be listed in the Attachments section. Both sections are shown in Figure 8–8.

The Contacts section of the Tasks Detail screen can be a valuable piece of information for a resource. This section names the project manager and approval manager for the project. It also lists all other resources who are on the project team, and also lists who else is assigned to the task. You may remember that for this task, we have two resources assigned—Tanya Foster and David Pelton—as shown in Figure 8–9. In some cases, if you have e-mail and communicator tools setup, the ability to instant message or e-mail the other resources will become available when you hover over their names.

The next section of the Tasks Detail screen is Related Assignments. This is information that allows the resource to see what task(s) should be completed before they can do their work and to see which task(s) are waiting for their task to be completed. As shown in Figure 8–10, a task (Task 3) is waiting for Task 2 to be completed, and Task 4 is the next task. It also shows the percentage completed of each task in the Status column. Because there are two resources assigned to this task, they will both be listed.

The final section, the Notes section, will display any notes that have been created. It also will allow the resource to enter notes that pertain to his or her task. In the next section of this chapter, The Update Cycle, we will demonstrate how the Notes section is modified.

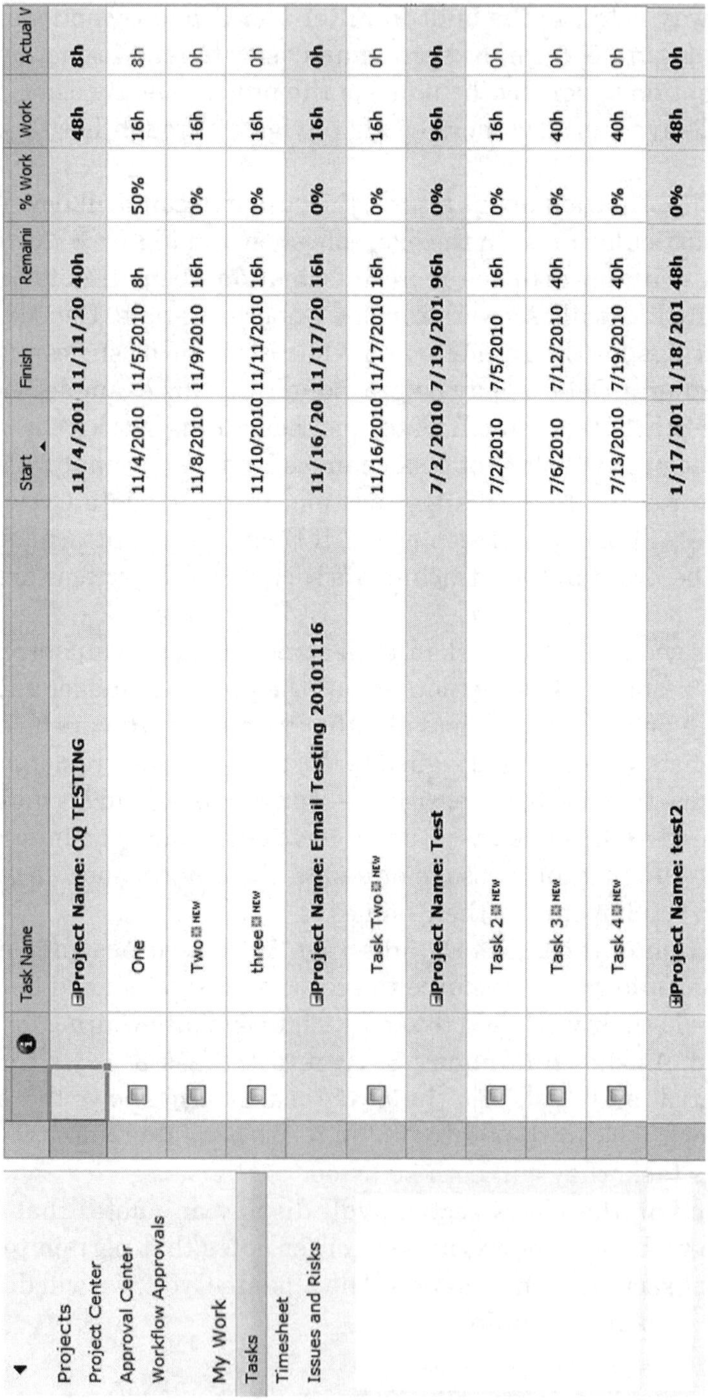

Projects
Project Center
Approval Center
Workflow Approvals

My Work
Tasks
Timesheet
Issues and Risks

Task Name	Start	Finish	Remaini	% Work	Work	Actual V
⊟Project Name: CQ TESTING	**11/4/201**	**11/11/20**	**40h**		**48h**	**8h**
One	11/4/2010	11/5/2010	8h	50%	16h	8h
Two NEW	11/8/2010	11/9/2010	16h	0%	16h	0h
three NEW	11/10/2010	11/11/2010	16h	0%	16h	0h
⊟Project Name: Email Testing 20101116	**11/16/20**	**11/17/20**	**16h**	**0%**	**16h**	**0h**
Task Two NEW	11/16/2010	11/17/2010	16h	0%	16h	0h
⊟Project Name: Test	**7/2/2010**	**7/19/201**	**96h**	**0%**	**96h**	**0h**
Task 2 NEW	7/2/2010	7/5/2010	16h	0%	16h	0h
Task 3 NEW	7/6/2010	7/12/2010	40h	0%	40h	0h
Task 4 NEW	7/13/2010	7/19/2010	40h	0%	40h	0h
⊞Project Name: test2	**1/17/201**	**1/18/201**	**48h**	**0%**	**48h**	**0h**

Figure 8–6

Task 3

Recalculate | Save

⊟ General Details

View and update status on this assignment

Task Progress

Total work: 5d

Timephased work: 0d of 5d (0%)

Task Properties

Start: 7/6/2010

Finish: 7/12/2010

Remaining Work: 40h

Figure 8–7

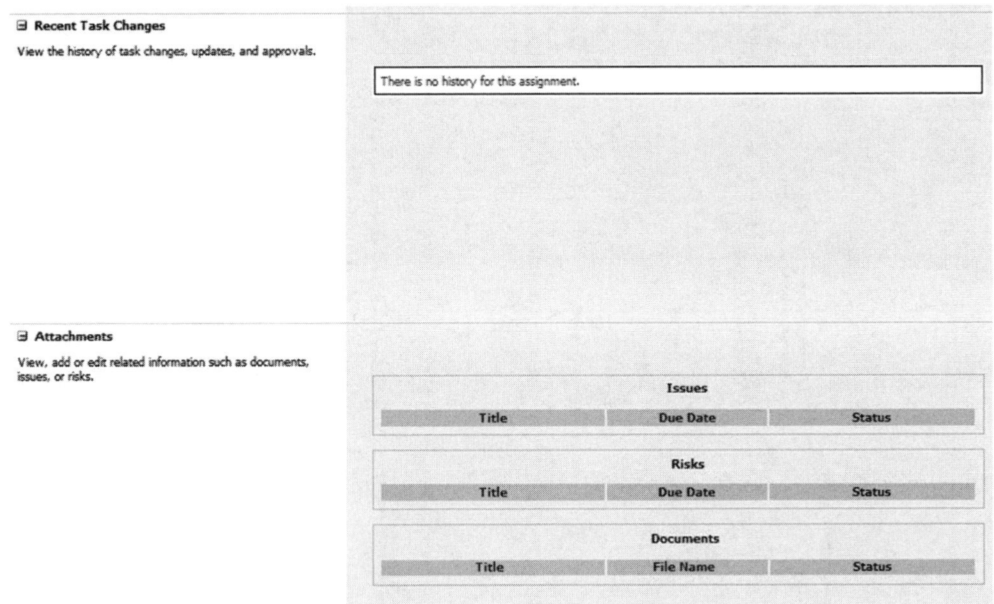

Figure 8–8

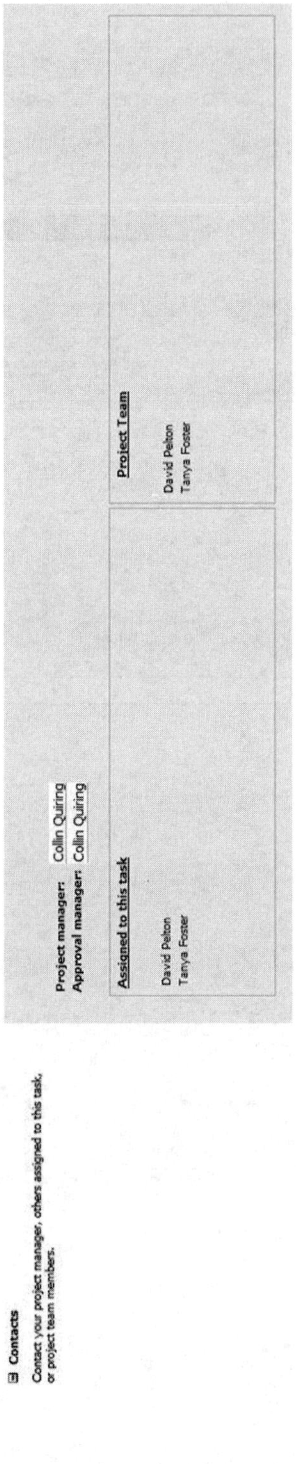

Contacts

Contact your project manager, others assigned to this task, or project team members.

Project manager: Collin Quiring
Approval manager: Collin Quiring

Assigned to this task	Project Team
David Pelton	David Pelton
Tanya Foster	Tanya Foster

Figure 8–9

Related Assignments

View related assignments with enterprise resources assigned. To view contact options, click on the resource name.

Tasks scheduled to finish before this task can start:

Task name:	Start	End	Status	Assigned To
Task 2	7/2/2010	7/5/2010	0%	David Pelton
Task 2	7/2/2010	7/5/2010	0%	Tanya Foster

Tasks dependent on this task's finish date:

Task name:	Start	End	Status	Assigned To
Task 4	7/13/2010	7/19/2010	0%	Tanya Foster

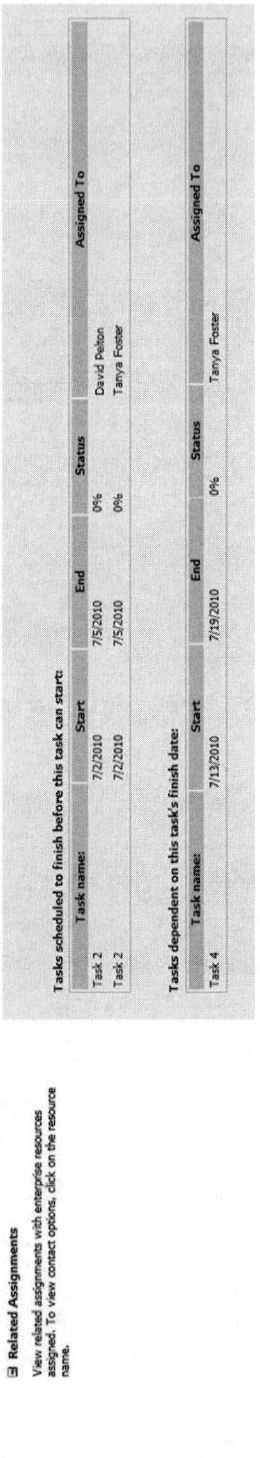

Figure 8–10

The Update Cycle

In Microsoft Project Server, you have the ability to allow resources to update their tasks directly through the Project Web App. This can be a huge time-saver for resources and resource managers. It also allows for instant communication between the resource, resource manager, and project manager. Depending upon the settings in the Project Web App , an e-mail can be sent for every update that a resource applies to his or her tasks.

In the accepted methodology and terminology of Microsoft, and project management in general, a project manager builds a project file, a resource manager assigns the resources to the tasks, and the project manager publishes the project file when it is ready. We understand that in many organizations the project manager and the resource manager are the same person. That same person is also sometimes the resource. We have also worked with organizations that have multiple project managers and multiple resource managers for a single project file.

The Update Cycle is relatively easy to understand, in theory. In practicality, it is technically easy, but a bit difficult to implement efficiently. We cover some of the practical aspects of implementing the Update Cycle in the Chapter 14, Questions and Answers, at the end of this book.

From a high-level view, the steps for the Update Cycle are as follows:

1. First, the project manager builds the work breakdown structure (WBS), preferably from a template.
2. The resource manager adds resources.
3. The project manager confirms timelines; the added resources may have moved some of the timelines.
4. The project manager publishes the project file to the Server.
5. Resources begin execution of tasks.
6. Resources update their task progress.
7. The project manager (and resource manager or other as needed) updates the project based on resource updates.
8. The project manager publishes the revised version of the project.

Visually, this is represented in Figure 8–11. The right half of the diagram is the initial creation and publishing of the project file while the left half of the diagram is where the updates and ongoing time will take place. As the smaller circle indicates, the Update Cycle can be repeated numerous times throughout the lifetime of the project file.

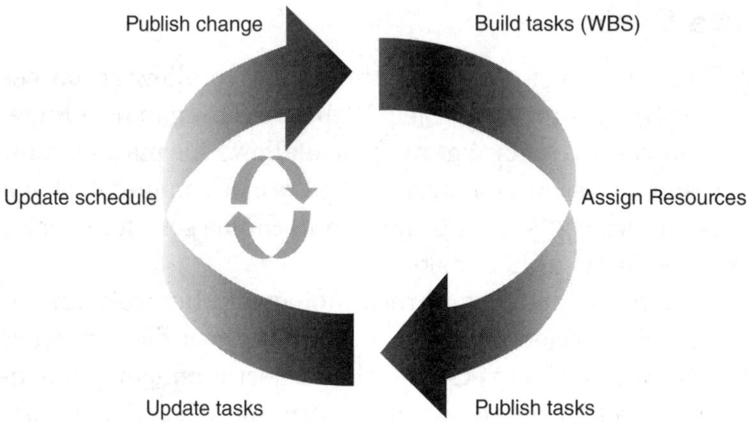

Figure 8–11

There are a few different methods available to update a task, but the most common way is to use a "percentage completed" method, where the resource enters a percentage to indicate how much of the task is completed. Other methods include allowing the resource to enter the hours of work done per time period, or the actual hours worked and the hours remaining. In this example, we are not using timesheets for updating. At this point, we are only using the Tasks screens. We cover how to use timesheets in Chapter 9.

Depending upon the workload and type of tasks, it may be possible to update tasks daily. Let's go through the process of a task update. We will use the same Test project file and Task 3 that we used earlier in this chapter.

Since we are going to use the percentage update method, we will go to the Tasks screen and enter the percentage into the box as shown in Figure 8–12.

In this case, we stated that the task is half finished by entering 50% in the *% Work* field. After entering a percentage in that column, the system will automatically provide a notice that the task has had a change that has not been saved. The notice appears on the task row itself in the Process Status column, and in the yellow bar at the top of the Task screen (just below the Ribbon), as shown in Figure 8–13.

Many tasks can be updated before they are saved as a batched group, or you can save each update as you do them. It may be beneficial to save each update as you do them in case something happens to your computer (just as backing up files is better to be safe than sorry). To save task update(s), select the task(s) and then click on the Save icon in the Ribbon, as shown in Figure 8–14.

Task Name	Start	Finish	Remaini	% Work	Work	Actual V	Process Status
Project Name: Test	7/2/2010	7/19/2010	96h	0%	96h	0h	
Task 2 NEW	7/2/2010	7/5/2010	16h	0%	16h	0h	
Task 3	7/6/2010	7/12/2010	40h	0%	40h	0h	
Task 4 NEW	7/13/2010	7/19/2010	40h	0%	40h	0h	

Figure 8–12

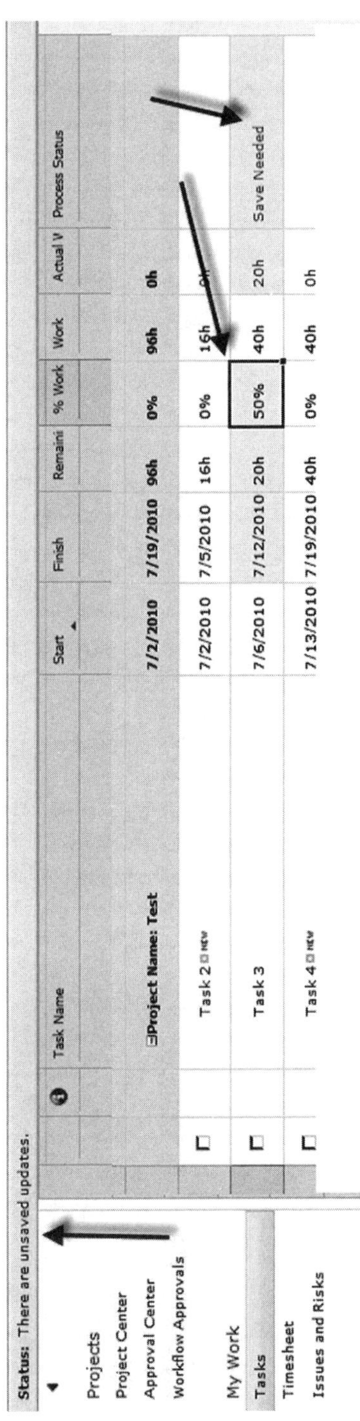

Figure 8–13

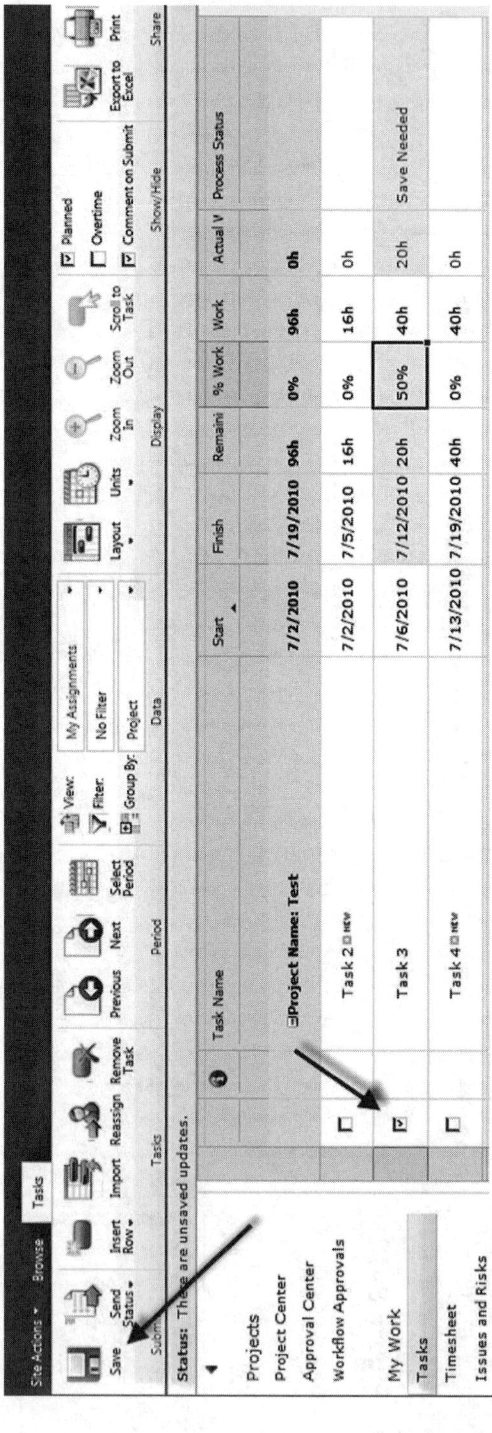
Site Actions
Browse
Tasks
Save
Send Status
Insert Row
Import
Reassign
Remove Task
Previous
Next
Select Period
View: My Assignments
Filter: No Filter
Group By: Project
Layout
Units
Zoom In
Zoom Out
Scroll to Task
Planned
Overtime
Comment on Submit
Export to Excel
Print
Status: There are unsaved updates.
Projects
Project Center
Approval Center
Workflow Approvals
My Work
Tasks
Timesheet
Issues and Risks
Task Name
Start
Finish
Remaini
% Work
Work
Actual V
Process Status
Project Name: Test
7/2/2010
7/19/2010
96h
0%
96h
0h
Task 2
7/2/2010
7/5/2010
16h
0%
16h
0h
Task 3
7/6/2010
7/12/2010
20h
50%
40h
20h
Save Needed
Task 4
7/13/2010
7/19/2010
40h
0%
40h
0h

Figure 8–14

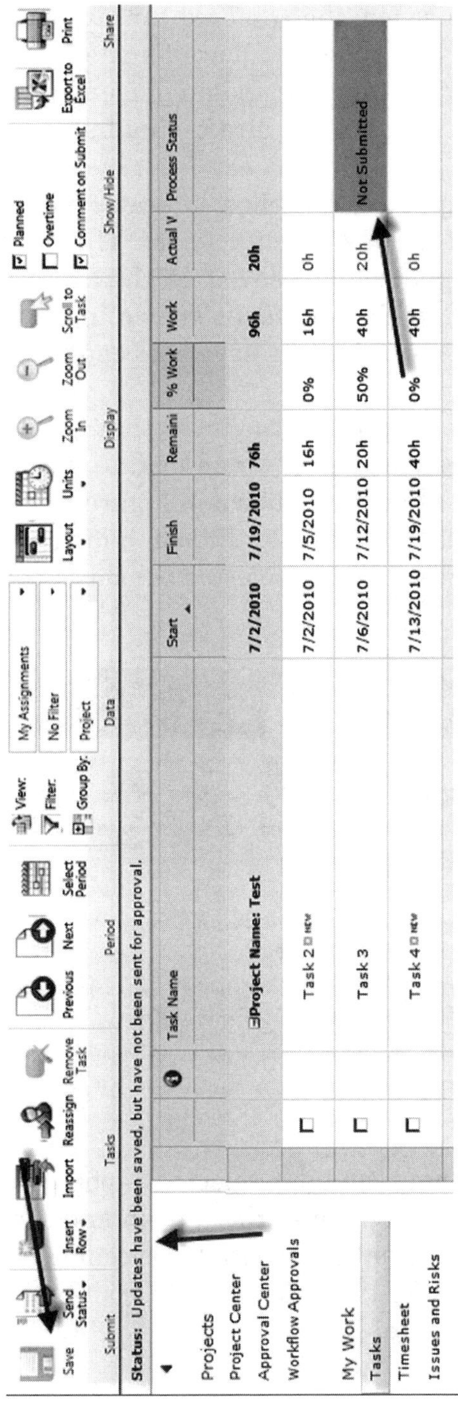
Save
Send Status
Insert Row
Import
Reassign
Remove Task
Previous
Next
Select Period
View: My Assignments
Filter: No Filter
Group By: Project
Layout
Units
Zoom In
Zoom Out
Scroll to Task
Planned
Overtime
Comment on Submit
Export to Excel
Print
Submit
Tasks
Period
Data
Display
Show/Hide
Share
Status: Updates have been saved, but have not been sent for approval.
Projects
Project Center
Approval Center
Workflow Approvals
My Work
Tasks
Timesheet
Issues and Risks
Task Name
Start
Finish
Remaini
% Work
Work
Actual W
Process Status
Project Name: Test
7/2/2010
7/19/2010
76h
96h
20h
Task 2
7/2/2010
7/5/2010
16h
0%
16h
0h
Task 3
7/6/2010
7/12/2010
20h
50%
40h
20h
Not Submitted
Task 4
7/13/2010
7/19/2010
40h
0%
40h
0h

Figure 8–15

Once a task update is saved, the resource can exit the Project Web App or send the update. Since Project Server allows for the updates to be batched together, there is no urgency to send the update immediately. How your organization wants updates to be received will direct what business policy you institute within the Update Cycle.

After saving the task updates, the yellow indicator bar will change to indicate that an update has been saved, but not yet sent. The Save icon will be grayed out when there are no updates to be saved. In the Process Status column, the message will change to Not Submitted, as shown in Figure 8–15. This allows the resource to quickly see which tasks have not been sent to the resource manager yet.

After the resource has updated all the tasks that he or she wants to update, a specific task can be selected to send for an update, or all task updates can be sent at the same time in a batch. As shown in Figure 8–16, updates are sent by selecting the Send Status icon from the Ribbon and choosing either All Tasks or Selected Tasks, if the resource has selected the check box next to one or more tasks.

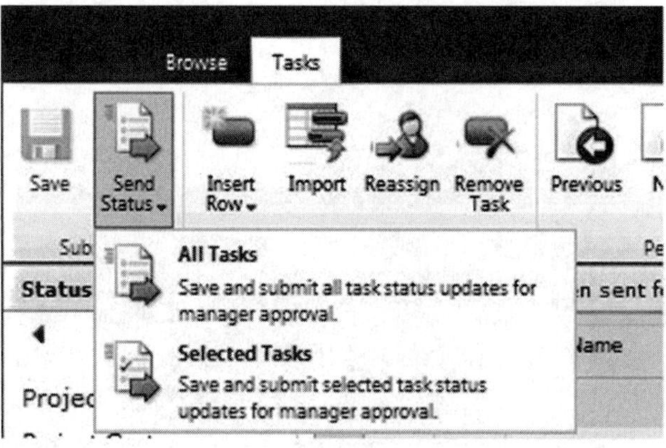

Figure 8–16

If the Comment on Submit option is selected, a pop-up box for notes will appear. Figure 8–17 shows the option in the Ribbon and the comment box called Submit Changes. It is important to note that this comment is not specific to any one task. This comment is for the entire update, so it will be "attached" to each task in this particular update.

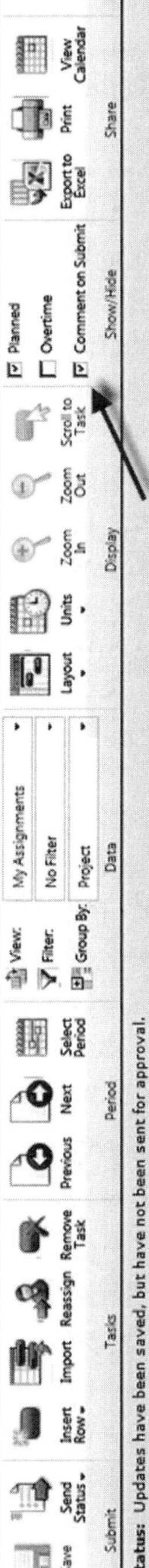
Save
Send Status
Submit
Insert Row
Import
Reassign
Remove Task
Tasks
Previous
Next
Select Period
Period
View: My Assignments
Filter: No Filter
Group By: Project
Data
Layout
Units
Zoom In
Zoom Out
Scroll to Task
Display
Planned
Overtime
Comment on Submit
Show/Hide
Export to Excel
Print
View Calendar
Share
Status: Updates have been saved, but have not been sent for approval.

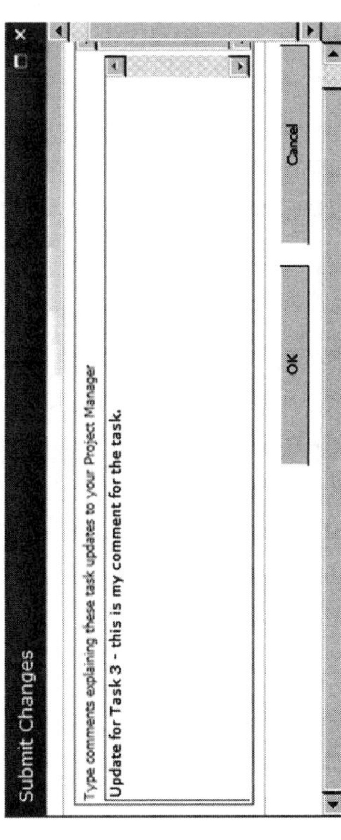
Submit Changes
Type comments explaining these task updates to your Project Manager
Update for Task 3 - this is my comment for the task.
OK
Cancel

Figure 8–17

After the update is sent, the yellow bar will change to blue, and the Process Status column will change to Awaiting Approval, since the resource is now waiting for the resource manager to approve this task. This is demonstrated in Figure 8–18.

To follow the Update Cycle through the entire process, let's switch hats from the resource to the resource manager. Depending on the settings for the resource manager, an e-mail notification might be sent for each update, or it might be a daily e-mail. Even if there are no notification e-mails being sent to the resource manager, the task updates will appear on the Project Web App home screen for the resource manager. Figure 8–19 shows how the homepage will look for the resource manager.

Clicking on the link that states how many updates are pending will take the resource manager to the Approval Center screen. In the Approval Center, any updates that have been sent from any resource will be displayed. Just as a resource can batch his or her updates to be sent, the resource manager can wait and run a batch update. In this example, the only update waiting for the resource manager is the one for Task 3 that the resource recently sent. The field that has been updated by the resource will be highlighted in red in the Approval Center if it is one of the columns in the view. In this case, the percent complete column is the updated field, as shown in Figure 8–20.

When the resource manager selects the task(s) that they want to update, the Ribbon icons for Accept, Reject, and Preview Updates become active and

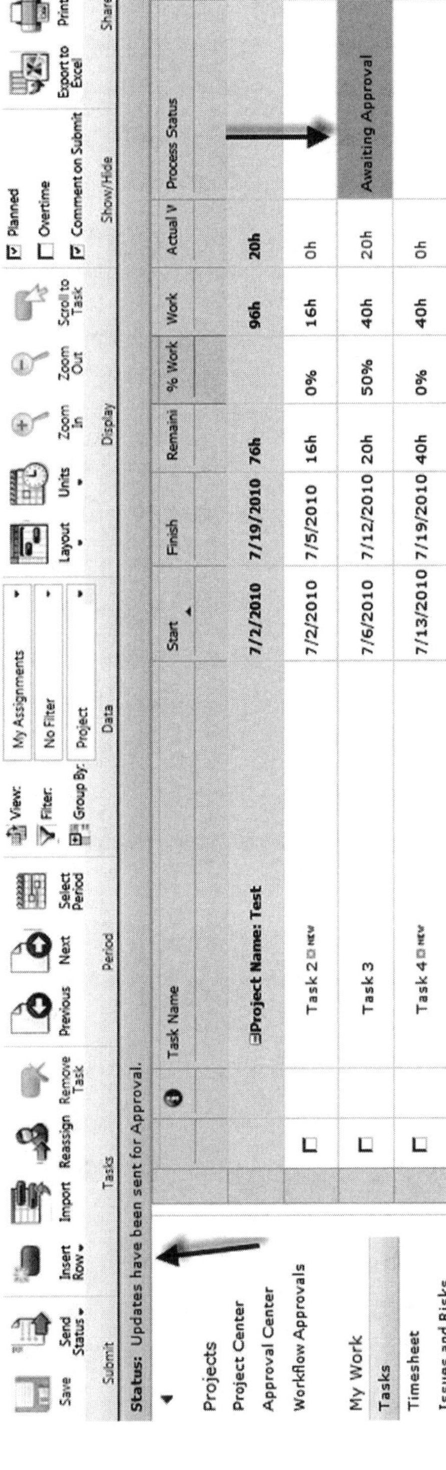
Save
Send Status
Insert Row
Import
Reassign
Remove Task
Previous
Next
Select Period
View: My Assignments
Filter: No Filter
Group By: Project
Layout
Units
Zoom In
Zoom Out
Scroll to Task
Planned
Overtime
Comment on Submit
Export to Excel
Print
Submit
Tasks
Period
Data
Display
Show/Hide
Share
Status: Updates have been sent for Approval.
Projects
Project Center
Approval Center
Workflow Approvals
My Work
Tasks
Timesheet
Issues and Risks
Task Name
Start
Finish
Remaini
% Work
Work
Actual W
Process Status
Project Name: Test
7/2/2010
7/19/2010
76h
96h
20h
Task 2
7/2/2010
7/5/2010
16h
0%
16h
0h
Task 3
7/6/2010
7/12/2010
20h
50%
40h
20h
Awaiting Approval
Task 4
7/13/2010
7/19/2010
40h
0%
40h
0h

Figure 8–18

Project Web App ▸ Home
Project Web App
Home
Projects
Project Center
Approval Center
Workflow Approvals
My Work
Tasks
Timesheet
Issues and Risks
Reminders
Tasks
You have 3449 new tasks assigned to you.
Timesheets
You are the timesheet manager for resources with 78 unsubmitted timesheets in periods ending prior to 1/17/2011.
You have 78 unsubmitted timesheets.
Approvals
You have 1 task update from resources pending your approval.
You have no timesheets from resources pending your approval.
You have no timesheet lines from resources pending your approval.
You have no administrative time-off requests from resources pending your approval.
Status Reports
You have no overdue status reports.
Issues and Risks
You have no active risks assigned to you.
You have no active issues assigned to you.

Figure 8–19

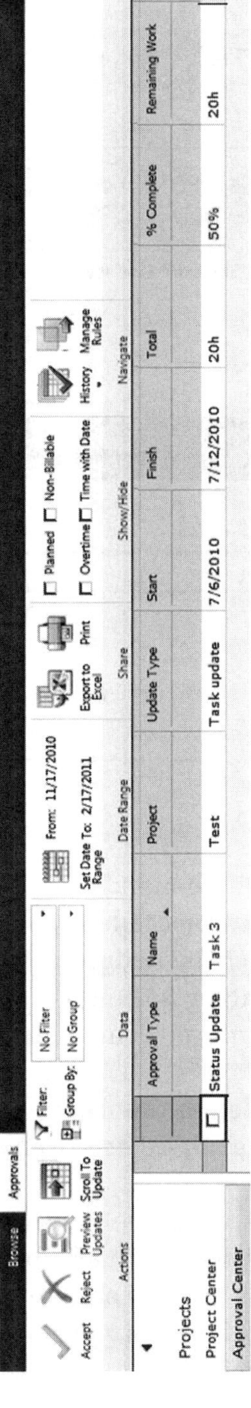

Browse
Approvals
Accept
Reject
Preview Updates
Scroll To Update
Actions
Filter:
No Filter
Group By:
No Group
Data
Set Date Range
From: 11/17/2010
To: 2/17/2011
Date Range
Export to Excel
Print
Share
Planned
Non-Billable
Overtime
Time with Date
Show/Hide
History
Manage Rules
Navigate
Projects
Project Center
Approval Center
Approval Type
Name
Project
Update Type
Start
Finish
Total
% Complete
Remaining Work
Status Update
Task 3
Test
Task update
7/6/2010
7/12/2010
20h
50%
20h

Figure 8–20

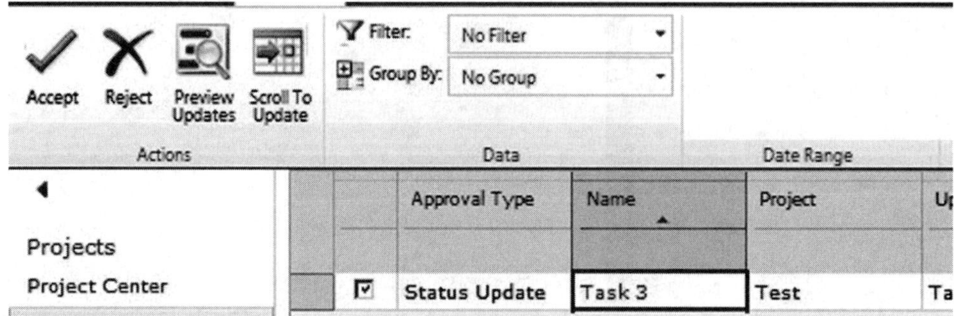

Figure 8–21

Confirmation

Help

Optionally type comments for your team members:

Figure 8–22

available. At this point, the resource manager can preview what the update(s) will do to the other tasks in the project file (by selecting the Preview Updates icon) or choose to Accept or Reject the update, as shown in Figure 8–21.

When the resource manager accepts the task, a confirmation box appears in which the resource manager can type comments if desired. The confirmation box is shown in Figure 8–22.

After all approvals are completed, the Approval Center screen will change to display a message, stating that there aren't any more updates to accept (or reject), as shown in Figure 8–23.

When a resource manager wants to see the history of the project's updates, he or she can click on the History icon in the Ribbon. The resource manager can select the Status Updates option to view a history of status updates, or select the Timesheets option to view a history of timesheet updates. For this example, the Status Updates option is shown in Figure 8–24.

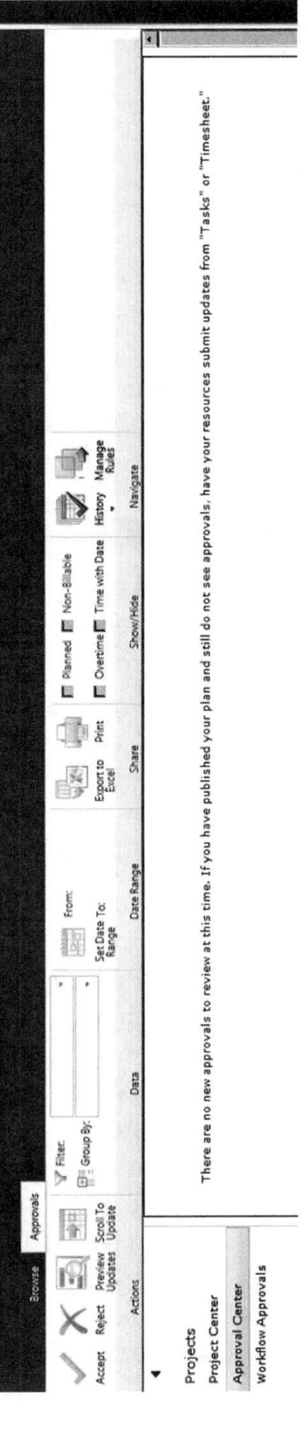
Browse
Approvals
Accept
Reject
Preview Updates
Scroll To Update
Actions
Filter:
Group By:
Data
Set Date Range
From:
To:
Date Range
Export to Excel
Print
Share
Planned
Non-Billable
Overtime
Time with Date
Show/Hide
History
Manage Rules
Navigate
Projects
Project Center
Approval Center
Workflow Approvals
There are no new approvals to review at this time. If you have published your plan and still do not see approvals, have your resources submit updates from "Tasks" or "Timesheet."

Figure 8–23

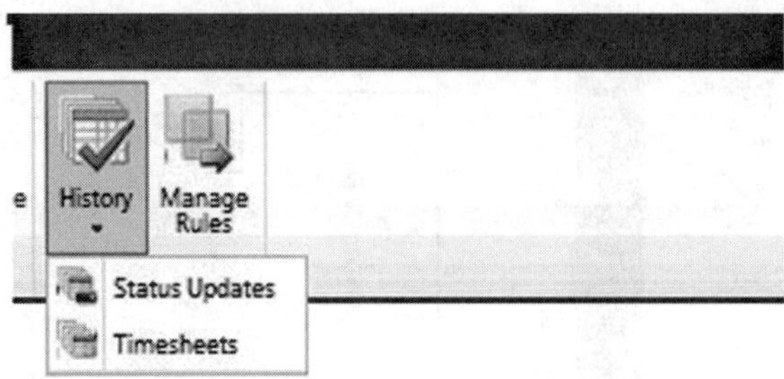

Figure 8–24

The Status Updates History is shown in Figure 8–25. In this case, there is only one update. As also available in the Ribbon, a Date Range selection can be made.

Figure 8–25

If you select the Task Name link, the Task Details box will appear, as shown in Figure 8–26. This box shows what the update was when it was submitted and approved (the % Work Complete information changed from 0% to 50%).

There are different methods for viewing task change approvals. Usually, the resource manager is done at this point. When the project manager next opens the schedule, he or she will see that an update has been done and the information is changed, according to that approved update. However, for purposes of this example, let's say the Project Professional file was open prior to the update. If the project manager has the file open while the resource manager accepts an update, then the project manager will get a message box like the one shown in Figure 8–27. Note that the box won't appear the moment the update is accepted; it will appear when a change is made in the file.

Since the project file was open at the time of the approval, either the project manager has to Save and Publish the file to complete the update, or the resource

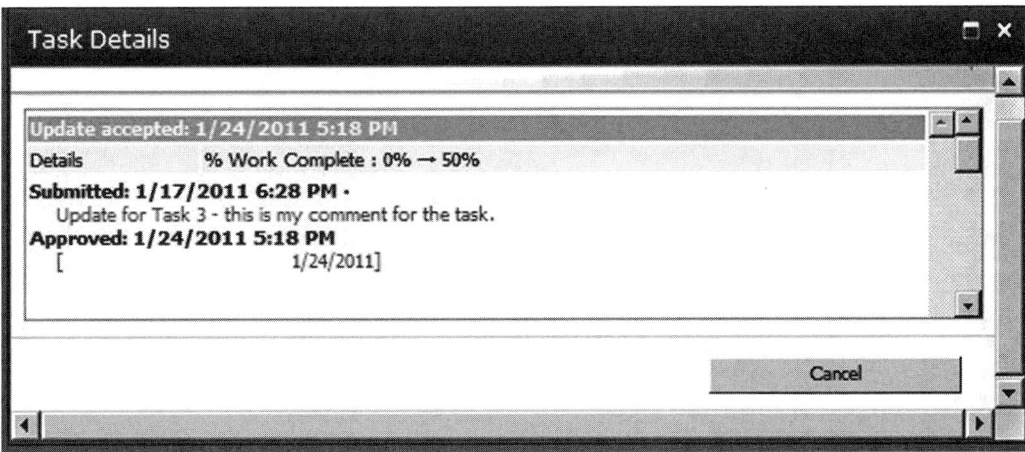

Figure 8–26

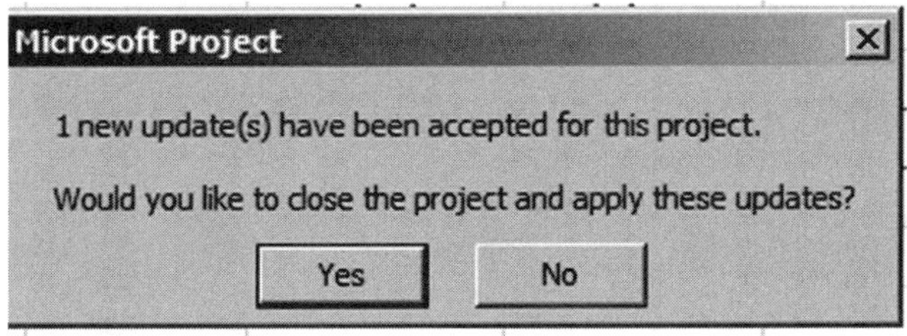

Figure 8–27

manager will need to publish the update. This is not the usual case, since the resource manager doesn't publish schedules in the usual Update Cycle process. However, to demonstrate another function of Project Server, in this example the resource manager will publish the update directly. As shown in Figure 8–28, this is done by selecting the task row in the check box, and then selecting the Publish icon in the Ribbon.

After clicking on the Publish icon, the Message from Webpage box appears, indicating that the Publish action was placed into the queue. This is shown in Figure 8–29.

Regardless of the way that the project file is finally saved and published, the updated task will now show the information that was approved in both the Project Detail views and in Project Professional. As Figure 8–30 shows, the task that was updated in this example, Task 3, now displays as 50% Complete.

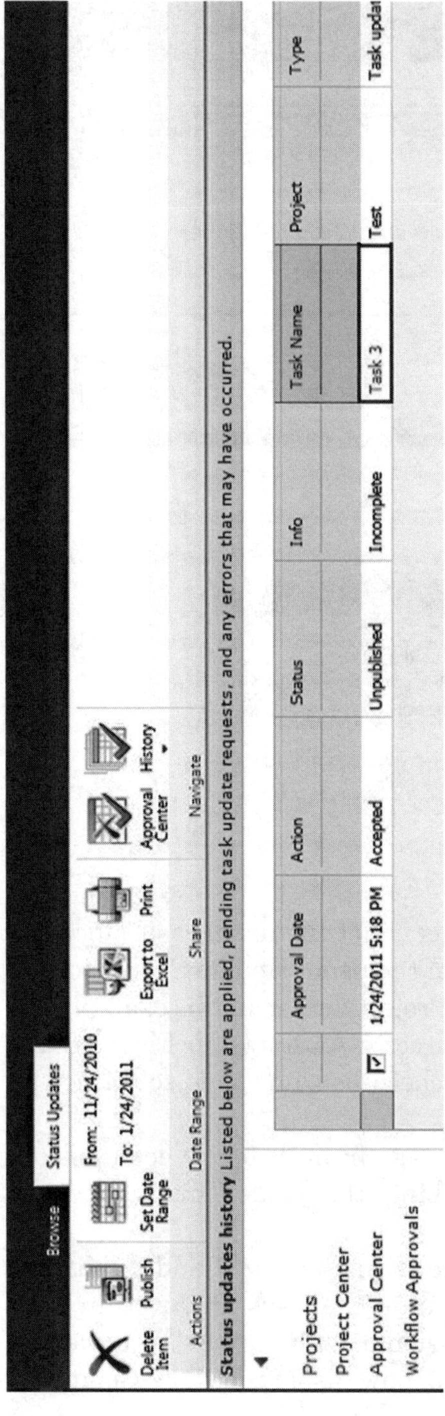

Figure 8–28

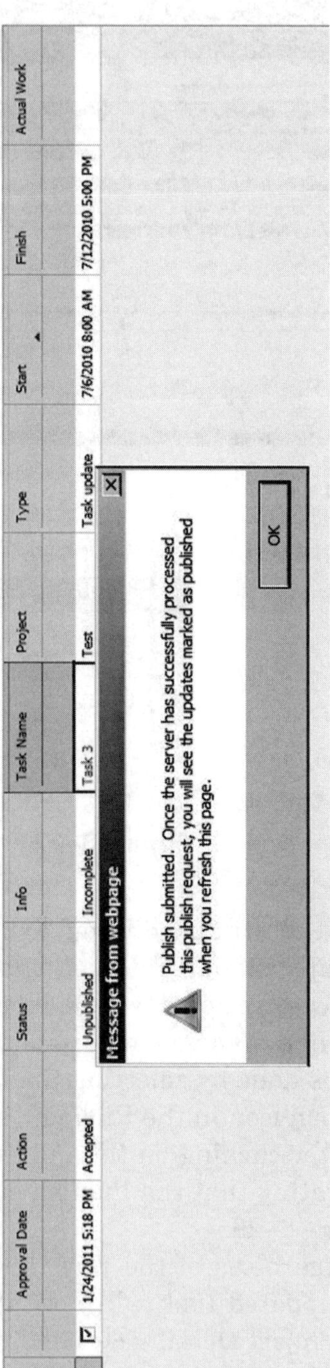

Figure 8–29

		Task Mode	% Complete	Task Name	Duratior	Work	Start	Finish	Predecessc
0			16%	**Test**	**16 days**	**176 hrs**	**Mon 6/28/10 8:0**	**Mon 7/19/10**	
1			0%	Task 1	4 days	24 hrs	Mon 6/28/10 8:00 A	Thu 7/1/10 5:0	
2			0%	Task 2	2 days	32 hrs	Fri 7/2/10 8:00 AM	Mon 7/5/10 5:(	1
3			50%	Task 3	5 days	80 hrs	Tue 7/6/10 8:00 AM	Mon 7/12/10 5	2
4			0%	Task 4	5 days	40 hrs	Tue 7/13/10 8:00 A	Mon 7/19/10 5	3

Figure 8–30

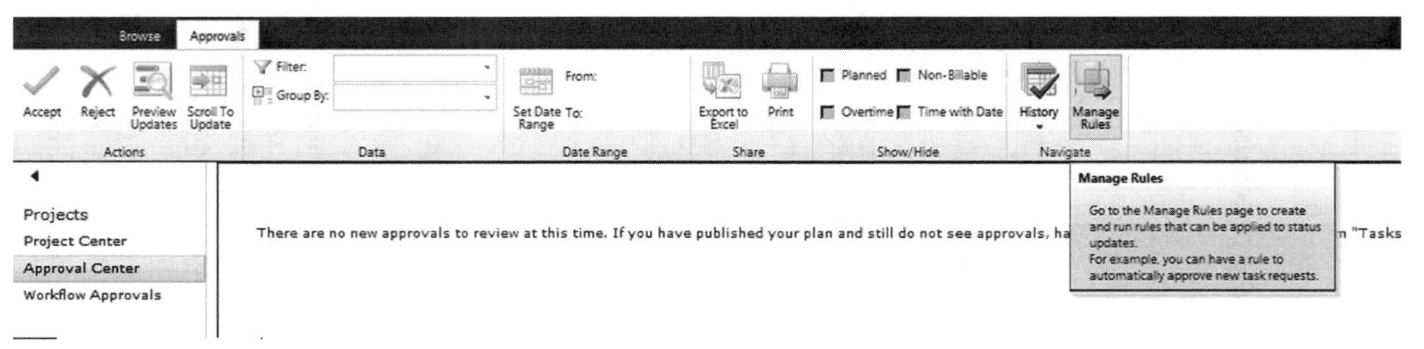

Figure 8–31

In addition, the system automatically updated the Project Summary task to show, with this one task being 50% complete, the entire project file is now 16% complete.

Automatic Approvals

Automatic approvals can be used to expedite the entire approval process. The resource manager can set up rules that automatically approve tasks. The following screenshots will demonstrate the setup for automatic approvals and how they can be done. To start, the Manage Rules icon is shown on the Ribbon of the Approval Center in Figure 8–31.

The Manage Rules option shows all of the current rules that are created. In the case of Figure 8–32, there are no rules set up yet. However, in the Ribbon, the New icon is available to create a rule.

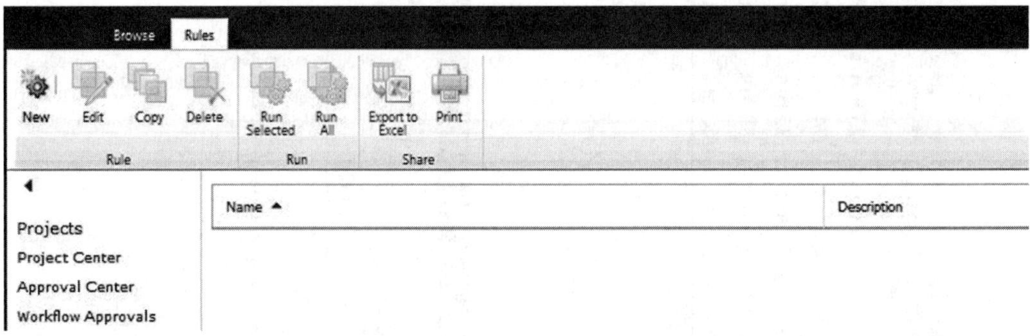

Figure 8–32

After clicking on the New icon, the Edit/Create New Rule screen will display, as shown in Figure 8–33. The first section of this screen allows the resource manager to give this rule a name and description. The key to making an update happen automatically is to select the check box in the Automatic Updates section to *Automatically run this rule*. The third section of this screen determines what types of updates to automatically approve.

The bottom half of the screen allows the resource manager to be specific about which tasks to update automatically. In the Projects section, the *All my current and future projects* option can be chosen, or the *Specific Projects* option can be chosen. When the Specific Projects option is chosen, the screen automatically adjusts to allow the resource manager to select which projects to include in the new rule. The resource section works the same way by allowing the resource

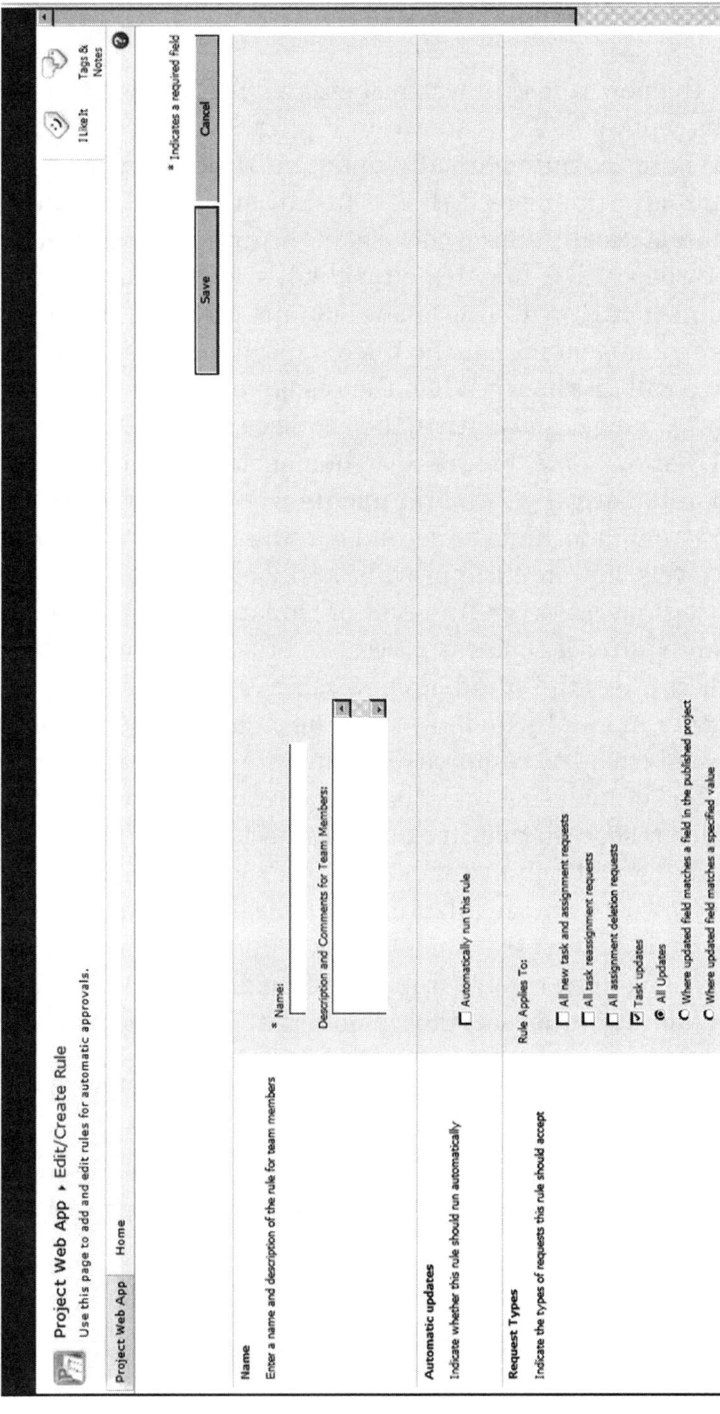
Project Web App ▸ Edit/Create Rule
Use this page to add and edit rules for automatic approvals.
Project Web App
Home
I Like It
Tags & Notes
* Indicates a required field
Save
Cancel
Name
Enter a name and description of the rule for team members
* Name:
Description and Comments for Team Members:
Automatic updates
Indicate whether this rule should run automatically
Automatically run this rule
Request Types
Indicate the types of requests this rule should accept
Rule Applies To:
All new task and assignment requests
All task reassignment requests
All assignment deletion requests
Task updates
All Updates
Where updated field matches a field in the published project
Where updated field matches a specified value

Figure 8–33

manager to select specific resources to automatically accept updates from, as shown in Figure 8–34.

The name of the new rule that was just created is Example One and is set to automatically accept updates, as shown in Figure 8–35.

When a rule is set to automatically update a task, no further action is required by the resource manager. When a task that meets the rule's criteria is updated, it is automatically approved without any interaction from the resource manager. The resource that updates a task will see the message *Awaiting Approval* for a moment or two after he or she submits the task. However, once they refresh the screen, depending on the queue speed, the task will be approved and the message will disappear. When the resource drills down to their task or looks at the Task Change information, they will see that the task was automatically approved. For example, Figure 8–36 demonstrates two task updates that were approved automatically. The first update was to change the task from 0% complete to 75% complete, and the second one was from 75% to 80%.

The Update Cycle, automatic approvals, and views discussed in this chapter are all specific to Project Server. Any type of Update Cycle on stand-alone Project Professional requires a business process to be set up. Usually, the process of updating a project file in the stand-alone version is when the resource manager or project manager manually updates the project, based upon information that they have received from the resource directly.

Another method of updating tasks is for the resource to use Outlook. This is only available for resources that are using Project Server. There are some differences when using Outlook instead of using Project Web App, and those are outlined below. However, for organizations that desire the convenience of allowing resources to update directly from Outlook, and that do not require as much information as they might receive from a task update in PWA, this is an easy-to-use tool in a familiar interface. Please note that if your organization chooses to use Outlook, this does not have to be the only way to update tasks. Resources can use Outlook or PWA to update their tasks.

One of the benefits of using Outlook in Project Server 2010 is that the resource does not have to download an Active-X control or an add-in to their own copy of Outlook. The setup is done by the exchange administrator and the project server administrator.

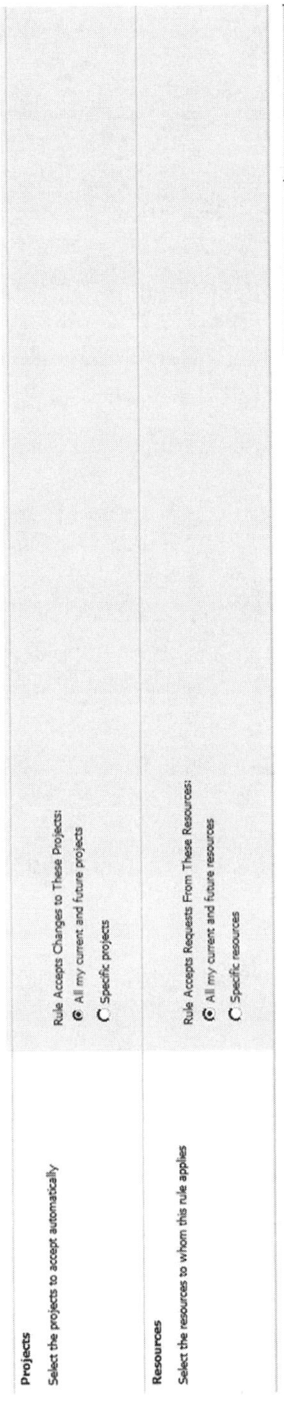

Figure 8–34

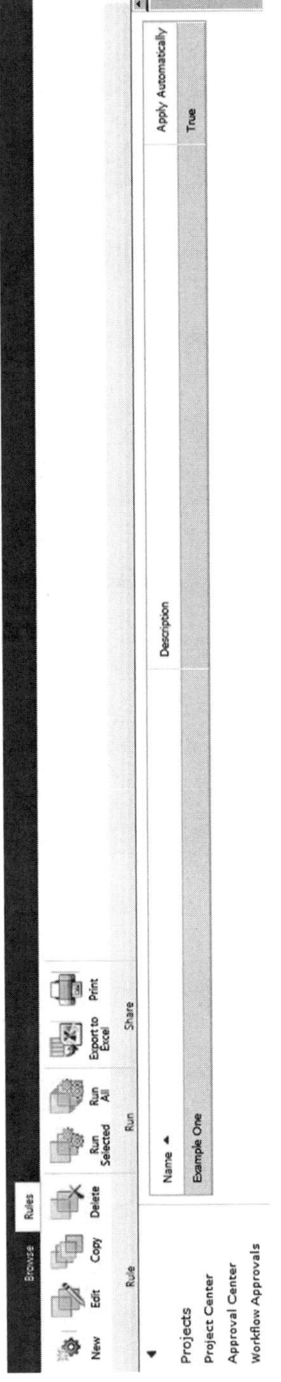

Figure 8–35

Recent Task Changes

View the history of task changes, updates, and approvals.

Update accepted: 75% complete on 1/24/2011 9:25 PM

Details % Work Complete : 0% → 75%

Submitted: 1/24/2011 9:25 PM <Collin Quiring>
Approved: 1/24/2011 9:25 PM <Collin Quiring>
Update accepting automatically by rules engine.

Update accepted: 80% complete on 1/24/2011 9:27 PM

Details % Work Complete : 75% → 80%

Submitted: 1/24/2011 9:27 PM <Collin Quiring>
Approved: 1/24/2011 9:27 PM <Collin Quiring>
Update accepting automatically by rules engine.

Figure 8–36

Other benefits of using Outlook for task updates are:

- Embedded user interface: This can become part of the Outlook experience and the interface is already familiar to users.
- Low training requirements:
  - Since this is in Outlook and has fewer fields to update, the amount of training needed for resources is minimal.
  - If the resource knows how to update in Project Web App, the update options in Outlook are already familiar and even less training is required.
- Appearance: Project Tasks will appear as Outlook tasks.
- Update process: Outlook will synchronize with Project Web App and the resource does not have to use Project Web App directly.
- Exchange integration: Since this feature uses exchange integration, updates can be done through Outlook, Outlook Web Access, or Outlook Mobile Access (in some cases).

Ease of implementation: This might be a great solution for creating more detailed task updates in Project Web App later. For organizations beginning their experience with resource management, this can be a relatively easy starting point for resources instead of diving into all the aspects of Project Web App. The following restrictions to using Outlook as an update method may be benefits or detractions, depending on your perspective.

- Resources are able to update the following items in Outlook:
  - Percentage complete
  - Amount of work completed
  - Amount of remaining work
- Update Types: Using Outlook works fine for task updates, but does not work for timesheet updates. For Single Entry Mode timesheet entry, the task portion of the entries will work.
- Exchange Type: This functionality works for both Exchange Server 2007 and 2010.
- Outlook Calendar: The project tasks cannot be placed on the Outlook Calendar.

9

Timesheets

In Chapter 8, we talked about resources updating their tasks and the Update Cycle, and demonstrated how the My Tasks page works. In this chapter, we will demonstrate another method of updating that involves using timesheets. Timesheets are not available in the stand-alone Project Professional version. Timesheets also require a timesheet manager. The timesheet manager is the person responsible for approving the time entries that resources put on their timesheets. The timesheet manager may or may not be the resources themselves, a resource manager, or anyone interested in the project file.

In Microsoft Project Server, there are three different types of time entry: Task, Timesheet, and Single Entry Mode. The Task mode is the method that was covered in Chapter 8. This mode is for project file tasks only, and updates by the resource are sent to the resource manager. The Task mode also allows for timesheet entries to be imported.

The Timesheet mode can import tasks from the project file, but can also import administrative time, billing categories, and personal tasks. This allows for non-project file tasks to be accounted for in addition to project file tasks. Individual timesheet lines, or the entire timesheet, are approved by the timesheet manager.

Timesheet Entry

Timesheets can be thought of as "this is how many hours I worked this week and this is what I worked on." That includes work on project file tasks *and* on non-project file (administrative) items. From the perspective of the resource manager, the work input against scheduled tasks is important and affects the schedule's time. The resource manager is not concerned with the amount of time a person worked in total during the week; he or she only cares how much time that resource worked on scheduled tasks. However, from the perspective of the timesheet manager, the total amount of hours worked last week, and what was worked on, are what matters. The timesheet manager wants to classify the work for budget/payroll, paperwork, or human resource reporting purposes. In this situation, the timesheet manager has nothing to do with the project file tasks for certain projects.

To help illustrate the differences and methods of Timesheet and Task entry, let's work through a quick example. In this example, the resource will be Tanya, who will enter time into her timesheet, and then import that time into her Tasks page. Tanya will go through these steps to update her timesheet:

1. Tanya enters all of her timesheet time at once, and so she opens her timesheet for the week she wants to update.
2. She enters the following time:

   Monday—8 hours on Task 1 of Project A

   Tuesday—8 hours of vacation time

   Wednesday—2 hours on Task 2 of Project B and 6 hours in meetings

   Thursday—8 hours of jury duty

   Friday—8 hours of jury duty
3. Tanya saves and submits her timesheet, imports it into her Task page, and sends the update.

Now that Tanya has completed her Timesheet and Task entry, the timesheet information is important to the timesheet manager and the task information is important to the resource manager. After Tanya submits her timesheet, these are the steps the timesheet manager goes through:

4. The timesheet manager can approve or reject the timesheet. In this example, the timesheet manager looks to see if the approved number of hours, type of work, and other timesheet criteria are met. Tanya had worked 40

hours total, using 8 hours of available and approved vacation time, spent 16 hours in jury duty, 6 hours in approved meetings, and worked 10 hours on project file tasks.

5. The timesheet manager approves Tanya's timesheet since it meets the appropriate criteria and the timesheet manager is finished with it.

Since Tanya also imported her timesheet information into her Task entry and submitted that information, the resource manager is able to accept or reject the task information:

6. The resource manager looks at the Task Updates and sees that Tanya worked 10 hours on two different tasks.
7. The resource manager accepts the work and updates the two schedules accordingly.

This example is demonstrated in Figure 9–1, showing the workflow of the Timesheet and Task entries.

Using Timesheet entry requires that the time updates be separately imported into the Task entry screen. However, in Project Server 2010, a new method to update Timesheets and Tasks together has been created. This is the Single Entry Mode and allows for resources to update both their project file tasks and administrative time tasks in one location. In this case, the timesheet is approved by the timesheet manager, and the project file tasks are sent to the resource manager for approval.

As is often the case, the setup for the timesheets is critical to how they work and how effective they are within your organization. For these reasons, we include information about how to set up timesheets at the end of this chapter. While timesheet setup can only be done by the project server administrator, the resource manager(s) should be consulted as to how they expect to receive updates from the resources.

The following screenshots are taken from the Single Entry Mode, where the use of other variables is possible, some of which are described. For example, you can get to timesheets from the Home Page in Project Server by clicking on *Timesheet* under the My Work section, or by clicking on any of the blue links under the main Timesheets section. You can also see under the main Timesheets section how many timesheets for which you are the resource manager. If you are a resource as well as a resource manager, you can also see how

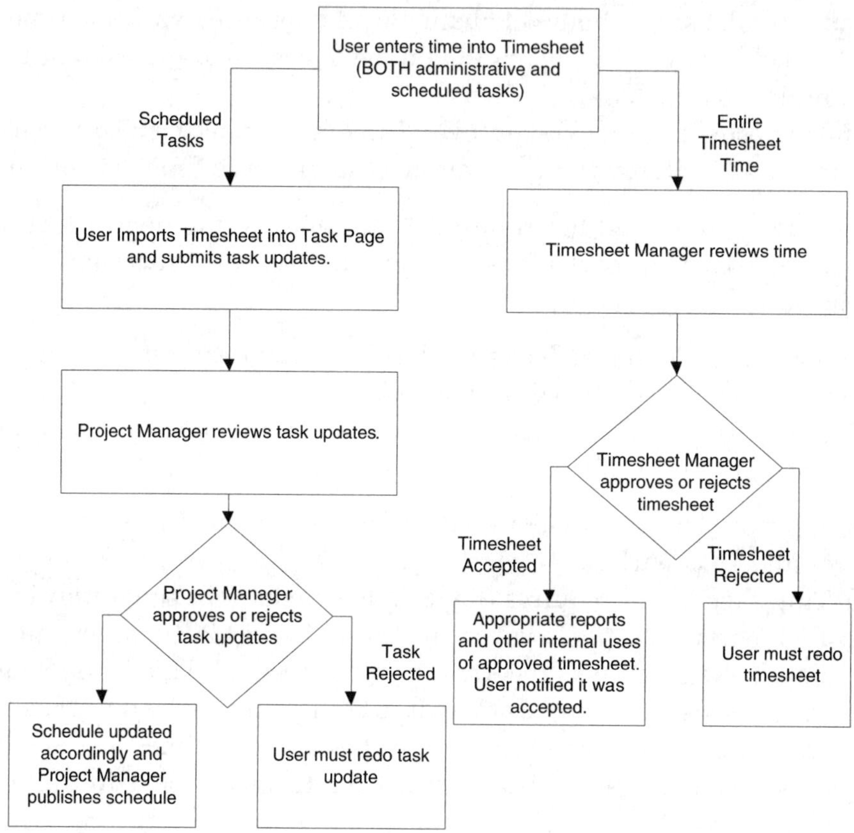

Figure 9–1

many timesheets that you are responsible for, which have not been submitted, as shown in Figure 9–2.

Clicking on any of the links will bring you to the main Timesheet page. Depending on your security permissions, you can create a new task, insert a new task, or enter time against a task and then save and submit that information to the timesheet manager and resource manager for approval. Even though this example is in Single Entry Mode, as shown in Figure 9–3, the screen has been cut off so that you can only see the project file tasks. (The administrative tasks will be discussed a bit later.) In this example, there are two project files (Admin TEST and Process Point Sample) with tasks to be updated. When the timesheet for a specific time period opens, the date range for the timesheet is displayed in the Status bar just below the Ribbon. The timesheet period is 9/12/10 – 9/18/10.

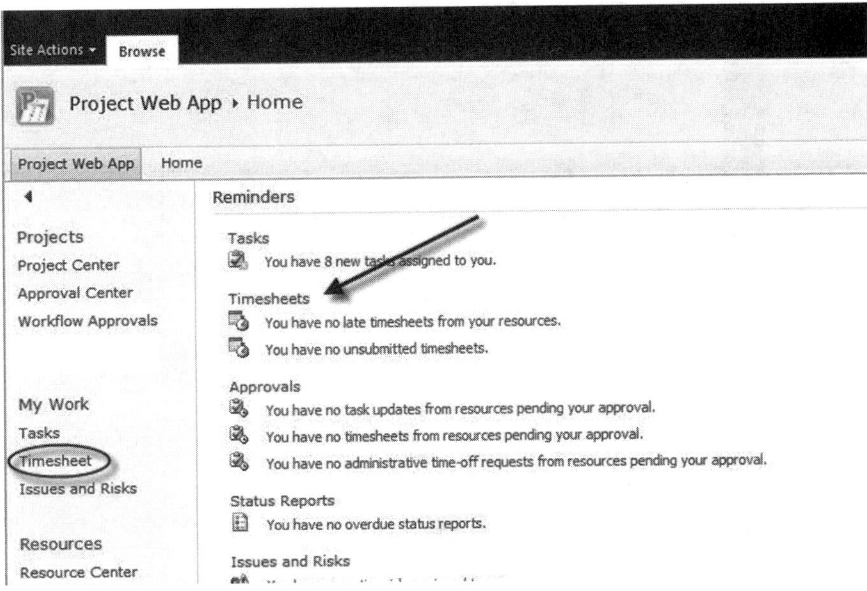

Figure 9–2

The date range determines which tasks are displayed on the timesheet since it will automatically find any tasks that should be worked on during that date range.

Since it is possible that we did work on a task that was originally outside the date range for this timesheet, we can insert those tasks into this timesheet. Please note that we are only inserting tasks that already exist in a project file. We are not creating new tasks and assigning them to a project file. Figure 9–4 shows how to insert a task. Click the Insert Row icon in the Ribbon to open the drop-down menu. Select *Insert Task* to add an existing task to the timesheet.

Once the Add an Existing Task pop-up box opens, select a project file from the Project drop-down box, shown in Figure 9–5.

The Test project file was chosen. When a project file is chosen, the available tasks appear in the *Select from Existing Assignments* section. Before selecting a task, you can also select a task hierarchy from the Task Hierarchy drop-down box. The task hierarchy helps to differentiate tasks under various summary tasks in the project file. The default setting is *All Tasks*, which will show all the available tasks in the project file. After selecting a task, select a line classification from the Line Classification drop-down menu, and type any comments in the Comment section. (We cover line classification later in this chapter.) When finished, click the OK button to add the tasks.

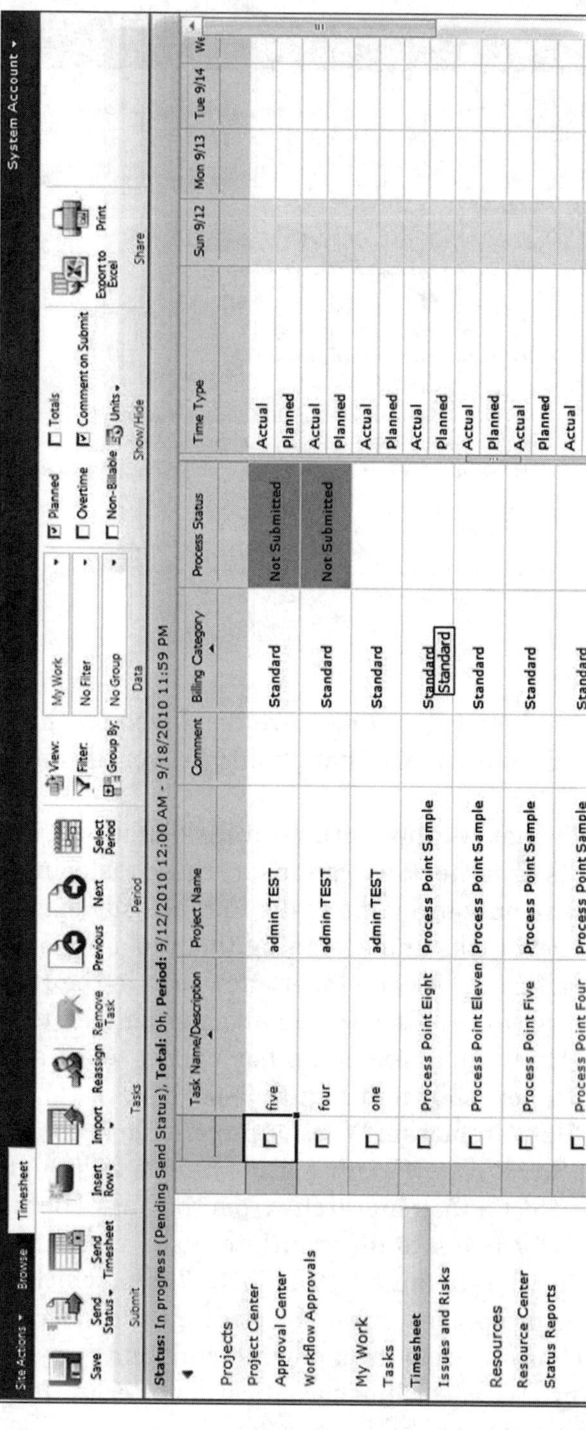
Site Actions
Browse
Timesheet
System Account
Save
Send Status
Send Timesheet
Submit
Insert Row
Import
Reassign
Remove Task
Tasks
Previous
Next
Select Period
Period
View: My Work
Filter: No Filter
Group By: No Group
Data
Planned
Overtime
Non-Billable
Totals
Comment on Submit
Units
Show/Hide
Export to Excel
Print
Share
Status: In progress (Pending Send Status), Total: 0h, Period: 9/12/2010 12:00 AM - 9/18/2010 11:59 PM
Projects
Project Center
Approval Center
Workflow Approvals
My Work
Tasks
Timesheet
Issues and Risks
Resources
Resource Center
Status Reports
Task Name/Description
Project Name
Comment
Billing Category
Process Status
Time Type
Sun 9/12
Mon 9/13
Tue 9/14
five
admin TEST
Standard
Not Submitted
four
one
Process Point Eight
Process Point Sample
Process Point Eleven
Process Point Five
Process Point Four
Actual
Planned

Figure 9–3

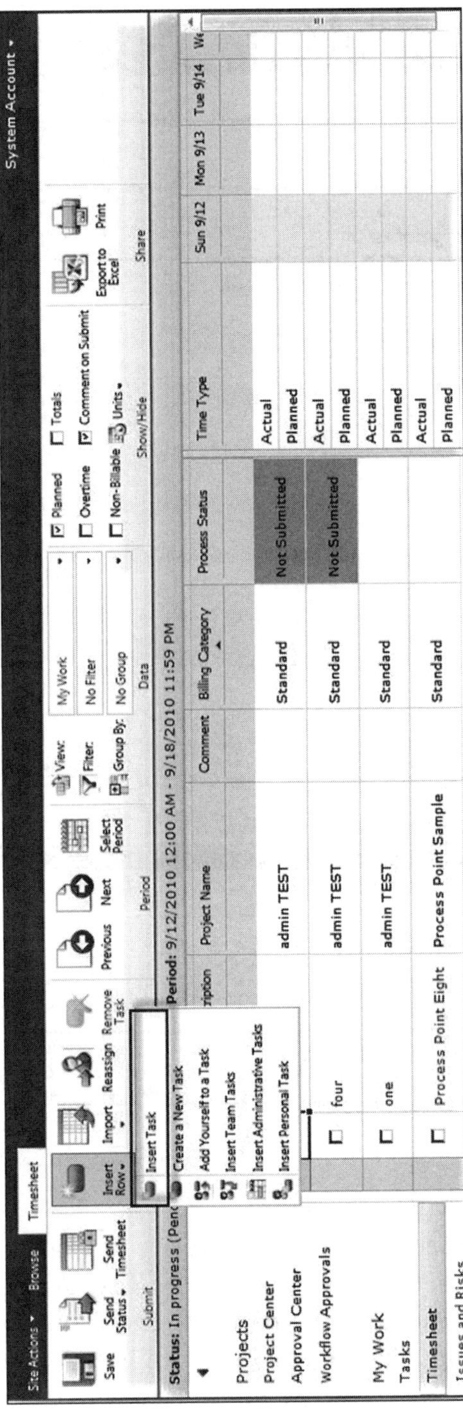
Site Actions
Browse
Timesheet
System Account
Save
Send Status
Send Timesheet
Submit
Insert Row
Import
Reassign
Remove Task
Previous
Next
Select Period
Period
View: My Work
Filter: No Filter
Group By: No Group
Data
Planned
Overtime
Non-Billable
Totals
Comment on Submit
Units
Show/Hide
Export to Excel
Print
Share
Status: In progress (Pend
Period: 9/12/2010 12:00 AM - 9/18/2010 11:59 PM
Insert Task
Create a New Task
Add Yourself to a Task
Insert Team Tasks
Insert Administrative Tasks
Insert Personal Task
Projects
Project Center
Approval Center
Workflow Approvals
My Work
Tasks
Timesheet
Issues and Risks
Project Name
Comment
Billing Category
Process Status
Time Type
Sun 9/12
Mon 9/13
Tue 9/14
four
one
Process Point Eight
admin TEST
Process Point Sample
Standard
Not Submitted
Actual
Planned

Figure 9–4

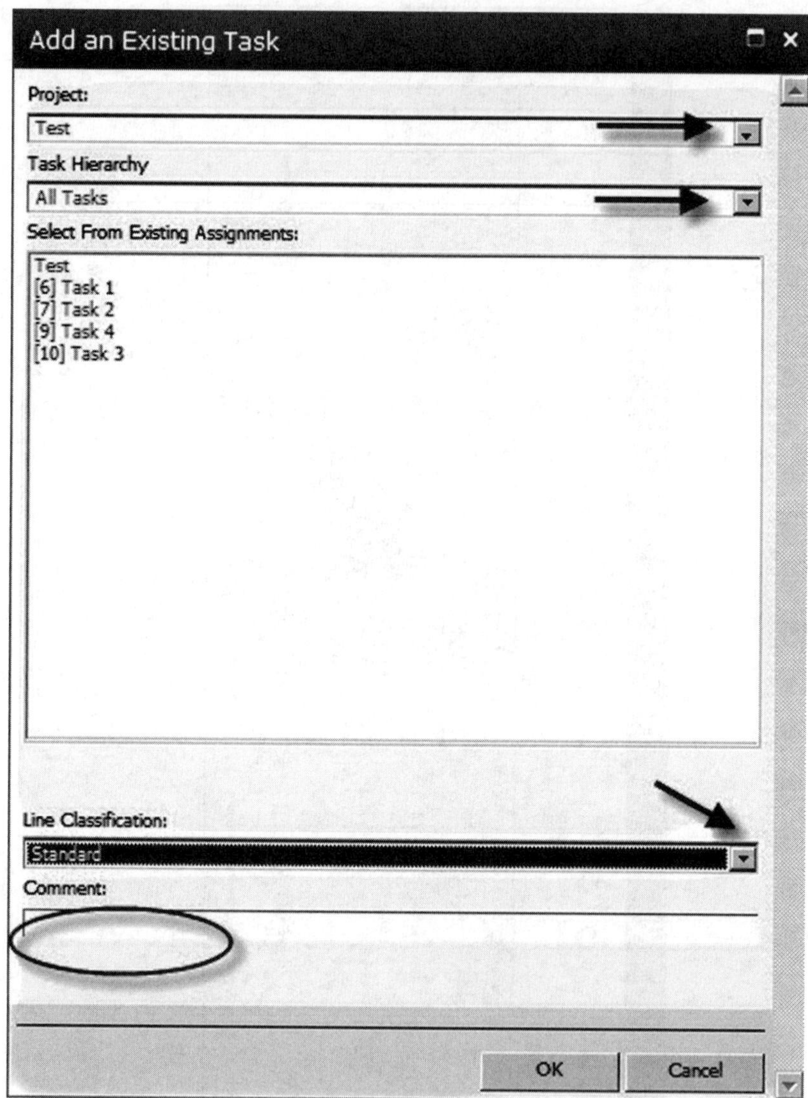

Figure 9–5

In this example, we chose all the tasks. Notice in Figure 9–6 that the tasks were added to the timesheet successfully for the Test project file.

Depending upon the Project Server settings and the resource's security permissions, the columns displayed in this view can be modified. In many cases, a resource will update the task directly from this screen. However, in the interest

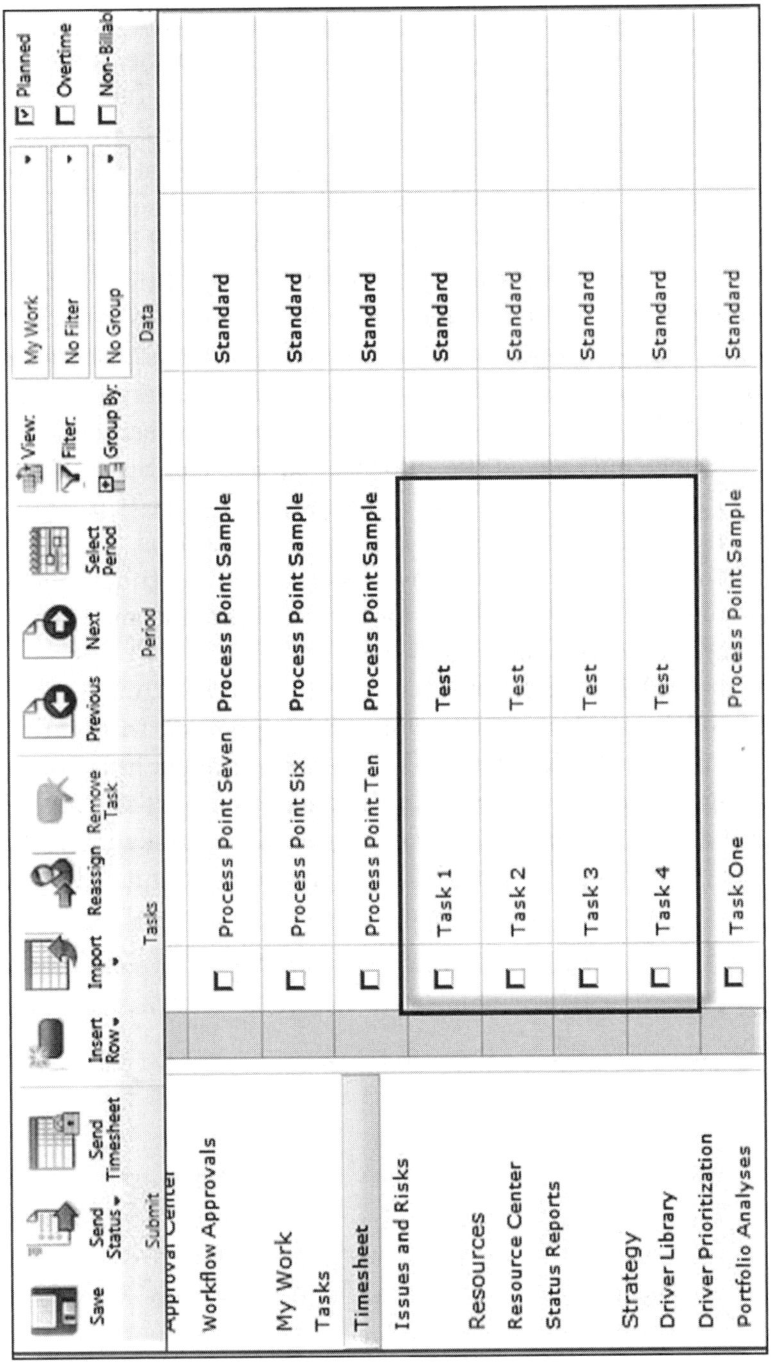

Figure 9–6

of demonstrating the available detail on a task, let's look at the details of one of the tasks that were just added to the timesheet. Click on the name of the task to open it. Figure 9–7 demonstrates the information from Task 1. This screen looks like the Tasks Detail Page in Tasks entry. In Chapter 8, we demonstrated the sections of the Task Detail Page, so we won't cover that again here. However, we did put some notes on the Timesheet screenshot as a reminder.

The Task information can be updated at this point, or on the Timesheet Entry page. For this example, let's update the task information and save it, as shown in Figure 9–8.

Once the task has been updated, the information needs to be saved. Once saved, you will be brought back to the Timesheet entry screen. The information that we just updated is now visible on the right side of the screen in the Hours section. Also, since we only saved the information, the Not Submitted message appears in the Process Status column. As shown in Figure 9–9, note that the Status bar shows that the timesheet is Pending Send Status.

Another way to enter time against an assignment in the timesheet, shown in Figure 9–10, is to simply find the dates for that assignment and type the hours in the 'Actual' row and corresponding date cell.

In Project Server 2010, you have the option to save the timesheet, and then send an update of the entire timesheet or of any one task. In Figure 9–11, we submit only a single task. The way to submit assignment information to the timesheet manager is to place a check in the check box next to the assignment and click on Send Status. Select *All Tasks* to submit all tasks in the timesheet for timesheet manager approval, or Selected Tasks to submit only those tasks with a check in the check box for timesheet manager approval. In this example, we have only selected Task 1, so that is all that will be sent.

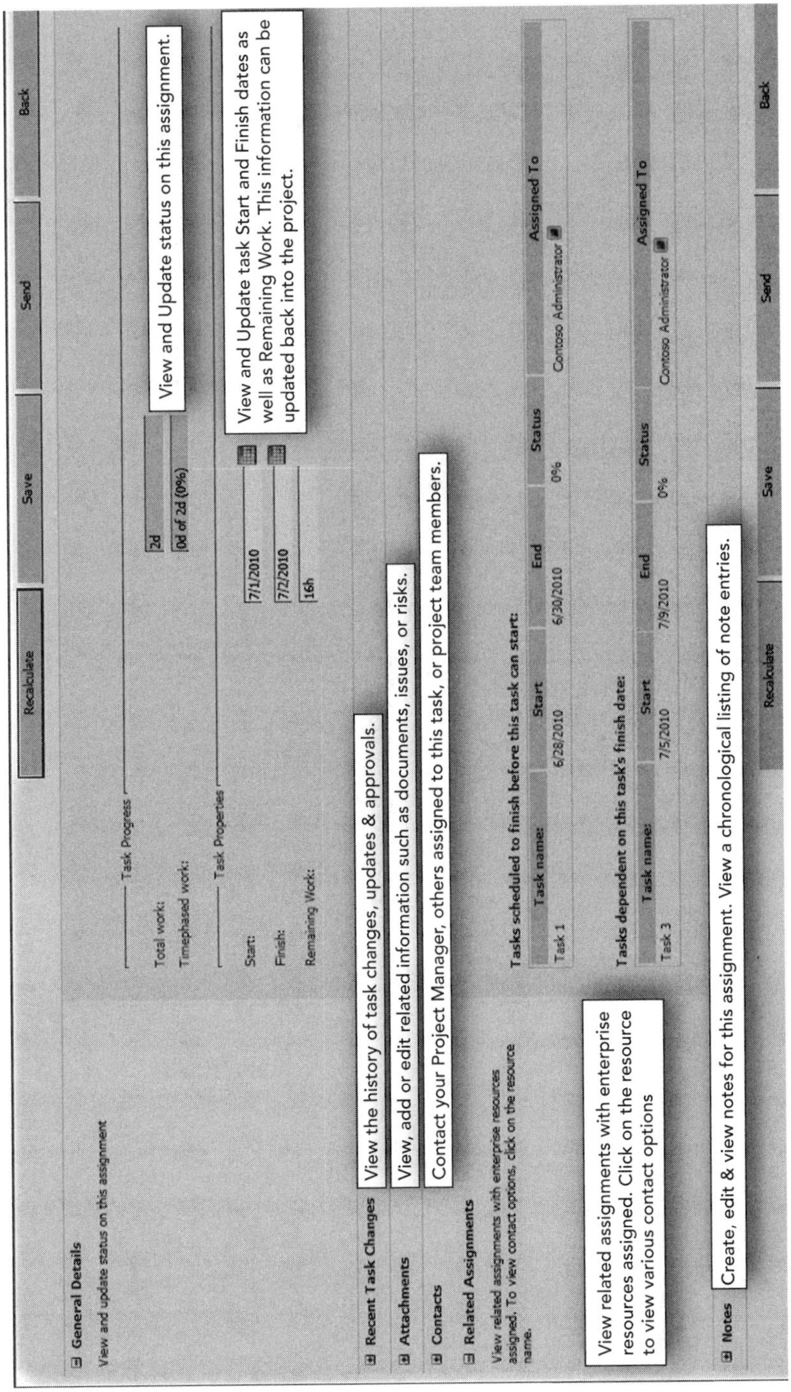

Recalculate | Save | Send | Back

⊟ General Details

View and update status on this assignment

Task Progress

Total work: 2d

Timephased work: 0d of 2d (0%)

View and Update status on this assignment.

Task Properties

Start: 7/1/2010

Finish: 7/2/2010

Remaining Work: 16h

View and Update task Start and Finish dates as well as Remaining Work. This information can be updated back into the project.

⊞ Recent Task Changes — View the history of task changes, updates & approvals.

⊞ Attachments — View, add or edit related information such as documents, issues, or risks.

⊞ Contacts — Contact your Project Manager, others assigned to this task, or project team members.

⊟ Related Assignments

View related assignments with enterprise resources assigned. To view contact options, click on the resource name.

Tasks scheduled to finish before this task can start:

Task name:	Start	End	Status	Assigned To
Task 1	6/28/2010	6/30/2010	0%	Contoso Administrator

Tasks dependent on this task's finish date:

Task name:	Start	End	Status	Assigned To
Task 3	7/5/2010	7/9/2010	0%	Contoso Administrator

View related assignments with enterprise resources assigned. Click on the resource to view various contact options

⊞ Notes — Create, edit & view notes for this assignment. View a chronological listing of note entries.

Recalculate | Save | Send | Back

Figure 9–7

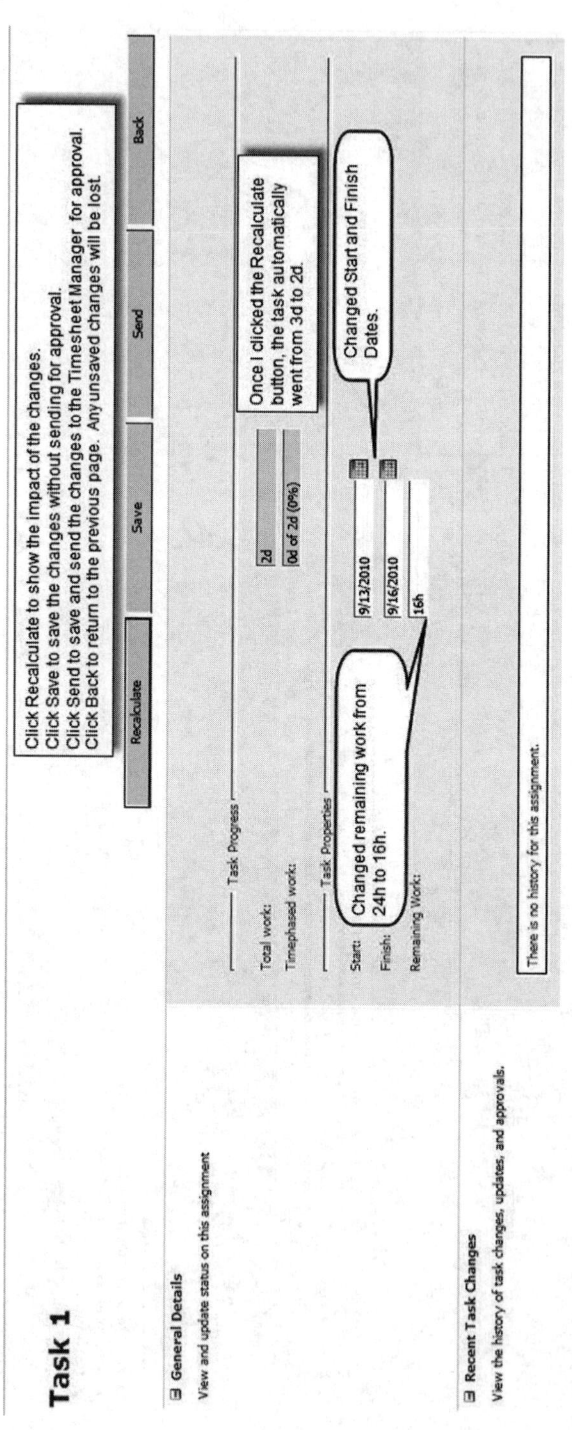
Task 1
Click Recalculate to show the impact of the changes.
Click Save to save the changes without sending for approval.
Click Send to save and send the changes to the Timesheet Manager for approval.
Click Back to return to the previous page. Any unsaved changes will be lost.
Recalculate
Save
Send
Back
General Details
View and update status on this assignment
Task Progress
Total work:
2d
Timephased work:
0d of 2d (0%)
Once I clicked the Recalculate button, the task automatically went from 3d to 2d.
Task Properties
Start:
9/13/2010
Finish:
9/16/2010
Remaining Work:
16h
Changed remaining work from 24h to 16h.
Changed Start and Finish Dates.
Recent Task Changes
View the history of task changes, updates, and approvals.
There is no history for this assignment.

Figure 9–8

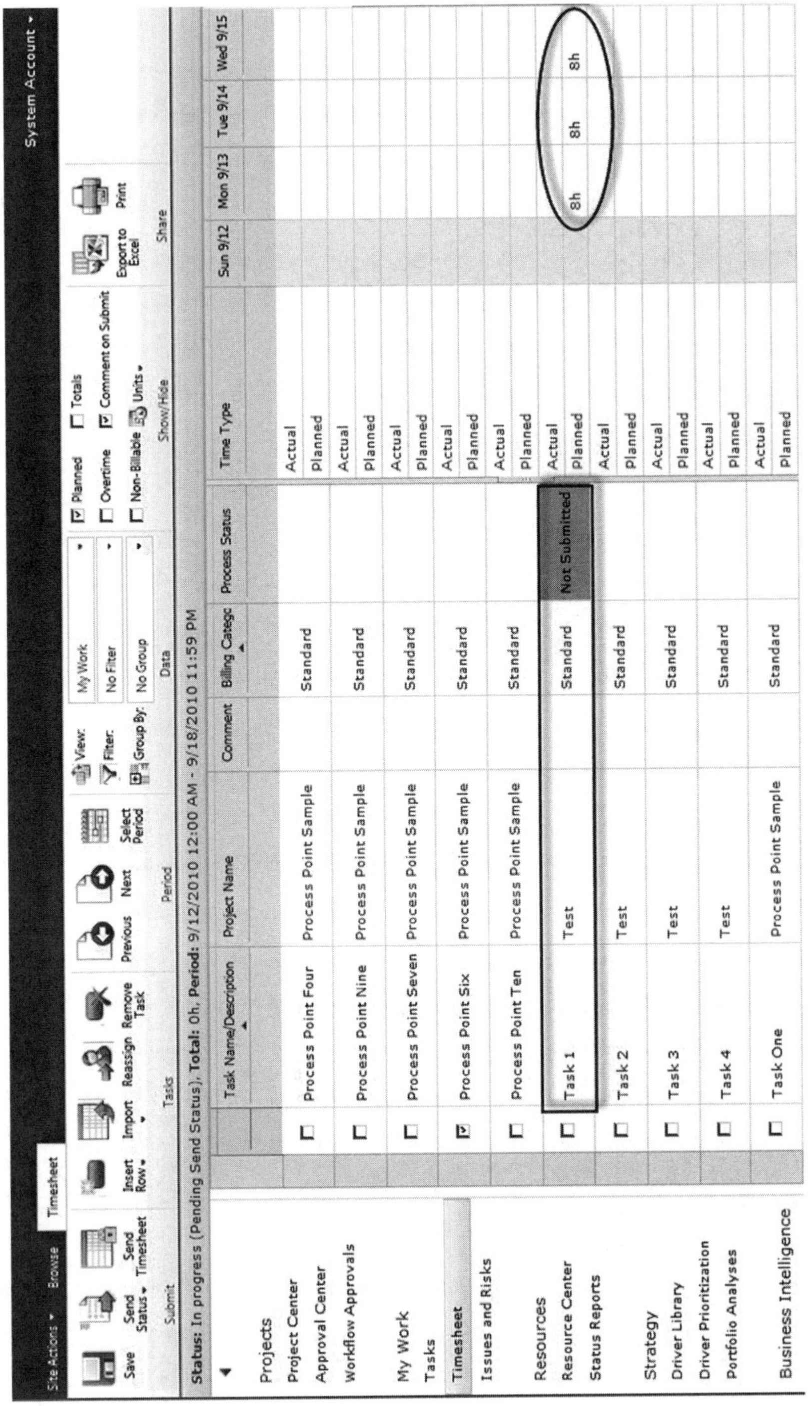

Site Actions
Browse
Timesheet
System Account
Save
Send Status
Send Timesheet
Submit
Insert Row
Import
Reassign
Remove Task
Tasks
Previous
Next
Select Period
Period
View: My Work
Filter: No Filter
Group By: No Group
Data
Planned
Totals
Overtime
Comment on Submit
Non-Billable
Units
Show/Hide
Export to Excel
Print
Share
Status: In progress (Pending Send Status), Total: 0h, Period: 9/12/2010 12:00 AM - 9/18/2010 11:59 PM
Projects
Project Center
Approval Center
Workflow Approvals
My Work
Tasks
Timesheet
Issues and Risks
Resources
Resource Center
Status Reports
Strategy
Driver Library
Driver Prioritization
Portfolio Analyses
Business Intelligence
Task Name/Description | Project Name | Comment | Billing Categc | Process Status | Time Type | Sun 9/12 | Mon 9/13 | Tue 9/14 | Wed 9/15
Process Point Four | Process Point Sample | Standard | Actual / Planned
Process Point Nine | Process Point Sample | Standard | Actual / Planned
Process Point Seven | Process Point Sample | Standard | Actual / Planned
Process Point Six | Process Point Sample | Standard | Actual / Planned
Process Point Ten | Process Point Sample | Standard | Actual / Planned
Task 1 | Test | Standard | Not Submitted | Actual / Planned | 8h | 8h | 8h
Task 2 | Test | Standard | Actual / Planned
Task 3 | Test | Standard | Actual / Planned
Task 4 | Test | Standard | Actual / Planned
Task One | Process Point Sample | Standard | Actual / Planned

Figure 9–9

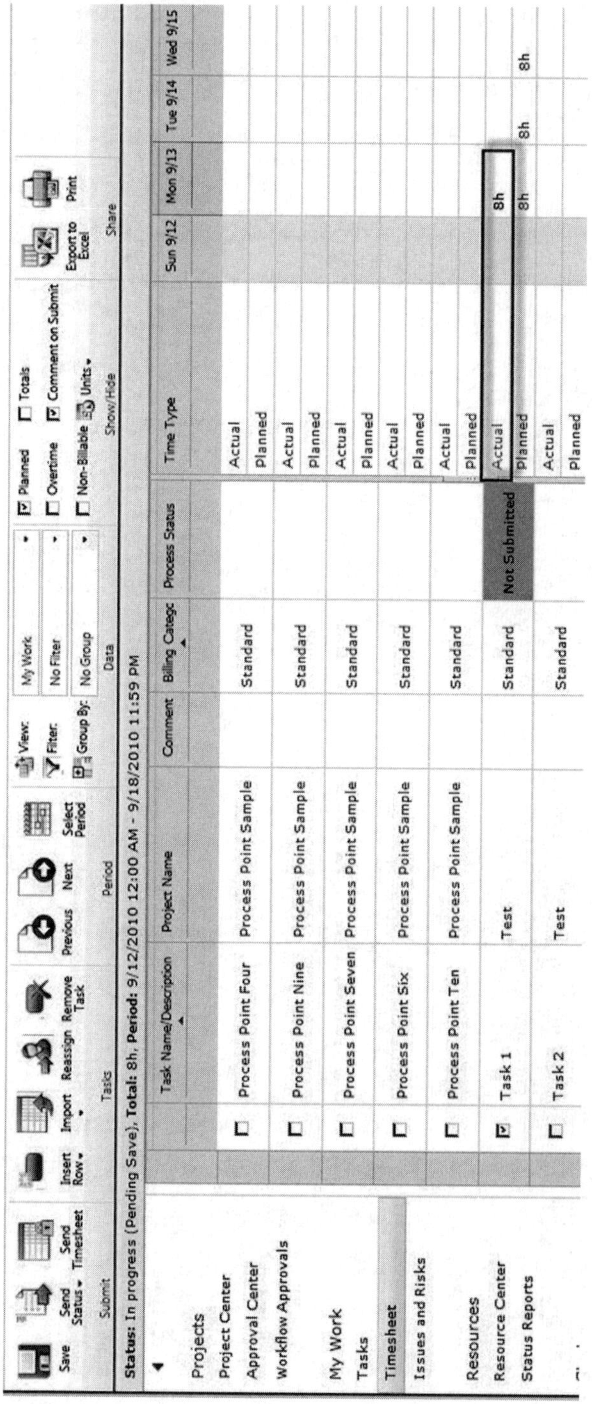

Figure 9–10

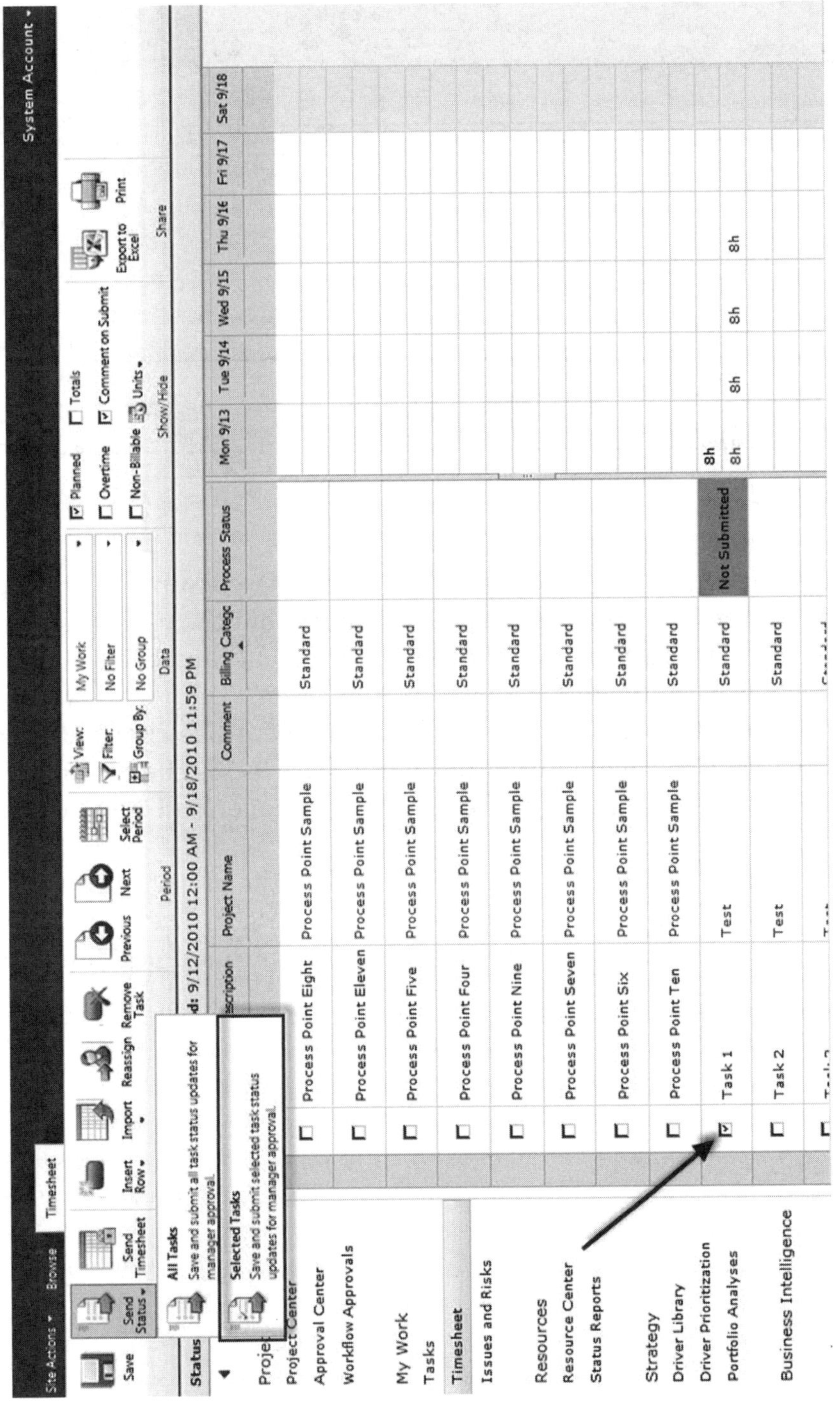

Figure 9–11

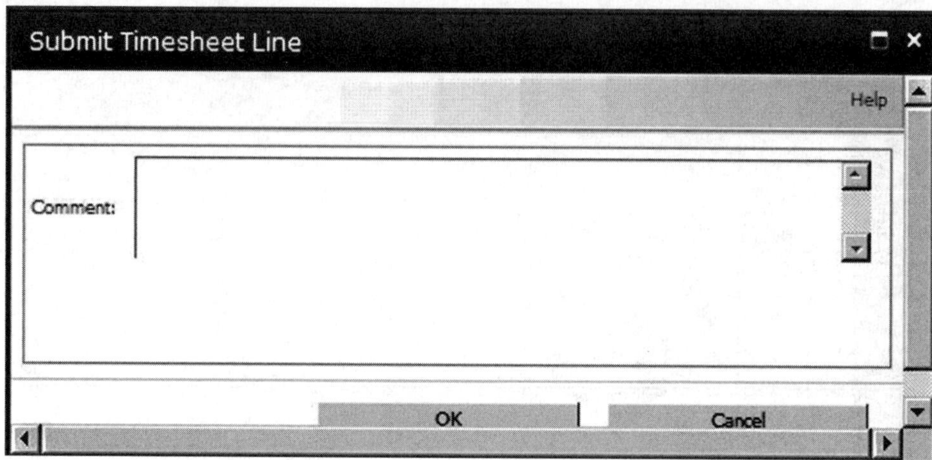

Figure 9–12

When submitting tasks, a Submit Timesheet Line pop-up box will appear, as shown in Figure 9–12. Any relevant comments about the assignment can be typed in for the timesheet manager to view, or the field can be left blank. Click OK to submit the assignment for approval.

Note that now the Process Status of the assignment has changed from Not Submitted to Awaiting Approval, as shown in Figure 9–13. The timesheet manager will approve the update and the resource manager will update the project.

Up to this point the example has concentrated on the project file tasks. However, that is only half of the reason for Single Entry Mode. The other half is the administrative time portion of the timesheet. The purpose of administrative

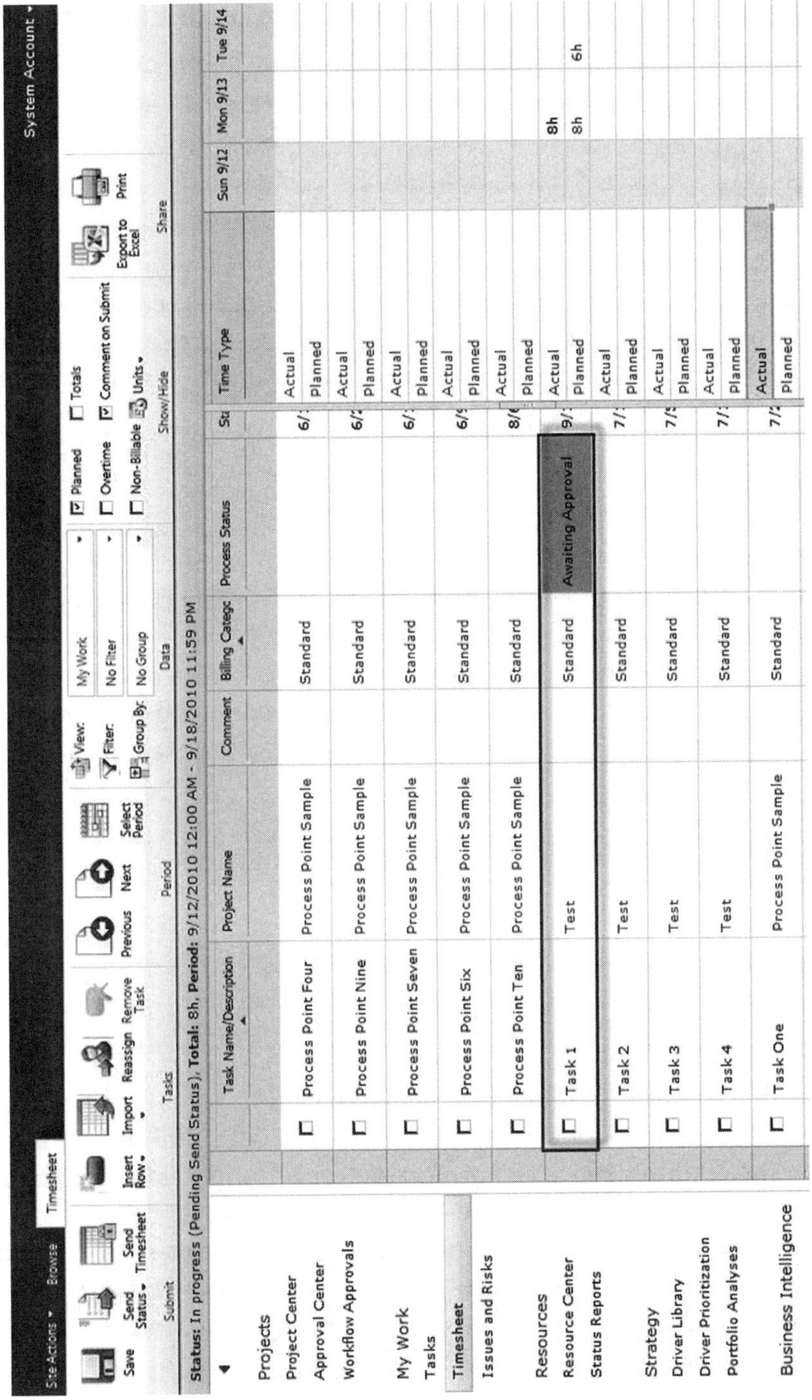

Figure 9–13

time is to allow you to report against exception (non-project file) time. Some of the typical categories that companies use are:

- Administrative
- Jury duty
- Sick time
- Vacation

Administrative time is important for resource utilization, capacity, and other reports. It is used when you still want to track a resource's time so that you can account for it, but you don't want to have to put it into a project file to keep track of it and have resources report against it.

In Figure 9–14, you can see the example shows two hours on 9/15 for administrative time. In this example, let's say that the resource had a two hour meeting that day, so was unable to work on project file tasks during that time. The resource wants to record that time so that the resource manager knows that they were working during that time, just not working on a specific project file task.

On 9/14, the resource took a vacation day and they want to record that time so that it doesn't reflect on their project file task work and appear as if they weren't doing anything that day! These updates are submitted to the timesheet manager just like a regular assignment.

When the entire timesheet is saved and submitted, the timesheet manager and the resource manager will each be able to review their respective needed information.

Miscellaneous Items

Up to this point, the example has shown how the resource updates his or her own timesheet. But, to update a timesheet, it has to be created. This is a Project Server term that might be a bit confusing. Note that by "created" we mean that the resource has to create their timesheet so that it is available for them to update—we are not talking about the project server administrator generating the timesheet periods on the Project Server.

When the project server administrator generates the timesheet periods, and allows resources to use them, then the resource can create them from the Manage Timesheets screen, shown in Figure 9–15. Highlighted in this figure is the view in the Ribbon that will show which timesheets the resource is viewing.

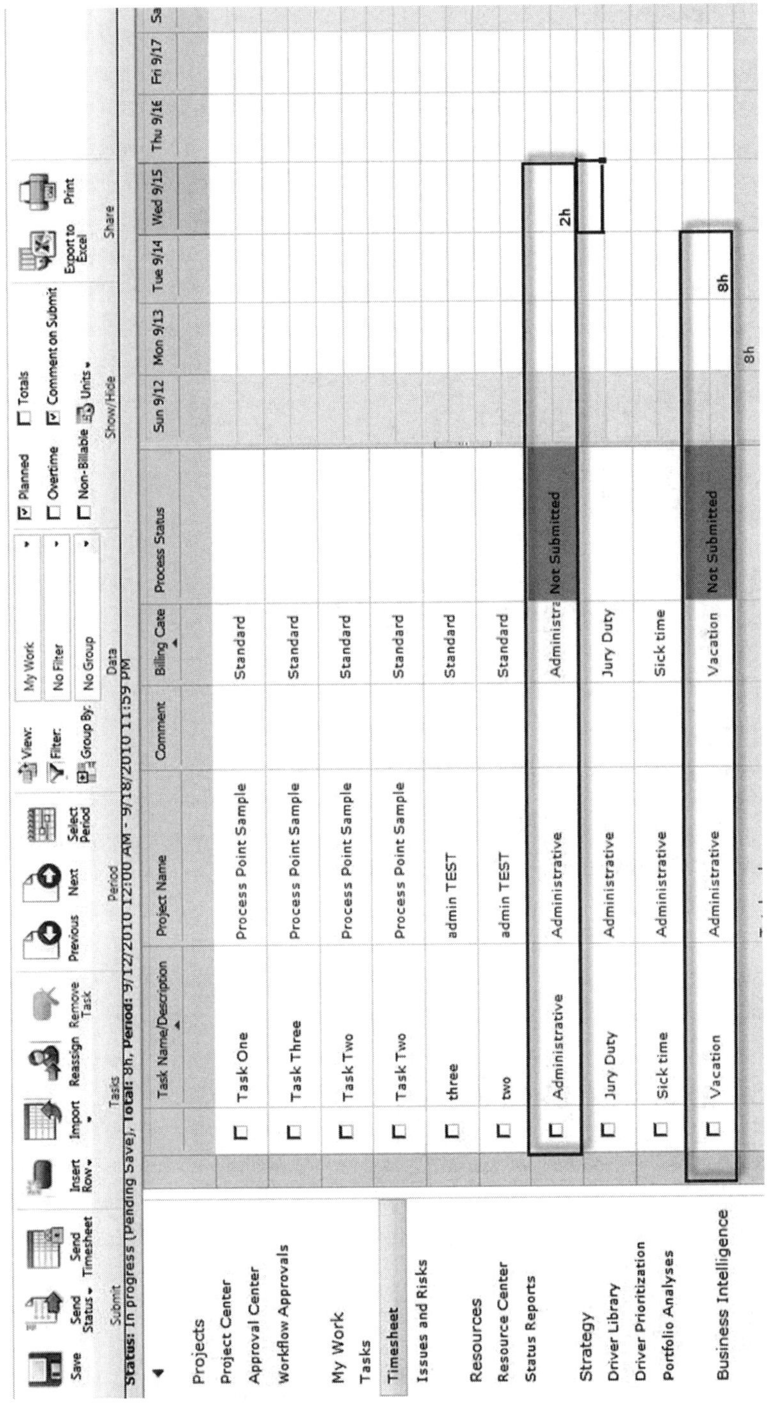

Save | Send Status | Send Timesheet | Insert Row | Import | Reassign | Remove Task | Previous | Next | Select Period | View: My Work | Filter: No Filter | Group By: No Group | Planned | Totals | Overtime | Comment on Submit | Non-Billable | Units | Export to Excel | Print

Submit | Tasks | Period | Data | Show/Hide | Share

Status: In progress (Pending Save), Total: 8h, Period: 9/12/2010 12:00 AM - 9/18/2010 11:59 PM

Projects
Project Center
Approval Center
Workflow Approvals

My Work
Tasks
Timesheet
Issues and Risks

Resources
Resource Center
Status Reports

Strategy
Driver Library
Driver Prioritization
Portfolio Analyses

Business Intelligence

Task Name/Description	Project Name	Comment	Billing Cate	Process Status	Sun 9/12	Mon 9/13	Tue 9/14	Wed 9/15	Thu 9/16	Fri 9/17	Sa
Task One	Process Point Sample		Standard								
Task Three	Process Point Sample		Standard								
Task Two	Process Point Sample		Standard								
Task Two	Process Point Sample		Standard								
three	admin TEST		Standard								
two	admin TEST		Standard								
Administrative	Administrative		Administra	Not Submitted				2h			
Jury Duty	Administrative		Jury Duty								
Sick time	Administrative		Sick time								
Vacation	Administrative		Vacation	Not Submitted			8h				
						8h					

Figure 9–14

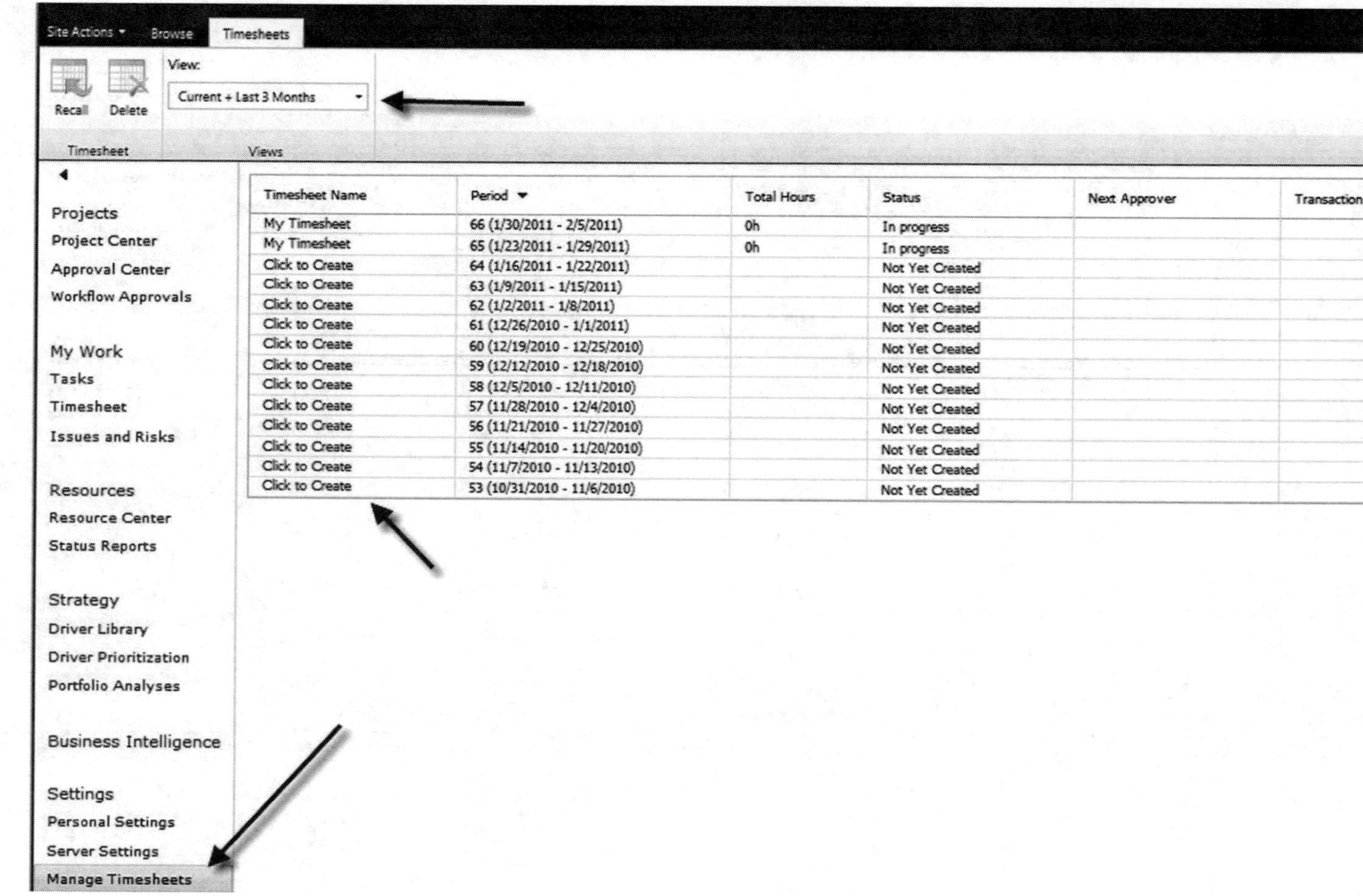
Site Actions
Browse
Timesheets
Recall
Delete
View:
Current + Last 3 Months
Timesheet
Views
Projects
Project Center
Approval Center
Workflow Approvals
My Work
Tasks
Timesheet
Issues and Risks
Resources
Resource Center
Status Reports
Strategy
Driver Library
Driver Prioritization
Portfolio Analyses
Business Intelligence
Settings
Personal Settings
Server Settings
Manage Timesheets
Timesheet Name
Period
Total Hours
Status
Next Approver
Transaction
My Timesheet | 66 (1/30/2011 - 2/5/2011) | 0h | In progress
My Timesheet | 65 (1/23/2011 - 1/29/2011) | 0h | In progress
Click to Create | 64 (1/16/2011 - 1/22/2011) | Not Yet Created
Click to Create | 63 (1/9/2011 - 1/15/2011) | Not Yet Created
Click to Create | 62 (1/2/2011 - 1/8/2011) | Not Yet Created
Click to Create | 61 (12/26/2010 - 1/1/2011) | Not Yet Created
Click to Create | 60 (12/19/2010 - 12/25/2010) | Not Yet Created
Click to Create | 59 (12/12/2010 - 12/18/2010) | Not Yet Created
Click to Create | 58 (12/5/2010 - 12/11/2010) | Not Yet Created
Click to Create | 57 (11/28/2010 - 12/4/2010) | Not Yet Created
Click to Create | 56 (11/21/2010 - 11/27/2010) | Not Yet Created
Click to Create | 55 (11/14/2010 - 11/20/2010) | Not Yet Created
Click to Create | 54 (11/7/2010 - 11/13/2010) | Not Yet Created
Click to Create | 53 (10/31/2010 - 11/6/2010) | Not Yet Created

Figure 9–15

Once the timesheet is created, it can be used by the resource to update his or her tasks.

At the beginning of this chapter, we stated that another entry method is to use both Timesheet and Task entry. In that situation, the information from the timesheet will need to be imported to the Task screen (or, vice-versa). Figure 9–16 shows the Import icon in the Ribbon. Since we are on the Task screen, the option is to import from the timesheet.

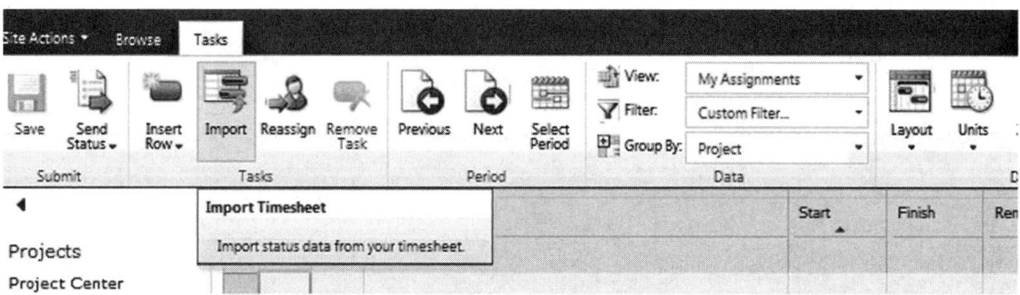

Figure 9–16

When clicking on the Import icon, the Import Timesheet screen appears. This screen allows the resource to select the timesheet they want, and is shown in Figure 9–17.

Once a timesheet is selected, the project file task information that is on that timesheet will appear. Administrative tasks will not appear. Figure 9–18 shows that in this example, Task Fifty and Task Fourty were both updated in the Timesheet entry to have had 16 hours of work completed. Note that the timesheet does not have to be submitted to import the time into the Task entry.

After clicking on the Import button, the tasks shown in the screen will be placed into the Tasks entry screen. They will also appear as Not Submitted in the Process Status column. Note that in Figure 9–18, the Current Progress column showed 0%. Now that the information has been updated, note in Figure 9–19 that the progress (as shown in the % Work column) changed because the task was updated with the timesheet information.

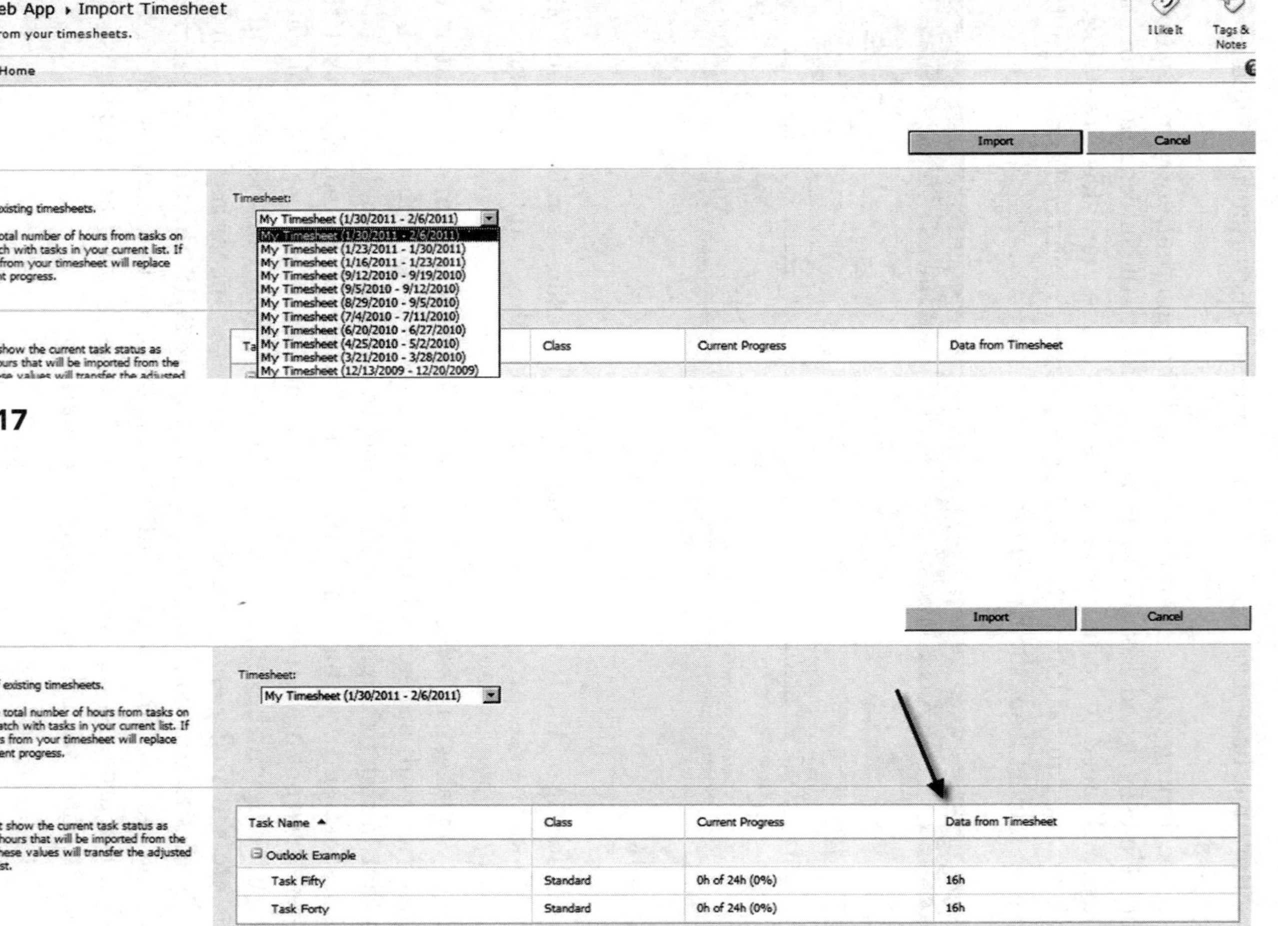

Figure 9–17

Figure 9–18

☐			Task Fifty	2/1/2011	2/3/2011	8h	67%	24h	16h	Not Submitted
☐			Task Forty	2/1/2011	2/3/2011	8h	67%	24h	16h	Not Submitted

Figure 9–19

Timesheet Setup

Documentation about how to set up timesheets is easily found, but we wanted to cover some of the settings from the perspective that we have used in the examples above, and to clarify the use of some of those settings.

In the Project Server Settings is the *Time and Task Management* section. This is where the timesheet setup information is contained, as shown in Figure 9–20.

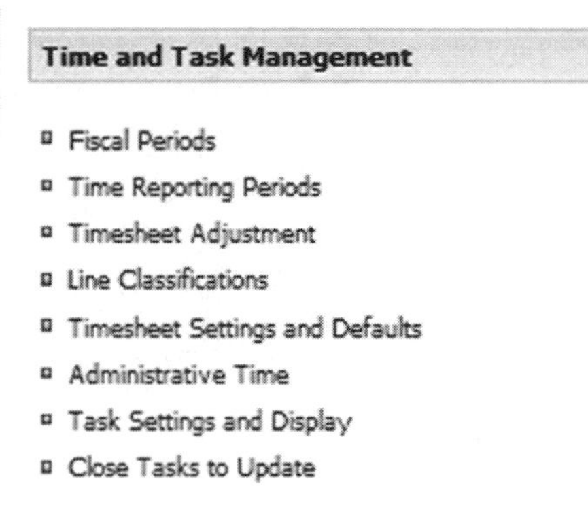

Figure 9–20

The items that pertain to timesheet setup are:

- Time Reporting Periods
- Line Classifications
- Timesheet Settings and Defaults
- Administrative Time
- Task Settings and Display

The settings of these screens all work together, so they should all be completed prior to creating time reporting periods. Figure 9–21 shows the top half

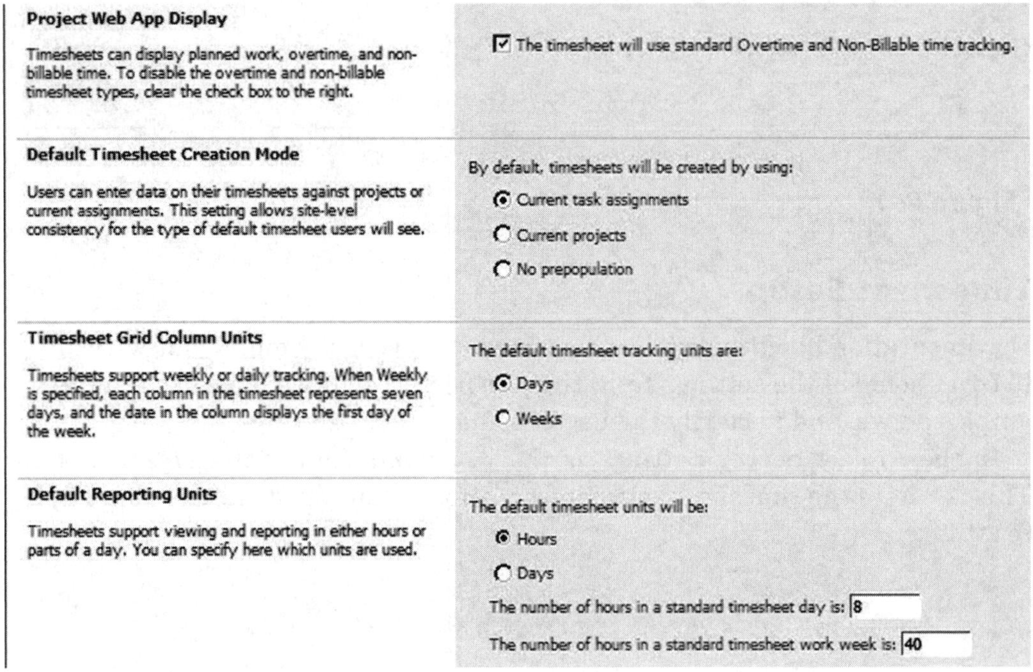

Project Web App Display Timesheets can display planned work, overtime, and non-billable time. To disable the overtime and non-billable timesheet types, clear the check box to the right.	☑ The timesheet will use standard Overtime and Non-Billable time tracking.
Default Timesheet Creation Mode Users can enter data on their timesheets against projects or current assignments. This setting allows site-level consistency for the type of default timesheet users will see.	By default, timesheets will be created by using: ◉ Current task assignments ○ Current projects ○ No prepopulation
Timesheet Grid Column Units Timesheets support weekly or daily tracking. When Weekly is specified, each column in the timesheet represents seven days, and the date in the column displays the first day of the week.	The default timesheet tracking units are: ◉ Days ○ Weeks
Default Reporting Units Timesheets support viewing and reporting in either hours or parts of a day. You can specify here which units are used.	The default timesheet units will be: ◉ Hours ○ Days The number of hours in a standard timesheet day is: 8 The number of hours in a standard timesheet work week is: 40

Figure 9–21

of the Timesheet Settings and Defaults screen, and in the following screenshots we discuss settings in more detail.

- **Project Web App Display.** Timesheets can display planned work, overtime, and non-billable time. To disable the Overtime and Non-Billable timesheet types, clear the check box. The Timesheet view allows the resource to toggle the Overtime and Non-Billable information in the view. When the check box is cleared, the option to toggle that in the view is not enabled, as shown in Figure 9–22.

Project Web App Display Timesheets can display planned work, overtime, and non-billable time. To disable the overtime and non-billable timesheet types, clear the check box to the right.	☑ The timesheet will use standard Overtime and Non-Billable time tracking.

Figure 9–22

- **Default Timesheet Creation Mode.** Users can enter data on their timesheets against projects or current assignments. This setting allows site-level consistency for the type of default timesheet users will see, as in Figure 9–23. This applies to the resource when he or she creates a timesheet.

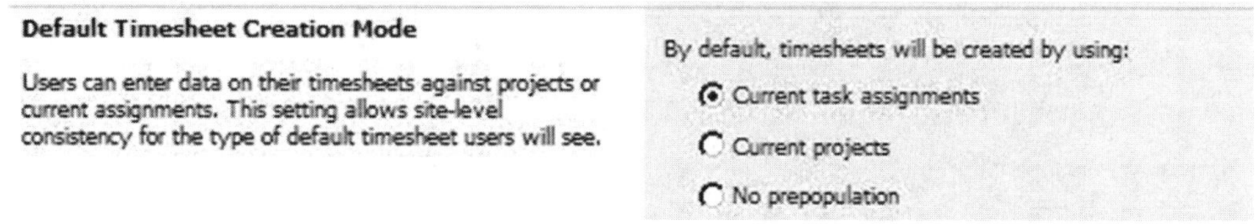

Default Timesheet Creation Mode

Users can enter data on their timesheets against projects or current assignments. This setting allows site-level consistency for the type of default timesheet users will see.

By default, timesheets will be created by using:

(•) Current task assignments

( ) Current projects

( ) No prepopulation

Figure 9–23

- **Timesheet Grid Column Units.** Timesheets support weekly or daily tracking. When weekly tracking is specified, each column in the display represents seven days, and the data in the column displays the first day of the week, as shown in Figure 9–24.

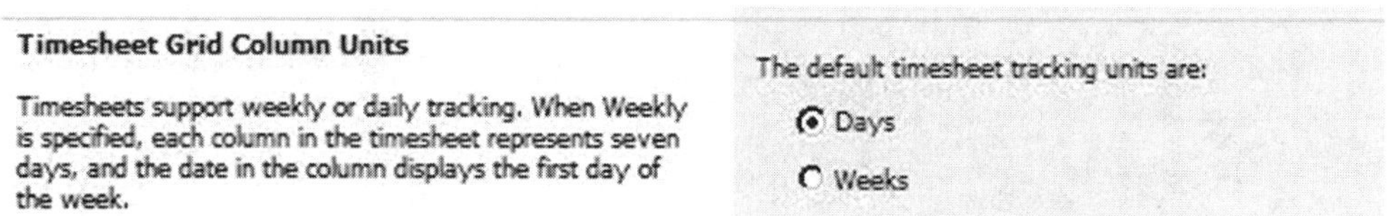
Timesheet Grid Column Units
Timesheets support weekly or daily tracking. When Weekly is specified, each column in the timesheet represents seven days, and the date in the column displays the first day of the week.
The default timesheet tracking units are:
Days
Weeks

Figure 9–24

- **Default Reporting Units.** Timesheets support viewing and reporting in either hours or parts of a day. You can specify which units are used, as shown in Figure 9–25. Since this is a Default option only, it can be modified in the Timesheet screen by selecting the appropriate option in the Ribbon.

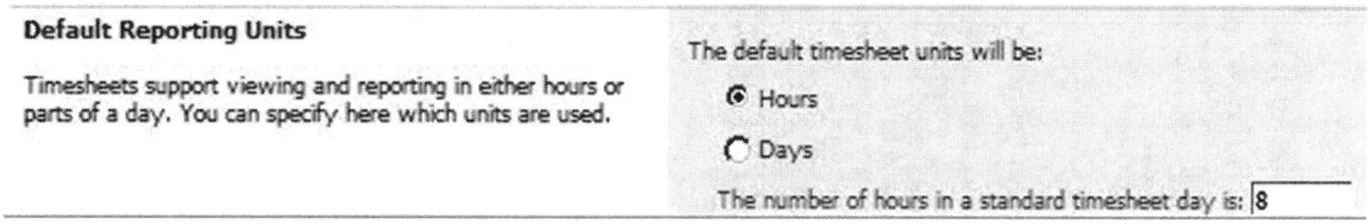

Default Reporting Units

Timesheets support viewing and reporting in either hours or parts of a day. You can specify here which units are used.

The default timesheet units will be:

(•) Hours

( ) Days

The number of hours in a standard timesheet day is: 8

Figure 9–25

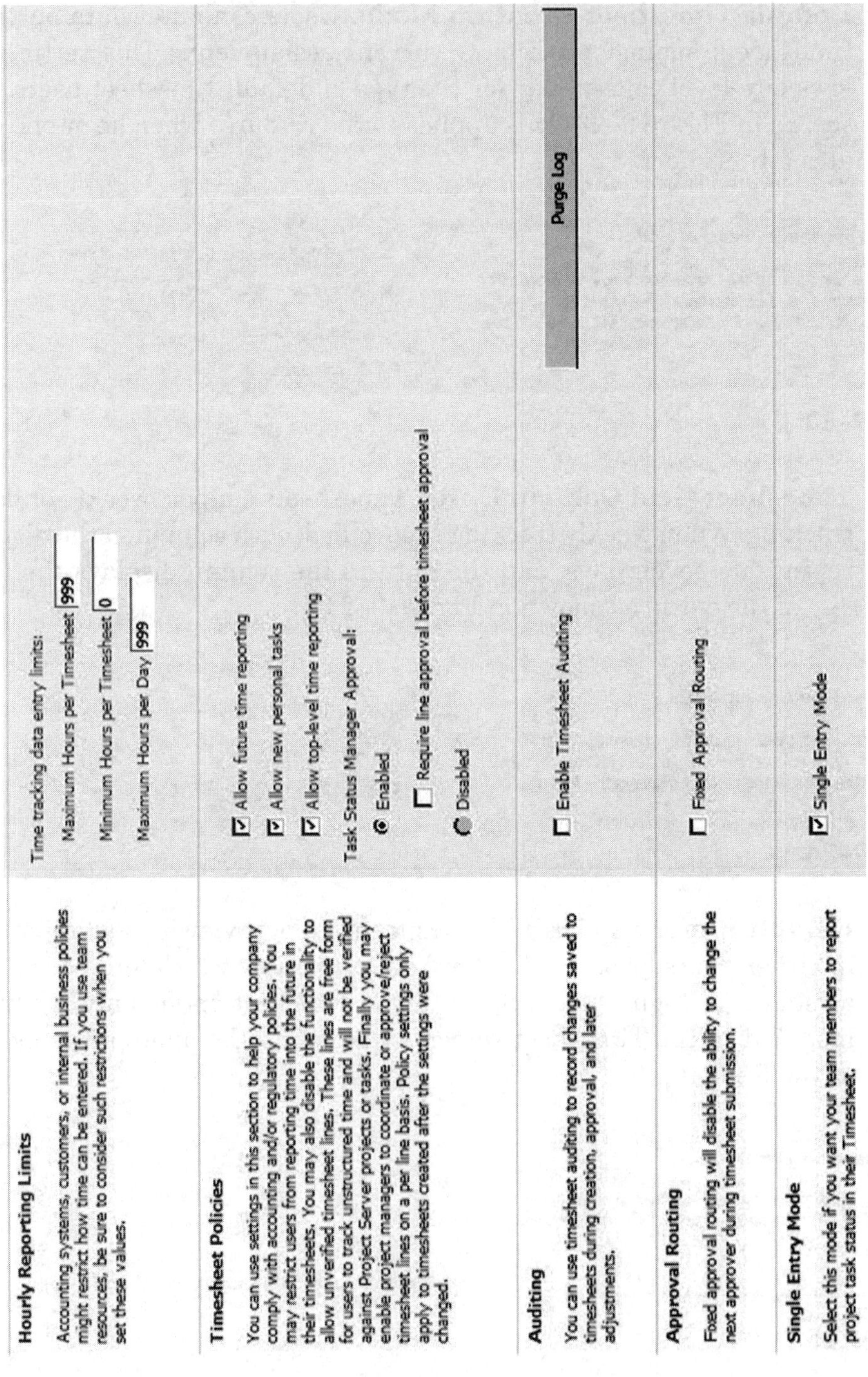

Hourly Reporting Limits

Accounting systems, customers, or internal business policies might restrict how time can be entered. If you use team resources, be sure to consider such restrictions when you set these values.

Time tracking data entry limits:

Maximum Hours per Timesheet 999

Minimum Hours per Timesheet 0

Maximum Hours per Day 999

Timesheet Policies

You can use settings in this section to help your company comply with accounting and/or regulatory policies. You may restrict users from reporting time into the future in their timesheets. You may also disable the functionality to allow unverified timesheet lines. These lines are free form for users to track unstructured time and will not be verified against Project Server projects or tasks. Finally you may enable project managers to coordinate or approve/reject timesheet lines on a per line basis. Policy settings only apply to timesheets created after the settings were changed.

☑ Allow future time reporting

☑ Allow new personal tasks

☑ Allow top-level time reporting

Task Status Manager Approval:

◉ Enabled

☐ Require line approval before timesheet approval

○ Disabled

Auditing

You can use timesheet auditing to record changes saved to timesheets during creation, approval, and later adjustments.

☐ Enable Timesheet Auditing

Purge Log

Approval Routing

Fixed approval routing will disable the ability to change the next approver during timesheet submission.

☐ Fixed Approval Routing

Single Entry Mode

Select this mode if you want your team members to report project task status in their Timesheet.

☑ Single Entry Mode

Figure 9–26

The bottom half of the Timesheet Settings and Display screen looks like Figure 9–26.

- **Hourly Reporting Limits.** Accounting systems, customers, or internal business policies might restrict how time can be entered. If you use team resources, be sure to consider such restrictions when you set these values. These determine the absolute maximum and minimum number of hours that a resource can put on a timesheet per day or within a timesheet period. If a resource tries to enter too many or too few hours, based on this setting, then they will receive an error message, and the timesheet will not be sent for approval. This error message is shown in Figure 9–27.

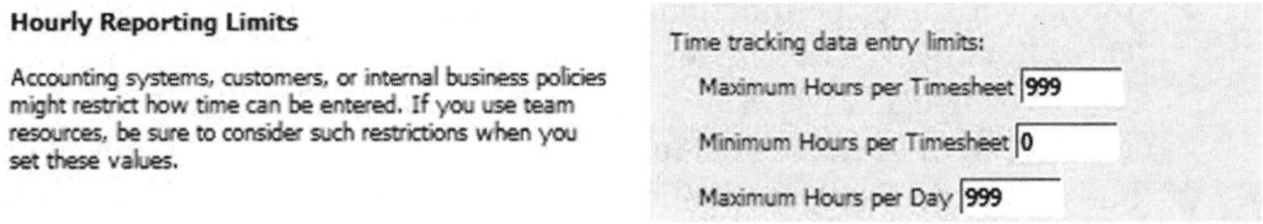

Hourly Reporting Limits

Accounting systems, customers, or internal business policies might restrict how time can be entered. If you use team resources, be sure to consider such restrictions when you set these values.

Time tracking data entry limits:
Maximum Hours per Timesheet 999
Minimum Hours per Timesheet 0
Maximum Hours per Day 999

Figure 9–27

- **Timesheet Policies.** Figure 9–28 shows this section of the Timesheet Settings and Default screen. You can use the settings in this section to help your company comply with accounting and/or regulatory policies. You may restrict users from reporting time into the future in their timesheets. But, note that business policies may affect some of these options—like the Allow Future Time Reporting option. If your organization requires a weekly timesheet update and a resource is going on vacation for two weeks, then they will need to be able to report into the future; or, they will have to complete the timesheets when they return. However, waiting until they return might be out of compliance with the business policy.

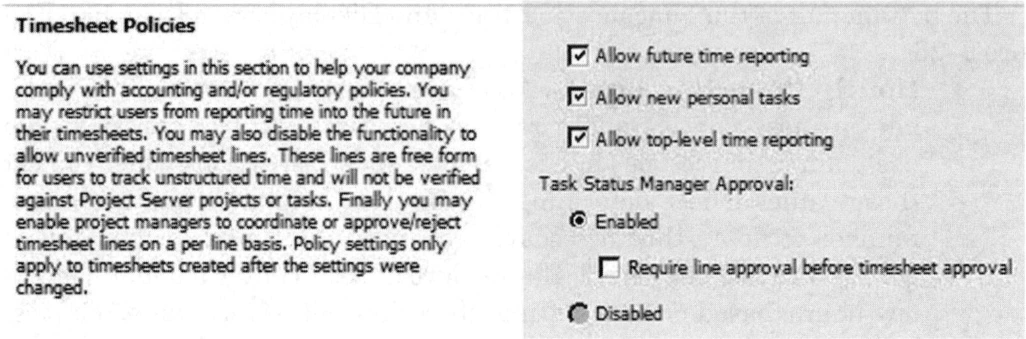

Timesheet Policies

You can use settings in this section to help your company comply with accounting and/or regulatory policies. You may restrict users from reporting time into the future in their timesheets. You may also disable the functionality to allow unverified timesheet lines. These lines are free form for users to track unstructured time and will not be verified against Project Server projects or tasks. Finally you may enable project managers to coordinate or approve/reject timesheet lines on a per line basis. Policy settings only apply to timesheets created after the settings were changed.

☑ Allow future time reporting
☑ Allow new personal tasks
☑ Allow top-level time reporting

Task Status Manager Approval:

◉ Enabled

☐ Require line approval before timesheet approval

○ Disabled

Figure 9–28

- You may disable the functionality to allow unverified timesheet lines. These lines are "free form" for users to track unstructured time and will not be verified against Project Server projects or tasks. Finally, you may enable resource managers to coordinate or approve/reject timesheet lines on a per line basis. Policy settings only apply to timesheets created after the settings were changed.
- **Auditing.** You can use timesheet auditing to record changes saved to timesheets during creation, approval, and later adjustments. Organizations that need to be compliant with the Defense Contract Audit Agency need to have this enabled. This allows an organization to record when changes are saved to timesheets, as shown in Figure 9–29.

Auditing

You can use timesheet auditing to record changes saved to timesheets during creation, approval, and later adjustments.

☐ Enable Timesheet Auditing

Purge Log

Figure 9–29

- **Approval Routing.** Fixed Approval routing will disable the ability to change the next approver during timesheet submission, as shown in Figure 9–30.

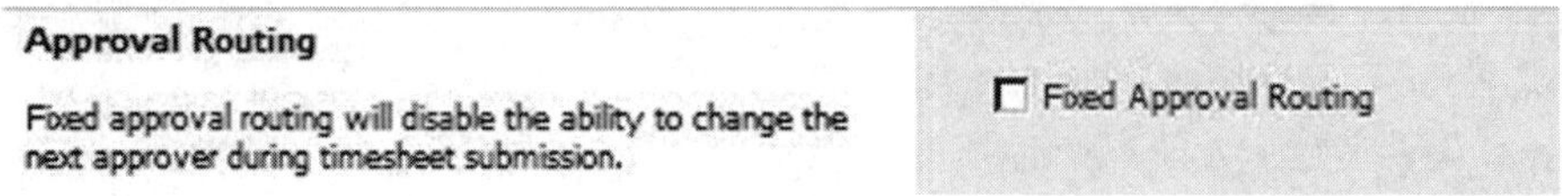

Approval Routing

Fixed approval routing will disable the ability to change the next approver during timesheet submission.

☐ Fixed Approval Routing

Figure 9–30

- **Single Entry Mode.** Select this mode if you want your team to report project file task status in their timesheets. This was selected to allow the demonstration of the main example of this chapter, and is shown in Figure 9–31.

Single Entry Mode

Select this mode if you want your team members to report project task status in their Timesheet.

☑ Single Entry Mode

Figure 9–31

The Line Classifications screen creates lines that can be used on timesheets for resources to enter different types of time on the same task. Also, since classifications may change over time, the Status can be changed from Active to Inactive, if necessary, in the future. This is often referred to as the Billing Category, and is an easy way to split the time between two activities that are associated with one task. An example of how this might work is shown in Figure 9–32.

While the Line Classification information appears as the Billing Category column in the timesheet, don't get too focused on this being a "billing" item. It might be a simple way for accounting to clarify time. For example, if a resource is assigned to a three-day task that involves one day of travel, and your organization accounts for travel differently, they can add that information to the same task, as demonstrated in Figure 9–33. In a project file called Line Classification Example, the resource has allocated time for the task called Three Day Task to both the Standard and Travel line classifications, and put in the appropriate amount of time for each line. The resource appropriately placed four hours of Travel on the first and last day of the task, and assigned the rest of their time to the Standard classification.

Administrative time is designed to allow the project server administrator to set up the categories where resources can input their administrative time when they complete their timesheets, as shown in Figure 9–34. Some common categories to create are personal time off, funeral, jury duty, sick time, and vacation. The project server administrator can determine if these options will display every time a timesheet is created by selecting the check box in the Always Display column. This does not mean that it is a required column to be completed by the resource.

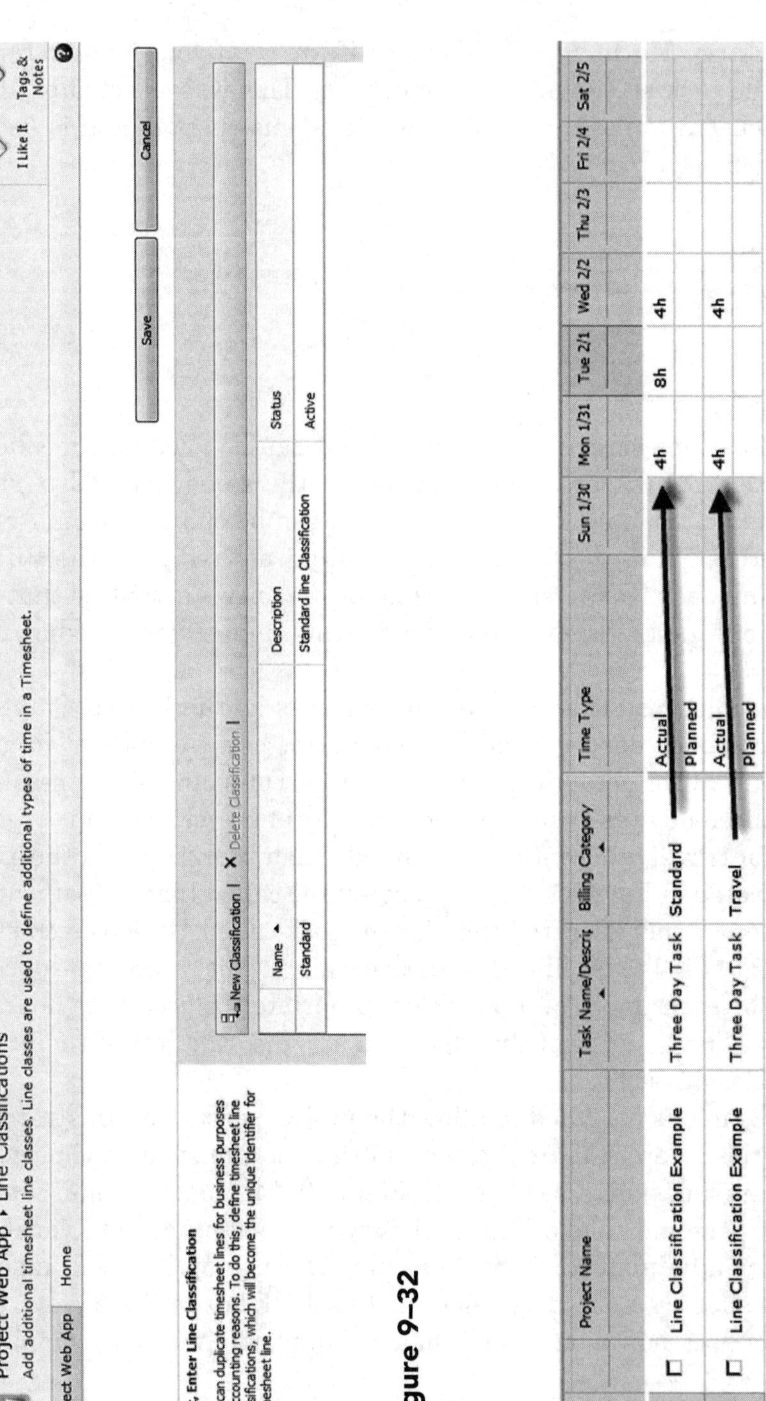

Figure 9–32

Figure 9–33

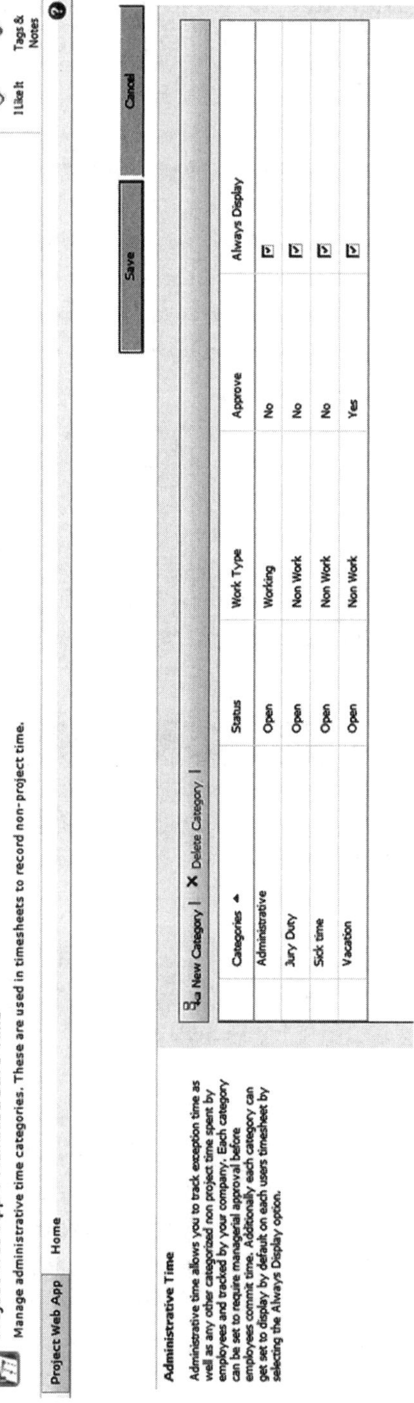
Project Web App › Administrative Time
Manage administrative time categories. These are used in timesheets to record non-project time.
I Like It
Tags & Notes
Project Web App
Home
Save
Cancel
Administrative Time
Administrative time allows you to track exception time as well as any other categorized non project time spent by employees and tracked by your company. Each category can be set to require managerial approval before employees commit time. Additionally each category can get set to display by default on each users timesheet by selecting the Always Display option.
New Category
Delete Category
Categories
Status
Work Type
Approve
Always Display
Administrative
Open
Working
No
Jury Duty
Open
Non Work
No
Sick time
Open
Non Work
No
Vacation
Open
Non Work
Yes

Figure 9–34

When a resource is in the Timesheet entry screen and the Administrative Time categories are checked to Always Display, the categories will be visible every time, as shown in Figure 9–35.

☐	Administrative	Administrative	Administrative	Actual Planned
☐	Administrative	Jury Duty	Jury Duty	Actual Planned
☐	Administrative	Sick time	Sick time	Actual Planned
☐	Administrative	Vacation	Vacation	Actual Planned

Figure 9–35

When a resource is in the Timesheet entry screen and they choose to Insert Administrative Tasks from the Insert Row icon, they are presented with options in the Administrative Time categories. Selecting the Insert Row icon is shown in Figure 9–36.

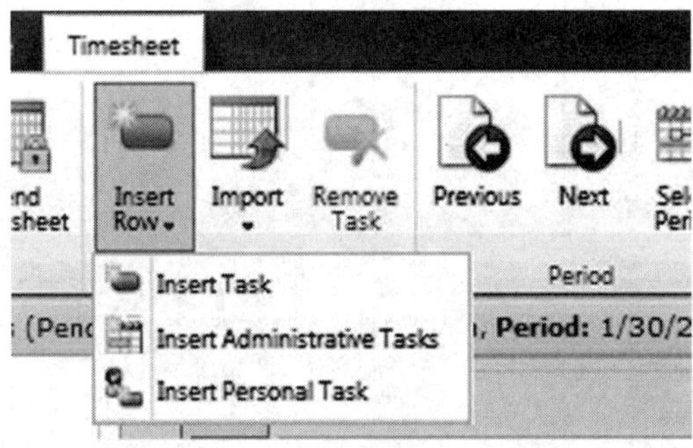

Figure 9–36

After selecting the Insert Administrative Tasks option, the Administrative Time option box will appear. In the Category drop-down, the list of available options is from the list as set up in the Administrative Time settings, shown in Figure 9–37. The Description field is populated with the default description from the Administrative Time settings. However, the resource can type anything they need to in that box.

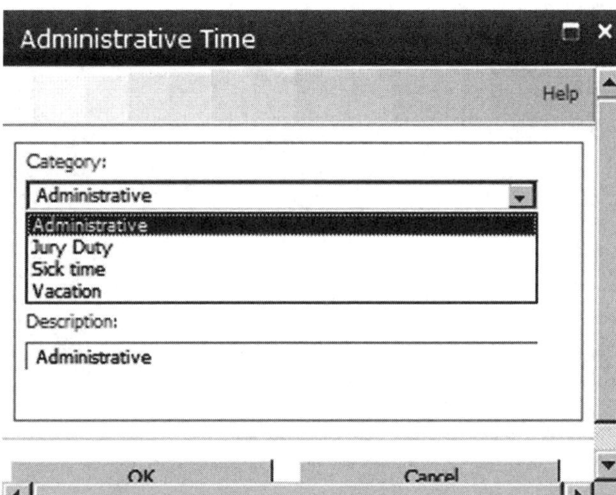

Figure 9–37

The next part of the Time and Task Management section to set up is the Task Settings and Display, shown in Figure 9–38.

Options for Time and Task Management are:

- **Tracking Method.** Timesheets can be updated in different methods. This option allows the project server administrator to choose one of the four methods that resources will have to update their timesheets, as shown in Figure 9–39. The check box can be selected to require every project file to use the same method for tracking. If not selected, it is possible for some project files to require percentage updates while others require hour entry. This can be confusing to resources and can cause reporting to show some unexpected results. For example, if you were running a report to display Actual Work information, and you were expecting all the hours to be in whole numbers but some resources were using percentages, then the system will have calculated some of their Actual Work based on the percentage. This means that the Actual Work for a task might display as 6.43 hours. It is for this reason that a level of consistency is desired in Project Server.
- **Reporting Display.** The two options in this section determine if resources will report their time in daily increments, or by the total number

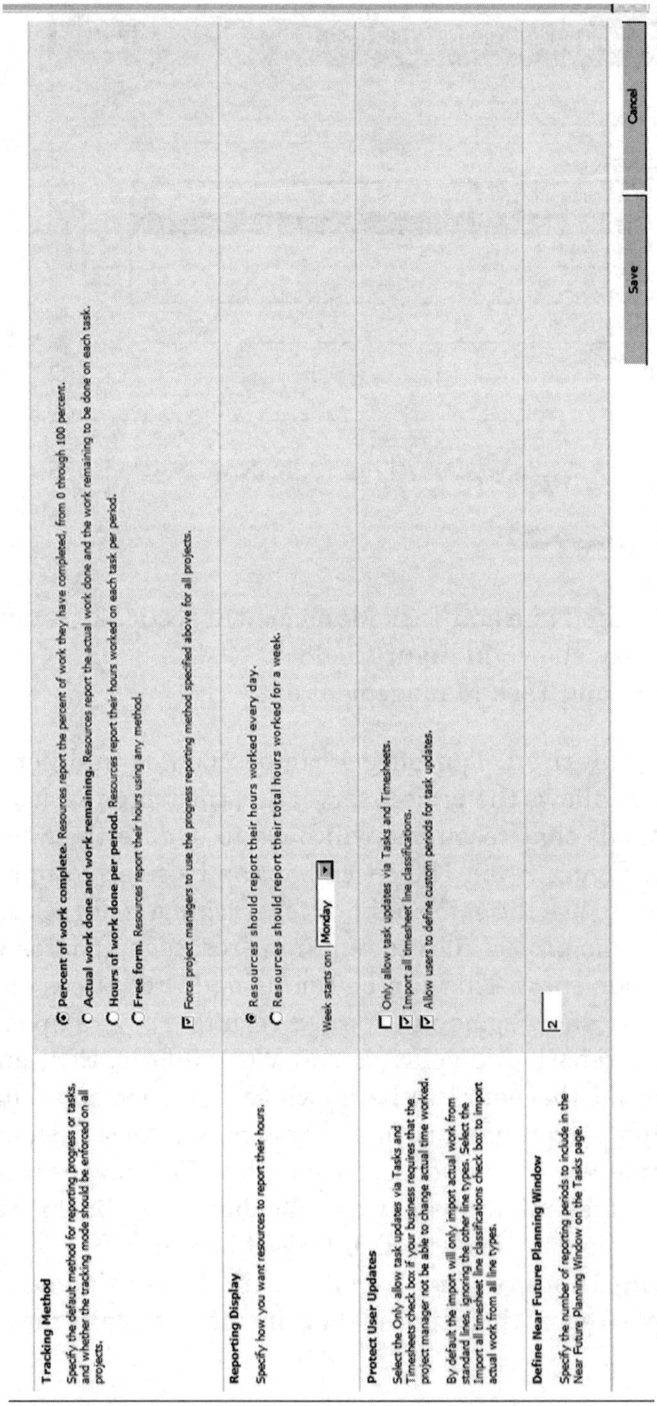

Tracking Method

Specify the default method for reporting progress or tasks, and whether the tracking mode should be enforced on all projects.

- (•) **Percent of work complete.** Resources report the percent of work they have completed, from 0 through 100 percent.
- ( ) **Actual work done and work remaining.** Resources report the actual work done and the work remaining to be done on each task.
- ( ) **Hours of work done per period.** Resources report their hours worked on each task per period.
- ( ) **Free form.** Resources report their hours using any method.

[x] Force project managers to use the progress reporting method specified above for all projects.

Reporting Display

Specify how you want resources to report their hours.

- (•) Resources should report their hours worked every day.
- ( ) Resources should report their total hours worked for a week.

Week starts on: Monday

Protect User Updates

Select the Only allow task updates via Tasks and Timesheets check box if your business requires that the project manager not be able to change actual time worked.

By default the import will only import actual work from standard lines, ignoring the other line types. Select the Import all timesheet line classifications check box to import actual work from all line types.

- [ ] Only allow task updates via Tasks and Timesheets.
- [x] Import all timesheet line classifications.
- [x] Allow users to define custom periods for task updates.

Define Near Future Planning Window

Specify the number of reporting periods to include in the Near Future Planning Window on the Tasks page.

2

Save Cancel

Figure 9–38

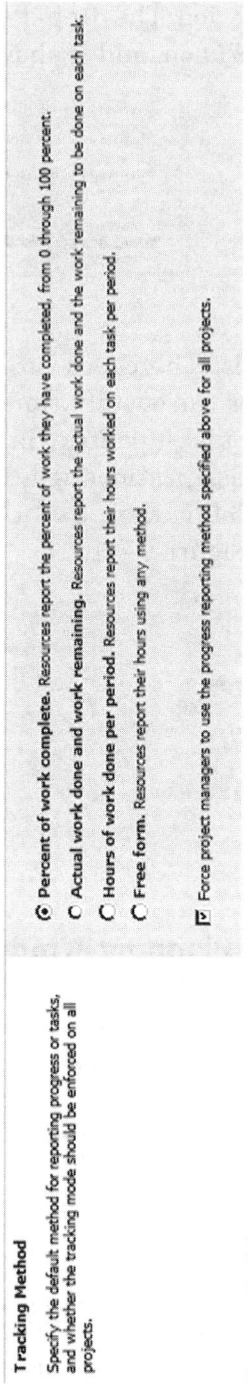

Tracking Method

Specify the default method for reporting progress or tasks, and whether the tracking mode should be enforced on all projects.

- (•) **Percent of work complete.** Resources report the percent of work they have completed, from 0 through 100 percent.
- ( ) **Actual work done and work remaining.** Resources report the actual work done and the work remaining to be done on each task.
- ( ) **Hours of work done per period.** Resources report their hours worked on each task per period.
- ( ) **Free form.** Resources report their hours using any method.

[x] Force project managers to use the progress reporting method specified above for all projects.

Figure 9–39

of hours for the whole period. The drop-down also indicates what day of the week your week starts on, and is shown in Figure 9–40.

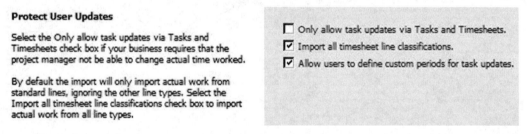

Reporting Display

Specify how you want resources to report their hours.

◉ Resources should report their hours worked every day.
○ Resources should report their total hours worked for a week.

Week starts on: Monday

Figure 9–40

- **Protect User Updates.** The check boxes in this section determine if the resource manager can modify time on project file task updates (choosing to only allow task updates via Tasks and Timesheets), how the Timesheet Line Classifications will be imported, and whether or not the resources can define their own time periods for task updates, with options shown in Figure 9–41.

Protect User Updates

Select the Only allow task updates via Tasks and Timesheets check box if your business requires that the project manager not be able to change actual time worked.

By default the import will only import actual work from standard lines, ignoring the other line types. Select the Import all timesheet line classifications check box to import actual work from all line types.

☐ Only allow task updates via Tasks and Timesheets.
☑ Import all timesheet line classifications.
☑ Allow users to define custom periods for task updates.

Figure 9–41

- **Define Near Future Planning Window.** This setting affects how the Planning Window displays the Near Future tasks section of the My Tasks view. The number in the box represents the number of time reporting periods that are shown, as in Figure 9–42.

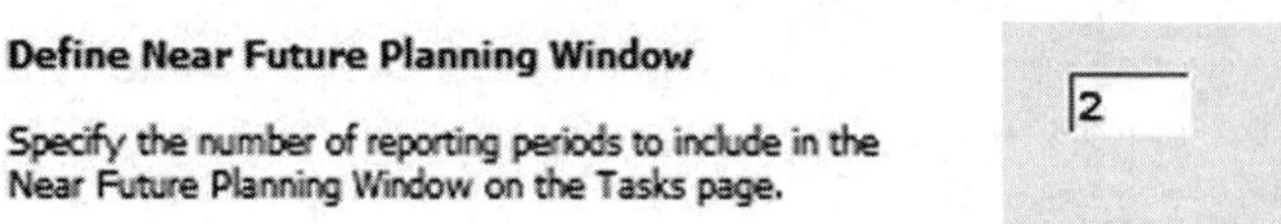

Figure 9–42

The final section to set up so that timesheets can be used is the time reporting periods. Figure 9–43 shows this screen. This is the section where you actually

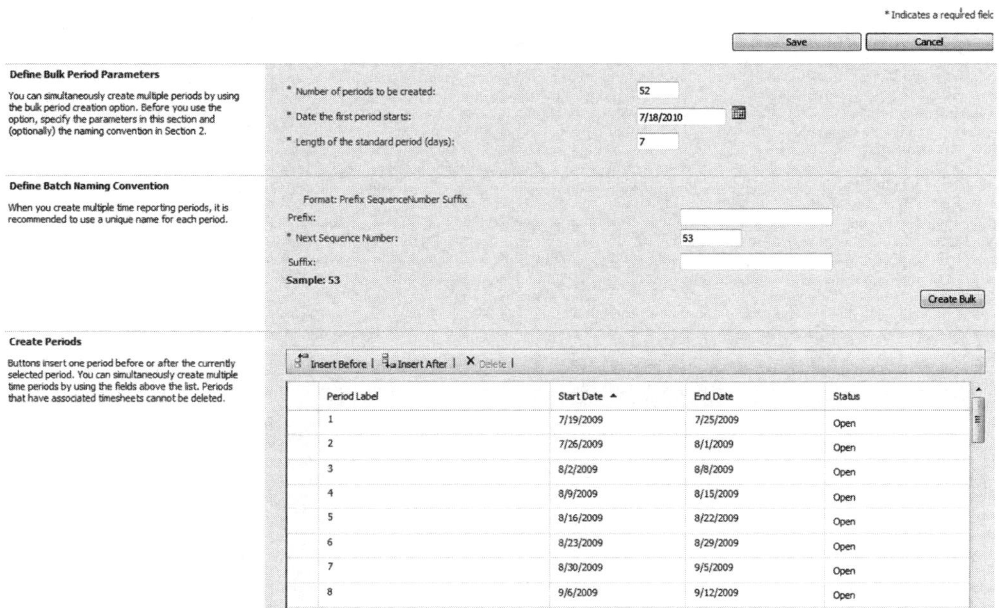

Figure 9–43

create the time periods that resources will use and see in their timesheet views. It is common to create a year's worth of time periods when this is done.

Options for time reporting periods are:

- **Define Bulk Period Parameters.** You can simultaneously create multiple periods by using the Bulk Period option. Before you use the option, specify the parameters in this section and (optionally) the naming convention in Section 2, as shown in Figure 9–44.
- **Define Batch Naming Convention.** When you create multiple time reporting periods, it is recommended to use a unique name for each period. Whatever prefix and suffix you enter here will be in the label for each period that you create, as shown in Figure 9–45.
- **Create Periods.** Buttons insert one period before or after the currently selected period. You can simultaneously create multiple time periods by using the fields above the list. Periods that have associated timesheets cannot be deleted (see Figure 9–46). You can also close a time period that will not allow anyone to update timesheets any longer.

Define Bulk Period Parameters

You can simultaneously create multiple periods by using the bulk period creation option. Before you use the option, specify the parameters in this section and (optionally) the naming convention in Section 2.

* Number of periods to be created: 52

* Date the first period starts: 10/30/2011

* Length of the standard period (days): 7

Figure 9–44

Define Batch Naming Convention

When you create multiple time reporting periods, it is recommended to use a unique name for each period.

Format: Prefix SequenceNumber Suffix

Prefix:

* Next Sequence Number: 1

Suffix:

Sample: 1

Create Bulk

Figure 9–45

Create Periods

Buttons insert one period before or after the currently selected period. You can simultaneously create multiple time periods by using the fields above the list. Periods that have associated timesheets cannot be deleted.

Insert Before | Insert After | ✕ Delete |

Period Label	Start Date ▲	End Date	Status
New Period :7/19/2009-7/25/2009	7/19/2009	7/25/2009	Open
New Period :7/26/2009-8/1/2009	7/26/2009	8/1/2009	Open
New Period :8/2/2009-8/8/2009	8/2/2009	8/8/2009	Open
New Period :8/9/2009-8/15/2009	8/9/2009	8/15/2009	Open

Figure 9–46

In the Time and Task Management section of the Project Server Settings, you may have noticed that there are a few other options. These are:

- Fiscal Periods
- Timesheet Adjustment
- Close Tasks to Update

The Fiscal Periods screen is for organizations that do not use a calendar year for fiscal reporting purposes. This screen is available to the project server administrator, and affects reporting and where timesheet information will fall. For example, if your organization's fiscal year starts in June and ends in May, this screen will look like Figure 9–47. This screen shows that even though the year is 2009 and the date is 6/1/2009, it is the first month (represented in the Fiscal Period column) and it is in the first quarter.

The Timesheet Adjustment screen is available to resource managers and timesheet managers to review or modify the history of Timesheet updates and approvals. This is where they can correct any issues that they may discover about a Timesheet after they have already approved it.

The Close Tasks to Update option can be used by resource managers and resources with the appropriate security permissions. The goal of this item is to select a task from a specific project file that you no longer want to have updated by any resources. This is effective for times when a task is not deleted, but no more time can be logged against it.

Timesheets can benefit an organization by helping to track the non-project file tasks and to better track resource utilization and capacity. Timesheets allow an organization to reach another level of information and detail about their resources, where the resources spend time and what work they are doing that might not be directly related to a project file. While regular task updates allow an organization to understand the work that a resource is doing for a specific project file, or a group of project files, the timesheet gives a picture of what the resource is doing with the rest of their time. And, depending upon how your organization uses the timesheet information, the data collected here can be used for billing customers or even tying into a payroll system.

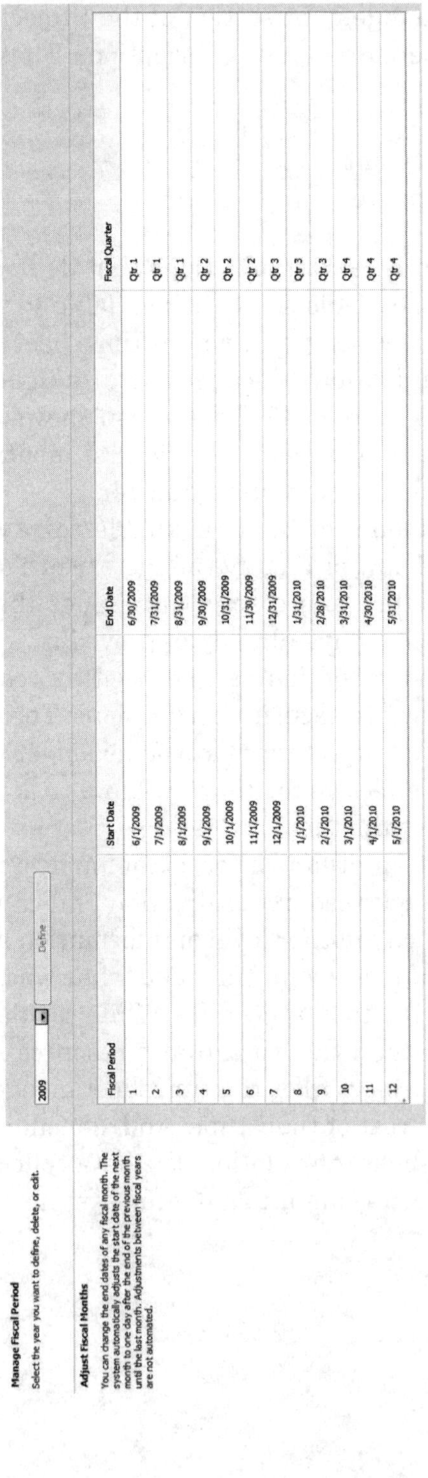

Manage Fiscal Period

Select the year you want to define, delete, or edit.

2009 Define

Adjust Fiscal Months

You can change the end dates of any fiscal month. The system automatically adjusts the start date of the next month to one day after the end of the previous month until the last month. Adjustments between fiscal years are not automated.

Fiscal Period	Start Date	End Date	Fiscal Quarter
1	6/1/2009	6/30/2009	Qtr 1
2	7/1/2009	7/31/2009	Qtr 1
3	8/1/2009	8/31/2009	Qtr 1
4	9/1/2009	9/30/2009	Qtr 2
5	10/1/2009	10/31/2009	Qtr 2
6	11/1/2009	11/30/2009	Qtr 2
7	12/1/2009	12/31/2009	Qtr 3
8	1/1/2010	1/31/2010	Qtr 3
9	2/1/2010	2/28/2010	Qtr 3
10	3/1/2010	3/31/2010	Qtr 4
11	4/1/2010	4/30/2010	Qtr 4
12	5/1/2010	5/31/2010	Qtr 4

Figure 9–47

10

Leveling Resource Assignments

One capability of Microsoft Project Professional is to level resource assignments automatically. When a resource is overallocated in their work assignments, and the resource managers want to eliminate as much of that overallocation as possible, the choices are to do it manually or to have the system do it for them. This chapter explains how resource leveling works. This is a function within Project Professional that basically works the same on Server as it does in the stand-alone version.

How resource leveling is performed is the topic of this chapter, but it is the authors' general recommendation that resource managers use this capability sparingly and discriminately. It has been our experience that the system's algorithms are mathematically correct and very logical; and, the algorithms can be quite complex when leveling multiple resources across multiple project files. However, the results are rarely what the resource manager expects to occur, and the end result is often a significantly time-expanded project file.

In most situations, a resource manager can manually level a resource's assignments to more accurately reflect their business needs than the system's algorithms. While the act of using the system's resource leveling is relatively straightforward, it is the setup behind the scenes that affects how the leveling actually works. For resource managers who constantly maintain this information, using the system for resource leveling will more closely represent what they would do manually. It is the initial setup, maintenance, and business needs that factor into whether or not a resource manager should manually or systematically accomplish their resources' leveling. After the example shown below, some leveling options will be explained in more detail.

At its most basic, the goal of resource leveling is to reduce resource overallocations to none. Leveling delays or splits tasks for resources, generic resources, and committed resources. Material and cost resources are not leveled. Proposed resources are not leveled by default, but can be selected.

An example can demonstrate the system's resource leveling capability. For instance, let's say that there are two project files and two resources. The project files are called The Project and Project 3. The resource names are simply Resource 1 and Resource 2. While viewing the following screenshots, it is important to note that The Project project file is originally set to 35 days for the five tasks (sequentially linked), which are assigned to both Resource 1 and Resource 2.

On the left side of Figure 10–1, in the indicator column, is a *person* icon. This indicator represents that one or more resources assigned to that task are overallocated. In this case, only one resource is assigned to the task so we know that Resource 1 is the overallocated resource.

Figure 10–2 shows the second project file, Project 3. Resource 1 has overlapping work based on the dates from this project file and The Project project file. Again, a little person icon appears in the left indicator column.

		Task Mode	Task Name	Duration	Start	Finish	Predecessors	Resource Names
0			The Project	**35 days**	**Mon 1/3/11**	**Fri 2/18/11**		
1			Task 1	5 days	Mon 1/3/11	Fri 1/7/11		Resource 1
2			Task 2	10 days	Mon 1/10/11	Fri 1/21/11	1	Resource 1
3			Task 3	5 days	Mon 1/24/11	Fri 1/28/11	2	Resource 2
4			Task 4	10 days	Mon 1/31/11	Fri 2/11/11	3	Resource 1
5			Task 5	5 days	Mon 2/14/11	Fri 2/18/11	4	Resource 2

Figure 10–1

		Task Mode	Task Name	Duration	Start	Finish	Predecessors	Resource Names	Ac
0			**Project3**	**88 days**	**Mon 1/3/11**	**Wed 5/4/11**			
1			Task 1	10 days	Mon 1/3/11	Fri 1/14/11		Resource 1	
2			Task 2	15 days	Mon 1/17/11	Fri 2/4/11	1	Resource 1	
3			Task 3	20 days	Mon 2/7/11	Fri 3/4/11	2	Resource 1	
4			Task 4	25 days	Mon 3/7/11	Fri 4/8/11	3	Resource 2	
5			Task 5	1 day	Mon 4/11/11	Mon 4/11/11	4	Resource 2	
6			Task 6	1 day	Tue 4/12/11	Tue 4/12/11	5	Resource 1	
7			Task 7	1 day	Wed 4/13/11	Wed 4/13/11	6	Resource 2	
8			Task 8	5 days	Thu 4/14/11	Wed 4/20/11	7	Resource 1	
9			Task 9	5 days	Thu 4/21/11	Wed 4/27/11	8	Resource 2	
10			Task 10	5 days	Thu 4/28/11	Wed 5/4/11	9	Resource 1	

Figure 10–2

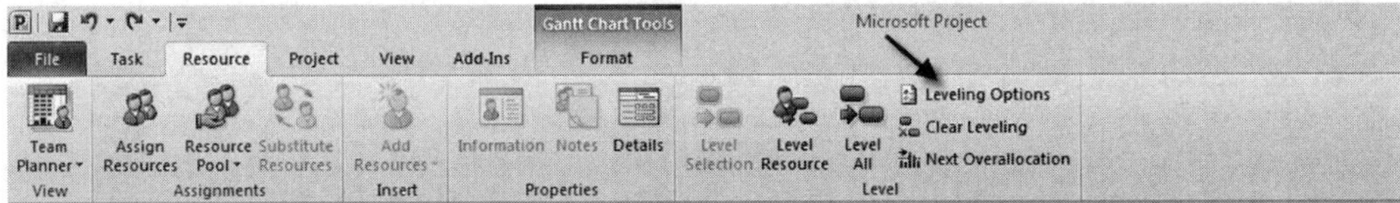

Figure 10–3

In Project Professional, in the resource Ribbon, is the Leveling Options icon, as shown in Figure 10–3. When that icon is selected, the Resource Leveling box appears.

As shown in Figure 10–4, the Resource Leveling box has three sections. The first section is to determine if leveling is performed automatically or manually.

Resource Leveling

Leveling calculations

Automatic ◉ Manual

Look for overallocations on a Day by Day basis

☑ Clear leveling values before leveling

Leveling range for 'The Project'

◉ Level entire project

Level From: Mon 1/3/11

To: Fri 2/18/11

Resolving overallocations

Leveling order: Standard

☐ Level only within available slack

☑ Leveling can adjust individual assignments on a task

☑ Leveling can create splits in remaining work

☐ Level resources with the proposed booking type

☑ Level manually scheduled tasks

Help | Clear Leveling... | Level All | OK | Cancel

Figure 10–4

The *Automatic* option means that the system will automatically level every time it finds an overallocation. The *Manual* option means that leveling will only occur when the resource manager requests it. The *Look for overallocations on a* option is to select the level of detail that the resource manager wants to level. The options are from "minute by minute" to "month by month." Since most project files are scheduled in day increments by default, "day to day" is the most common choice. The *Clear leveling values before leveling* check box is to clear out previous leveling delays.

The second section of the Resource Leveling box allows the resource manager to select a specific date range to use for leveling or to use the project file's entire date range. The third section contains the options to determine the order and the methodology of the leveling.

It is important to understand the drop-down options in the first line titled *Leveling order.* The options are ID only, Standard, and Priority, Standard. *ID only* means that the system uses the Task ID and starts with the higher ID number. *Standard* means that the system will level in this order:

- Task Dependencies
- Slack
- Start Date
- Priority
- Constraint

The third option, *Priority, Standard,* means that the system will level in this order:

- Priority
- Task Dependencies
- Slack
- Start Date
- Constraint

Here is a brief explanation of the other check boxes:

- **Level only within available slack:** This option will have the least effect on a project file as it assumes that slack exists and that resource overallocations can be made within that slack. Selecting this check box will often result in an error message, stating that the project file can't be leveled by the system, which would happen if there was no slack.

- **Leveling can adjust individual assignments on a task:** This option modifies when the resource works on a task independently of other tasks.
- **Leveling can create splits in remaining work:** This option allows for tasks to be split during leveling.
- **Level resources with the proposed booking type:** This option allows for leveling to modify proposed resources in addition to committed resources.
- **Level manually scheduled tasks:** This option will allow leveling to modify the dates on manually scheduled tasks, so it is important to think about this option since it might defeat the purpose of having a manually scheduled task if leveling can change the dates.

After the resource manager modifies the selection to the desired settings, selecting OK will save the option for when leveling is selected.

Figure 10–5 shows the Level Resource icon in the Resource Ribbon in Project Professional. Once this is selected, the Level Resources box appears.

Figure 10–6 shows the Level Resources box. The options are to select all the project files that are open and the resources. In the example, since we know that Resource 1 is the overallocated resource, that is the only one selected. Multiple resources can be selected if so desired.

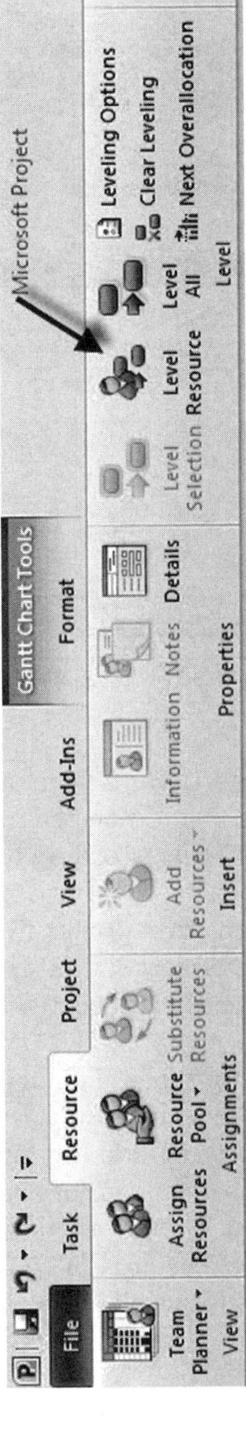
Microsoft Project
File
Task
Resource
Project
View
Add-Ins
Gantt Chart Tools
Format
Team Planner
Assign Resources
Resource Pool
Substitute Resources
Add Resources
Information
Notes
Details
Level Selection
Level Resource
Level All
Leveling Options
Clear Leveling
Next Overallocation
View
Assignments
Insert
Properties
Level

Figure 10–5

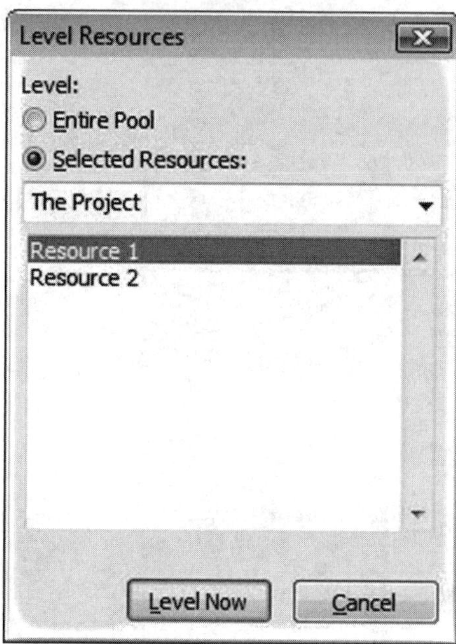

Figure 10–6

After clicking Level Now in the Level Resource box, the schedules will be modified according to settings that were selected in the Resource Leveling box. Note that the system worked correctly according to the algorithms and the selections. However, for this example, we only have two project files for Resource 1. As Figure 10–7 demonstrates, the first project file, The Project, went from 35 to 55 days. The second project file, Project 3, went from 88 days to 108 days. Also notice that the resource is no longer overallocated, and the little person icon is no longer in the indicator column.

This example of resource leveling is based on default settings for project and task priorities. On each task within a project file, the resource manager has the ability to set a priority. The priority field is the level of importance given to a task in relation to other tasks. The default priority is 500, with the range of the priority field between 0 and 1000. The lowest priority is 0 and the highest is 1000. This means that a task given a priority of 1000 will not be leveled because the task is such a high priority that it won't be split or moved based on resource

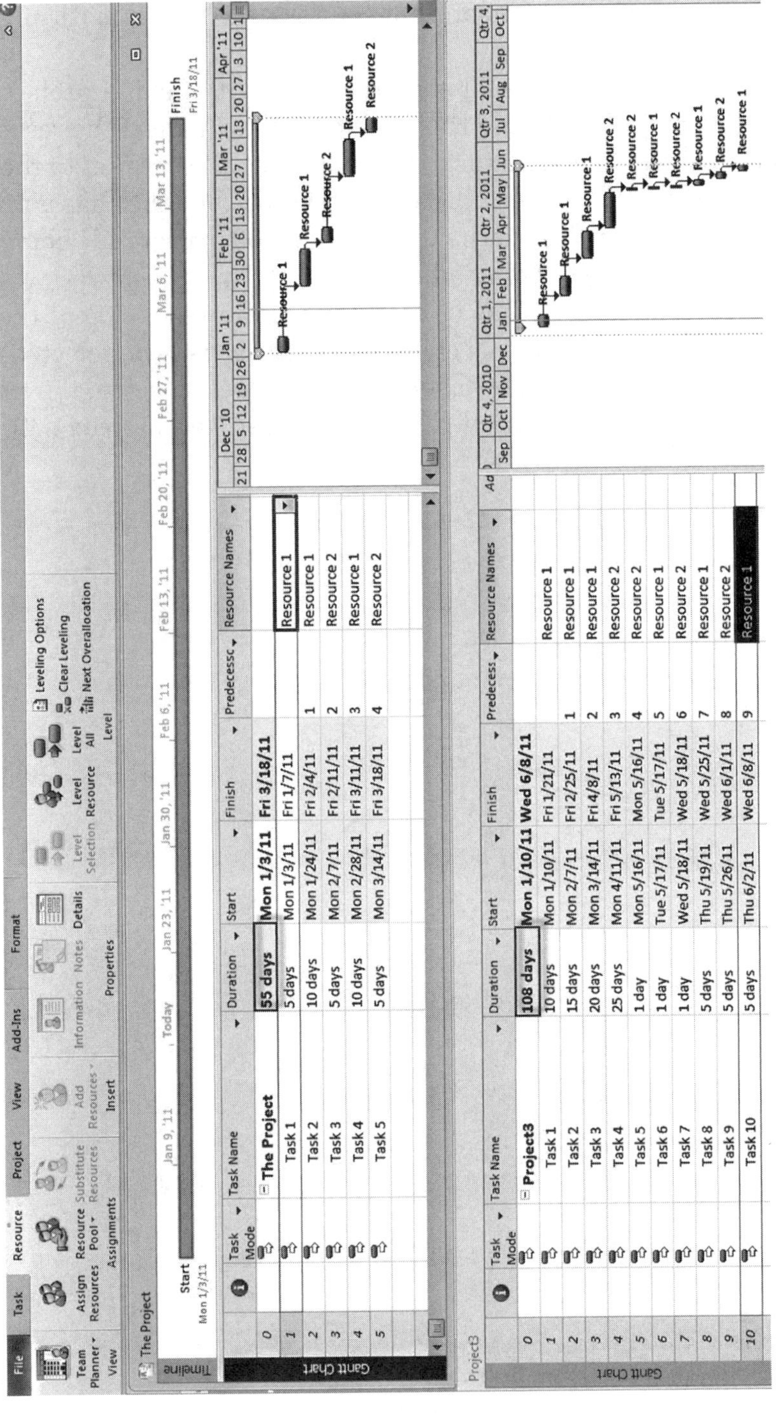

File
Task
Resource
Project
View
Add-Ins
Format
Team Planner
Assign Resources
Resource Pool
Substitute Resources
Add Resources
Information
Notes
Details
Level Selection
Level Resource
Level All
Leveling Options
Clear Leveling
Next Overallocation
View
Assignments
Insert
Properties
Level
The Project
Timeline
Start
Mon 1/3/11
Finish
Fri 3/18/11
Gantt Chart
Task Mode
Task Name
Duration
Start
Finish
Predecessors
Resource Names
0 The Project 55 days Mon 1/3/11 Fri 3/18/11
1 Task 1 5 days Mon 1/3/11 Fri 1/7/11 Resource 1
2 Task 2 10 days Mon 1/24/11 Fri 2/4/11 1 Resource 1
3 Task 3 5 days Mon 2/7/11 Fri 2/11/11 2 Resource 2
4 Task 4 10 days Mon 2/28/11 Fri 3/11/11 3 Resource 1
5 Task 5 5 days Mon 3/14/11 Fri 3/18/11 4 Resource 2
Project3
0 Project3 108 days Mon 1/10/11 Wed 6/8/11
1 Task 1 10 days Mon 1/10/11 Fri 1/21/11 Resource 1
2 Task 2 15 days Mon 2/7/11 Fri 2/25/11 1 Resource 1
3 Task 3 20 days Mon 3/14/11 Fri 4/8/11 2 Resource 1
4 Task 4 25 days Mon 4/11/11 Fri 5/13/11 3 Resource 2
5 Task 5 1 day Mon 5/16/11 Mon 5/16/11 4 Resource 2
6 Task 6 1 day Tue 5/17/11 Tue 5/17/11 5 Resource 1
7 Task 7 1 day Wed 5/18/11 Wed 5/18/11 6 Resource 2
8 Task 8 5 days Thu 5/19/11 Wed 5/25/11 7 Resource 1
9 Task 9 5 days Thu 5/26/11 Wed 6/1/11 8 Resource 2
10 Task 10 5 days Thu 6/2/11 Wed 6/8/11 9 Resource 1

Figure 10–7

leveling. A priority of 20 would mean that the task can be dramatically moved, based upon resource leveling.

The same principle holds true for the project priority field. A project file can be set to a priority of 0 to 1000, and the priority field will affect the resource leveling function. For example, if all tasks in two project files are set to the default of 500, but one project file has a priority of 300 while the other has a priority of 1000, that setting would result in the tasks in the 300 priority file being moved, but tasks in the 1000 file not being adjusted.

It is also important to note that in the Manage Users section of the Server Settings in Project Server, there is a check box that needs to be selected for each resource so that their tasks can be leveled. If this is not selected, the resource's tasks won't be leveled, regardless of resource leveling and priority settings.

11

Utilizing Resources

Key questions that resource managers ask are, when and where are resources working, and what specific tasks are they working on? Along with these, are questions about the capacity and utilization of those resources. The resources themselves may have the same questions about their own assignments.

The ways to discover this information is quite a bit different, depending on whether or not you are using Project Professional stand-alone or Project Server. With Project Server, the first step is to go to the Resource Center and select the resource names that you want to view. In Chapter 12, we discuss how to customize those views to better meet the needs for information, but for now we will use default views.

The Resource Center

Figure 11–1 shows the Resource Center with the list of resources in the middle of the screen and the resources that we have selected to review on the right side of the screen. In this case, we selected a total of five resources. Two of them are named resources, and three are generic resources.

After selecting the resources, select the Resource Availability icon from the Ribbon, as shown in Figure 11–2.

Resources

System Account ▾

Open | Outline | View: All Resources | Filter: No Filter | Group By: Type | Data

Selected Resources | Time with Date | Show/Hide

Export to Excel | Print | Share

Resource Assignments | Resource Availability | Navigate

	Resource Name	ID	Checked Out	Email Address	Generic
	⊟ **Type: Work**		**No**		
☑	Aaron Painter	152	No	AaronP@contoso	No
☑	Accountant	27	No		Yes
☑	Adam Barr	50	No	adamb@contoso.	No
☐	Amy Strande	51	No	amys@contoso.c	No
☐	Analyst	28	No		Yes
☐	Ari Bixhorn	52	No	arib@contoso.co	No
☐	Attila Biber	53	No	attilab@contoso.	No
☐	Barry Johnson	54	No	barryj@contoso.	No
☐	Ben Spain	55	No	bens@contoso.c	No
☐	Brian Burke	56	No	brianb@contoso.	No
☐	Brian Groth	155	No	briang@contoso.	No
☐	Brian Perry	57	No	brianp@contoso.	No
☐	Carol Troup	58	No	CarolT@contoso	No
☐	Catherine Boeger	59	No	catherineb@cont	No
☐	Chris Barry	60	No	chrisb@contoso.	No
☐	Chris Gray	61	No	chrisg@contoso.	No
☐	Consultant	29	No		Yes
☐	Contoso Administrator	6	No	Administrator@c	No
☐	Creative Designer	30	No		Yes
☐	Customer	31	No		Yes
☐	David Pelton	62	No	davidp@contoso.	No
☐	Denise Smith	63	No	denises@contos	No
☐	Developer	32	No		Yes
☐	Dimple Arya	64	No	dimplea@contos	No

Selected Resources
Aaron Painter
Accountant
Adam Barr
Tester
Trainer

ce

Figure 11–1

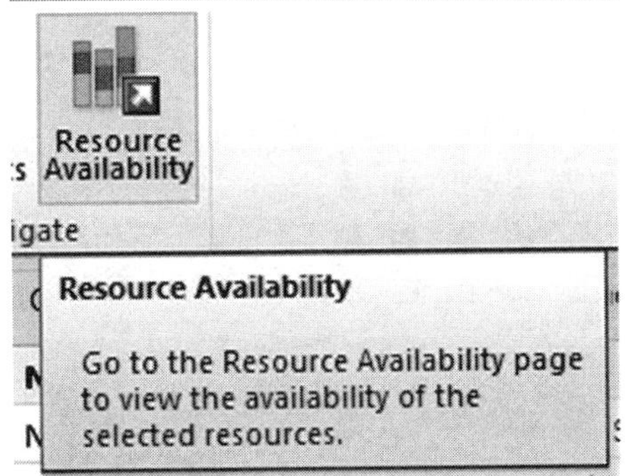

Figure 11–2

After clicking on the Resource Availability icon, the default view for that screen will open. In Figure 11–3, that view is the Assignment Work by Resource view. It is important to note that this is in "real time." If a project file was created and published before selecting this screen, the update assignment work by resource information will appear.

This is an important screen with lots of information, so let's take a moment to review it. On the right side, the resources that we selected have a check box next to them. This means that all of these resources listed are being viewed in the graph in the middle of the screen. Each resource is color coded to more easily visualize their utilization on the graph.

The graph in the middle of the screen has a capacity line. In this example, all of the resources are on a default standard calendar so they work Monday through Friday, 8 hours per day. The capacity line is cumulative, and five resources mean that there are 40 hours of cumulative working capacity per day. Notice that there is no capacity on Saturday and Sunday, but we also have no assignments on those days.

Also notice that in the second and third weeks of this graph, there is excess capacity. This means that there is more time available for these resources than there are resource assignments. However, it appears that most of the time utilized in those weeks is that of the Trainer. We will dive deeper into the Trainer's capacity and utilization in the next few screenshots.

The last part of this screen that we want to highlight is at bottom right: View Options. Figure 11–4 shows the Date Range selected for this view, the Units available, and the critical *Include proposed bookings* check box. This check box will determine if we decide to include proposed bookings, or not. It is important

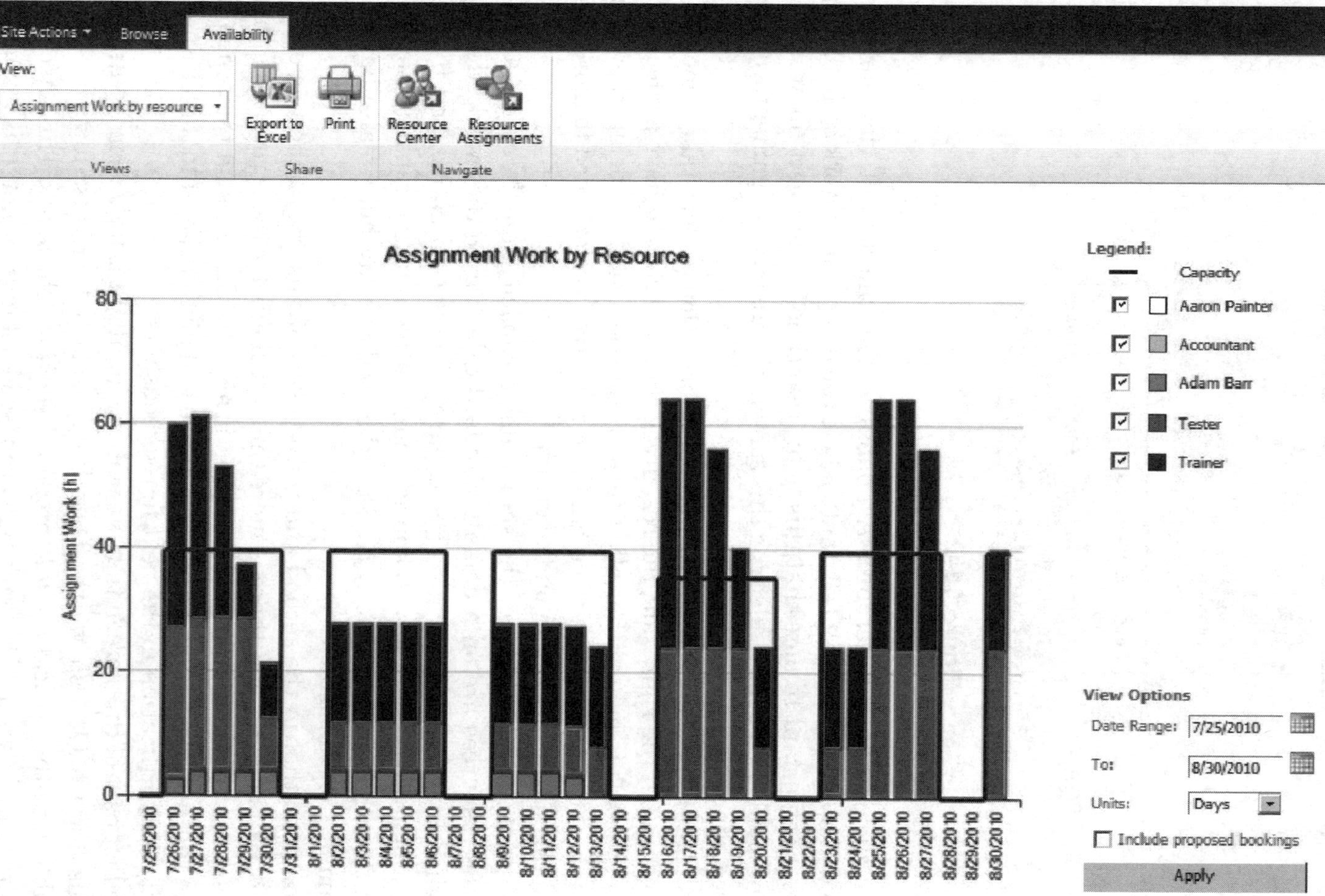
Site Actions
Browse
Availability
View:
Assignment Work by resource
Export to Excel
Print
Resource Center
Resource Assignments
Views
Share
Navigate
Assignment Work by Resource
Assignment Work (h)
80
60
40
20
0
7/25/2010
7/26/2010
7/27/2010
7/28/2010
7/29/2010
7/30/2010
7/31/2010
8/1/2010
8/2/2010
8/3/2010
8/4/2010
8/5/2010
8/6/2010
8/7/2010
8/8/2010
8/9/2010
8/10/2010
8/11/2010
8/12/2010
8/13/2010
8/14/2010
8/15/2010
8/16/2010
8/17/2010
8/18/2010
8/19/2010
8/20/2010
8/21/2010
8/22/2010
8/23/2010
8/24/2010
8/25/2010
8/26/2010
8/27/2010
8/28/2010
8/29/2010
8/30/2010
Legend:
Capacity
Aaron Painter
Accountant
Adam Barr
Tester
Trainer
View Options
Date Range: 7/25/2010
To: 8/30/2010
Units: Days
Include proposed bookings
Apply

Figure 11–3

because if we have resources set with that booking type, or if we have proposals with those types of resources, we need to understand whether or not that information is reflected in this view.

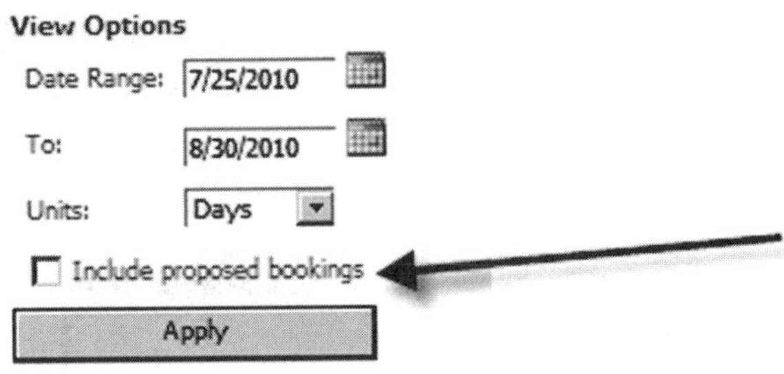

Figure 11–4

Figure 11–5 shows the options that are available to us in the Units section. While this example shows Days, it may be more beneficial to see the data in a different format, particularly when looking at a large date range.

Figure 11–5

Since we noticed that the Trainer might have a lion's share of the work in the second and third week of this graph, we will modify the view—without having to go to any other views. Just by de-selecting the other resource names and only leaving the Trainer resource selected, the graph will change. Notice that the capacity line has changed to 8 hours. It also appears that in the date range, the generic resource called Trainer is seriously overallocated, as shown in Figure 11–6. It also appears that the Trainer is overallocated for all the weeks of the selected Date Range, not just the second and third weeks.

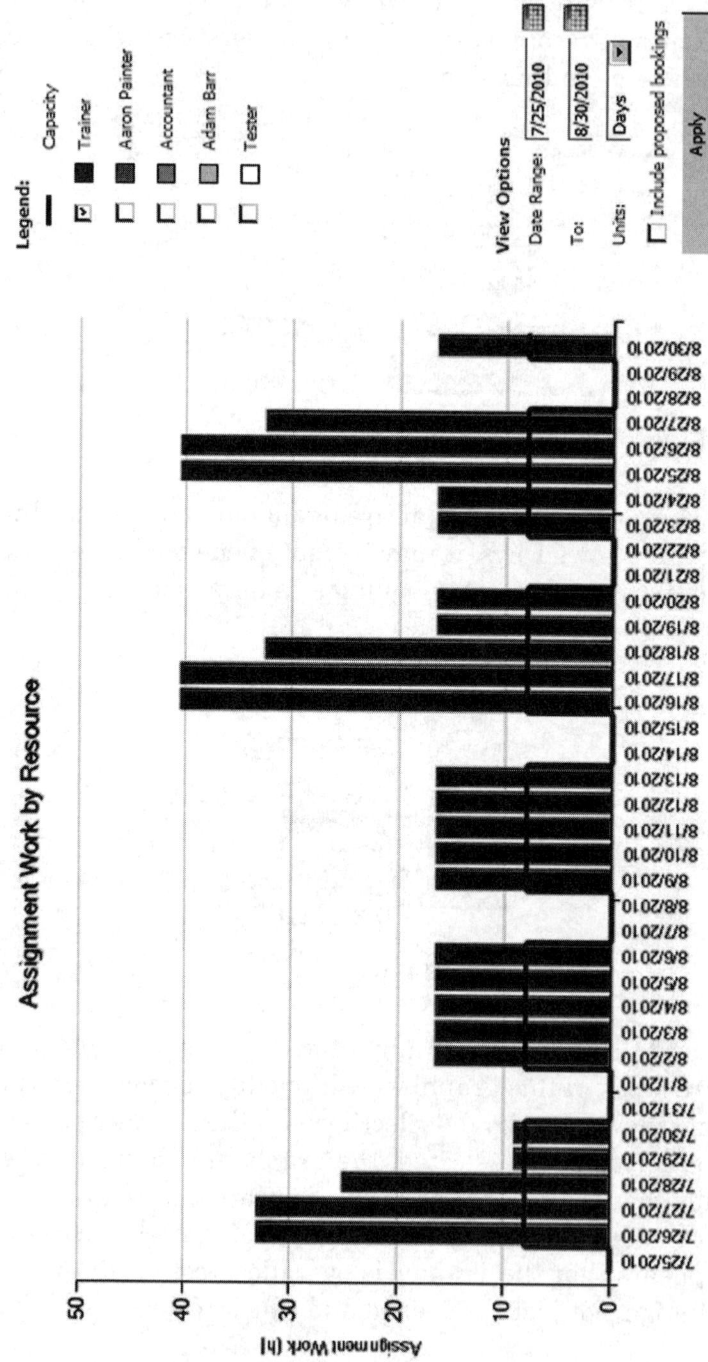
Assignment Work by Resource
Assignment Work (h)
0
10
20
30
40
50
7/25/2010
7/26/2010
7/27/2010
7/28/2010
7/29/2010
7/30/2010
7/31/2010
8/1/2010
8/2/2010
8/3/2010
8/4/2010
8/5/2010
8/6/2010
8/7/2010
8/8/2010
8/9/2010
8/10/2010
8/11/2010
8/12/2010
8/13/2010
8/14/2010
8/15/2010
8/16/2010
8/17/2010
8/18/2010
8/19/2010
8/20/2010
8/21/2010
8/22/2010
8/23/2010
8/24/2010
8/25/2010
8/26/2010
8/27/2010
8/28/2010
8/29/2010
8/30/2010
Legend:
Capacity
Trainer
Aaron Painter
Accountant
Adam Barr
Tester
View Options
Date Range: 7/25/2010
To: 8/30/2010
Units: Days
Include proposed bookings
Apply

Figure 11–6

To this point, we have only shown the top half of this view. The bottom half shows the graphical information in a data format, as in Figure 11–7. The data is broken out by resource name, availability, capacity, and the name of the project files where work is assigned in the rows and the date range appears in the columns.

In this case, we are interested in the Trainer. So, we will look at the detailed information for the Trainer for the first week of the date range. In Figure 11–8 we can see that the Trainer has a daily capacity of 8 hours, but is currently at an availability of –25.067 hours *per day*. That means that the Trainer is assigned 33.067 hours a day and we have to determine where. When looking at the data, it appears that the project file named *Warehouse Pick-n-Pack solution* is the culprit—with 24 hours being assigned per 8 hour day.

From this view, we can go directly to the list of assignments and look at the details of the file Warehouse Pick-n-Pack solution, and see exactly what tasks are being assigned. To do so, we select the Resource Assignments icon in the Ribbon at the top of the view, as shown in Figure 11–9.

This will open the assignments view with the project file information. Since we had five resources selected at first and we left this view when we selected the Trainer, all five of those resources' assignment information details are being displayed, as shown in Figure 11–10.

We want to look specifically at the Warehouse Pick-n-Pack solution project file to see what tasks are assigned to the Trainer. As shown in Figure 11–11, for the first week of the date range that we selected earlier, the tasks are:

- Develop training specifications for end users.
- Develop training specifications for help-desk support staff.
- Identify training delivery methodology.

We can see that the resource is assigned anywhere from 16 to 24 hours *per day*. Therefore, we can see that we need to do something with these assignments to solve this overallocation. The resource manager will need to manage this work, along with the other assignments for the same date range, and the various project file priorities to determine what needs to be done.

Stand-alone Resource Pool

The stand-alone method of using Project Professional is a bit more difficult to use to get capacity and utilization information. The best method is to use a

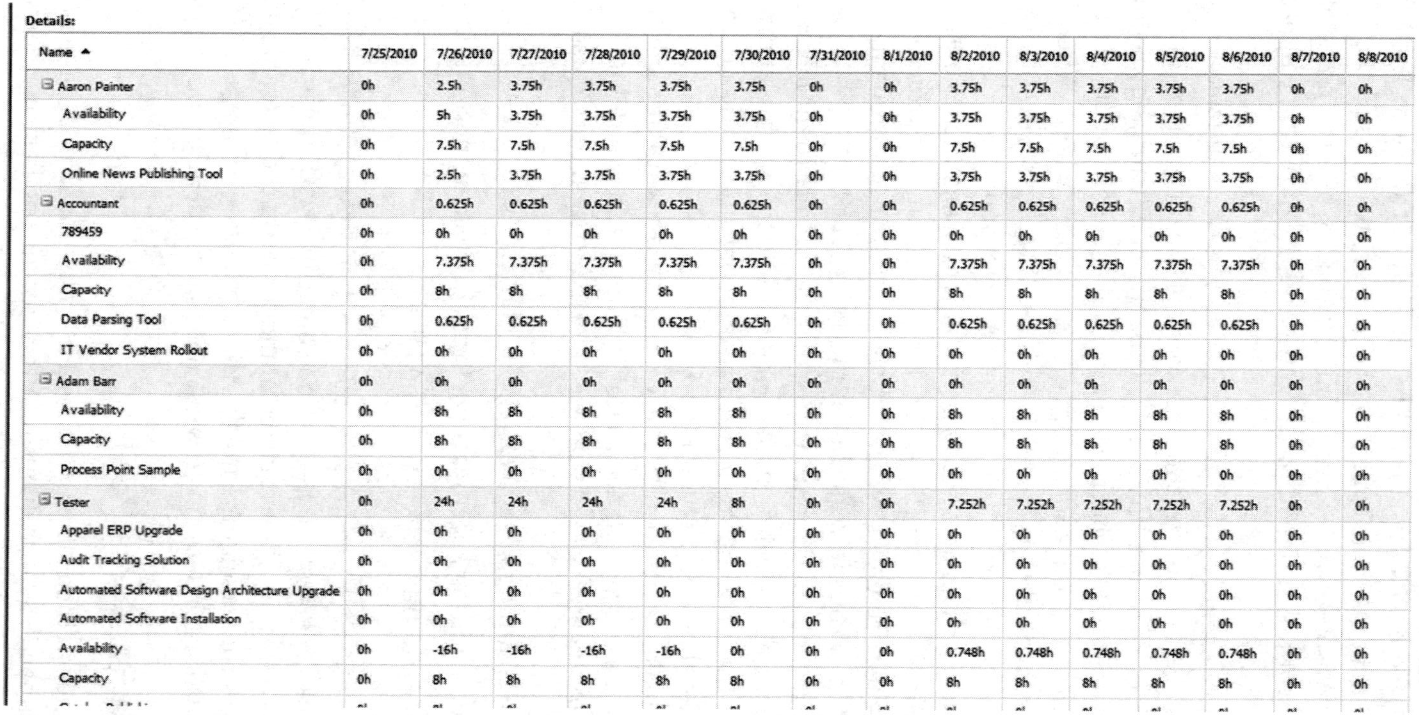

Details:

Name ▲	7/25/2010	7/26/2010	7/27/2010	7/28/2010	7/29/2010	7/30/2010	7/31/2010	8/1/2010	8/2/2010	8/3/2010	8/4/2010	8/5/2010	8/6/2010	8/7/2010	8/8/2010
⊟ Aaron Painter	0h	2.5h	3.75h	3.75h	3.75h	3.75h	0h	0h	3.75h	3.75h	3.75h	3.75h	3.75h	0h	0h
Availability	0h	5h	3.75h	3.75h	3.75h	3.75h	0h	0h	3.75h	3.75h	3.75h	3.75h	3.75h	0h	0h
Capacity	0h	7.5h	7.5h	7.5h	7.5h	7.5h	0h	0h	7.5h	7.5h	7.5h	7.5h	7.5h	0h	0h
Online News Publishing Tool	0h	2.5h	3.75h	3.75h	3.75h	3.75h	0h	0h	3.75h	3.75h	3.75h	3.75h	3.75h	0h	0h
⊟ Accountant	0h	0.625h	0.625h	0.625h	0.625h	0.625h	0h	0h	0.625h	0.625h	0.625h	0.625h	0.625h	0h	0h
789459	0h	0h	0h	0h	0h	0h	0h	0h	0h	0h	0h	0h	0h	0h	0h
Availability	0h	7.375h	7.375h	7.375h	7.375h	7.375h	0h	0h	7.375h	7.375h	7.375h	7.375h	7.375h	0h	0h
Capacity	0h	8h	8h	8h	8h	8h	0h	0h	8h	8h	8h	8h	8h	0h	0h
Data Parsing Tool	0h	0.625h	0.625h	0.625h	0.625h	0.625h	0h	0h	0.625h	0.625h	0.625h	0.625h	0.625h	0h	0h
IT Vendor System Rollout	0h	0h	0h	0h	0h	0h	0h	0h	0h	0h	0h	0h	0h	0h	0h
⊟ Adam Barr	0h	0h	0h	0h	0h	0h	0h	0h	0h	0h	0h	0h	0h	0h	0h
Availability	0h	8h	8h	8h	8h	8h	0h	0h	8h	8h	8h	8h	8h	0h	0h
Capacity	0h	8h	8h	8h	8h	8h	0h	0h	8h	8h	8h	8h	8h	0h	0h
Process Point Sample	0h	0h	0h	0h	0h	0h	0h	0h	0h	0h	0h	0h	0h	0h	0h
⊟ Tester	0h	24h	24h	24h	24h	8h	0h	0h	7.252h	7.252h	7.252h	7.252h	7.252h	0h	0h
Apparel ERP Upgrade	0h	0h	0h	0h	0h	0h	0h	0h	0h	0h	0h	0h	0h	0h	0h
Audit Tracking Solution	0h	0h	0h	0h	0h	0h	0h	0h	0h	0h	0h	0h	0h	0h	0h
Automated Software Design Architecture Upgrade	0h	0h	0h	0h	0h	0h	0h	0h	0h	0h	0h	0h	0h	0h	0h
Automated Software Installation	0h	0h	0h	0h	0h	0h	0h	0h	0h	0h	0h	0h	0h	0h	0h
Availability	0h	-16h	-16h	-16h	-16h	0h	0h	0h	0.748h	0.748h	0.748h	0.748h	0.748h	0h	0h
Capacity	0h	8h	8h	8h	8h	8h	0h	0h	8h	8h	8h	8h	8h	0h	0h

Figure 11–7

⊟ Trainer	0h	33.067h	33.067h	25.067h	9.067h	9.067h
Apparel ERP Upgrade	0h	0h	0h	0h	0h	0h
Audit Tracking Solution	0h	0h	0h	0h	0h	0h
Auditing Services Training	0h	0.4h	0.4h	0.4h	0.4h	0.4h
Automated Software Design Architecture Upgrade	0h	0h	0h	0h	0h	0h
Availability	0h	-25.067h	-25.067h	-17.067h	-1.067h	-1.067h
Capacity	0h	8h	8h	8h	8h	8h
Catalog Publishing	0h	0h	0h	0h	0h	0h
Corporate Web Site Server Software Upgrade	0h	0h	0h	0h	0h	0h
Data Exchange and Integration	0h	0h	0h	0h	0h	0h
E-commerce Portal Development	0h	0h	0h	0h	0h	0h
Employee Retention Tracking System	0h	0h	0h	0h	0h	0h
EPM Software Implementation	0h	0h	0h	0h	0h	0h
ERP System Equipment Upgrade	0h	0h	0h	0h	0h	0h
Voice Recognition Software	0h	0h	0h	0h	0h	0h
Warehouse Inventory Tracking Upgrade	0h	0h	0h	0h	0h	0h
Warehouse Pick-n-Pack solution	0h	24h	24h	16h	0h	0h
Warranty Tracking Database Upgrade	0h	0h	0h	0h	0h	0h

Figure 11–8

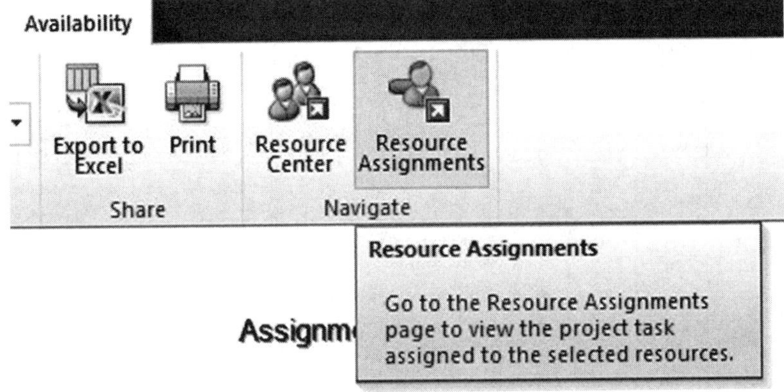

Figure 11–9

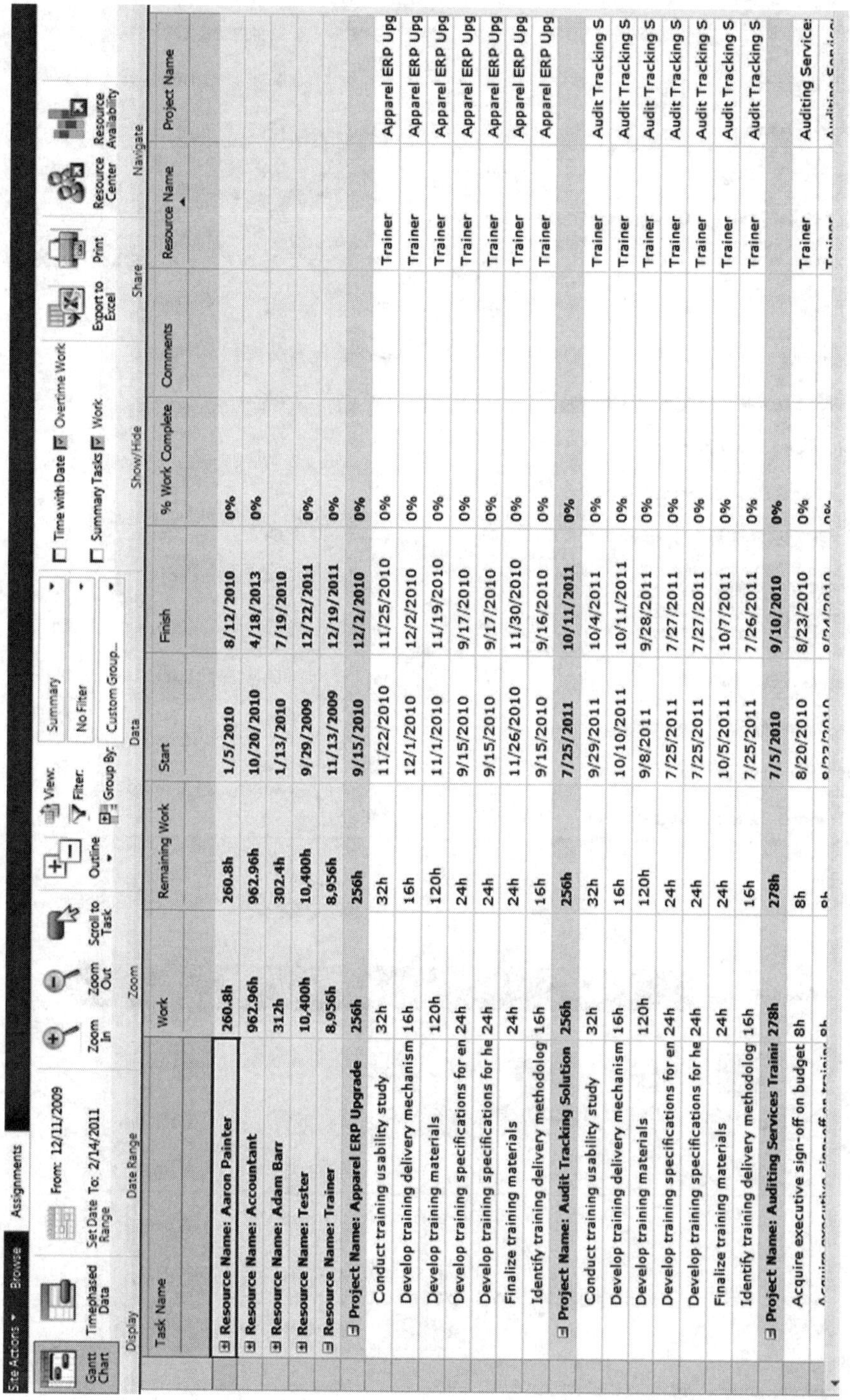

Site Actions ▾ Browse Assignments

Gantt Chart | Timephased Data | Set Date Range From: 12/11/2009 To: 2/14/2011 | Zoom In | Zoom Out | Scroll to Task | Outline | View: Summary | Filter: No Filter | Group By: Custom Group... | Time with Date | Overtime Work | Summary Tasks | Work | Export to Excel | Print | Resource Center | Resource Availability

Display | Date Range | Zoom | Data | Show/Hide | Share | Navigate

Task Name	Work	Remaining Work	Start	Finish	% Work Complete	Comments	Resource Name	Project Name
⊞ Resource Name: Aaron Painter	**260.8h**	**260.8h**	**1/5/2010**	**8/12/2010**	**0%**			
⊞ Resource Name: Accountant	**962.96h**	**962.96h**	**10/20/2010**	**4/18/2013**	**0%**			
⊞ Resource Name: Adam Barr	**312h**	**302.4h**	**1/13/2010**	**7/19/2010**				
⊞ Resource Name: Tester	**10,400h**	**10,400h**	**9/29/2009**	**12/22/2011**	**0%**			
⊟ Resource Name: Trainer	**8,956h**	**8,956h**	**11/13/2009**	**12/19/2011**	**0%**			
⊟ Project Name: Apparel ERP Upgrade	**256h**	**256h**	**9/15/2010**	**12/2/2010**	**0%**			
Conduct training usability study	32h	32h	11/22/2010	11/25/2010	0%		Trainer	Apparel ERP Upg
Develop training delivery mechanism	16h	16h	12/1/2010	12/2/2010	0%		Trainer	Apparel ERP Upg
Develop training materials	120h	120h	11/1/2010	11/19/2010	0%		Trainer	Apparel ERP Upg
Develop training specifications for en	24h	24h	9/15/2010	9/17/2010	0%		Trainer	Apparel ERP Upg
Develop training specifications for he	24h	24h	9/15/2010	9/17/2010	0%		Trainer	Apparel ERP Upg
Finalize training materials	24h	24h	11/26/2010	11/30/2010	0%		Trainer	Apparel ERP Upg
Identify training delivery methodolog	16h	16h	9/15/2010	9/16/2010	0%		Trainer	Apparel ERP Upg
⊟ Project Name: Audit Tracking Solution	**256h**	**256h**	**7/25/2011**	**10/11/2011**	**0%**			
Conduct training usability study	32h	32h	9/29/2011	10/4/2011	0%		Trainer	Audit Tracking S
Develop training delivery mechanism	16h	16h	10/10/2011	10/11/2011	0%		Trainer	Audit Tracking S
Develop training materials	120h	120h	9/8/2011	9/28/2011	0%		Trainer	Audit Tracking S
Develop training specifications for en	24h	24h	7/25/2011	7/27/2011	0%		Trainer	Audit Tracking S
Develop training specifications for he	24h	24h	7/25/2011	7/27/2011	0%		Trainer	Audit Tracking S
Finalize training materials	24h	24h	10/5/2011	10/7/2011	0%		Trainer	Audit Tracking S
Identify training delivery methodolog	16h	16h	7/25/2011	7/26/2011	0%		Trainer	Audit Tracking S
⊟ Project Name: Auditing Services Trainin	**278h**	**278h**	**7/5/2010**	**9/10/2010**	**0%**			
Acquire executive sign-off on budget	8h	8h	8/20/2010	8/23/2010	0%		Trainer	Auditing Service

Figure 11–10

	Identify training delivery methodology (computer based training,	16h	16h	11/13/2009	11/16/2009	0%
	⊟ Project Name: Warehouse Pick-n-Pack solution	**256h**	**256h**	**7/26/2010**	**10/12/2010**	**0%**
	Conduct training usability study	32h	32h	9/30/2010	10/5/2010	0%
	Develop training delivery mechanism	16h	16h	10/11/2010	10/12/2010	0%
	Develop training materials	120h	120h	9/9/2010	9/29/2010	0%
	Develop training specifications for end users	24h	24h	7/26/2010	7/28/2010	0%
	Develop training specifications for helpdesk support staff	24h	24h	7/26/2010	7/28/2010	0%
	Finalize training materials	24h	24h	10/6/2010	10/8/2010	0%
	Identify training delivery methodology (computer based training,	16h	16h	7/26/2010	7/27/2010	0%
	⊟ Project Name: Warranty Tracking Database Upgrade	**256h**	**256h**	**2/21/2011**	**5/10/2011**	**0%**

Figure 11–11

		Resource Name	Type	Material	Initials	Group	Max.	Std. Rate	Ovt. Rate	Cost/Use	Accrue At	Base Calendar	Code
1		Jessica	Work		J		100%	$0.00/hr	$0.00/hr	$0.00	Prorated	Standard	
2		Ryan	Work		R		100%	$0.00/hr	$0.00/hr	$0.00	Prorated	Standard	
3		Shelly	Work		S		100%	$0.00/hr	$0.00/hr	$0.00	Prorated	Standard	
4		Michael	Work		M		100%	$0.00/hr	$0.00/hr	$0.00	Prorated	Standard	
5		Chrystal	Work		C		100%	$0.00/hr	$0.00/hr	$0.00	Prorated	Standard	
6		Mercedes	Work		M		100%	$0.00/hr	$0.00/hr	$0.00	Prorated	Standard	
7		Nick	Work		N		100%	$0.00/hr	$0.00/hr	$0.00	Prorated	Standard	
8		Mario	Work		M		100%	$0.00/hr	$0.00/hr	$0.00	Prorated	Standard	

Figure 11–12

Resource Pool as discussed in Chapter 5. By using the Pool, all the information about a resource is in one place. This allows you to use the built-in or customized views for resources to see information.

The Resource Pool that we are using for this example is shown in Figure 11–12. Our first two resources, Jessica and Ryan, are both overallocated. The first indication is that they are a different color than the other resources in the list. The second indication is that they each have a diamond in the indicator column.

In Figure 11–13, you can see that by hovering over the diamond indicator, a message warns about an overallocation.

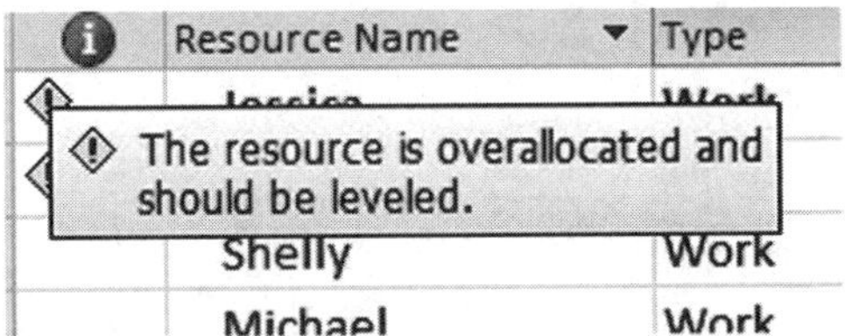

Figure 11–13

In Chapter 10, we discussed how to use the system to level a resource's assignments. However, at this point, we don't want to just level the resource, we want to investigate and determine what is causing the overallocation. Also, we still don't know the capacity of this resource or how overallocated the resource actually is.

In the Resource Usage view, you can look at the resource's assignments. We have modified the default view to include the Work Availability row and the Overallocation row to the Detail portion of this view. (In Chapter 12, we discuss how to modify views.) As seen in Figure 11–14, the resource named Jessica has a daily capacity (Work Availability) of 8 hours; for the week we are reviewing, she has 16 hours of work assigned and is overallocated by 8 hours.

Just as with the Project Server example in the beginning of this chapter, we still want to know exactly where the overallocation is coming from. To view that information, we can drill down on the resource name and view this information on a task basis. We have added the Project column to this view to better understand which project file each task is coming from. Figure 11–15 shows that Jessica is only overallocated on two tasks. She is assigned 8 hours each on two tasks (Task 4a and Task 4c) from the project file named Project 4.

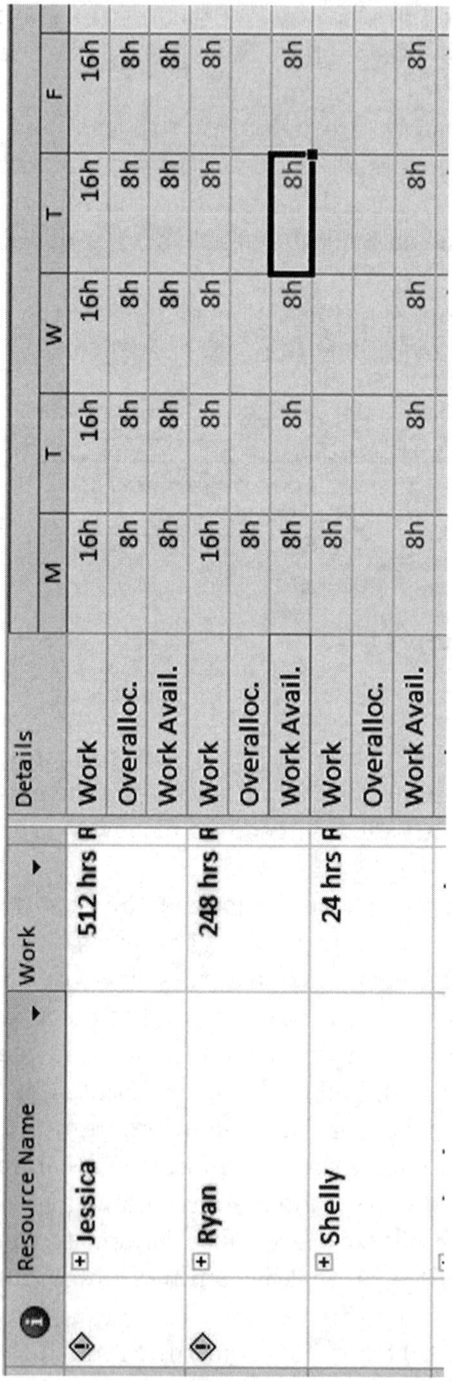

Resource Name	Work	Details	M	T	W	T	F
Jessica	512 hrs	Work	16h	16h	16h	16h	16h
		Overalloc.	8h	8h	8h	8h	8h
		Work Avail.	8h	8h	8h	8h	8h
Ryan	248 hrs	Work	16h	8h	8h	8h	8h
		Overalloc.	8h				
		Work Avail.	8h	8h	8h	8h	8h
Shelly	24 hrs	Work	8h				
		Overalloc.					
		Work Avail.	8h	8h	8h	8h	8h

Figure 11–14

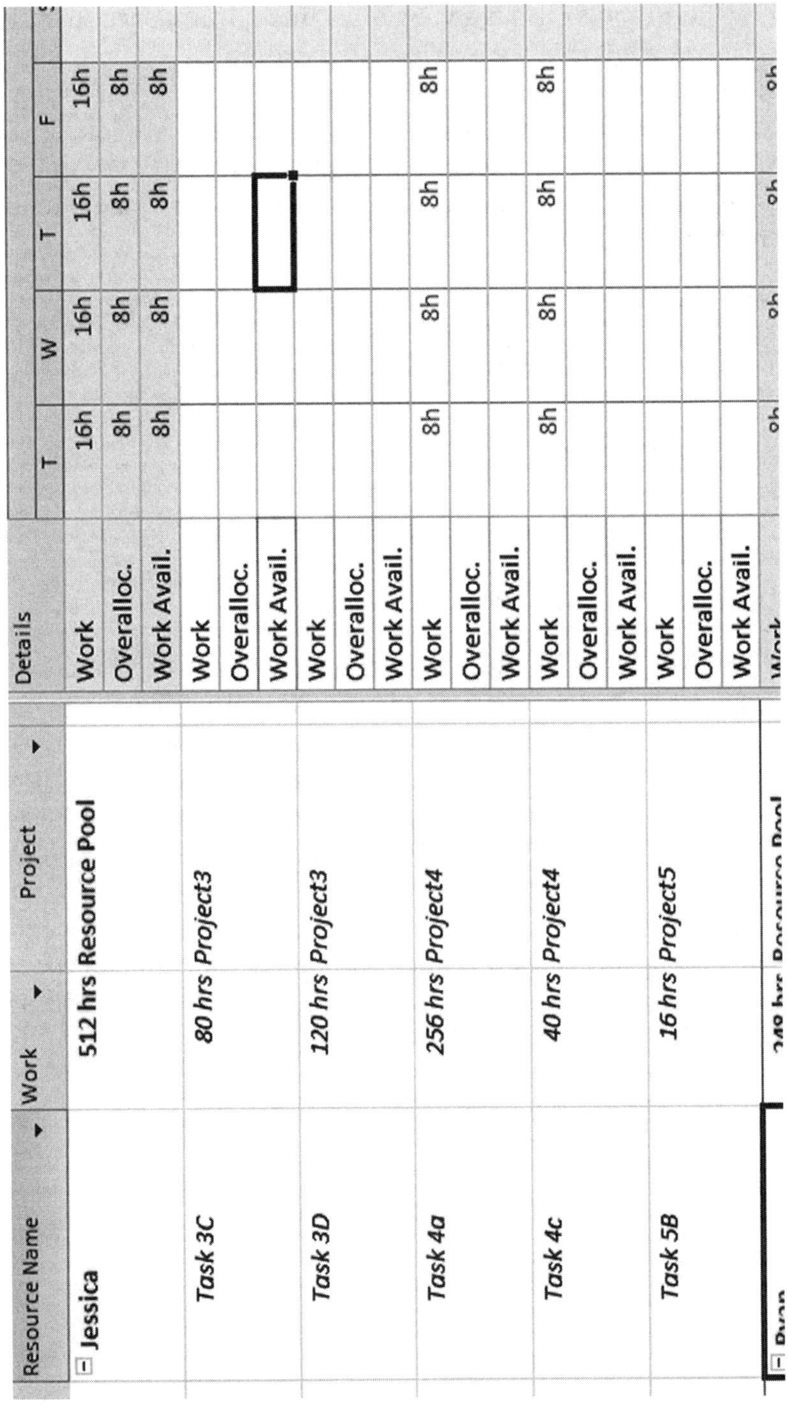

Resource Name	Work	Project	Details	T	W	T	F
⊟ Jessica	512 hrs	Resource Pool	Work	16h	16h	16h	16h
			Overalloc.	8h	8h	8h	8h
			Work Avail.	8h	8h	8h	8h
Task 3C	*80 hrs*	*Project3*	Work				
			Overalloc.				
			Work Avail.				
Task 3D	*120 hrs*	*Project3*	Work				
			Overalloc.				
			Work Avail.				
Task 4a	*256 hrs*	*Project4*	Work	8h	8h	8h	8h
			Overalloc.				
			Work Avail.				
Task 4c	*40 hrs*	*Project4*	Work	8h	8h	8h	8h
			Overalloc.				
			Work Avail.				
Task 5B	*16 hrs*	*Project5*	Work				
			Overalloc.				
			Work Avail.				
⊟ Ryan	248 hrs	Resource Pool	Work	8h	8h	8h	8h

Figure 11–15

In looking at the Resource Usage view a bit more, it appears that Ryan has plenty of free time during this week. This is an example of why it is important to drill down to view where the overallocations are occurring. Even though Ryan shows overallocated, he isn't overallocated during this week, and we may be able to transfer some of the work from Jessica to Ryan. The same week for Ryan appears in Figure 11–16, and it shows that he is available 8 hours every day and has nothing assigned.

Resource Name	Work	Project	Details	T	W	T	F
Ryan	**248 hrs**	**Resource Pool**	Work	8h	8h	8h	8h
			Overalloc.				
			Work Avail.	8h	8h	8h	8h
Task 3E	*40 hrs*	*Project3*	Work				
			Overalloc.				
			Work Avail.				

Figure 11–16

In Project Professional there is also a graph view similar to the Resource Availability view on Project Server. This view is called the Resource Graph, and it helps to see some overallocations. However, it isn't informative in relation to data when viewed by itself. In Figure 11–17, the Resource Graph is showing the overallocation based on percentages in relation to the amount of work availability. So, the middle of the screen is 100% capacity based on available time, and the top of this graph is at 200%.

Regardless of how you view the data, it is important to understand each resource's capacity and utilization. This information can provide the resource manager with details about *who* is overallocated and *when* this will affect the ability to complete work on time or effectively.

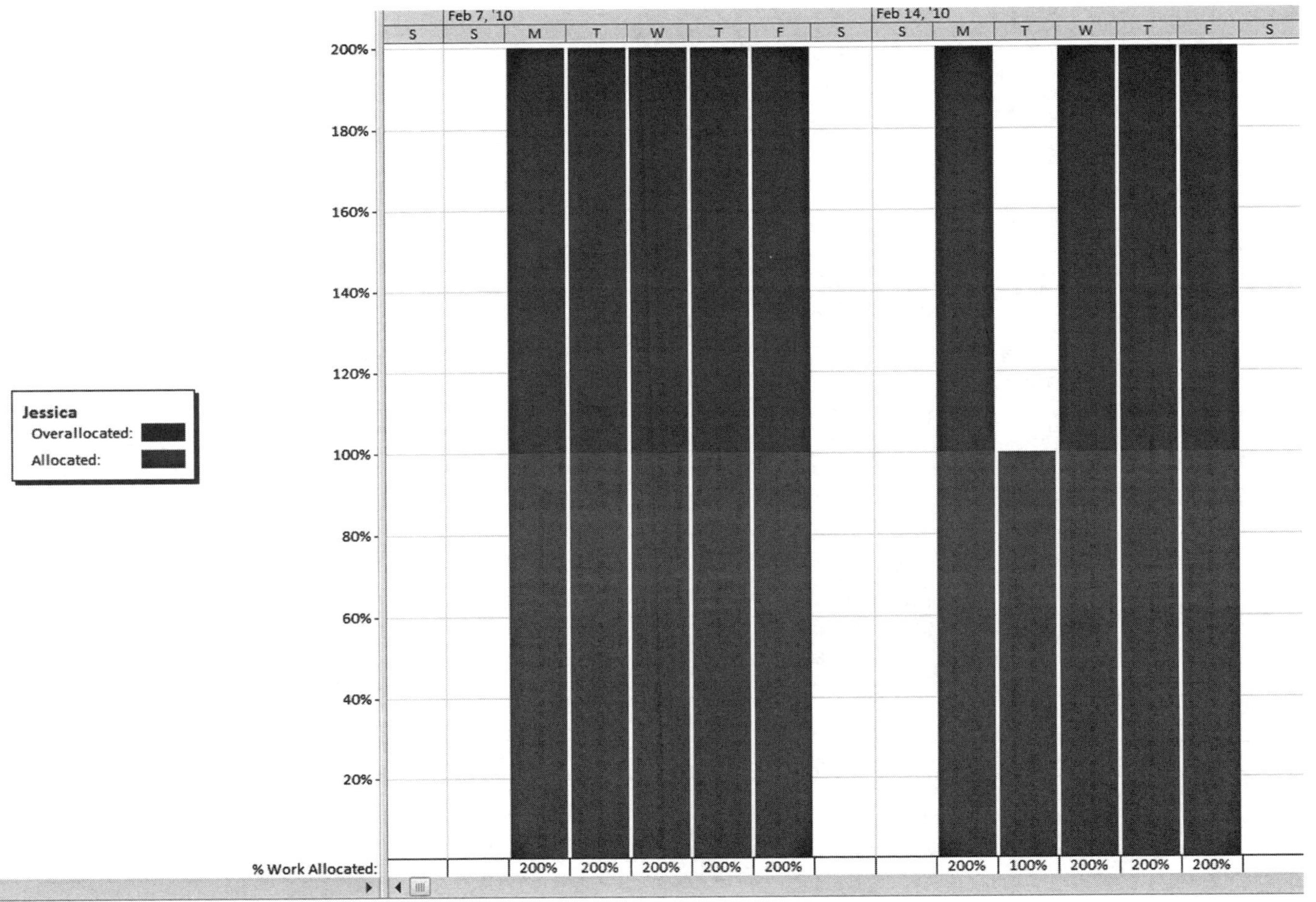
Feb 7, '10
Feb 14, '10
S
S
M
T
W
T
F
S
S
M
T
W
T
F
S
200%
180%
160%
140%
120%
100%
80%
60%
40%
20%
% Work Allocated:
200%
200%
200%
200%
200%
200%
100%
200%
200%
200%
Jessica
Overallocated:
Allocated:

Figure 11–17

12

Information Is Everywhere

The volume of information that can be contained in one single project file in Microsoft Project Professional 2010 can be overwhelming. Multiply that volume of information by the number of project files and proposals that have been created, and the entire amount of data can become indecipherable without proper and well-defined reporting.

Project Professional has reporting for each project file that can be comprehensive and customized to the needs of each type of user. There are volumes of documentation regarding how to setup and use reporting with Project Professional, but we want to demonstrate some resource specific information and to explain some of the terminology.

You do not have to be a database expert or a certified report writer to get information in Project Professional. Different people in an organization will have diverse needs and you may need to make multiple views or add columns to existing views for them.

In Chapter 5, we discussed the Resource Pool and how to add information for resources to that pool. The columns, fields, and tables that are part of the Resource Pool are what make up what is referred to as the Resource Global file. This is really a set of views and tables in the Enterprise Global template. The Enterprise Global template is what determines which settings Project Professional uses when it first opens. Every computer with Project Professional has a Global template, and users on Project Server will use the Global template that is provided by the Project Server. This is important to note because any changes made in Professional will be done on the local computer for the open project file unless specifically added to the Global template (whether locally or on the Server).

Views in Project Professional

For users who understand databases and reporting, some definitions of views are slightly different in Project Server than in Project Professional. In Professional, each piece of data resides in a *Field,* and each field resides in a *Table.* The tables are shown in a *View*. The fields are shown in *Columns*.

For example, if there is a resource named Catherine Rivera visible in the Resource Sheet, we might be looking at a row of information that looks like Figure 12–1.

In this example, the information is interpreted this way:

- **Data:** Catherine Rivera
- **Field:** Resource Name
- **Column:** Resource Name
- **View:** Resource Sheet
- **Table:** Entry

The information to determine the View and Table are easy to find. The left hand side of the screen will show the name of the view for which you are currently looking. In Figure 12–2 the name of the view is highlighted with an arrow.

Or, as shown in Figure 12–3, if you click on the icon in the View Group of the Resource Tab Ribbon, you can also see the name of the view checked.

From this drop-down, if you select the More Views option, a box will appear, listing all of the views, as shown in Figure 12–4. You now have the opportunity to create a new view, edit an existing view, or copy the view and make a new one. If you want to transfer the view to allow others to use it, you can use the Organizer to copy it to a network share, if on Project Professional, or to the Global file if on Project Server (and you have the appropriate permissions).

To see the table that a view is using, you can select the Edit button and look at the Table information. Note that, in Figure 12–5, along with the Table information is the ability to set a Group and/or Filter as well as to select whether or not this view is shown in the menu. It can be effective to uncheck this box if you have a view that you don't need right now, but don't want to permanently delete.

Resource Name	Type	Material	Initials	Group	Max.	Std. Rate	Ovt. Rate	Cost/Use	Accrue At	Base Calendar
Catherine Rivera	Work		C		100%	$0.00/hr	$0.00/hr	$0.00	Prorated	Standard
Victoria Rivera	Work		V		100%	$0.00/hr	$0.00/hr	$0.00	Prorated	Standard
Alexandra Rivera	Work		A		100%	$0.00/hr	$0.00/hr	$0.00	Prorated	Standard

Figure 12–1

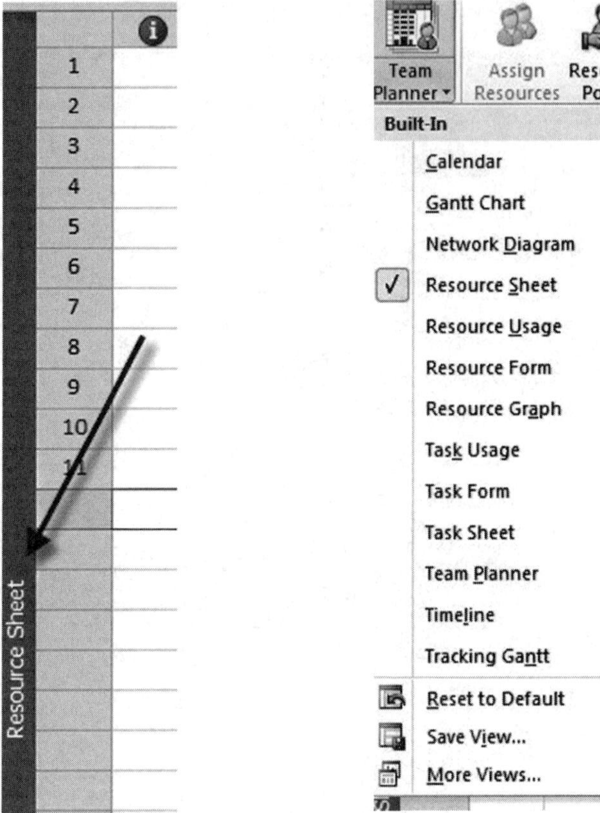

Figure 12–2 **Figure 12–3**

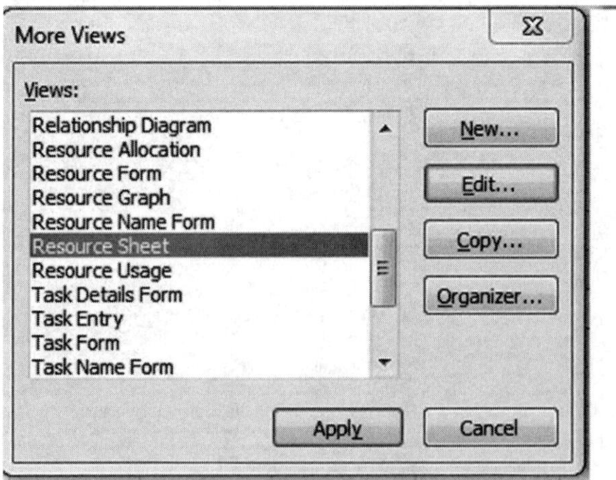

Figure 12–4

Figure 12–5

Just because a field isn't shown in the view doesn't mean that the field isn't in the table. For example, the field for the resource's e-mail is in the table. But, this column isn't in the default view. To add this column to the view, all you have to do is right click in the column headers area where you want to insert it, and select Insert Column from the drop-down, as shown in Figure 12–6.

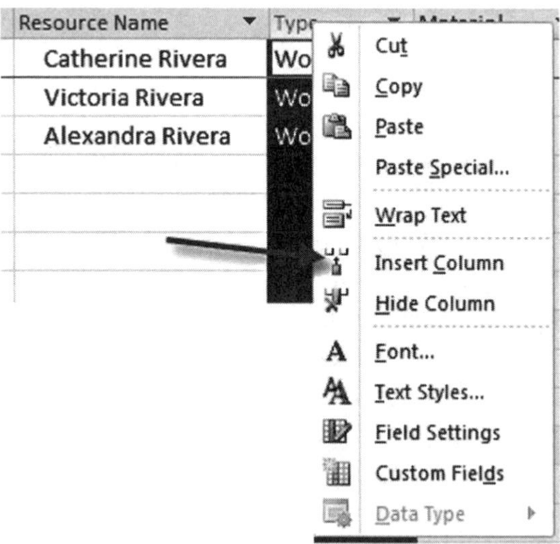

Figure 12–6

Figure 12–7 shows that in the drop down of available column names is the choice for Email Address. Selecting this will add it to the view.

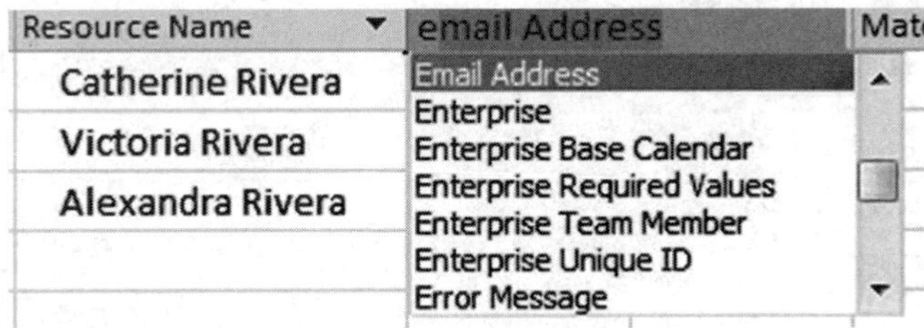

Figure 12–7

As Figure 12–8 shows, this column is now part of the view.

Resource Name	Email Address
Catherine Rivera	Catherine@pmpspecialists.com
Victoria Rivera	Victoria@pmpspecialists.com
Alexandra Rivera	Alexandra@pmpspecialists.com

Figure 12–8

Creating a New View

However, a selected column will *not* stay as part of the view beyond the current session. The next time that you open Project Professional and go to the Resource Sheet, the view is automatically set to the default. The way to have a selected column stay in a view is to either make it a new view or edit an existing view. To make it a new view, select Save View from the View Group drop-down options, shown in Figure 12–9.

After selecting the Save View option, the Name field appears to let you name this view whatever you want. In this example, we will call it *Res Sheet with Email*, which is shown in Figure 12–10.

Now that we have saved this as a new view, it will be available in the Custom section of the view group drop-down, shown in Figure 12–11.

Also, when a new view is created, a corresponding table is created as well. When looking at the View Definition box for the new view (Res Sheet with Email), we see that the Table has automatically become *Res Sheet with Email Table 1*, as shown in Figure 12–12.

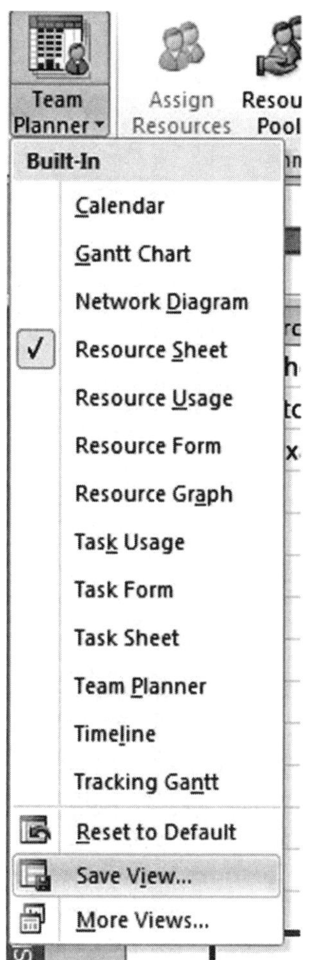

Figure 12–9

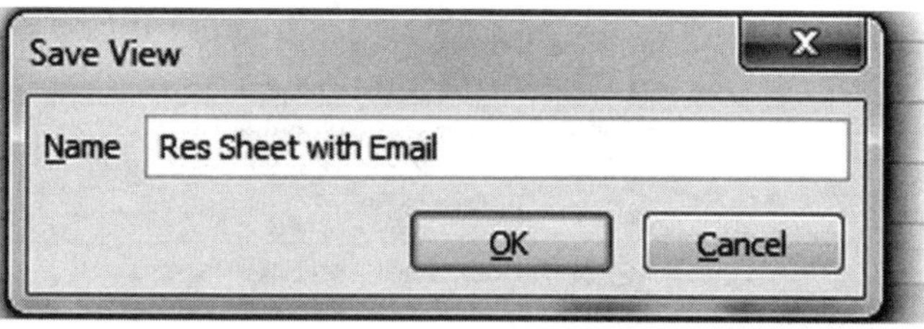

Figure 12–10

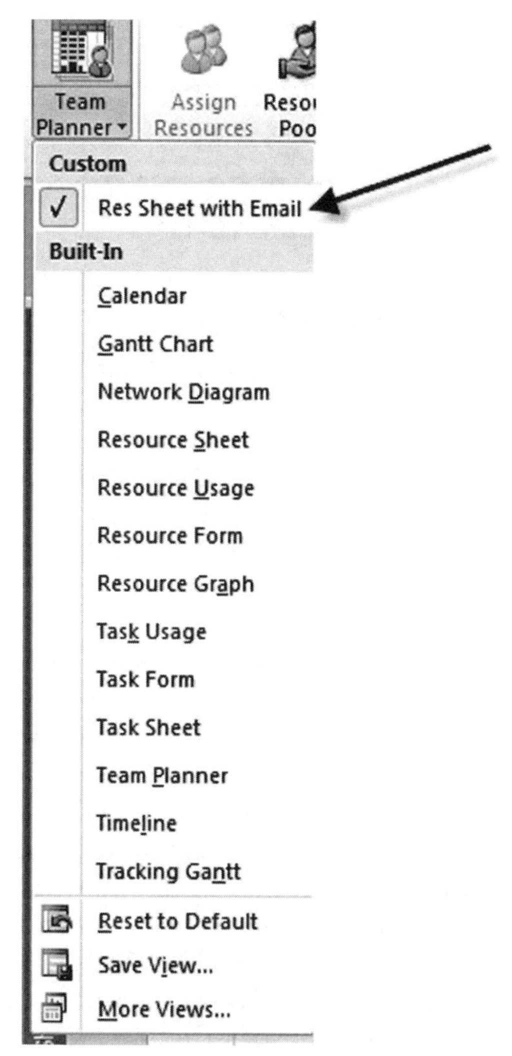

Figure 12–11

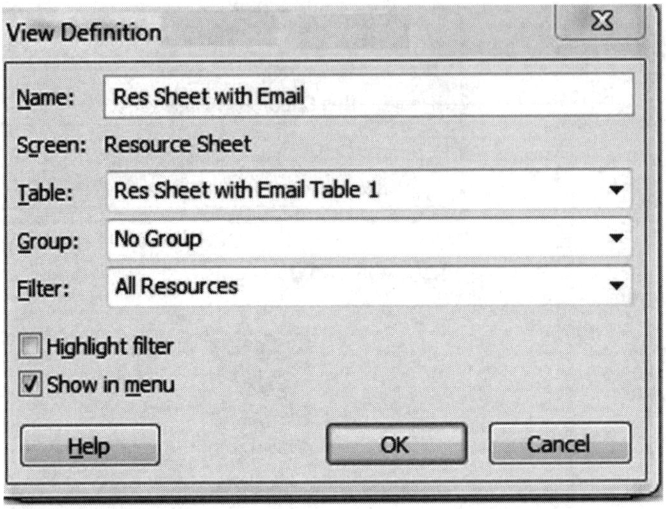

Figure 12–12

Editing an Existing View

The other option—to edit the existing view—is a little different. If you want to modify the existing view, you have to modify the table. So, to add the Email Address column to your Resource Sheet view, you will have to modify the Entry table. If you go to the Data Group of the View tab and select the Tables icon, the drop-down will appear with the option to select *More Tables*. In Figure 12–13, you can see that we have reverted back to the default Resource Sheet view without the Email Address column. And, you can see the More Tables entry.

Similarly to the More Views option earlier, this option brings up the list of available tables in a More Tables box. Since our goal is to edit the Entry table, we will select it and then click on Edit, as shown in Figure 12–14.

After selecting the Edit button, the Table Definition box for this table appears. This shows the list of fields that are currently being displayed in this table and the corresponding view. Note that in the top right corner is the ability to add or remove this table from the menu drop-down by checking or unchecking the box. The Title column shows the friendly name that you want to give a column. To this point, we have said that the field was named *Resource Name,* but in reality, the field name is actually just *Name*. This is another user friendly feature of Project 2010—it doesn't matter if you look for the real name of the field (Name) or the title (Resource Name), as they will both be displayed. Figure 12–15 shows the Table Definition box.

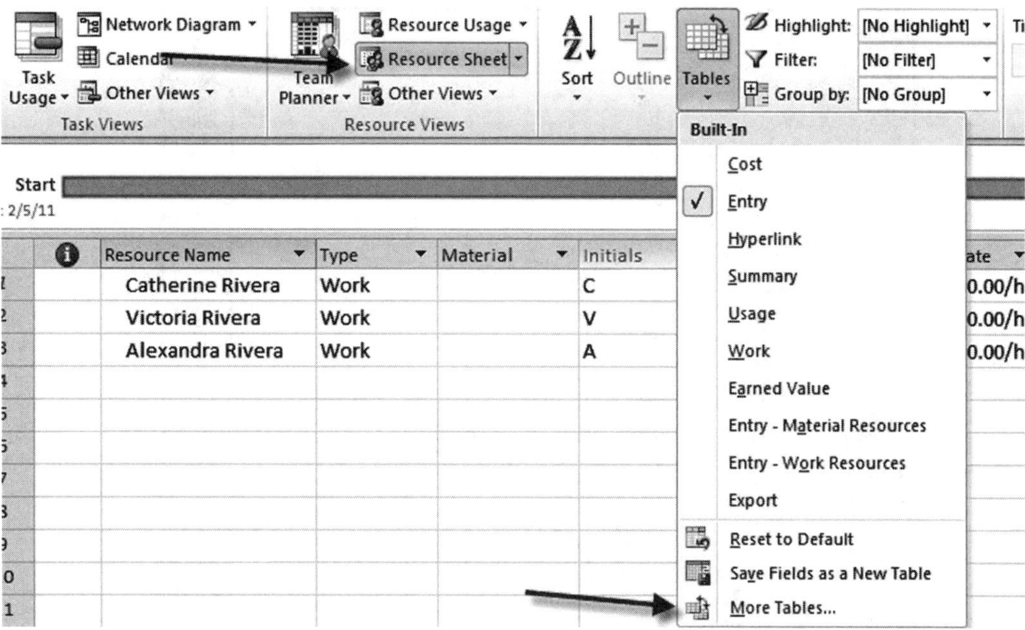

Figure 12–13

More Tables

Tables: ○ Task ◉ Resource

Cost
Earned Value
Entry
Entry - Material Resources
Entry - Work Resources
Export
Hyperlink
Res Sheet with Email Table 1
Summary
Usage
Work

New...
Edit...
Copy...
Organizer...

Apply
Cancel

Figure 12–14

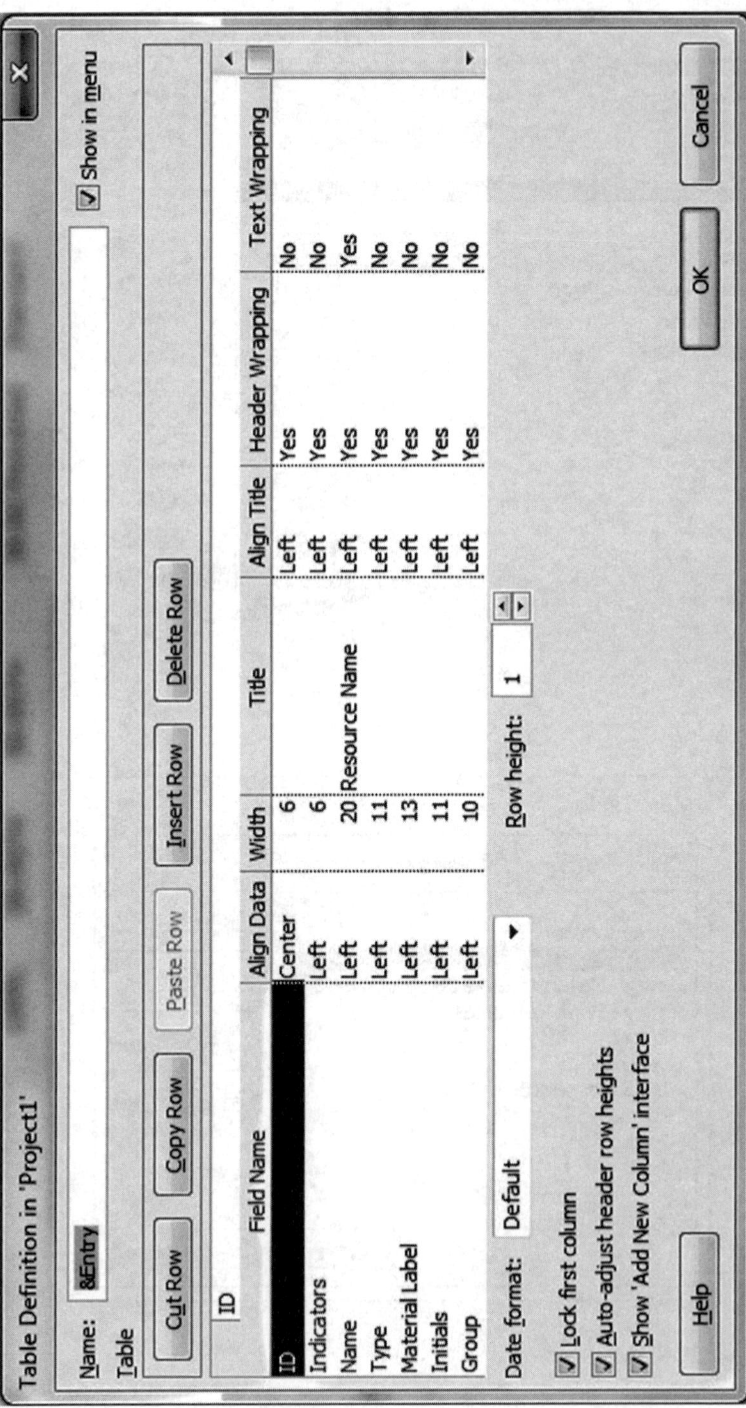
Table Definition in 'Project1'
Name: &Entry
Show in menu
Table
Cut Row
Copy Row
Paste Row
Insert Row
Delete Row
ID
Field Name
Align Data
Width
Title
Align Title
Header Wrapping
Text Wrapping
ID
Center
6
Left
Yes
No
Indicators
Left
6
Left
Yes
No
Name
Left
20
Resource Name
Left
Yes
Yes
Type
Left
11
Left
Yes
No
Material Label
Left
13
Left
Yes
No
Initials
Left
11
Left
Yes
No
Group
Left
10
Left
Yes
No
Date format: Default
Row height: 1
Lock first column
Auto-adjust header row heights
Show 'Add New Column' interface
Help
OK
Cancel

Figure 12–15

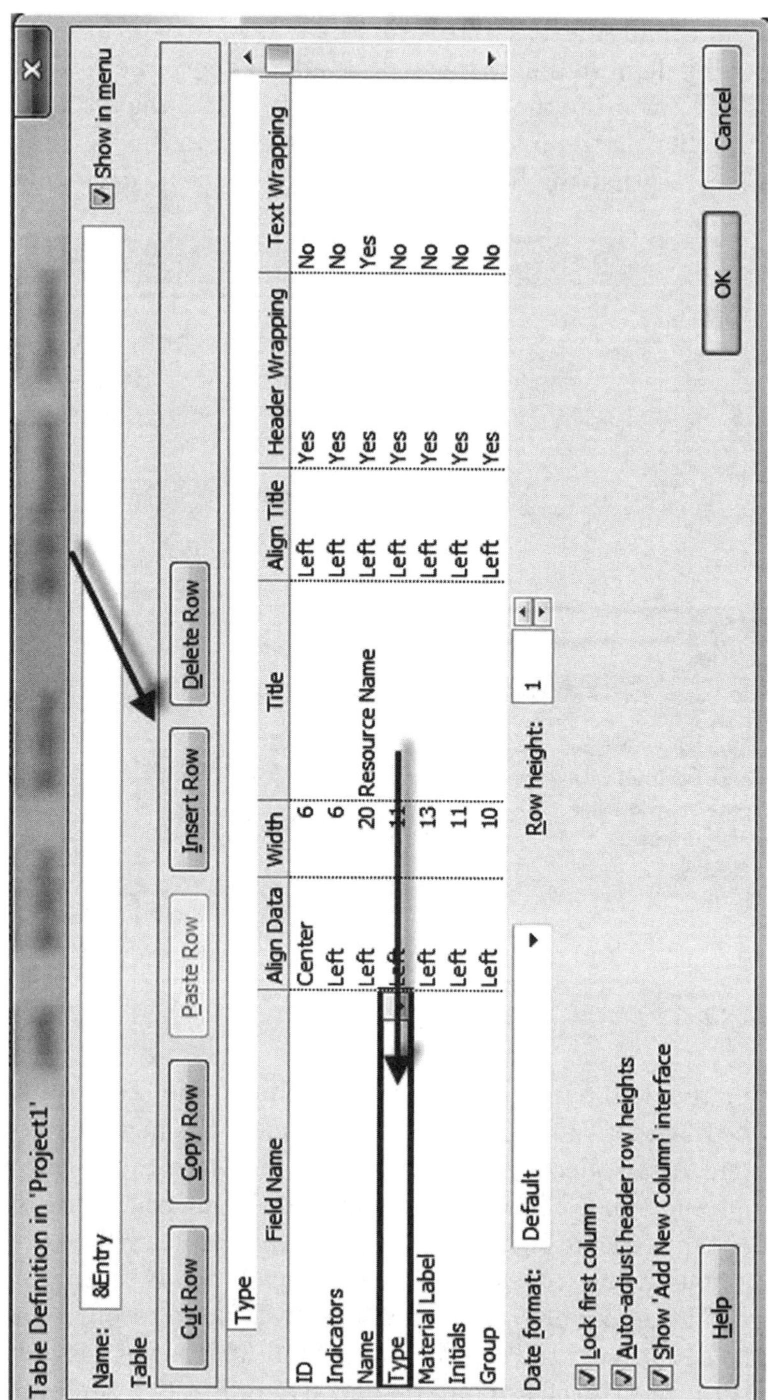
Table Definition in 'Project1'
Name: &Entry
Show in menu
Table
Cut Row
Copy Row
Paste Row
Insert Row
Delete Row
Type
Field Name
Align Data
Width
Title
Align Title
Header Wrapping
Text Wrapping
ID
Center
6
Left
Yes
No
Indicators
Left
6
Left
Yes
No
Name
Left
20
Resource Name
Left
Yes
Yes
Type
11
Left
Yes
No
Material Label
Left
13
Left
Yes
No
Initials
Left
11
Left
Yes
No
Group
Left
10
Left
Yes
No
Date format: Default
Row height: 1
Lock first column
Auto-adjust header row heights
Show 'Add New Column' interface
Help
OK
Cancel

Figure 12–16

To add the field Email Address to this table, we have to determine where we want to insert it. By default, a new row will be added *above* the row you select. Since we want the row after the Name, we need to select the Type row. After selecting the row, click on the Insert Row button, shown in Figure 12–16.

Figure 12–17 shows that the field can be selected from the drop-down.

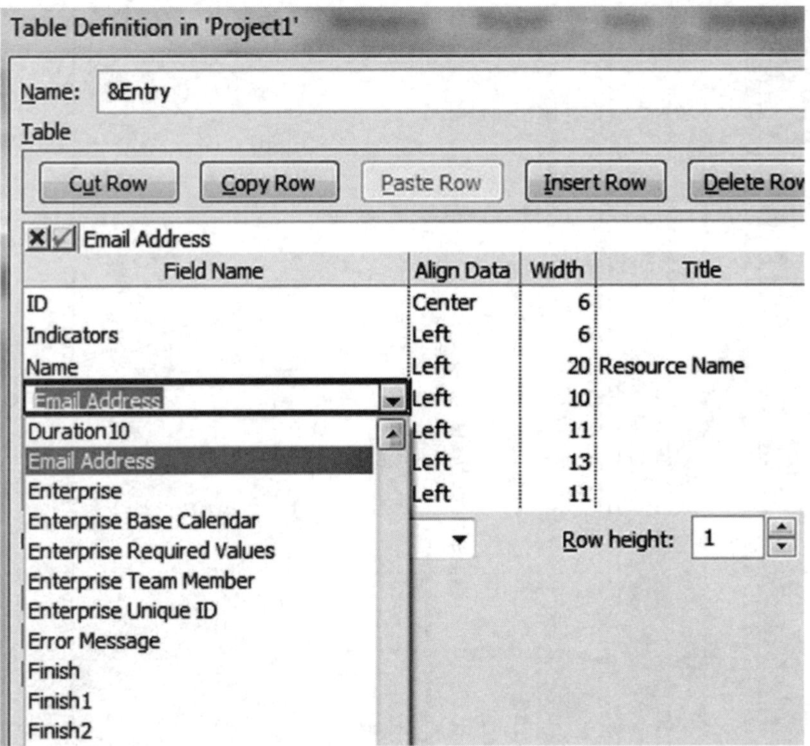

Figure 12–17

After selecting the field name, the Align Data, Width, and other columns will automatically be filled in. You can adjust these to meet the needs that you may have for each field. After selecting OK on this box, the More Tables box will still be open. Click on Apply in the More Tables box and the modifications that were just made to the table, including any views using that table, will be displayed.

It can be valuable to add tables and views, or to add fields to existing tables or views, to expand the amount of information available to resource managers and other people with access to Project Professional. This is not the only source of information in Project Professional, though. There are two separate sets of reports that are provided by default.

Reports in Project Professional

As shown in Figure 12–18, the Project tab Ribbon contains the Reports group, which includes the icons for Reports and Visual Reports.

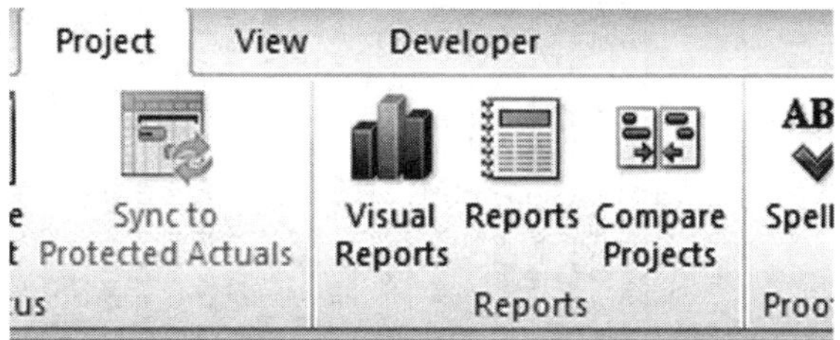

Figure 12–18

As Figure 12–19 shows, the Reports icon opens the Reports box, which contains the links to reports that have been available for at least a few versions of Project. These are reports that have options for you as the report writer and that are generally linear in nature. Some people have written fairly complex reports of their own and continue to update them with new versions. That is partly why the ability to run those reports still exists.

Figure 12–19

For example, Figure 12–20 shows the report that would result if you were to select Assignments, and then "Who does What When."

Who Does What
Audit Tracking Solution

ID	Indicators	Resource Name	Work
1		Analyst	164 hrs

Project	ID	Task Name	Units	Work	Delay	Start	Finish
Audit Tracking Solution	11	Review software specifications/budget with team	100%	4 hrs	0 days	Tue 6/28/11 1:00 PM	Tue 6/28/11 5:00 PM
Audit Tracking Solution	19	Develop functional specifications	100%	40 hrs	0 days	Wed 7/6/11 1:00 PM	Wed 7/13/11 12:00 PM
Audit Tracking Solution	20	Develop prototype based on functional specifications	100%	32 hrs	0 days	Wed 7/13/11 1:00 PM	Tue 7/19/11 12:00 PM
Audit Tracking Solution	18	Review preliminary software specifications	100%	16 hrs	0 days	Mon 7/4/11 1:00 PM	Wed 7/6/11 12:00 PM
Audit Tracking Solution	12	Incorporate feedback on software specifications	100%	8 hrs	0 days	Wed 6/29/11 8:00 AM	Wed 6/29/11 5:00 PM
Audit Tracking Solution	9	Draft preliminary software specifications	100%	24 hrs	0 days	Tue 6/21/11 1:00 PM	Fri 6/24/11 12:00 PM
Audit Tracking Solution	8	Conduct needs analysis	100%	40 hrs	0 days	Tue 6/14/11 1:00 PM	Tue 6/21/11 12:00 PM

ID	Indicators	Resource Name	Work
2		Developer	360 hrs

Project	ID	Task Name	Units	Work	Delay	Start	Finish
Audit Tracking Solution	79	Deploy software	100%	8 hrs	0 days	Tue 11/1/11 8:00 AM	Tue 11/1/11 5:00 PM
Audit Tracking Solution	30	Developer testing (primary debugging)	100%	120 hrs	0 days	Thu 8/18/11 8:00 AM	Wed 9/7/11 5:00 PM
Audit Tracking Solution	78	Train support staff	100%	8 hrs	0 days	Mon 10/31/11 8:00 AM	Mon 10/31/11 5:00 PM
Audit Tracking Solution	72	Evaluate testing information	100%	8 hrs	0 days	Tue 10/25/11 8:00 AM	Tue 10/25/11 5:00 PM
Audit Tracking Solution	71	Obtain user feedback	100%	40 hrs	0 days	Tue 10/18/11 8:00 AM	Mon 10/24/11 5:00 PM
Audit Tracking Solution	75	Determine final deployment strategy	100%	8 hrs	0 days	Wed 10/26/11 8:00 AM	Wed 10/26/11 5:00 PM
Audit Tracking Solution	70	Install/deploy software	100%	8 hrs	0 days	Mon 10/17/11 8:00 AM	Mon 10/17/11 5:00 PM
Audit Tracking Solution	27	Identify modular/tiered design parameters	100%	8 hrs	0 days	Tue 7/26/11 8:00 AM	Tue 7/26/11 5:00 PM
Audit Tracking Solution	26	Review functional specifications	100%	8 hrs	0 days	Mon 7/25/11 8:00 AM	Mon 7/25/11 5:00 PM
Audit Tracking Solution	28	Assign development staff	100%	8 hrs	0 days	Wed 7/27/11 8:00 AM	Wed 7/27/11 5:00 PM
Audit Tracking Solution	77	Secure deployment resources	100%	8 hrs	0 days	Fri 10/28/11 8:00 AM	Fri 10/28/11 5:00 PM
Audit Tracking Solution	29	Develop code	100%	120 hrs	0 days	Thu 7/28/11 8:00 AM	Wed 8/17/11 5:00 PM
Audit Tracking Solution	76	Develop deployment methodology	100%	8 hrs	0 days	Thu 10/27/11 8:00 AM	Thu 10/27/11 5:00 PM

Figure 12–20

These reports are informative, but may not be as flexible as desired or formatted in a preferred manner. That is partly why the newer versions of reports are called Visual Reports. These reports allow you to view data in either Excel or Visio. If you choose Visio, you can use all the features of Visio, including Pivot Diagrams. And, if you choose to use Excel, PivotTables and PivotCharts will be available along with all of the other features of Excel.

Visual Reports

As shown in Figure 12–21, click on the Visual Reports icon in the Ribbon to access the Visual Reports—Create Report box.

The Visual Reports—Create Report box is shown in Figure 12–22. This box has some default templates already created that are very useful. However, you can also create your own reports. In addition, you can click on each report and see a sample of the report in the Sample window. To be able to use the Excel or Visio report features you must have Excel or Visio installed on your computer.

Let's take a look at a resource report as an example of how reports created in this box can be used. Since the *Show report templates* selection box at the top of the box are checked for both Visio and Excel, we need a method to tell them apart easily. You can tell which ones are Excel by this icon and which ones are Visio by this icon . To view a report, click on the report name, then click the View button. In Figure 12–23, we show some of the features of this box, and then select the Excel-based Resource Work Summary Report.

In Figure 12–24, a sample of the report is displayed. In the next few screenshots, we will look more closely to see what is displaying with this particular report, and then we can modify it if necessary.

Figure 12–25 displays the main part of this visual report. At the left side of the report, you can see Work is listed along with numbers representing hours. At the bottom of the report, you can see that resource names are listed with bars representing the data values.

As Figure 12–26 shows, the right side of the main report is the PivotTable Field List. You can add or remove fields simply by clicking in the check boxes next to the field names. Keep in mind that changing these selections will change the data in the report. The four areas below the field list can also be modified. You can change the filter, fields and values by clicking the drop-down arrow and moving it, or you can click and hold the mouse button down and simply drag and drop it where you want it in the report. If you modify the report in this manner, while you are in the main report view, it can be a little tricky to

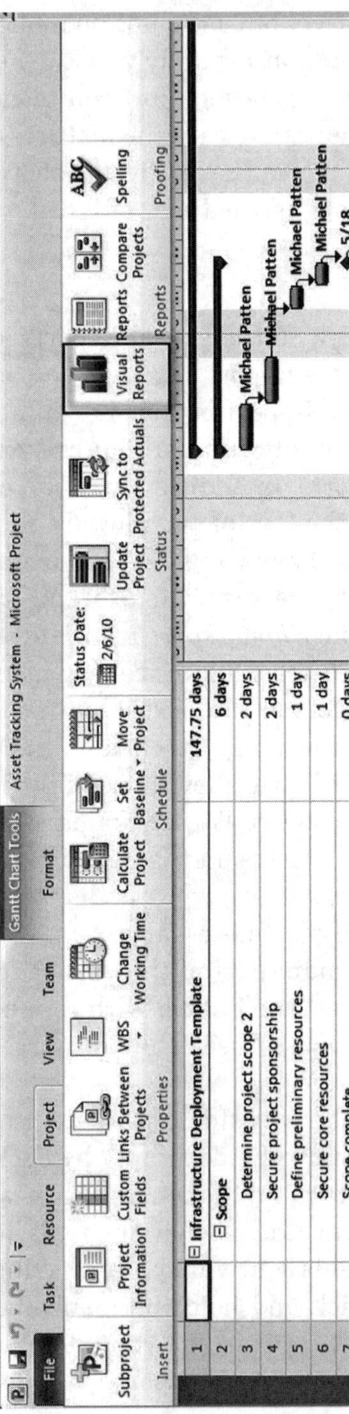
Asset Tracking System - Microsoft Project
Gantt Chart Tools
File
Task
Resource
Project
View
Team
Format
Subproject
Insert
Project Information
Custom Fields
Links Between Projects
WBS
Change Working Time
Properties
Calculate Project
Set Baseline
Move Project
Schedule
Status Date:
2/6/10
Update Project
Sync to Protected Actuals
Status
Visual Reports
Reports
Compare Projects
Reports
Spelling
Proofing
Infrastructure Deployment Template
Scope
Determine project scope 2
Secure project sponsorship
Define preliminary resources
Secure core resources
Scope complete
147.75 days
6 days
2 days
2 days
1 day
1 day
0 days
Michael Patten
Michael Patten
Michael Patten
Michael Patten
5/18

Figure 12–21

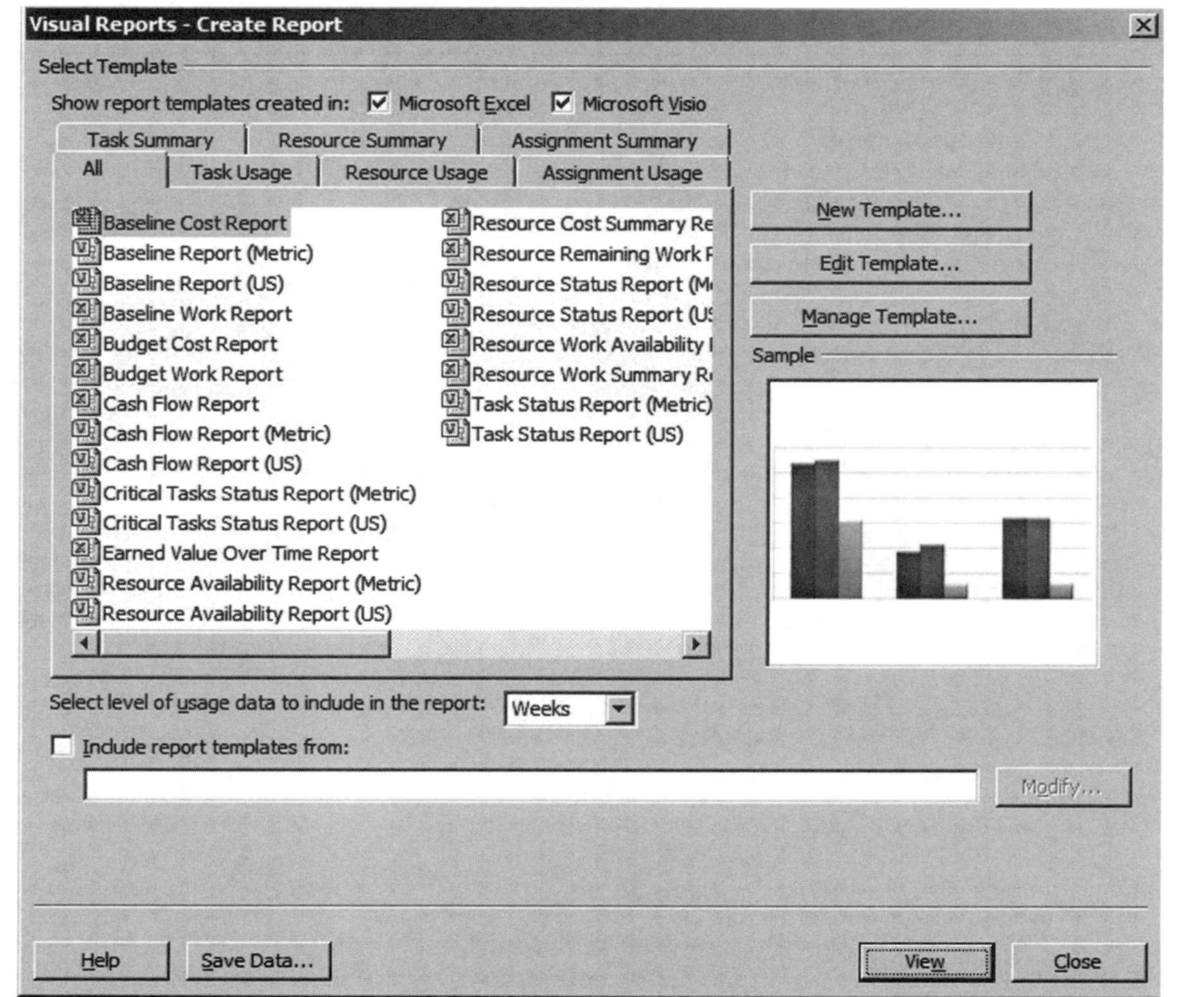
Visual Reports - Create Report
Select Template
Show report templates created in: Microsoft Excel Microsoft Visio
Task Summary
Resource Summary
Assignment Summary
All
Task Usage
Resource Usage
Assignment Usage
Baseline Cost Report
Baseline Report (Metric)
Baseline Report (US)
Baseline Work Report
Budget Cost Report
Budget Work Report
Cash Flow Report
Cash Flow Report (Metric)
Cash Flow Report (US)
Critical Tasks Status Report (Metric)
Critical Tasks Status Report (US)
Earned Value Over Time Report
Resource Availability Report (Metric)
Resource Availability Report (US)
Resource Cost Summary Re
Resource Remaining Work F
Resource Status Report (M
Resource Status Report (US
Resource Work Availability I
Resource Work Summary R
Task Status Report (Metric)
Task Status Report (US)
New Template...
Edit Template...
Manage Template...
Sample
Select level of usage data to include in the report: Weeks
Include report templates from:
Modify...
Help
Save Data...
View
Close

Figure 12–22

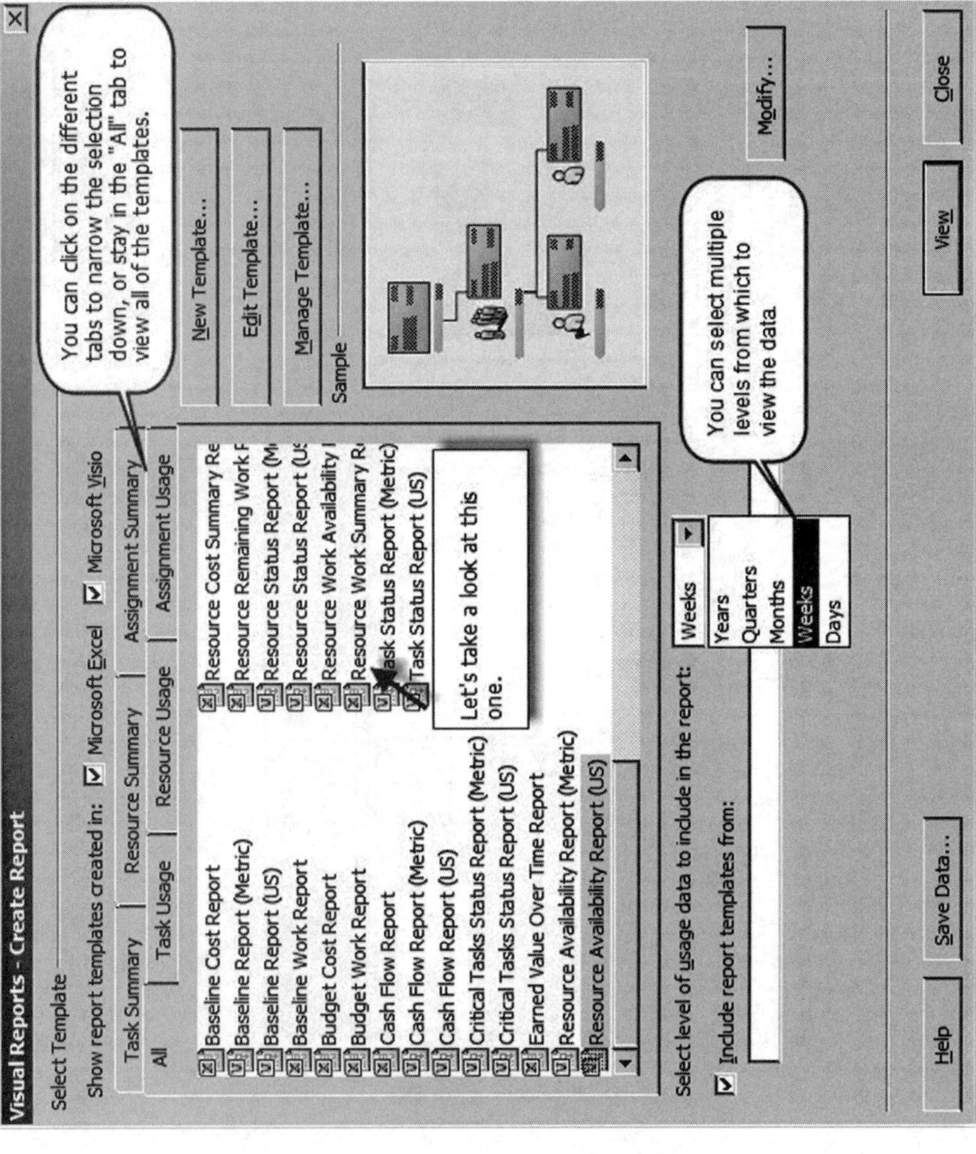
Visual Reports - Create Report
Select Template
Show report templates created in: Microsoft Excel Microsoft Visio
Task Summary
Resource Summary
Assignment Summary
All
Task Usage
Resource Usage
Assignment Usage
Baseline Cost Report
Baseline Report (Metric)
Baseline Report (US)
Baseline Work Report
Budget Cost Report
Budget Work Report
Cash Flow Report
Cash Flow Report (Metric)
Cash Flow Report (US)
Critical Tasks Status Report (Metric)
Critical Tasks Status Report (US)
Earned Value Over Time Report
Resource Availability Report (Metric)
Resource Availability Report (US)
Resource Cost Summary Re
Resource Remaining Work R
Resource Status Report (M
Resource Status Report (US
Resource Work Availability
Resource Work Summary R
Task Status Report (Metric)
Task Status Report (US)
Let's take a look at this one.
You can click on the different tabs to narrow the selection down, or stay in the "All" tab to view all of the templates.
New Template...
Edit Template...
Manage Template...
Sample
Select level of usage data to include in the report:
Weeks
Years
Quarters
Months
Weeks
Days
You can select multiple levels from which to view the data
Include report templates from:
Modify...
Help
Save Data...
View
Close

Figure 12–23

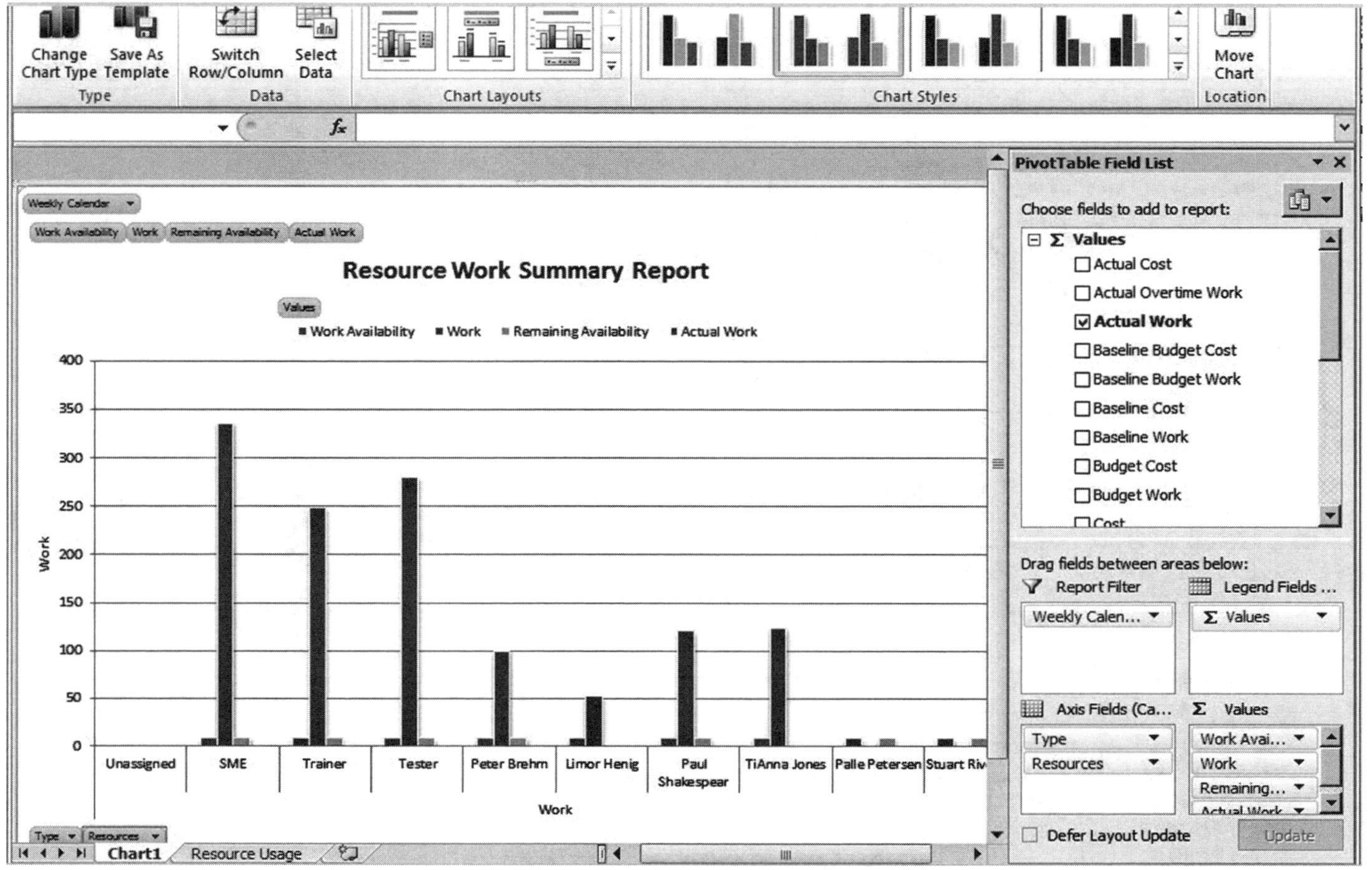
Change Chart Type
Save As Template
Type
Switch Row/Column
Select Data
Data
Chart Layouts
Chart Styles
Move Chart
Location
Weekly Calendar
Work Availability
Work
Remaining Availability
Actual Work
Resource Work Summary Report
Values
Work Availability
Work
Remaining Availability
Actual Work
400
350
300
250
200
150
100
50
0
Work
Unassigned
SME
Trainer
Tester
Peter Brehm
Limor Henig
Paul Shakespear
TiAnna Jones
Palle Petersen
Work
Type
Resources
Chart1
Resource Usage
PivotTable Field List
Choose fields to add to report:
Values
Actual Cost
Actual Overtime Work
Actual Work
Baseline Budget Cost
Baseline Budget Work
Baseline Cost
Baseline Work
Budget Cost
Budget Work
Drag fields between areas below:
Report Filter
Legend Fields ...
Weekly Calen...
Values
Axis Fields (Ca...
Values
Type
Resources
Work Avai...
Work
Remaining...
Defer Layout Update
Update

Figure 12–24

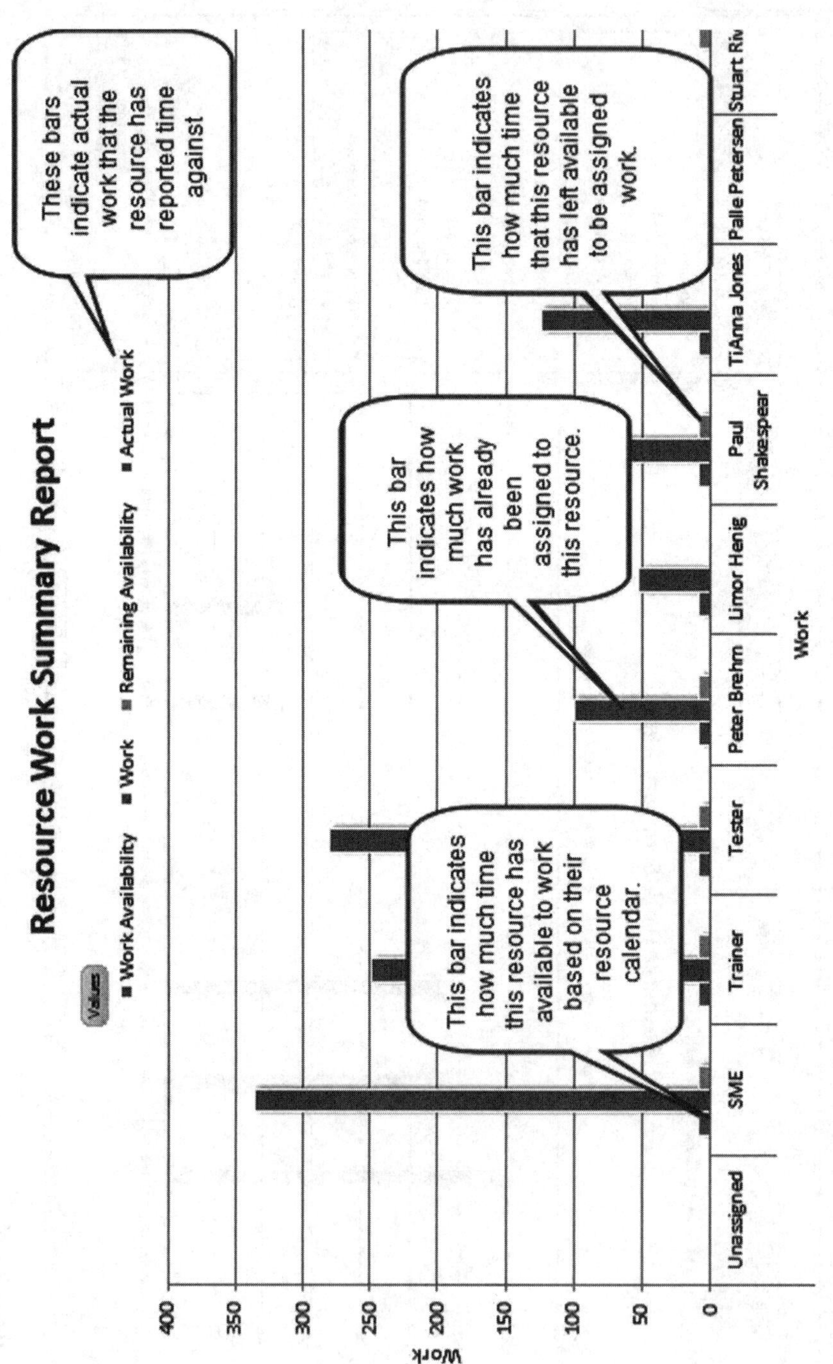
Resource Work Summary Report
Values
■ Work Availability ■ Work ■ Remaining Availability ■ Actual Work
These bars indicate actual work that the resource has reported time against
This bar indicates how much time this resource has available to work based on their resource calendar.
This bar indicates how much work has already been assigned to this resource.
This bar indicates how much time that this resource has left available to be assigned work.
Work
400
350
300
250
200
150
100
50
0
Unassigned
SME
Trainer
Tester
Peter Brehm
Limor Henig
Paul Shakespear
TiAnna Jones
Palle Petersen
Stuart Riv
Work

Figure 12–25

see what data changed and how it impacted the report. It might be easier to see the data instead of the chart when modifying the report. Modifying the report in this manner allows you to see exactly what parts of the report are impacted by adding or removing values or filters.

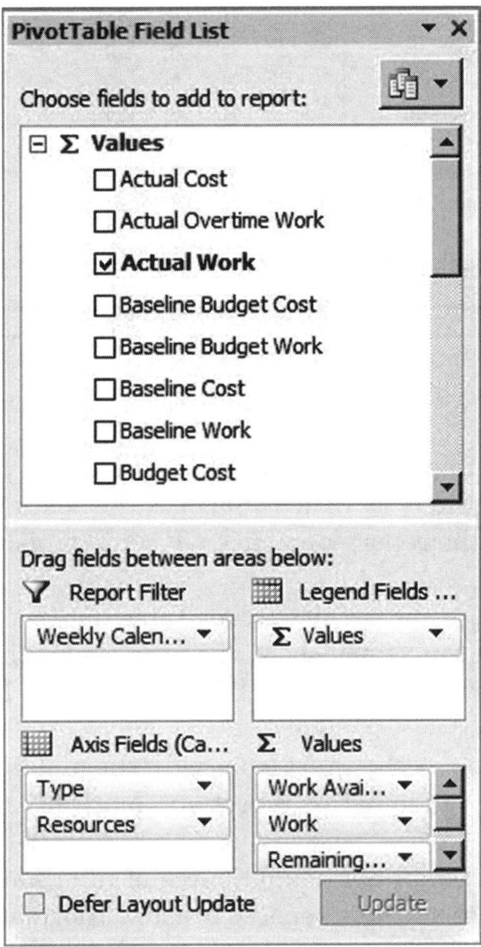

Figure 12–26

Figure 12–27 shows the data behind the report in the Excel Pivot Table. When looking at this data, you can see that the report is pulling in some generic resources; for the purposes of this example, we don't want to compare them. Data can be modified from this table directly.

A	B	C	D	E	F
Weekly Calendar	All				
		Data			
Type	Resources	Work Availability	Work	Remaining Availability	Actual Work
Work	Unassigned	0	0	0	0
	SME	8	336	8	0
	Trainer	8	248	8	0
	Tester	8	280	8	0
	Peter Brehm	8	100	8	0
	Limor Henig	8	52	0	0
	Paul Shakespear	8	120	8	0
	TiAnna Jones	8	124	0	0
	Palle Petersen	8	0	8	0
	Stuart Rivchun	8	0	8	0
Work Total		72	1260	56	0
Grand Total		72	1260	56	0

Figure 12–27

To remove the generic resources from the report, click the drop-down arrow next to Resources. All you need to do is uncheck the boxes next to the resources to remove them from the report, and click OK when finished, as shown in Figure 12–28.

Figure 12–29 shows what the new Pivot Table data looks like when the generic resources have been removed. To view the visual chart with the generic resource information removed, simply click on the Chart 1 tab at the bottom of the Excel spreadsheet.

Figure 12–30 shows how the chart looks with the updated information. All of the changes that were made to this report automatically modified the chart at the same time.

Visual Reports can be an abundant source of information. This is particularly true when you create new reports to view information in the way that best suits your needs. The recommended way to determine which report might be the best template for you is to open your project and click through all of the different reports to see what information each provides. You can also go into the Pivot Table and modify the data to see how it changes the report.

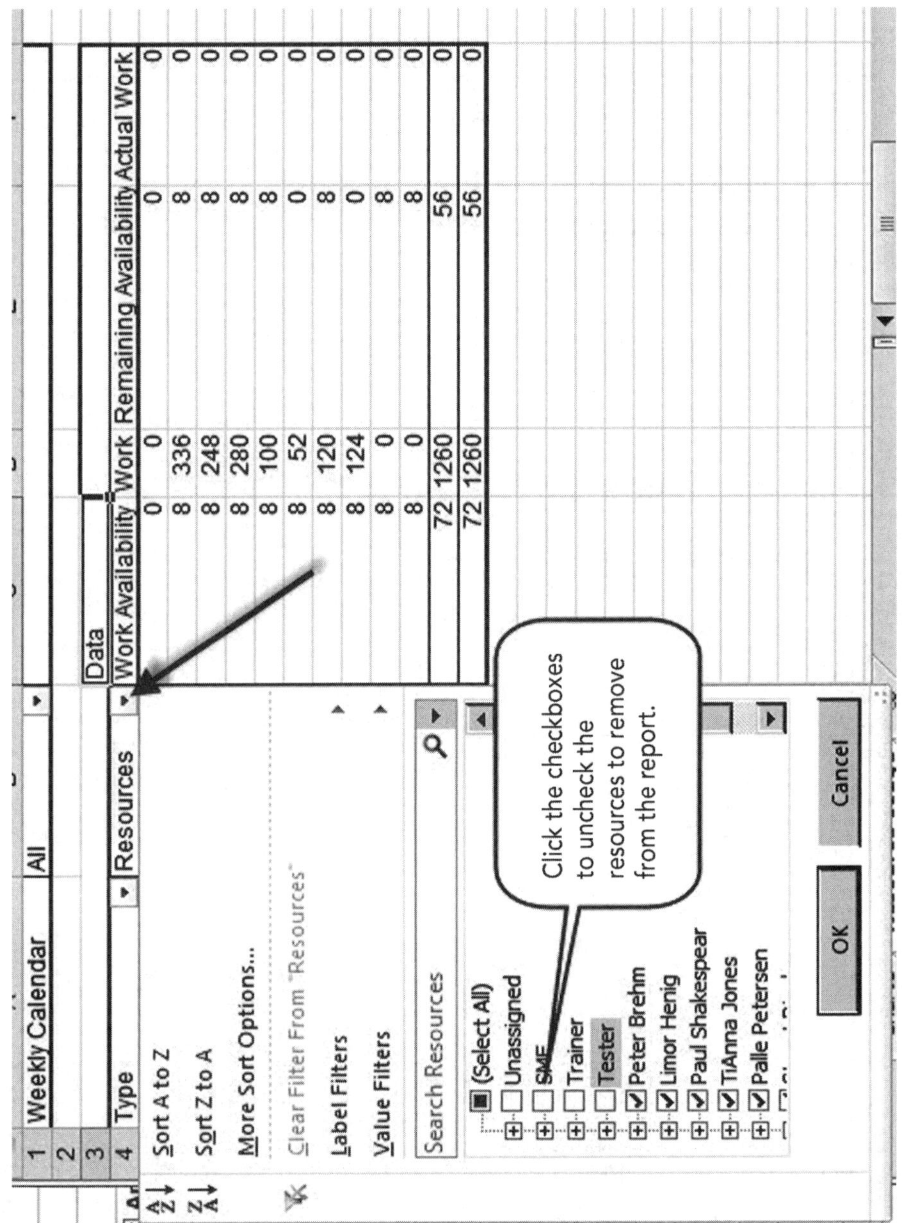
Weekly Calendar
All
Data
Type
Resources
Work Availability
Work
Remaining Availability
Actual Work
Sort A to Z
Sort Z to A
More Sort Options...
Clear Filter From "Resources"
Label Filters
Value Filters
Search Resources
(Select All)
Unassigned
SME
Trainer
Tester
Peter Brehm
Limor Henig
Paul Shakespear
TiAnna Jones
Palle Petersen
OK
Cancel
Click the checkboxes to uncheck the resources to remove from the report.

Figure 12–28

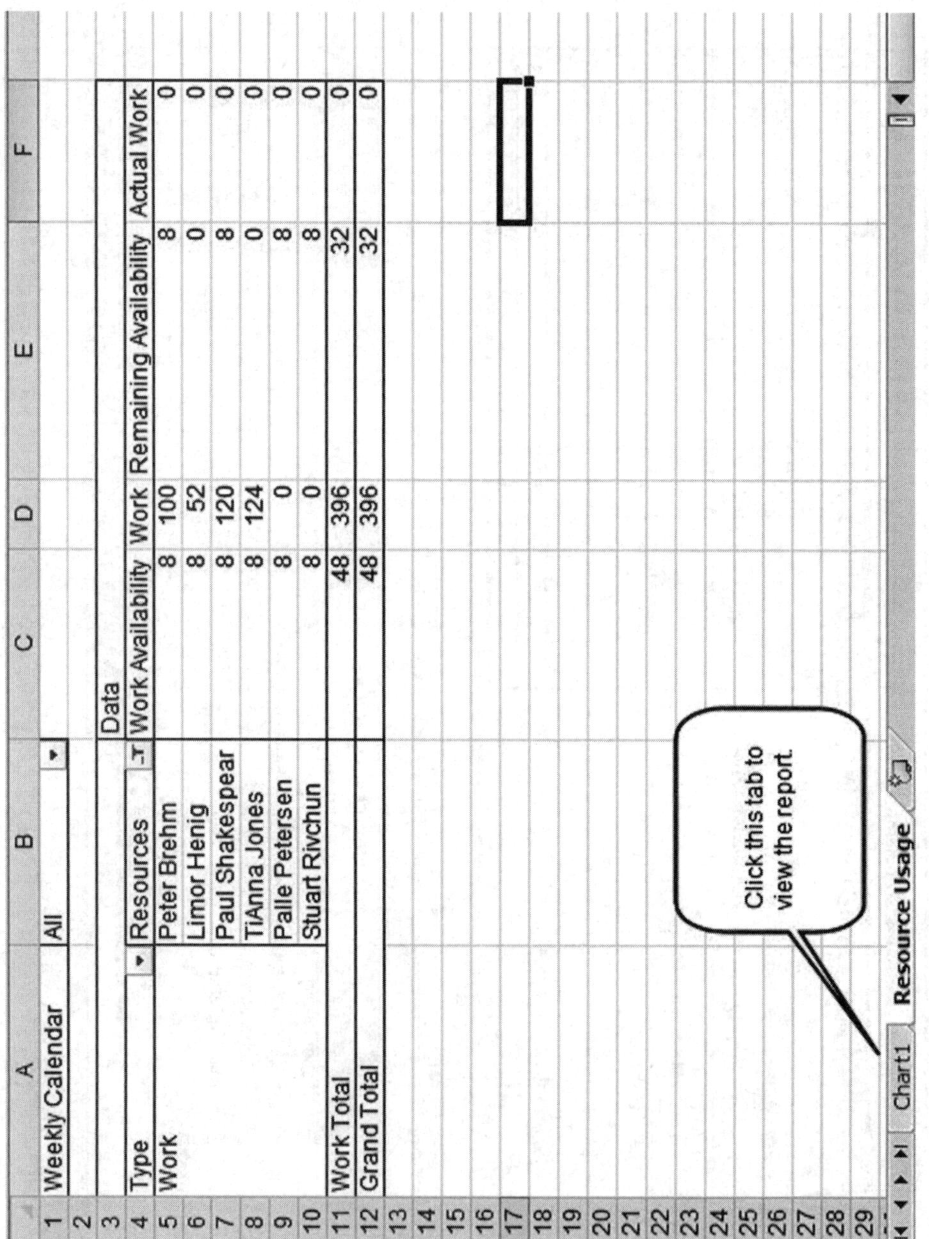

	A	B	C	D	E	F
1	Weekly Calendar	All				
2						
3			Data			
4	Type	Resources	Work Availability	Work	Remaining Availability	Actual Work
5	Work	Peter Brehm	8	100	8	0
6		Limor Henig	8	52	0	0
7		Paul Shakespear	8	120	8	0
8		TiAnna Jones	8	124	0	0
9		Palle Petersen	8	0	8	0
10		Stuart Rivchun	8	0	8	0
11	Work Total		48	396	32	0
12	Grand Total		48	396	32	0

Figure 12–29

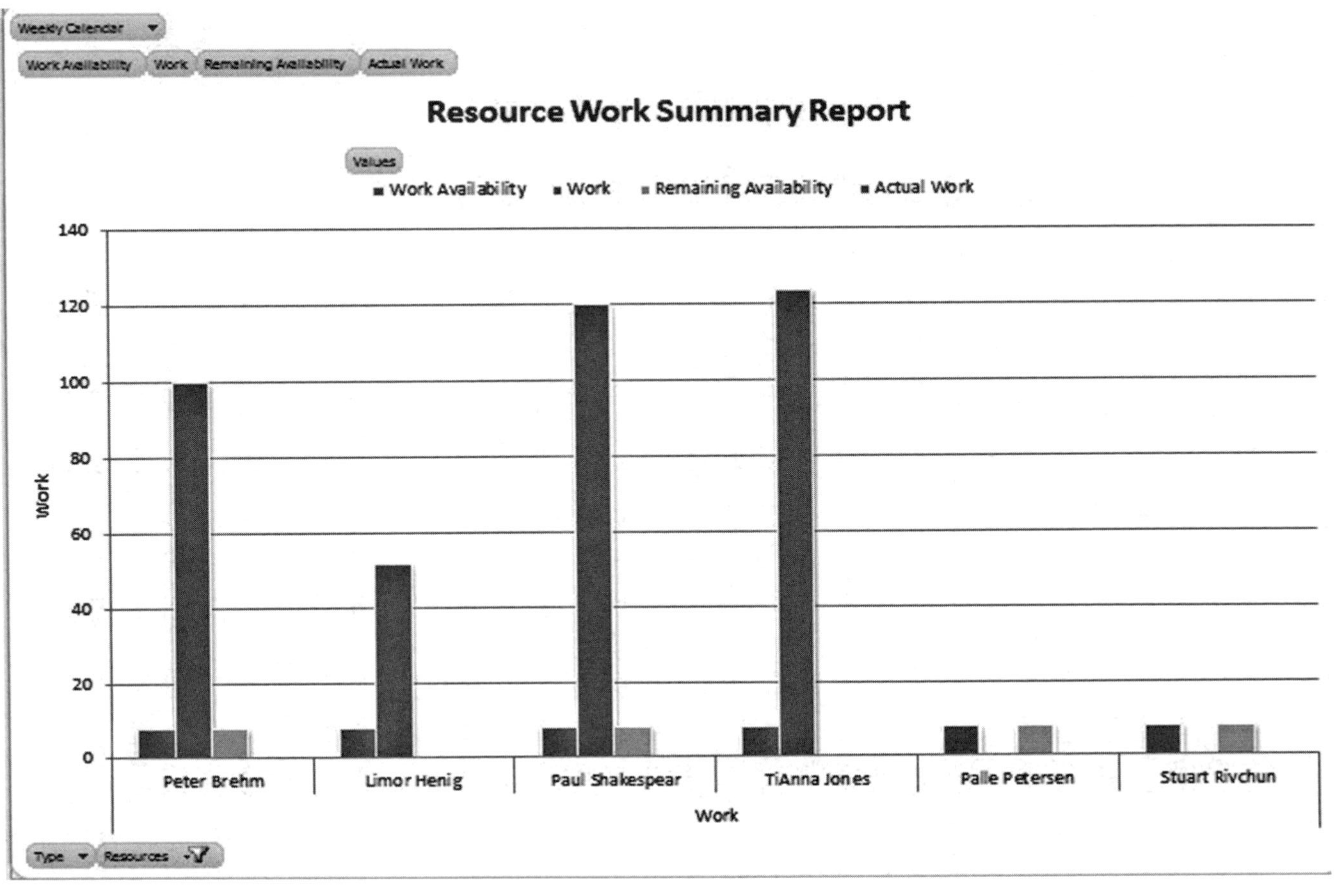
Weekly Calendar
Work Availability
Work
Remaining Availability
Actual Work
Resource Work Summary Report
Values
Work Availability
Work
Remaining Availability
Actual Work
Work
140
120
100
80
60
40
20
0
Peter Brehm
Limor Henig
Paul Shakespear
TiAnna Jones
Palle Petersen
Stuart Rivchun
Work
Type
Resources

Figure 12–30

Views in Project Server

The views in Project Server for resource information are similar to the way views work in Project Professional. Data resides in fields, which is displayed in columns, in different views. The notion of *tables* is not important at this point. The biggest difference is that the views in Project Server can't be modified by users directly. Only the project server administrator can modify the views.

However, it is very easy to make views that have specific columns of information and then only have certain people see those views. For example, it might be appropriate to have views with costing information only available to executives, while having views with resource assignments only available to resource managers. There is no need to have every possible view available to every user of the Project Server.

The main view for the resource manager in Project Server is the Resource Center. This view is shown in Figure 12–31 with the selected view shown by an arrow at the top of the Ribbon. The resources that have been selected for other information are on the right side. In this example, no resources have been selected. In Chapter 11, we had selected resources to determine their availability.

The drop-down selections that are available to the user are based on their security permissions. In this example, the user logged on has the ability to see seven different views, as shown in Figure 12–32.

Selecting a different view immediately changes the view of the selected view. It is possible that a resource manager might want to Print or Export a particular view to Excel to do further work with the data. Printing or exporting can be done by selecting either icon, as shown in Figure 12–33.

Choosing the Print or Export icon will open the report in Excel and allow the user to manipulate the data as desired.

Since modification of fields, columns, views, and tables were demonstrated in Project Professional, we will briefly demonstrate how this is done in Project Server. The project server administrator needs to go to the Manage Views link of the Project Server settings. From there, the project server administrator can create or modify the view, name, and other information.

As an example, we will create a new view called Sample Resource Data. The top section of the new view is shown in Figure 12–34.

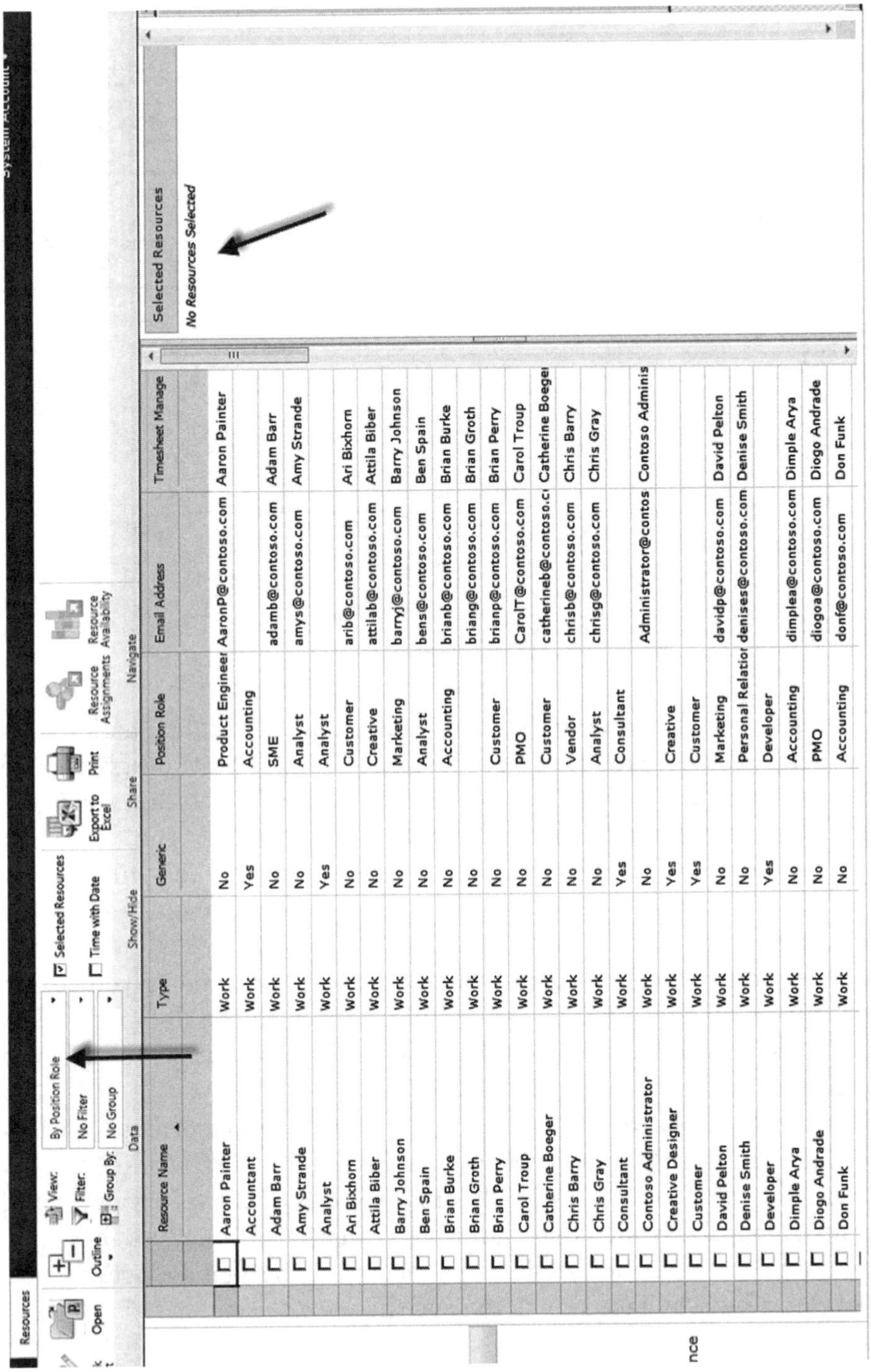

Resources

View: By Position Role
Filter: No Filter
Group By: No Group
Open | Outline | Data
☑ Selected Resources
☐ Time with Date
Show/Hide
Export to Excel | Print | Share
Resource Assignments | Resource Availability | Navigate

	Resource Name	Type	Generic	Position Role	Email Address	Timesheet Manage
☐	Aaron Painter	Work	No	Product Engineer	AaronP@contoso.com	Aaron Painter
☐	Accountant	Work	Yes	Accounting		
☐	Adam Barr	Work	No	SME	adamb@contoso.com	Adam Barr
☐	Amy Strande	Work	No	Analyst	amys@contoso.com	Amy Strande
☐	Analyst	Work	Yes	Analyst		
☐	Ari Bixhorn	Work	No	Customer	arib@contoso.com	Ari Bixhorn
☐	Attila Biber	Work	No	Creative	attilab@contoso.com	Attila Biber
☐	Barry Johnson	Work	No	Marketing	barryj@contoso.com	Barry Johnson
☐	Ben Spain	Work	No	Analyst	bens@contoso.com	Ben Spain
☐	Brian Burke	Work	No	Accounting	brianb@contoso.com	Brian Burke
☐	Brian Groth	Work	No		briang@contoso.com	Brian Groth
☐	Brian Perry	Work	No	Customer	brianp@contoso.com	Brian Perry
☐	Carol Troup	Work	No	PMO	CarolT@contoso.com	Carol Troup
☐	Catherine Boeger	Work	No	Customer	catherineb@contoso.c	Catherine Boeger
☐	Chris Barry	Work	No	Vendor	chrisb@contoso.com	Chris Barry
☐	Chris Gray	Work	No	Analyst	chrisg@contoso.com	Chris Gray
☐	Consultant	Work	Yes	Consultant		
☐	Contoso Administrator	Work	No		Administrator@contos	Contoso Adminis
☐	Creative Designer	Work	Yes	Creative		
☐	Customer	Work	Yes	Customer		
☐	David Pelton	Work	No	Marketing	davidp@contoso.com	David Pelton
☐	Denise Smith	Work	No	Personal Relatior	denises@contoso.com	Denise Smith
☐	Developer	Work	Yes	Developer		
☐	Dimple Arya	Work	No	Accounting	dimplea@contoso.com	Dimple Arya
☐	Diogo Andrade	Work	No	PMO	diogoa@contoso.com	Diogo Andrade
☐	Don Funk	Work	No	Accounting	donf@contoso.com	Don Funk

Selected Resources

No Resources Selected

Figure 12–31

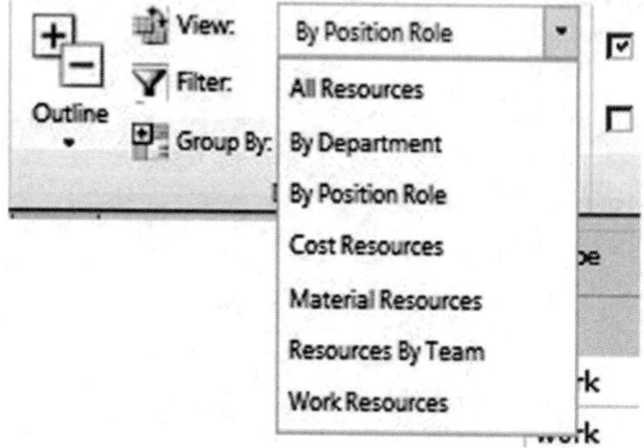

Figure 12–32

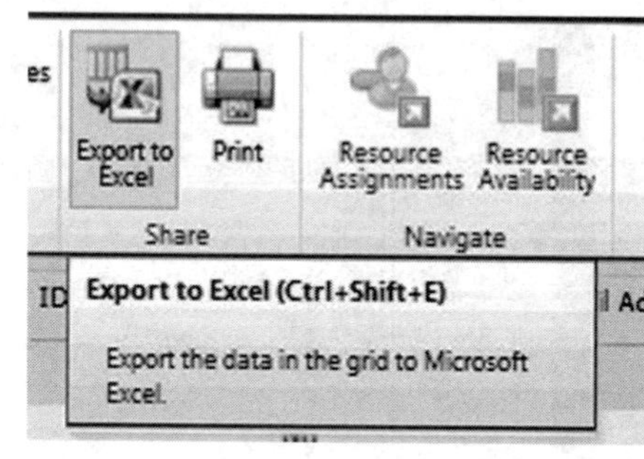

Figure 12–33

Name and Type

View Type: Resource Center
* Name: Sample Resource Report
Description: Report to show data

Figure 12–34

The next section of the new view screen is the Table and Fields section, shown in Figure 12–35. The left side lists the Available Fields, and the right side lists the fields to show in the new view. Note that the Field Width and the Custom Label fields can be modified. This will allow you to increase the width of the field to better show the information. The Custom Label is just like the Title column in Project Professional—it allows you to give your own friendly name to the field name.

Format View is the next section of the new view, and allows you to group and sort the view. In this example, we will leave it with the default *Grouping Format* of Timesheet, but we will add the Sort By information to sort by the Resource Name, as shown in Figure 12–36.

The Filter section, shown in Figure 12–37, allows you to provide a Custom Filter for the view. The Resource Breakdown Structure (RBS) filter allows you to use an RBS if you have set it up. The final section of the new view contains the Security Categories, which determine who can see this view. As shown, with none of the Available categories selected on the right-hand side, nobody will be able to see this view. The last step is to save the view.

Table and Fields

Select the type of information and fields you want to display in this view.

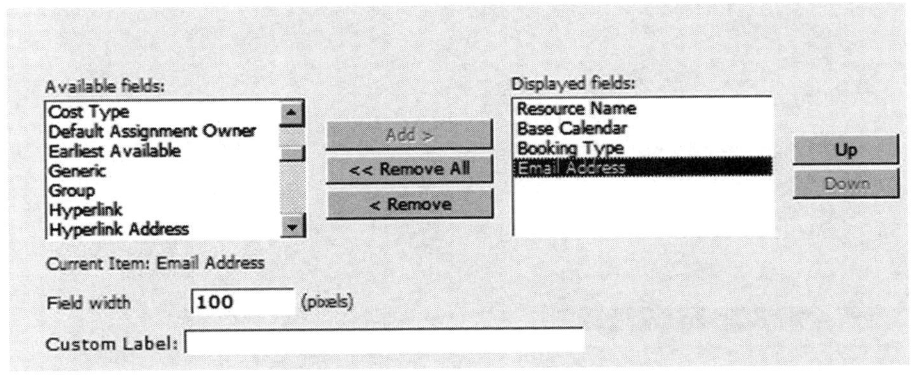

Figure 12–35

Format View

Specify the format setting for this view.

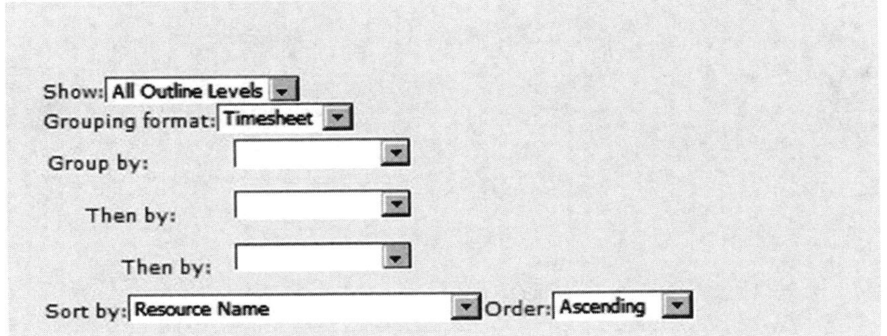

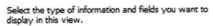

Figure 12–36

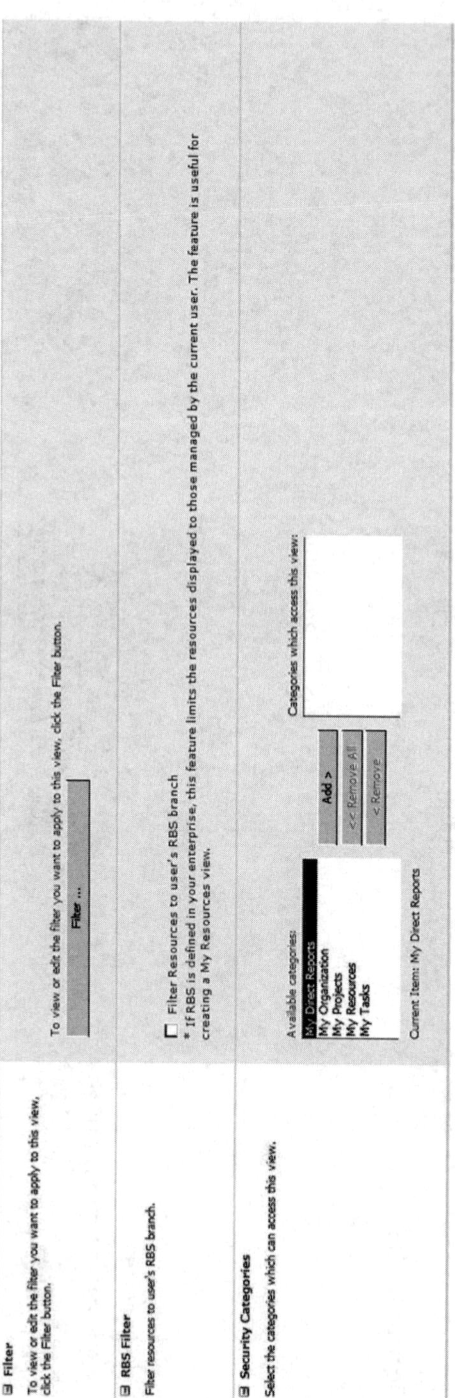
Filter
To view or edit the filter you want to apply to this view, click the Filter button.
To view or edit the filter you want to apply to this view, click the Filter button.
Filter ...
RBS Filter
Filter resources to user's RBS branch.
Filter Resources to user's RBS branch
* If RBS is defined in your enterprise, this feature limits the resources displayed to those managed by the current user. The feature is useful for creating a My Resources view.
Security Categories
Select the categories which can access this view.
Available categories:
My Direct Reports
My Organization
My Projects
My Resources
My Tasks
Add >
<< Remove All
< Remove
Categories which access this view:
Current Item: My Direct Reports
Save
Cancel

Figure 12–37

Once the view has been created and saved, users who have the correct security permissions will see it available in the drop-down, as shown in Figure 12–38.

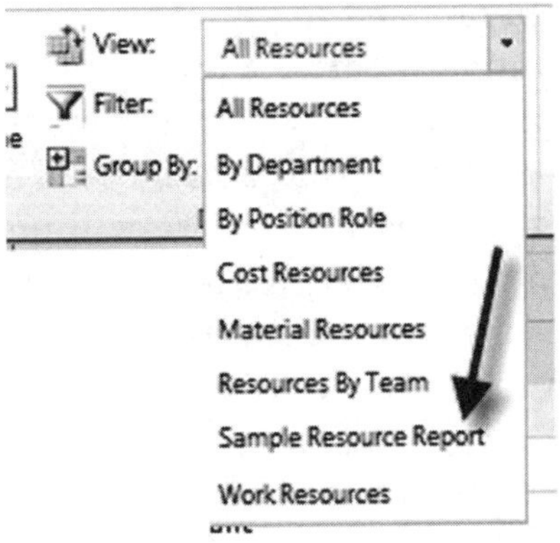

Figure 12–38

As shown in Figure 12–39, the new view has the columns that were just created in the view as we developed it.

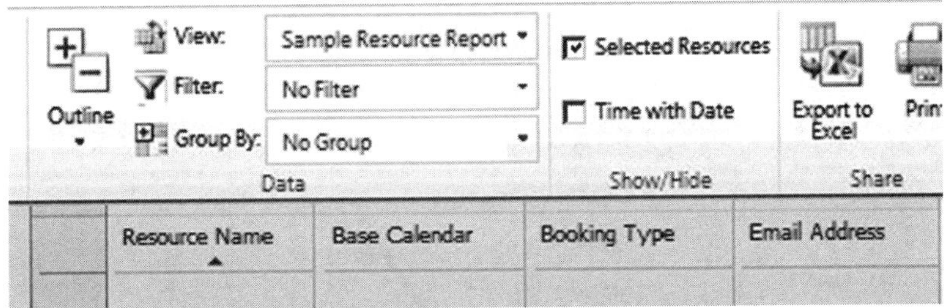

Figure 12–39

Just like creating new views and tables within Professional, it can be beneficial to create new views for resource managers, resources, and other users. However, just as there are reporting capabilities within Project Professional, there are other report options when using Project Server. The two main types of reports on Project Server are Reporting Services and Business Intelligence.

Reports in Project Server

When the views in Project Professional and the views in Project Server are not enough, the ability to access information is built into the software. Unlike the other reporting functions, you do need to understand fields, tables, databases and SharePoint to write effective reports. As with all areas of Project Server, you have to have the appropriate security permissions to create these types of reports. It is important to note though that a number of default sample reports come with the installation of Project Server. We will not go into the creation and modification of these types of reports since it requires a knowledge of SQL and there are many other books and sources of documentation on how to add these reports to Project Server. However, we will show some of the capabilities of these reports.

The Reporting Services reports are the reports created directly from the Reporting database or OLAP data. These reports are accessed by a link on the PWA Home Page created by the project server administrator. In Figure 12–40, the link is called *Reporting Services Reports*. However, in your organization this link could be called anything that the project server administrator named it.

Figure 12–40

When that link is selected, the project server administrator could have it go to any spot, but in our example, this link opens the list of available reports, as shown in Figure 12–41.

When selecting a report, the report will open using the Microsoft SQL Server Reporting Services window. If there are any parameters to the report, they will

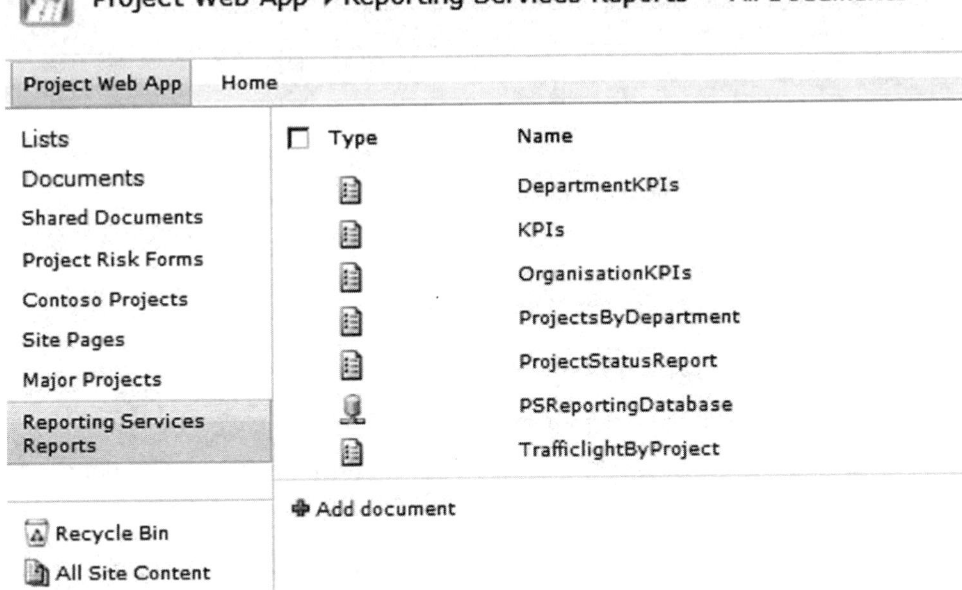

Figure 12–41

be visible on the right side of the screen, as shown in Figure 12–42. In this example, the KPI report has been chosen.

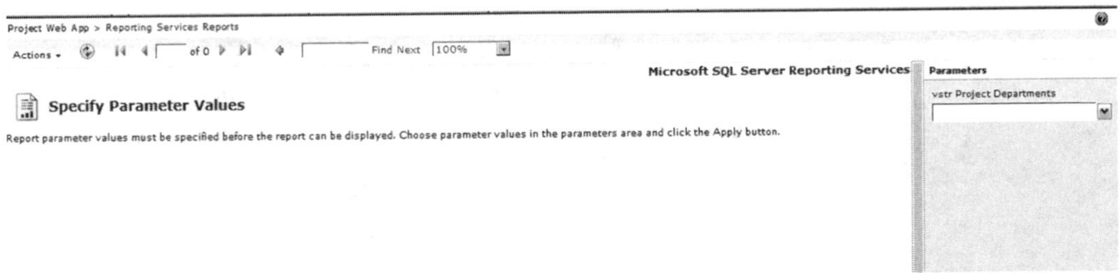

Figure 12–42

The parameters for reports will display based on the type of parameters—date fields, drop-downs, selections, or whatever was created for the report. In this case, the report has only one parameter and it is a multi-select drop-down. We will use the Select All check box, shown in Figure 12–43.

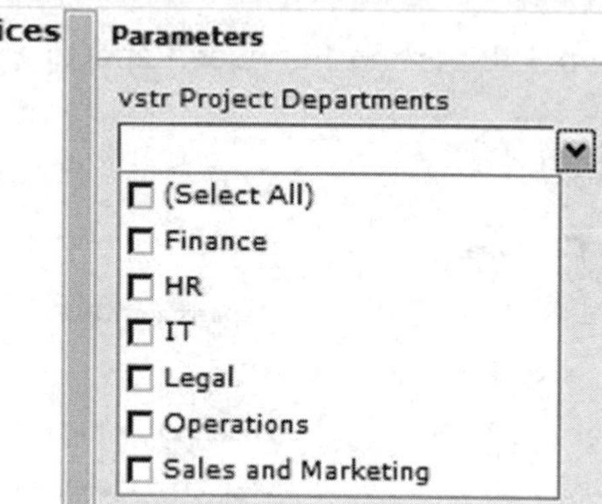

Figure 12–43

For this example, when the report is displayed, it has icons instead of data to make it easier to read, as shown in Figure 12–44.

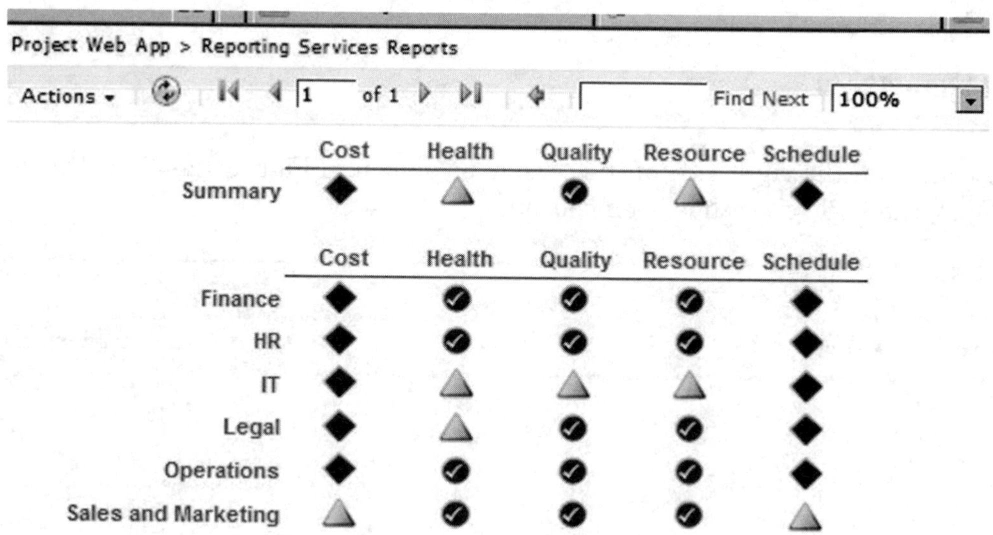

Figure 12–44

Reporting Services is a powerful reporting tool and numerous types of reports can be created. These can be data-centric, like the report shown in Figure 12–45.

Project Details

Project Milestones

Task Name	Finish Date	% Complete	Milestone Status
Scope complete	1/4/2010	0%	
Analysis complete	1/22/2010	0%	
Design complete	2/11/2010	0%	
Development complete	3/31/2010	0%	
Documentation complete	4/7/2010	0%	
Unit testing complete	4/21/2010	0%	
Training materials complete	5/4/2010	0%	
Integration testing complete	5/7/2010	0%	
Pilot complete	5/25/2010	0%	
Deployment complete	6/1/2010	0%	
Post implementation review complete	6/4/2010	0%	

Figure 12–45

Or, the report can contain icons, charts, dials, and other visual items that the administrator chooses when creating the report, as shown in Figure 12–46.

The last consideration about the Reporting Services reports is to note that these reports can be subscribed to so that they are sent to you or other members of your organization at a specific time and with specific report options selected. This means that users can automatically get a copy of the report. The subscriptions option is in the drop-down under the Actions icon, shown in Figure 12–47.

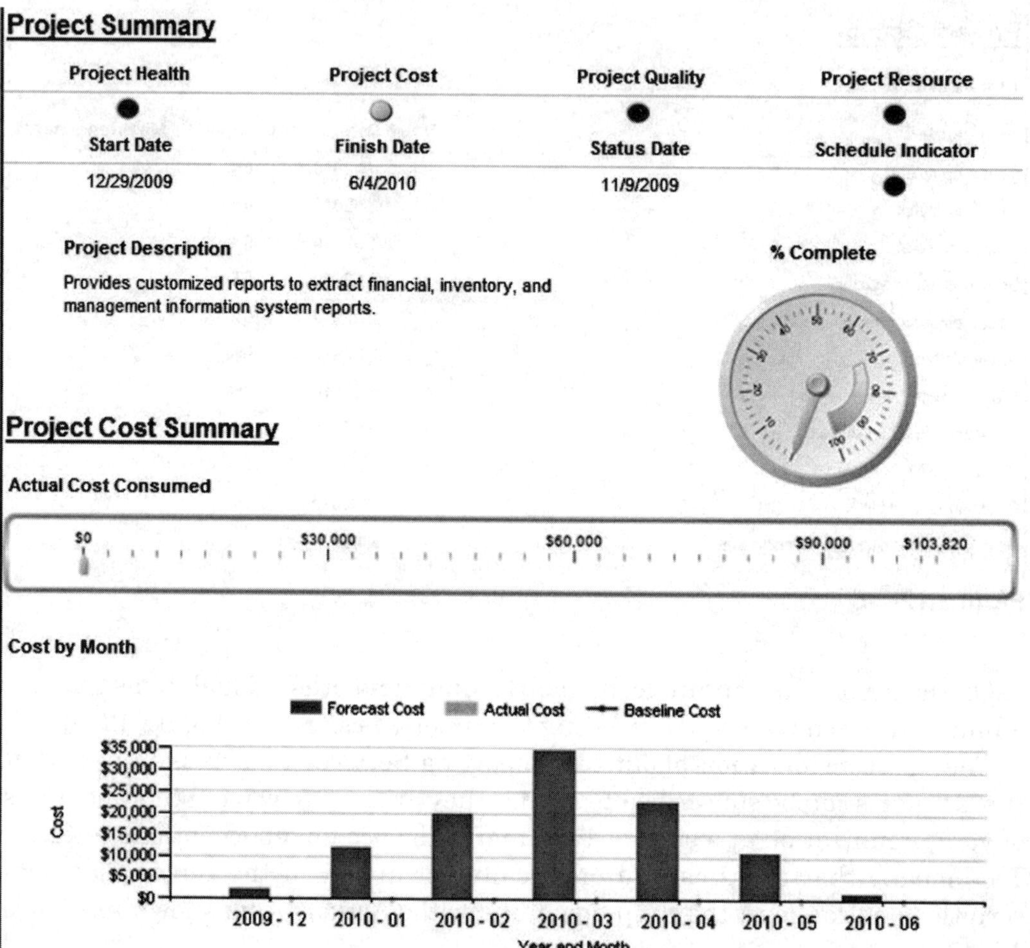
Project Summary
Project Health
Project Cost
Project Quality
Project Resource
Start Date
Finish Date
Status Date
Schedule Indicator
12/29/2009
6/4/2010
11/9/2009
Project Description
Provides customized reports to extract financial, inventory, and management information system reports.
% Complete
Project Cost Summary
Actual Cost Consumed
$0
$30,000
$60,000
$90,000
$103,820
Cost by Month
Forecast Cost
Actual Cost
Baseline Cost
$35,000
$30,000
$25,000
$20,000
$15,000
$10,000
$5,000
$0
Cost
2009 - 12
2010 - 01
2010 - 02
2010 - 03
2010 - 04
2010 - 05
2010 - 06
Year and Month

Figure 12–46

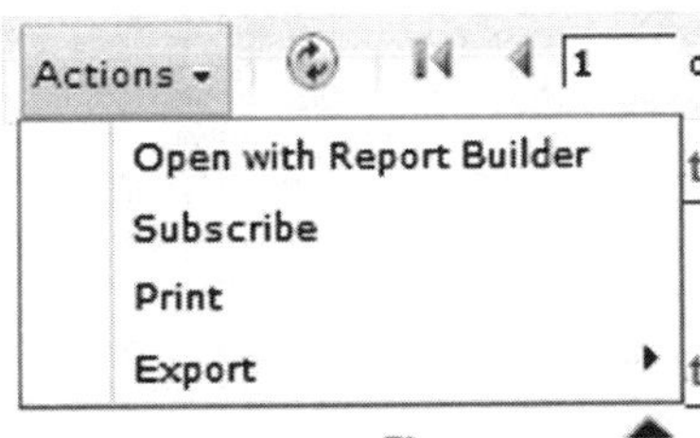

Figure 12–47

The subscription screen will open, and the method of delivery and other options will display. The methods of delivery may vary, depending on your organization's setup. In this example, we have the ability to e-mail the report, put it into a SharePoint library, or post to a Windows File Share, as shown in Figure 12–48.

Figure 12–48

Depending on the delivery method that is chosen, the rest of the options will populate accordingly. In this example, we have selected E-mail. This means that the Delivery Options appear for e-mail, including whom to send the e-mail to, the Subject line, and whether or not to include a link to the report or have the report as part of the message, as shown in Figure 12–49.

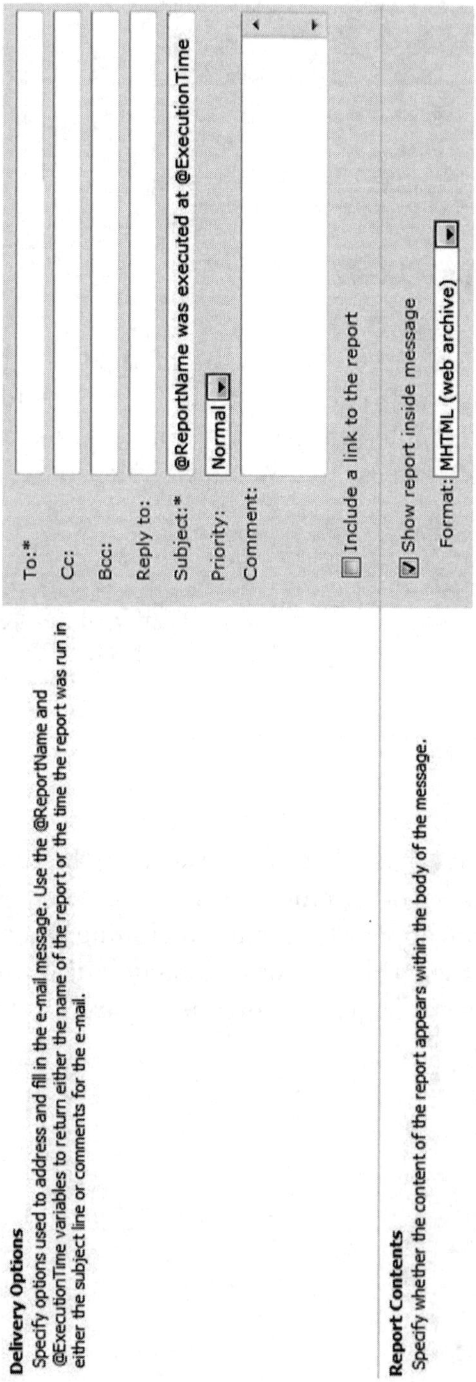

Delivery Options
Specify options used to address and fill in the e-mail message. Use the @ReportName and @ExecutionTime variables to return either the name of the report or the time the report was run in either the subject line or comments for the e-mail.

To:*
Cc:
Bcc:
Reply to:
Subject:* @ReportName was executed at @ExecutionTime
Priority: Normal
Comment:

☐ Include a link to the report

Report Contents
Specify whether the content of the report appears within the body of the message.

☑ Show report inside message
Format: MHTML (web archive)

Figure 12–49

If the report is included in the e-mail, rather than through a link, the format of the report can be selected, as shown in Figure 12–50.

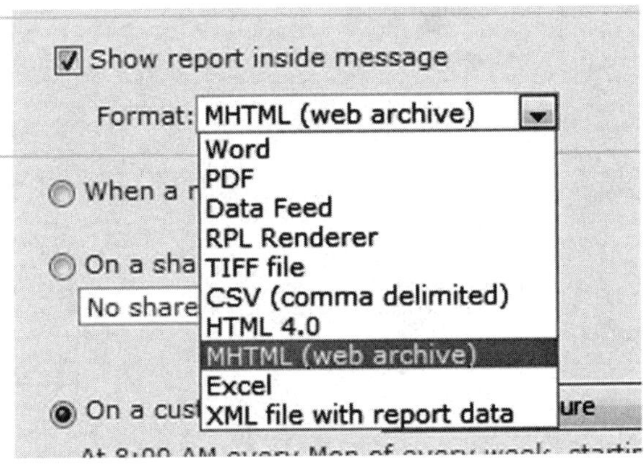

Figure 12–50

The last section of the Subscription screen determines when the report is sent and what parameters to use. As shown in Figure 12–51, you can configure the schedule and parameters.

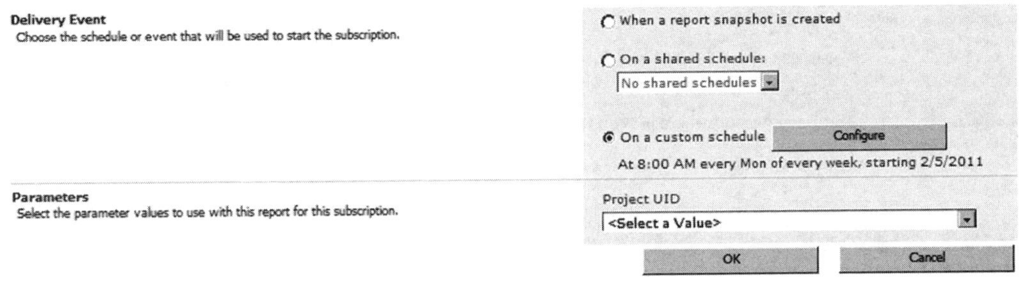

Figure 12–51

The Business Intelligence link may be renamed on your instance of PWA as well, but in this example, the link is located on the PWA homepage and is named *Business Intelligence*, as shown in Figure 12–52.

When clicking on the Business Intelligence link, the default view is the Business Intelligence Center with sample reports and guides located in the middle of the screen. The default page is shown in Figure 12–53.

My Work
Tasks
Timesheet
Issues and Risks

Resources
Resource Center
Status Reports

Strategy
Driver Library
Driver Prioritization
Portfolio Analyses

Business Intelligence

Figure 12–52

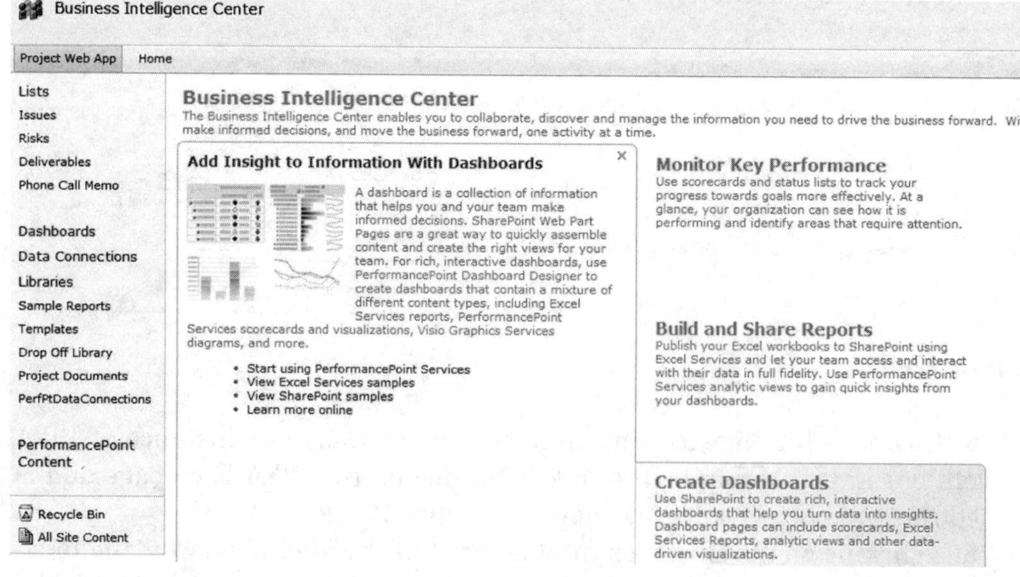

Figure 12–53

The Business Intelligence reports use PerformancePoint, Excel Services, and SharePoint for reporting. The types of reports can be placed into various web parts to display lots of information in one screen. Figure 12–54 is an example of a Business Intelligence report made up of four separate web parts.

Since each part of the web page is actually a separate report, it is possible to drill down or otherwise interact with any specific report without affecting the others. Again, this is determined by the project server administrator or person who prepares the reports.

While there are vast amounts of information in Project Professional and Project Server, there is a way to report on that information in a meaningful and practical method.

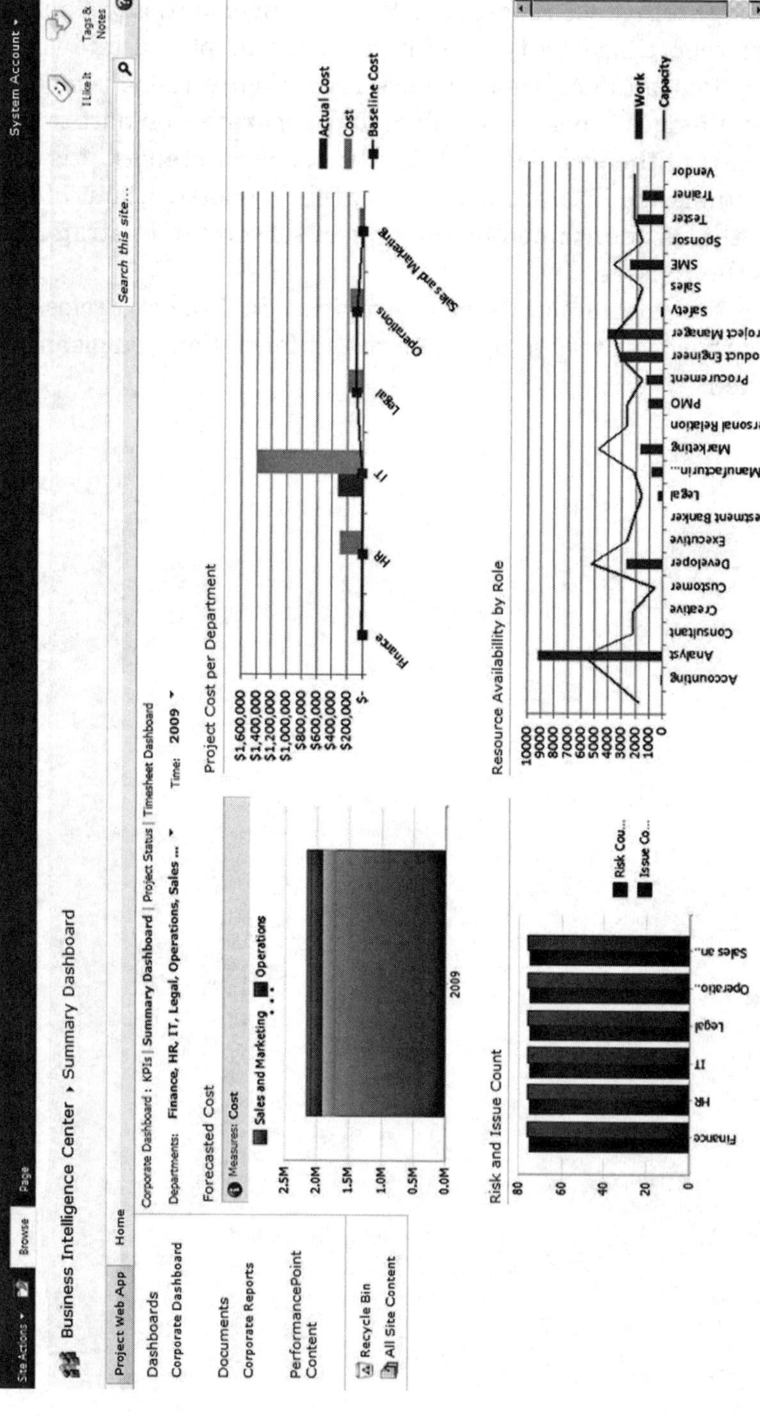
Site Actions
Browse
Page
System Account
Business Intelligence Center › Summary Dashboard
I Like It
Tags & Notes
Project Web App
Home
Search this site...
Dashboards
Corporate Dashboard
Documents
Corporate Reports
PerformancePoint Content
Recycle Bin
All Site Content
Corporate Dashboard : KPIs | Summary Dashboard | Project Status | Timesheet Dashboard
Departments: Finance, HR, IT, Legal, Operations, Sales ...
Time: 2009
Forecasted Cost
Measures: Cost
Sales and Marketing
Operations
2.5M
2.0M
1.5M
1.0M
0.5M
0.0M
2009
Project Cost per Department
$1,600,000
$1,400,000
$1,200,000
$1,000,000
$800,000
$600,000
$400,000
$200,000
$-
Finance
HR
IT
Legal
Operations
Sales and Marketing
Actual Cost
Cost
Baseline Cost
Risk and Issue Count
80
60
40
20
0
Finance
HR
IT
Legal
Operatio...
Sales an...
Risk Cou...
Issue Co...
Resource Availability by Role
10000
9000
8000
7000
6000
5000
4000
3000
2000
1000
0
Accounting
Analyst
Consultant
Creative
Customer
Developer
Executive
Legal
Manufacturin...
Marketing
PMO
Procurement
Safety
Sales
SME
Sponsor
Tester
Trainer
Vendor
Work
Capacity

Figure 12–54

13

A Portfolio Perspective

How resource information is viewed depends on the perspective of the person viewing it. An individual who is the resource is concerned with what work is assigned to them, and when and where to perform that work. Generally, most resources have a short-term perspective about the work—they want to know what they have to do today, this week, next week, or a little further into the future. Hopefully, they are aware of what work is the higher priority work in the case of conflicting assignments.

The resource managers view the same information for all of their resources and are concerned about what work is assigned to who, when, and where, as well as how the assignments affect other resources. They are also trying to balance overallocations and priorities between assignments, as well as looking far into the future to try to determine who has the skill sets and availability for assignments.

Most executives view information from a longer term perspective when it comes to resources. They are concerned about what project files are being worked on, what the work priorities are for current and future projects, and they are looking to the distant future to see what projects are coming up and how those will affect budgets—both monetary and resource. Executives want to see their organization's universe of project files—the entire portfolio.

Microsoft Project Server 2010 incorporates what used to be a separate product, called Portfolio Server, into one product. This merger allows for a seamless integration of information that can flow back and forth from the minute details of one specific task on one specific project file to a report showing the entire portfolio. Therefore, the capacity and utilization of a resource or a certain skill set can be used to help determine how the long-term portfolio is affected.

When referring to the long-term functions of Project Server, there are different terms that people use. Some terms include:

- Portfolio server
- Project portfolio server
- Portfolio analysis
- Portfolio management
- Project portfolio management

The concept of portfolio management has been around for quite some time, and there are many terms to describe it. However, the Project Management Institute usually refers to this concept as project portfolio management (PPM), and that is the term that we will use in this book. We just wanted you to be aware that there is more than one common term to describe this activity.

PPM within Project Server 2010 has its own set of terms and definitions. The authors' goal is not to explain every term, but to provide a few definitions that will make the rest of this chapter easier to understand:

- **Business drivers:** These are the objectives that your organization is trying to achieve. For example:
    - Expanding into new markets
    - Improving product quality
    - Reducing expenses
    - Increasing market share
    - Completing projects on time
    - Meeting a government mandate
- **Prioritization:** Putting business drivers into priority against each other. For example:
    - Meeting a government mandate might not be your organization's favorite activity, but it will have a higher priority than increasing

market share because people might go to jail if they don't do the mandate.

◇ Expanding into new markets might be more important (at least for now) than reducing expenses.

- **Portfolio analysis:** Comparing the prioritization of the business drivers in one list, based on criteria.
- **Proposal:** A request for a future project. Proposals can be created with different workflows, approvals, and required data fields.

As designed in Project Server 2010, the purpose of PPM is to look at all of the project files on the Server to determine which ones to work on. Depending on your organization's setup and use of PPM with Project Server, this can include everything from a "nice to have" proposed idea, to upcoming work (pre-sold but not yet begun), to current work. All types of work can be combined into one portfolio view.

Once in portfolio views, the information can be sorted and analyzed based on whatever criteria is important to management. The capability exists to allow each manager their own basis for prioritizing project files. For example, the Chief Financial Officer might want a priority based upon cost, while the Director of Human Resources wants to know how much labor is needed (in hours or by skill set), and the Vice President of Sales wants to prioritize work based on sales information. All three individuals can perform their own portfolio analysis. There can also be one combined, agreed upon, final version.

Yes, there is a way to force in (or force out) a project file. For example, if you have the best prioritization system in the world, and you come up with a perfect list of priorities based on your business drivers, it is still possible that the Chief Executive Officer states that he or she wants a certain project file to be worked on. You can select and force that project into the priority list.

By prioritizing items in the portfolio, management is allowing every individual from upper management to project managers, resource managers, and resources to understand what tasks they should be working on next. When the priorities change, the information can be updated and the priorities changed for everyone to see at once.

Setting up PPM in Project Server requires some effort and the strong support of upper management. But, as discussed elsewhere in this book, you do not have to set up every variable on the first day of use. Perhaps it is more beneficial to choose two or three variables that are important to upper management, use them as your business drivers, and then build in variables from there. It might be as simple as using two business drivers.

A lot of information exists on Microsoft's website and elsewhere on how to set up and use PPM with Project Server, so this book's intent is not to recreate that content. However, we will look at an example of PPM from the resource management perspective.

The proposal example will assume that some setup has been completed already, and includes a business process. The initial portfolio analysis criteria are based on *not* hiring any new resources. In this example, the business process is:

1. Proposals are created in the Project Server.
   a. Required data fields include:
      i. Project file name
      ii. Business purpose
      iii. Estimated duration
      iv. Enter high-level tasks.
         1. These are placeholder tasks only at this point.
         2. They may or may not end up in the final project.
         3. They are meant for general work buckets.
      v. Skill set types needed.
      vi. Number of hours for each skill set.
2. All proposals are reviewed and either approved, postponed, or rejected.
3. All recently approved proposals are compared against all other approved proposals and existing projects for their priority placement against the organization's business drivers.

The first required step is to enter the proposal. Permission to access this is security-based, so that your organization can control who may start new proposals. To start a new proposal from the Project Center, select the New icon, shown in Figure 13–1. The drop-down lists the available proposal types that have been set up in Project Server by the Project server administrator.

Once the proposal type is chosen, the appropriate workflow and required information becomes available for this proposal. In this example, the information is basic and the first screen that requires data to enter is the project information page, shown in Figure 13–2.

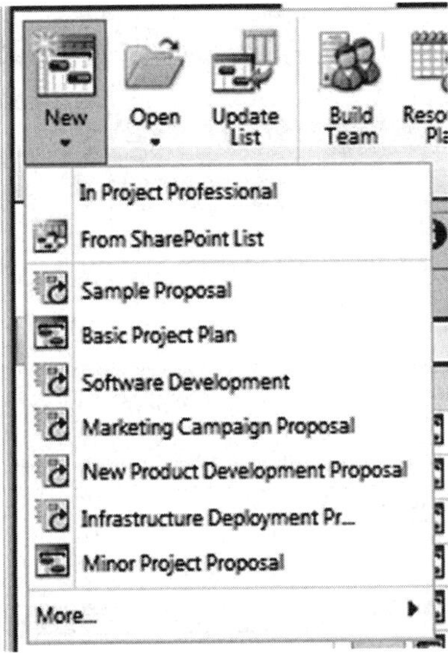

Figure 13–1

Project Fields

Project File Name Enter the name of the Project file you are proposing	
Business Purpose Enter the reason for this Proposal	
Estimated Duration How long will this project file last?	

Figure 13–2

Once the information is entered, the proposal example requires that the resources be selected who are expected to be needed. Since this is a proposal, it is required that only generic resources are used. These will be replaced by named resources with a matching skill set later. In Chapter 7, we discussed how to replace a resource based solely on skill set. The next screen allows you to add resources to the proposal by selecting the Build Team icon from the Ribbon, shown in Figure 13–3.

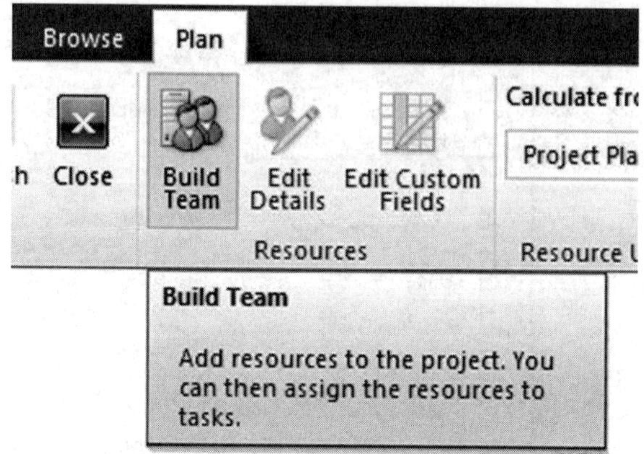

Figure 13–3

Resource Name	Type	Generic
Generic: Yes	Work	Yes
Accountant	Work	Yes
Analyst	Work	Yes
Consultant	Work	Yes
Creative Designer	Work	Yes
Customer	Work	Yes
Developer	Work	Yes
Executive	Work	Yes
Investment Banker	Work	Yes
Legal Assistant	Work	Yes
Manufacturing Engin	Work	Yes
Marketing Manager	Work	Yes
Personal Relationshi	Work	Yes
PMO	Work	Yes
Procurement Manag	Work	Yes
Product Engineer	Work	Yes
Project Manager	Work	Yes
Safety Manager	Work	Yes
Sales Associate	Work	Yes
SME	Work	Yes
Sponsor	Work	Yes
Tester	Work	Yes
Trainer	Work	Yes
Vendor	Work	Yes

Resource Name	Booking Type
Accountant	Committed
Analyst	Committed
Project Manager	Committed
Tester	Committed
Trainer	Committed

Figure 13–4

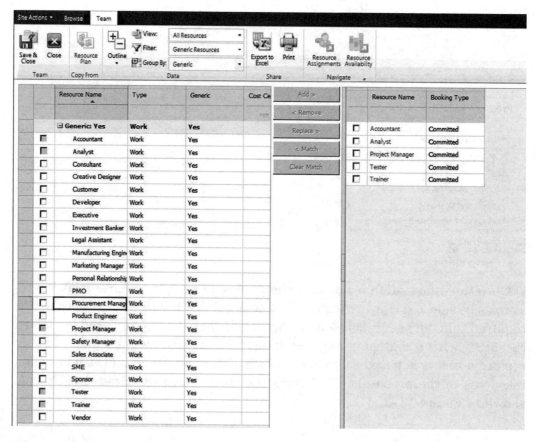

This works the same as the Build Team from Enterprise option that was demonstrated in Chapter 7. In this example, the default option is already set to only allow us to select generic resources. On the left side of the screen, we select the resources that we want for this proposal by clicking the check box. On the right side of the screen is the list of selected resources, which appears after you have clicked on the Add button in the middle, as shown in Figure 13–4.

Now that the resource team has been selected, the next requirement is to enter some high-level tasks. We have entered three tasks and given them an estimated duration and date range. Next, we will assign generic resources to these tasks, as shown in Figure 13–5.

	ID	Mode	Task Name	Duration	Start	Finish	Resource Names
	1		Manage Project	35d	2/4/2010	3/24/2010	Project Manager
	2		Construct Trainiing Material	11d	2/23/2010	3/9/2010	Trainer
	3		Test Material	10d	3/10/2010	3/23/2010	Tester

Figure 13–5

That is all of the required information needed for this type of new proposal. At this point, the new proposal can be used in a portfolio analysis. The Project server administrator set the business driver priorities already. For a portfolio analysis, we will use the already-created HR Prioritization analysis, shown in Figure 13–6.

	Name ▲	Department ▲
	CIO Priortization	
	Collin Priority	
	COO Priortization	
	Executive Consensus	
	HR Priortization	

Figure 13–6

We have also built a portfolio analysis that uses resource information as the key indicator for this business driver, shown in Figure 13–7. In this example, the goal is to prioritize project files (proposals and current work) based upon the number of resources required. Our goal is to prioritize the projects based on the ability to work on them without hiring any new resources.

Name	Type	Department	Constraint Type
Collin Analysis	Analysis		Cost
⊟ **FY11 Portfolio Analysis**	Analysis		Cost, Resource
⊟ **Baseline**	Portfolio Selection Scenario		Cost
Baseline	Portfolio Selection Scenario		Resource
Collin save portfolio	Portfolio Selection Scenario		Resource

Figure 13–7

Once we run the portfolio analysis and select the Analyze Resources icon in the Ribbon, we will get a list of project files. In the top left of Figure 13–8 is the Resource Constraint that we have established—that no new resources will be hired. Beneath that is the summary information that results from this constraint when it is used. In this example, 10 projects are chosen. This means that 10 separate projects can be worked on with this constraint. Note that this is a list of 10 projects that can be worked on simultaneously; not sequentially.

Earlier in this chapter we mentioned that some projects that do not necessarily fit the priority list can be forced into the list. This is shown in the project list's *Force in/out* column. In this case, we have a schedule that is the favorite project of an executive that we will do, even if it doesn't qualify for this portfolio analysis, as shown in Figure 13–9.

So far, we have looked at the project list that this analysis has resulted in based on one criterion. Another way to view this information is to look at the list of information from the resource perspective. Figure 13–10 shows how a list of projects appears when performing analysis based solely on resource information. The top half of this screen shows the generic resources that are available, and the bottom half of the screen shows the resource requirements for each project file.

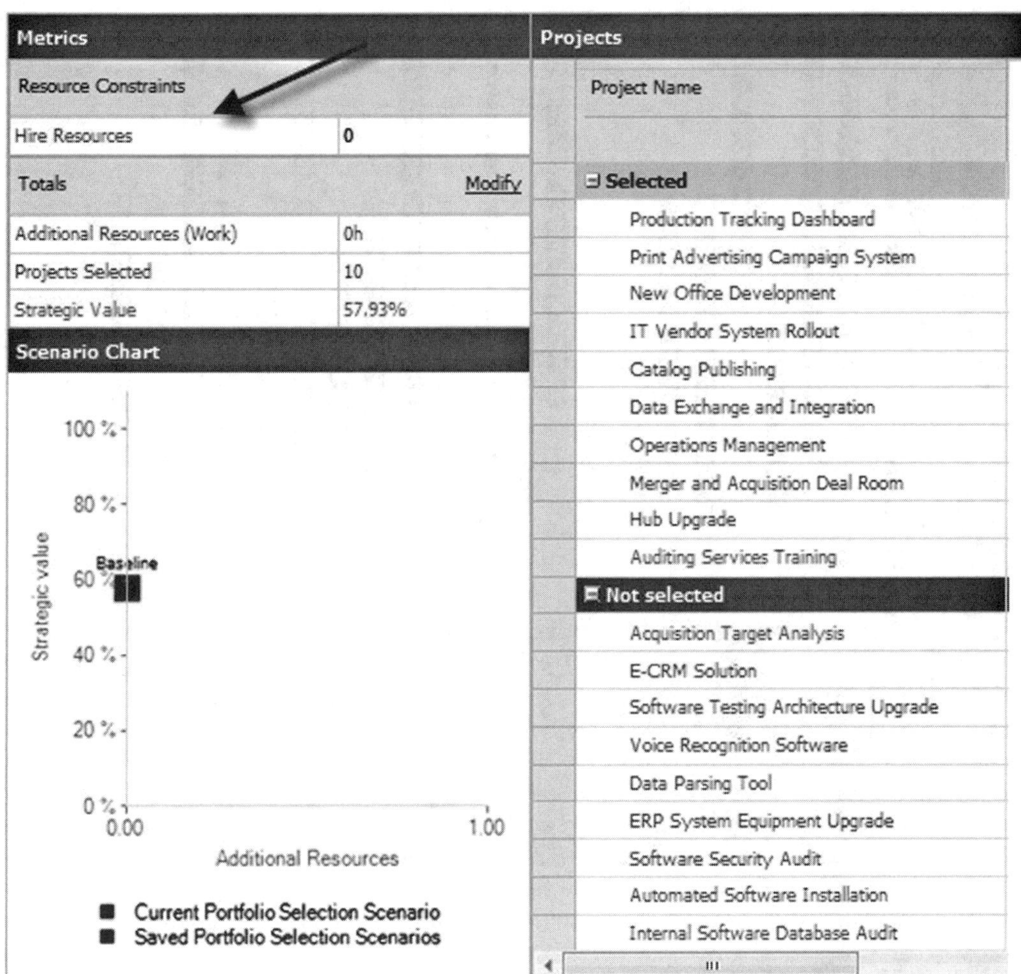

Figure 13–8

In the top right of the Resource Availability section is the Highlight Deficit check box. Selecting this will illustrate which generic resources skill sets (Roles) will be overallocated based on the project list, shown in Figure 13–11. In this case, we are viewing the Roles by month, so the highlighted amounts are for that Role for that specific month.

One of the generic resources assigned to the new proposal is overallocated. The role of Tester for the month of February is overallocated by 64.11 hours. As

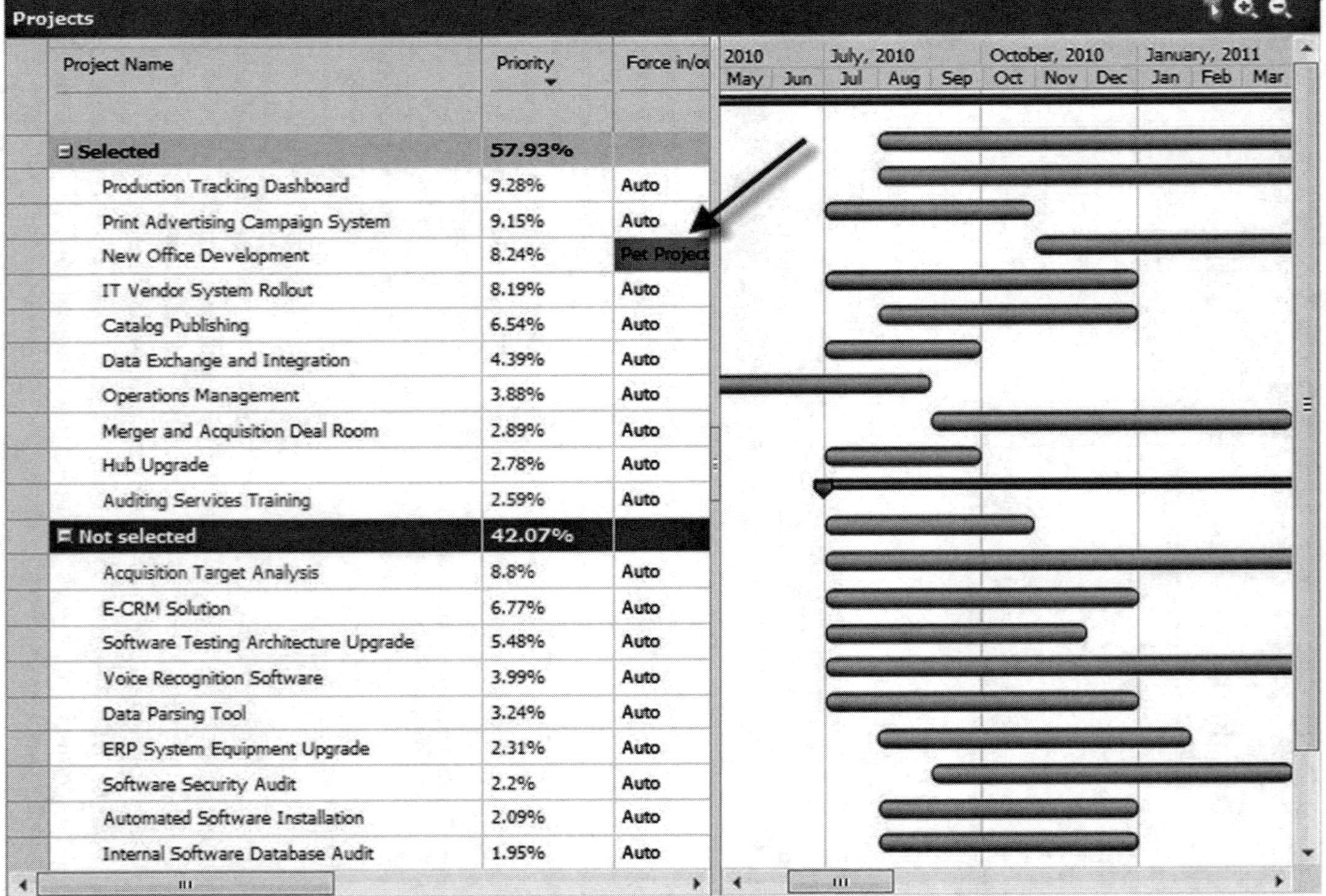
Projects
Project Name | Priority | Force in/ou
Selected | 57.93%
Production Tracking Dashboard | 9.28% | Auto
Print Advertising Campaign System | 9.15% | Auto
New Office Development | 8.24% | Pet Project
IT Vendor System Rollout | 8.19% | Auto
Catalog Publishing | 6.54% | Auto
Data Exchange and Integration | 4.39% | Auto
Operations Management | 3.88% | Auto
Merger and Acquisition Deal Room | 2.89% | Auto
Hub Upgrade | 2.78% | Auto
Auditing Services Training | 2.59% | Auto
Not selected | 42.07%
Acquisition Target Analysis | 8.8% | Auto
E-CRM Solution | 6.77% | Auto
Software Testing Architecture Upgrade | 5.48% | Auto
Voice Recognition Software | 3.99% | Auto
Data Parsing Tool | 3.24% | Auto
ERP System Equipment Upgrade | 2.31% | Auto
Software Security Audit | 2.2% | Auto
Automated Software Installation | 2.09% | Auto
Internal Software Database Audit | 1.95% | Auto
2010 | July, 2010 | October, 2010 | January, 2011
May | Jun | Jul | Aug | Sep | Oct | Nov | Dec | Jan | Feb | Mar

Figure 13–9

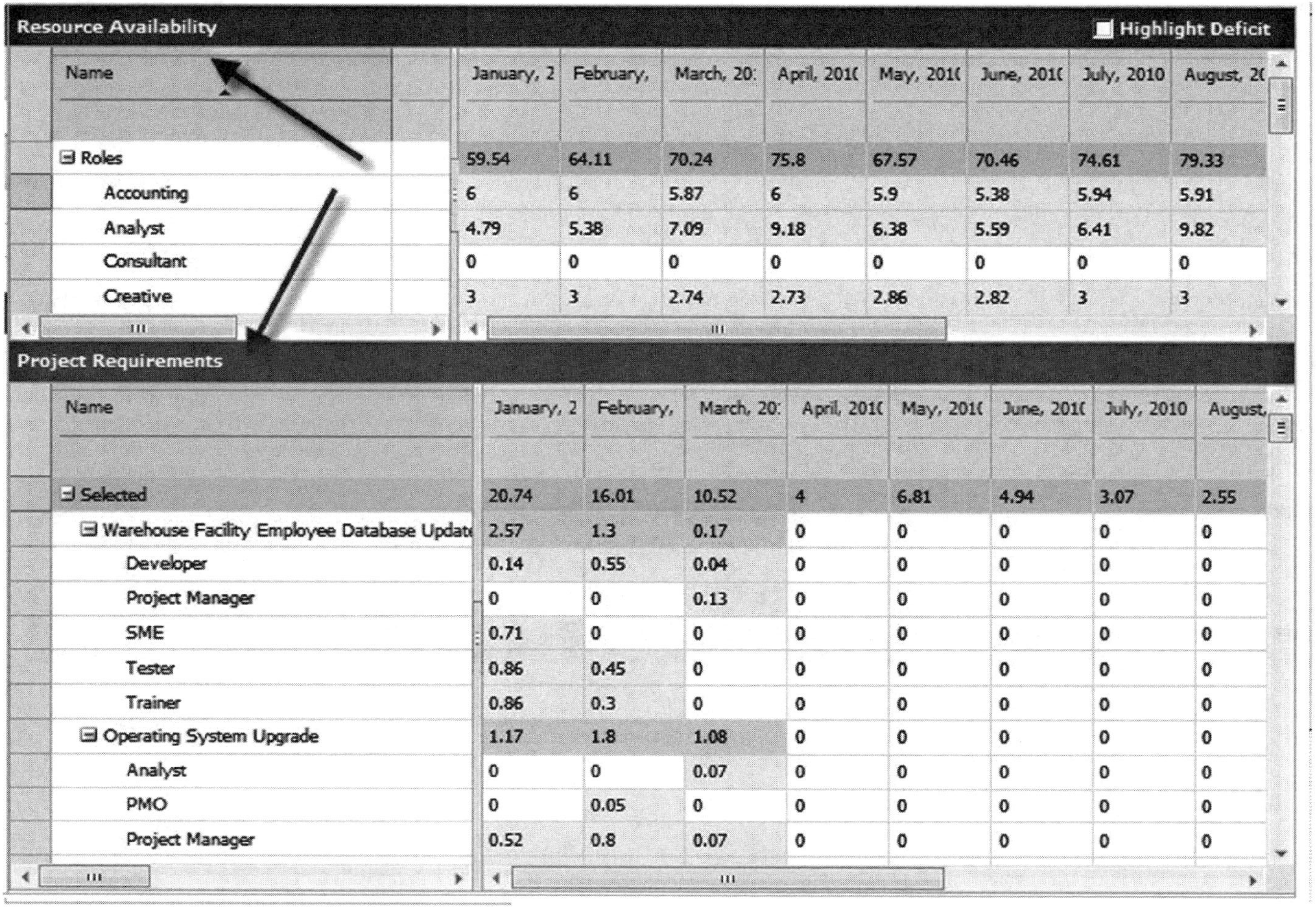

Resource Availability | Highlight Deficit

Name	January, 2	February,	March, 20:	April, 201(	May, 201(	June, 201(	July, 2010	August, 2(
⊟ Roles	59.54	64.11	70.24	75.8	67.57	70.46	74.61	79.33
Accounting	6	6	5.87	6	5.9	5.38	5.94	5.91
Analyst	4.79	5.38	7.09	9.18	6.38	5.59	6.41	9.82
Consultant	0	0	0	0	0	0	0	0
Creative	3	3	2.74	2.73	2.86	2.82	3	3

Project Requirements

Name	January, 2	February,	March, 20:	April, 201(	May, 201(	June, 201(	July, 2010	August,
⊟ Selected	20.74	16.01	10.52	4	6.81	4.94	3.07	2.55
⊟ Warehouse Facility Employee Database Updat	2.57	1.3	0.17	0	0	0	0	0
Developer	0.14	0.55	0.04	0	0	0	0	0
Project Manager	0	0	0.13	0	0	0	0	0
SME	0.71	0	0	0	0	0	0	0
Tester	0.86	0.45	0	0	0	0	0	0
Trainer	0.86	0.3	0	0	0	0	0	0
⊟ Operating System Upgrade	1.17	1.8	1.08	0	0	0	0	0
Analyst	0	0	0.07	0	0	0	0	0
PMO	0	0.05	0	0	0	0	0	0
Project Manager	0.52	0.8	0.07	0	0	0	0	0

Figure 13–10

Resource Availability

Highlight Deficit

Name	January, 2	February,	March, 20:	April, 201(	May, 201(	June, 201(	July, 2010	August, 2(	Sep
Roles	59.54	64.11	70.24	75.8	67.57	70.46	74.61	79.33	80.2
Accounting	6	6	5.87	6	5.9	5.38	5.94	5.91	6
Analyst	4.79	5.38	7.09	9.18	6.38	5.59	6.41	9.82	10
Consultant	0	0	0	0	0	0	0	0	0
Creative	3	3	2.74	2.73	2.86	2.82	3	3	3

Figure 13–11

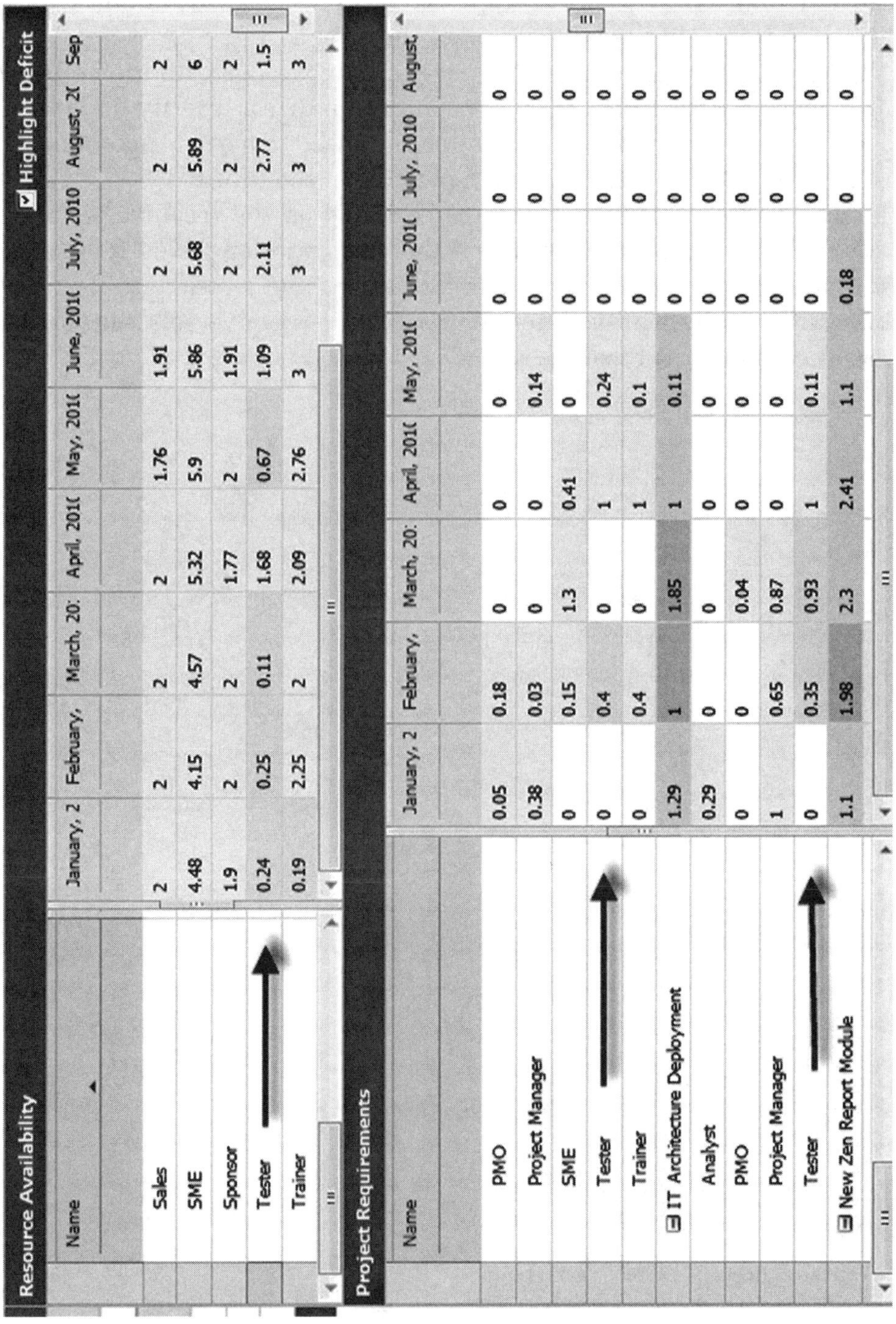

Resource Availability ☑ Highlight Deficit

Name	January, 2	February,	March, 20:	April, 201(	May, 201(	June, 201(	July, 2010	August, 2(	Sep
Sales	2	2	2	2	1.76	1.91	2	2	2
SME	4.48	4.15	4.57	5.32	5.9	5.86	5.68	5.89	6
Sponsor	1.9	2	2	1.77	2	1.91	2	2	2
Tester	0.24	0.25	0.11	1.68	0.67	1.09	2.11	2.77	1.5
Trainer	0.19	2.25	2	2.09	2.76	3	3	3	3

Project Requirements

Name	January, 2	February,	March, 20:	April, 201(	May, 201(	June, 201(	July, 2010	August,
PMO	0.05	0.18	0	0	0	0	0	0
Project Manager	0.38	0.03	0	0	0.14	0	0	0
SME	0	0.15	1.3	0.41	0	0	0	0
Tester	0	0.4	0	1	0.24	0	0	0
Trainer	0	0.4	0	1	0.1	0	0	0
⊟ IT Architecture Deployment	1.29	1	1.85	1	0.11	0	0	0
Analyst	0.29	0	0	0	0	0	0	0
PMO	0	0	0.04	0	0	0	0	0
Project Manager	1	0.65	0.87	0	0	0	0	0
Tester	0	0.35	0.93	1	0.11	0	0	0
⊟ New Zen Report Module	1.1	1.98	2.3	2.41	1.1	0.18	0	0

Figure 13–12

can be seen in Figure 13–12, two separate project files with Tester on them are highlighted by arrows in the bottom half of the screen.

This will help us view where we will have resource issues with the proposals in relation to our existing project files. When we finalize a priority list, we will be able to determine what project files will either need to move to accommodate our resources *or* resource needs that are possible in the future.

In the previous example, we concentrated solely on the resource effects on the portfolio, but we know that this isn't the only criterion for portfolio selection. We wanted to emphasize how the information from a task within a single project file will roll all the way up to the portfolio view. Conversely, the portfolio information rolls into the resource reports.

14

Questions and Answers

One objective of this book is to help you understand the *why* and not just the *how* of resource management. Hopefully, the previous chapters explained some of the *why* for different areas of resource management, and for Microsoft Project Server and Microsoft Project Professional. However, there are a few questions that are often encountered, so the authors decided to add this chapter to provide answers to those questions.

Please note that these answers are a blend of opinion and methodology, and are meant as food for thought more than as hard and fast business rules. Every organization is unique and has its own set of variables that may affect how an answer should be modified to better apply to those unique needs.

These questions are not necessarily in any order, and some answers may overlap while others should be taken in conjunction with other information provided in this book.

1. **Saving money and resource management—how do they tie together?**

   Saving money is an area that is difficult to quantify in some areas of resource management and extremely easy to do so in other areas. The difficult areas are related to productivity and information flow. How much money is being saved when resources are updating their tasks in real time and the resource manager doesn't have to spend half a day every week asking the individual resources on each schedule as to his or her progress.

In some of the easier areas to quantify, resource management brings the ability to see into the future. If you are using specific resource names or generic resources, you can look at upcoming assignments and determine what skill sets or people will be over-capacity and when that will occur. You can plan for that event if you can see it coming. If you don't have any resource management planned for the future, the solution will be forced upon you when you hit that time period—either throwing more money at it in the form of overtime, new hires, consultants, rush shipping, or missing the customer's deadline.

There are some areas that are both difficult to monetize and easy to see the benefit. For example, how much is saved by being able to tell a customer a realistic delivery date? If you can show a schedule to a customer, you are providing a service to them that is saving you future dollars and headaches. If you show a schedule that demonstrates why a project won't be completed until a specific date, you may be saving yourself from losing that customer on future projects if you were to just pick a date out of the air and then miss it.

2. **How do you encourage time reporting?**

   Any system, whether a business process or a new technology, is only as effective as what its inputs can produce. Therefore, it is important that the resources assigned tasks update their time appropriately so that you have reports that are realistic and valuable. We have a few thoughts regarding the question of how to encourage time reporting.

   First, we like to remind the resources that they already *are* updating their time in some way. It may be that they are sending an e-mail once a week or in response to a periodic request by a project manager or resource manager. Or, they are updating their progress by stating it in a meeting, participating in a hallway conversation, or responding when somebody shows up at their desk and asks them for their progress.

   The second part to the answer is that since they are already updating their progress, why not update progress easily and routinely in a web-based process? This makes it quicker and eliminates the need to send e-mails, respond to questions, or otherwise have to update progress haphazardly.

A third part to this answer is that time reporting is beneficial to the resources themselves. If they use the system, they will have the ability to view their utilization, capacity, and other information that can help them. They will have reports that they or their resource manager can use to show that they are overallocated or otherwise explain things like "Why are you late on this?" Having the ability to report on their current workloads and what work is coming up can be invaluable to a resource. As resources become more adept at using those reports, they will be able to discuss all sorts of situations with their resource managers—like demonstrating how they are overallocated for an upcoming week.

The fourth part ties back to the money issue. If a resource is constantly overallocated, but there is no system to prove that it is a work issue versus a productivity issue, then how do you know the solution? In some cases, the resource is over-capacity and if time is being reported and tracked, it is straightforward to see where the resource is overallocated. Conversely, if time is being reported, it is also easier to see if a resource is truly overallocated or if they may need more training or better tools to complete their work in a timely manner. In either case, the money saved from resolving the overallocations are more than worth the effort of tracking.

3. **How do you avoid the "90% done" approach?**

This is a common case where resources will say that all is going well and that their progress is "almost done" or "about 90% done," and that they just have to "finish up." Then, somehow, when the task due date is imminent, the resource starts explaining that they are not really quite as far along as they have been indicating.

This really comes down to a business process. The first step to remedy this situation might be to implement a regularly scheduled update time. Most companies seem to use Friday afternoon. This means that a resource has to have all their tasks updated before they leave the office on Friday. As a side note, updating on Friday afternoons is such a common practice that it is part of the reason for the cache system that Microsoft implemented in Project Server.

The second part of the business process is to set criteria for updates. This depends a bit on the project management maturity of the organization. At its most simple level, an organization might implement a system with four percentage updates. For example, when a task is started, the resource enters 25%, when they are about halfway through, they enter 50%, and when closer to the end, they enter 75%. When they complete the task, they enter 100%. A variation might be to do percentage and dates, having the resource enter a percentage and the estimated completion date.

Another method might be to use hours instead of percentages. If the resource enters the amount of hours of work done and the amount of hours remaining, the percentage field will automatically be calculated for them.

Note, though, that the more detailed the method of updating, the more detailed the project management and resource management is required of the organization. Using a specific set of percentages is easier to manage than using hours. The level of management should be reflected in the level of reporting that you need. If you have to report on a per-hour or resource unit percentage, rather than tracking updates with a few set percentages, it won't be sufficient. But, that may be enough information if you are not tracking at a deeper level.

4. **How do you account for non-project work to better portray resource availability?**

   There is no debate that accounting for non-project work is tough to do, and that there is no single solution for this issue. Part of the problem is that there is no way to schedule the break/fix work that might occur for a resource. So, solutions vary, depending on your organizational structure and the way that you track resource availability for scheduled work.

   In a case where a resource is almost entirely dedicated to scheduled work, the usage of calendars can help account for this time. If a resource has regularly scheduled meetings or other time that is for non-project work, then those can be added to their individual resource calendar.

   For a resource that has the possibility of working on non-scheduled work, but the amount of work is unknown, this becomes more difficult. Even if your organization doesn't use unit measurement for resources, this might be a case where a set amount of units can be determined for a resource. For example, if a resource spends half their time on scheduled tasks and half on break/fix/maintenance change his or her available working time (either on their calendar or in the Resource Information box's available time) to half-a-day, every day.

   Another method to account for non-project time is to create an administrative tasks schedule. The timesheet functions allow for administrative time to be accounted for, but this might be in addition to that set of functions. If a schedule is built that is designed only for the non-scheduled work, and it is updated regularly, then over time a larger picture will emerge for how much time the resource is available, helping to make work scheduling more predictable.

None of these solutions are perfect at the beginning, and they never get to be exactly precise. However, over time an organization can better predict how much non-scheduled or non-project work a resource will have.

5. **Should resource management be determined by an organization's level of project management maturity?**

Absolutely! Resource management is determined by an organization's level of project management maturity. One of the most common reasons for a failed implementation of project or resource management is trying to do everything at once. Implementing resource management should be done at the same pace as the ability and understanding of project management. If resource management is brand new to your organization, perhaps only getting resource names assigned to tasks and a level of information that can be maintained and used is a victory.

It is our experience that this becomes a spiral of information, where the business and the tool drive each other to more detail and more maturity. For example, if you start at the point of assigning a resource to a task, then you do have some valuable information—who is working on what and during what time frame. When you look at reports, the detail information won't be that great. But, once you become adept at managing that much information the natural tendency will be to get more information. So, perhaps the next thing to add is to put the resource onto a group calendar. Now we have better information about who is working on what and when they are available. Once management starts seeing reports (limited as they may be) about a resource, they will want more information about that resource until it is at the level of detail that they want in order to manage the organization.

6. **I am the resource manager and am responsible for obtaining updates from resources that are not in my line of authority. How can Microsoft Project help me accomplish this?**

This is a common situation where the resources have competing priorities that may not be schedule related or may not align to the priorities that you have been given. Many books have been written about how to function in this type of matrix environment. In the authors' opinion, this is a case where any tool will not be able to resolve the issue, but this tool can help to highlight the results.

Project Professional and Project Server have many reports (examples of some types of reports were covered in Chapter 12), and you can make a report that is very simple but will show the issue. For example, if one of the issues in a matrix environment is that resources are not updating their tasks and your work is suffering as a result, then a report that simply has a name and "who didn't update this week" information could be part of your regular reporting. In a matrix environment, sometimes it is difficult to ensure that resources update their tasks in a timely manner. Therefore, a report that simply has the list of resources who didn't update this week might be a good report to run on a regular basis. This report doesn't have to be used as a negative report, but could be used as a motivator.

Another report for matrix organizations might be to show who worked how many hours on what projects in the last reporting period. The people who do not update will have no time represented. Even though everybody knows that they worked on something, if they didn't update it then it didn't get on the report—and upper management doesn't like to see "0" for time worked.

Some people think of these types of reports as "negative," but we do not think of them in that way. Think about this type of reporting in relation to the end of the project. If you do not know the status of your project file, how do you know when to tell the customer to expect their product or service? You might be two weeks early or two weeks late. But, without a report on the timeliness of the schedule, how do you know? And, without having updates to the schedule, you can't tell the customer when you will deliver.

Think about updates in this way as well: Somehow it seems that everybody is able to turn in their timesheets to the Payroll department. Even if they are salaried and don't have to turn in a weekly time card, they are somehow still able to know how many vacation days they have accrued and how to take them and get paid. Why is that? Because there is a reward system in place—you turn in a time card or you don't get paid. The same concept works with updating time, but without the pay component.

If you don't update your time, then how does anybody know you are overworked? How does anybody know you are working at all on what you should be working on? How does the resource manager and project manager know when they can tell the customer (or upper management) that a project file will be completed?

7. **Why track time at all?**

The answer to this question is similar to the last paragraph in the answer to question 6: How do you know where the schedule stands if you don't track where you are? This is a great time to throw out a popular cliché: *You get what you measure.*

We think that with every client we have worked with, once a tracking system is in place, even a simple, high-level one, results in some surprises. One of those seems to be those forgotten "legacy" systems that somebody is spending time on, but nobody notices until their time is being tracked. It isn't that they are doing anything wrong. It is just that most people didn't realize that "so much time is being spent on that."

When you start to measure resources' time, you get a better picture as to what they are really working on, and how that is affecting the organization's productivity, effectiveness, utilization, and capacity for other work.

8. **How long does implementing resource management take?**

Resource management implementation time is the "magic bullet" question. This question is really, "How many days, weeks or months will this system take us to implement and become experts within our organization?" The answer is that there is always more to work on and become better at, and that you will never be done. This is not a "put a technology tool in place and our organization will reap instant rewards, and we will be good at it" kind of methodology. This isn't a fad. Resource management has been around for a long time in many forms and methodologies. For example, the ancient Egyptians must have used it when they built the pyramids!

Resource management implementation takes time. It takes understanding of what the organization is trying to accomplish. We will keep on repeating the mantra that you need to "Start small and build up your capability and experience over time." Creating a schedule and assigning some names to it is not resource management. But, assigning names to a schedule is the beginning of resource management because now you have some information from which to build.

Your organization will reach plateaus of capability (and desire) in resource management. The goal should be to understand where you are in your organizational maturity and where you want to be as an organization.

15

Conclusion

In the years of experience that the authors have worked with many organizations in various stages of resource management, it is always our great pleasure to help them with their needs in this discipline. We have written this book to help organizations get a better understanding of what is usually their largest area of investment—resources. The term *project management* is used quite often, and resource management is often considered to be just a part of project management, but we feel that it is a critical part. Without resource management, there is no project or portfolio management.

We know that within one book we can't cover every situation that every organization will encounter in their resource management or Microsoft Project experiences. That is part of the joy of this area—it is constantly churning at the edges even if it has a solid foundation. Resource management isn't a new discipline and Microsoft Project has been around for a number of years. However, how your organization uses them together *today* is where the work resides.

How you set up the organization's business processes and how you set up the technological tools should match each other. Our philosophy is that the technology should meet your business process as much as possible, rather than your business processes having to be modified to match technology. Having an understanding of how Microsoft Project can be modified (without add-ons or other software) is something that we consult with organizations about all the time. This is a tool that has capabilities and functionality most organizations don't realize.

Resource Planning

General Philosophy

This book concentrates on the actions of resource management and capabilities of Microsoft Project Professional 2010 and Microsoft Project Server 2010. The examples show why and how to do certain activities, but there are some assumptions behind those examples. One assumption is that the resource manager has a resource plan and a system to assign resources. In Chapter 5, we discuss the Resource Pool and the setup of resources. In Chapter 6, we discuss the resource calendar and project calendar, and in Chapter 7, we discuss skill sets.

Setup and Planning

There is setup and project planning that needs to be understood before diving into assigning a resource to a work breakdown structure (WBS) task. It is important that the "right" resource is assigned to the "right" task. In this book, we demonstrate how to determine if the resource you are assigning is available, and how to see other reports about utilization and capacity. But, is it always *right* to assign a resource simply because they are available? No. There should be a plan in place to determine which resources can be assigned when and for what reasons.

A planned strategy for setup, operations, and maintenance is important because every resource manager may try to assign the same resources to their own projects' tasks. It is understandable that each resource manager will try to get the "best" resource for his or her own schedules. Using the reporting capabilities of Microsoft Project (Professional and/or Server) helps managers understand who is assigned to what, but it doesn't help understand who *should* be assigned to what. Similarly, the project portfolio priority information helps this situation by giving clarity to the whole organization as to what should be worked on next; but, it doesn't put in place policies about when to reassign a resource from one task or priority to another, based upon those priorities. For example, if a person is assigned to work on one schedule and then gets assigned to another schedule with a task that is equal or higher, how is that resolved?

It isn't easy to just create a policy that states that the resource will always work on the higher priority project. That sounds good on paper, but there needs to be some sort of criteria. What if they are 10 minutes away from completing their work on the lower priority schedule—should they just stop? Or, what if they are 1 hour away? Or, what if they are 1 day away? These situations will almost always occur and can't be pre-qualified or pre-determined. However, if there is a framework for how to deal with these sorts of issues and situations, then dealing with them in a rush when they come up will be more efficient and effective.

There are numerous items that can and should be considered when assigning resources to tasks. Some organizations have created checklists to help the resource manager find the best resource for a task. For example, some of the items on a checklist could be:

- Determine approximate number of hours needed per task.
- Determine required skill sets for the task.
- Indicate approximately how many resources are needed per task.
- Assess if the schedule can be created with generic resources first.
- If using named resources, determine:
    - Current capacity and utilization.
    - Priority of the tasks.
    - If priorities of the project files will interfere with this one.
    - If the skill set of the resource will decrease (or increase) the duration of the assigned task.

  - If the skill set isn't exactly as needed, a method for resources to obtain the needed skill set (training or other education).
  - How much non-scheduled work the resource receives (e.g., if assigned to break/fix work).
  - Resource calendar(s) are current and accurate.
- Physical location of the resource:
  - Is the location remote or local?
- Backup plan for resource changes (promotion, transfer, or departure).

Checklists can be added to and may affect other documentation such as the communication plan. For example, if one or more of the resources on your project file are located at a remote site, the type and method of communication will be affected. Having a weekly meeting will require having at least a conference call number so that the remote resource(s) can join and participate.

Planning Skill Sets

Having a framework set up for evaluating resources against the needs of specific tasks for project files can be very important. Additionally, to assess resource's skills alongside each other, a common methodology needs to be implemented. One such area might be that of skill sets. In Chapter 7, we discussed how to use Microsoft Project to assign skill sets. However, there needs to be some planned structure for this before you can start creating and assigning skill sets to resources. Note that in this example, we are not discussing how Microsoft Project works; we are discussing how to be prepared to set up Microsoft Project and how to best use it.

How do you define skill sets? Creating a document with an outline of definitions for the terminology in the skill sets makes a common starting point when assigning skill sets to specific resources. This allows new resource managers to quickly determine who has what skill sets and to understand how to enter skill sets for new resources. For example, stating that a resource is a "Systems Administrator" means different things to different people. If you have three or four types of computer systems in the organization, then a "Systems Administrator" might mean Windows, Oracle, or Linux, and this could result in a different set of abilities and values in the schedule. A hierarchy should be created with terms, definitions, and some clarification.

For example, a skill set hierarchy might be something like the enclosed table. Here is a brief explanation of the fields and layout of Table A-1.

- **Skill Set Heading:** This is the top level category. It is rare to assign someone at this skill set level.
- **Skill Set:** This is the level that better defines the type of skill that the individual possesses.
- **Experience Level:** In this example, the experience level is broken down based upon the number of years that they have been this type of accountant. It does not necessarily represent how many years they have been with the organization.

Table A-1. Skill Sets Hierarchy of Headings

Skill Sets Heading	Skill Set	Experience Level (Years Range) A = 5 or less B = 5 or more	Hierarchy Level	Definition
Accountant		A	1	Top level selection-must be a CPA (or appropriately certified) to be considered an accountant
	Tax	A	2	Experienced in tax accounting.
	Tax	B	2	Experienced in tax accounting.
	Bookkeeper	A	2	Understanding of financial reporting systems and entry methods.
	Bookkeeper	B	2	Understanding of financial reporting systems and entry methods.
	Auditor	A	2	A person with the skills to examine accounting records and compare the records to verifiable items.
	Auditor	B	2	A person with the skills to examine accounting records and compare the records to verifiable items.

- **Hierarchy Level:** This is a helpful reminder where this skill set will fall when selecting it in Project. Each level of the hierarchy is shown as a numerical value with the first level being a "1", the second level a "2", and so on. This is the outline order for a specific skill set.
- **Definition:** To help all the readers get a basic understanding and to have a common agreement about what this skill set means, there is a short definitional statement in this field.

Therefore, an auditor with eight years of experience will have this selection in their skill set resource field: **Accountant/Auditor B**.

An accountant with three years of bookkeeping experience would have this in their skill set resource field: **Accountant/Bookkeeper A**.

A critical part of having a form or table for planning is to update it with meaningful information as changes are made in the organization. This isn't very hard to remember to do since resources will want to update their skill sets with the new education and skills that they develop over time. When your organization has resources helping the resource managers to update their information, keeping this information current is not difficult.

Custom Fields

Skill sets are just one area where a specific checklist or other documentation can be created. Other documentation might be to create custom fields or to establish a lookup table with definitions. This would allow the resource managers to have important information about resources that might be valuable for reporting or for assigning tasks. For example, it might be valuable to know which geographical location a resource resides in, and a custom field could be created for that purpose. Or, it might be important to be able to sort resources based on an organizational criteria that doesn't match the RBS. For example, if your organization has department names that don't match the RBS structure, it might be beneficial to have a field for this information. In Chapter 5, we discuss options for custom fields.

This book has free material available for download from the Web Added Value™ resource center at *www.jrosspub.com*

Resource Manager Guide

General Philosophy

There are a lot of items for the resource manager to remember to do every day, week, or month to keep the system in place and working as expected. Microsoft often creates a guidebook for these items for most versions of Microsoft Project. The guidebooks are normally lengthy and detailed manuals. If you obtain a guidebook for Microsoft Project 2010, then we recommend that you obtain a copy and determine which parts of it apply to you and your needs. For convenience, we put together an abbreviated list of what the resource manager should be checking as part of his or her routine.

It is our assumption that the resource manager is a separate individual from the project server administrator. This means that, in our view, the resource manager does not have the ability to modify server settings. This situation is represented in the list below by excluding some items, such as "modify the view" because that isn't something that the resource manager can do. In Project Professional 2010 stand-alone, the resource manager normally will have the ability to make changes to views and reports, so that action is represented in that list.

Project Professional (Stand-alone)

Daily

These are the items that the resource manager should check at least once per day:

- Tasks
  - Are there updates that you need?
  - Are there notes attached to updates that require action?
- Resources
  - Are there new project files requiring resources?
    - What are the requirements/skill sets needed for those tasks?
    - Who is available to be assigned?
  - Assign resources to new project files.

Weekly

These are the items that the resource manager should check at least once per week:

- Resources
  - Are all resource names current in the system?
    - Did anyone have a name change?
  - Has anyone left the company?
  - Has someone new been hired, and should she or he be a resource?
  - Do you need to replace or remove any resources from any project files?
  - Are any resources going to be unavailable in the near future?
    - Are their calendars updated?
    - What mitigation steps do you need to take to keep resources assigned to tasks?
- Training
  - Has anyone new been added as a resource who requires training on how to use the system?
  - Have any new resource managers been added who need to be trained?

Monthly

These are the items that the resource manager should check at least once per month:

- Views
    - Review current views for usage.
    - Review views for relevant information:
        - Do the views show the correct columns?
        - Are the columns in the right order?
    - Are some views no longer being used?
    - Are new views needed?
- Reports
    - Review current reports for usage.
    - Review reports for relevant information:
        - Do reports have the right columns?
        - Are reports in the right order?
    - How are the reports being used?
        - Should reports be updated to represent new business processes?
    - Should reports be removed?
- Communication
    - Are the resource managers communicating with the project managers?
        - What outages are there?
        - What can be done to correct any miscommunication so that resource managers and project managers can better do their work?
    - Are the resources and resource managers communicating?
        - What outages are there?
        - What can be done to correct any miscommunication so that resource managers and resources can better do their work?
- Resources
    - Are resources on the correct resource calendars?
    - Are the resource details correct in the Resource Information box for each resource?
    - Are the resource assignments updated and correct?

  - ◇ Are new generic resources required?
  - ◇ Should any of the existing generic resources be removed?
- ◆ Reports
  - ◇ What is the utilization and capacity of each resource for the next month?
  - ◇ What assignments are the resources currently working on?
  - ◇ What is the current status of the project file?
    - Is it late? On time? On hold?
    - How will that status affect your resource?
  - ◇ What is the current status of the predecessor task for your resource?
    - Is it late? Is it early?
    - How will the predecessor task status affect your resource's assignment?
- ◆ Training
  - ◇ Is there training documentation in a public site that needs to be updated?
  - ◇ Have there been some issues that might be corrected with more training?

Annually

These are the items that the resource manager should check at least once per year:

- ◆ Calendar
  - ◇ Review the standard calendar:
    - Update the calendar for organizational days off for the future.
    - This update should be for as many years ahead as your organization normally schedules.
  - ◇ Review other calendars:
    - Confirm that all custom calendars are appropriately updated.
- ◆ Training
  - ◇ Have new procedures been implemented that should be taught to system users?

  - ◇ Does documentation need to be updated?
  - ◇ Does documentation need to be removed?
- ◆ Resources
  - ◇ Are resources on the correct calendars?
  - ◇ Have any resources transferred to departments or teams that use different calendars?
  - ◇ Are you using a method for tracking resource time that meets your needs and the organization's needs?
  - ◇ Do you need to review the RBS?
  - ◇ Do you need to review skill sets (if using)?
  - ◇ What other custom fields need to be reviewed?
    - Any to remove?
    - Any to add?
  - ◇ Do you have the most current information for resources?
    - Have any resources obtained training this year that affects their Skill Sets?
- ◆ Resource Pool
  - ◇ Are there any changes needed in the Resource Pool settings? Check:
    - New columns.
    - Remove columns.
    - New custom fields.
    - Remove unused custom fields.

Project Server

Daily

These are the items that the resource manager should check at least once per day:

- ◆ Queue
  - ◇ Review the My Queued Jobs section:
    - Is there anything stuck in your queue?
- ◆ Timesheets
  - ◇ Are there updates that you need to accept or reject?
  - ◇ Are there notes attached to updates that require action?

- ◇ Do you have automated e-mails from the system that need your attention?
- ◆ Tasks
  - ◇ Are there any updates you need to accept or reject?
  - ◇ Are there any notes attached to updates that require action?
  - ◇ Do you have any automated e-mails from the system that need your attention?
- ◆ Status reports:
  - ◇ Have you received a required status report?
  - ◇ Have you sent a required status report?
- ◆ Resources
  - ◇ Are there new project files requiring resources?
    - What are the requirements/skill sets needed for those tasks?
    - Who is available to be assigned?
  - ◇ Assign resources to new project files.

Weekly

These are the items that the resource manager should check at least once per week:

- ◆ Delegates
  - ◇ Do you need to add or remove any delegate settings?
- ◆ Tasks
  - ◇ Are there tasks that should be closed to updates?
- ◆ Timesheets
  - ◇ Confirm that the data in the Manage Timesheets section is correct.
  - ◇ Are timesheets in the correct status?
  - ◇ Do timesheets need to be approved by you, or somebody else?
  - ◇ Do timesheets require adjustment?
- ◆ Resources
  - ◇ Are all of the resource names current in the system?
    - Did anyone have a name change?
  - ◇ Has anyone left the company?
  - ◇ Has someone new been hired, and should she or he be a resource?
  - ◇ Do you need to replace or remove a resource from any project file?

  - Are resources going to be unavailable in the near future?
    - Is his or her calendar updated?
    - What mitigation steps do you need to take to keep resources assigned to tasks?
- Training
  - Has anyone new been added as a resource who requires training on how to use the system?
  - Have new resource managers been added who need to be trained?

Monthly

These are the items that the resource manager should check at least once per month:

- Timesheets
  - Close old reporting periods that are still open so that they can't be accidentally updated.
- Approvals
  - Are there any automatic rules set up that should be modified?
  - Should a new approval or rule be added based on new project files that started this month?
  - Should any approvals or rules be deleted due to project files being completed this month?
- Views
  - Review current views for usage.
  - Review views for relevant information:
    - Do views have the correct columns?
    - Are columns in the right order?
  - Are any views no longer being used?
  - Are new views needed?
  - Review the views within Project Professional as well for these same criteria.
- Reports
  - Review current reports for usage.
  - Review reports for relevant information:
    - Do they have the correct columns?
    - Are the columns in the right order?

  - How are the reports being used?
    - Should reports be updated to represent new business processes?
  - Should any reports be removed?
  - Review the reports within Project Professional as well for these same criteria.
- E-mails
  - Review the Manage My Personal Alerts section:
    - Are the Task Alerts, Reminders, and Status Report Alerts set the way you want?
    - Is the Queue Job Failure Alert set the way you need it?
  - Review the Manage My Resource's Alerts and Reminders section:
    - Are the Task Alerts and Task Reminders set the way you want?
    - Have any projects recently started or finished that might warrant a change in these settings?
    - Are the Status Report Alerts set the way you need?
- Communication
  - Are the resource managers communicating with the project managers?
    - What outages are there?
    - What can be done to correct any miscommunication so that resource managers and project managers can better do their work?
  - Are the resources and resource managers communicating?
    - What outages are there?
    - What can be done to correct any miscommunication so that resource managers and resources can better do their work?
- Status report
  - Do you need to create any new recurring status reports for any of your resources or resource teams?
- Resources
  - Are all the active resources in the correct groups?
    - Do you need any new groups?
    - Can any groups be removed?

    - Are the groups in the right categories?
        - Do you need any new categories?
        - Can any categories be removed?
    - Are the views in the correct categories?
    - Are resources on the correct resource calendars?
    - Are the resource details correct in the Resource Information box for each resource?
    - Are the resource assignments updated and correct?
    - Are new generic resources required?
    - Should any of the existing generic resources be removed?
- Reports
    - What is the utilization and capacity of each resource for the next month?
    - What assignments are the resources currently working on?
    - What is the current status of the project file?
        - Is it late? On time? On hold?
        - How will that status affect your resource?
    - What is the current status of the predecessor task for your resource?
        - Is it late? Is it early?
        - How will that affect your resource's assignment?
- Training
    - Is there any training documentation in a public site that needs to be updated?
    - Have there been any issues that might be correct with more training?

Annually

These are the items that the resource manager should check at least once a year.

- Calendar
    - Review the standard calendar:

        - Update the Calendar for any organizational days off for the future.
        - This update should be for as many years ahead as your organization normally schedules.
    - Review other calendars:
        - Confirm that all custom calendars are appropriately updated.
- Timesheets
    - Have the project server administrator create timesheets for the next reporting period.
    - Is the method being used to update (% complete, work remaining, etc.) still pertinent to your organization and tracking methods?
    - Are there new timesheet lines classifications that should be activated?
    - Should any timesheet lines classifications be deactivated?
- Training
    - Have new procedures been implemented that should be taught to system users?
    - Does documentation need to be updated?
    - Does any documentation need to be removed?
- Resources
    - Are resources on the correct calendars?
    - Do resources who transferred to new departments or teams use different calendars?
    - Are you using a method for tracking resource time that meets your needs and the organization's needs?
    - Do you need to review the RBS?
    - Do you need to review skill sets (if using)?
    - What other custom fields need to be reviewed?
        - Any to remove?
        - Any to add?
    - Do you have the most current information for resources?
        - Have any resources obtained training this year that affects their skill sets?

- Resource Pool
  - Are there changes needed in the Resource Pool settings, such as:
    - New columns.
    - Remove columns.
    - New custom fields.
    - Remove unused custom fields.

Index

A

Active Directory Synchronization, 58
Actual Work information report, 201
Add an Existing Task, timesheet entry and, 173, 176
Administrative time
  timesheet and, 178, 186, 187
  timesheet setup and, 191, 197, 199
Administrator
  Enterprise Calendars and, 35
  security settings and, 25
Allow Future Time Reporting option, 195
Approval Center screen, 152, 155, 157
Approval Routing, timesheet setup, 196
Approvals. *See* Automatic approvals; Change approvals, viewing
Assigning a resource, 89–104. *See also* Team Planner
  Add Resources-Build Team, 90
  Build Team dialog box, 91, 95–100, 96
  custom filters, setting up, 92–95
  Existing Filters drop-down box, 92, 95
  filter, setting up, 92
  Generic Resource icon, 93
  Open Resource Pool option box, 102
  Save Filter button, 95
  selecting resources for team, 95–100
  Show Resource Availability checkbox, 95
  by skill set. *See* skill set, resource assigned by
  tasks, assigning, 100, 101
  Team Planner, 104–113
Assignment Work by Resource graph
  available reports list, 131, 133
  Legend, 127, 129
  new assigned resource, 132, 133
  Remaining Availability option, 131, 133
  View Options, 126, 127, 129
Assignment Work by Resource view, 221, 222
Auditing, timesheet setup, 196
Automatic approvals, 162–167
  Automatic Updates, 162, 164, 165
  Awaiting Approval message, 164
  Manage Rules icon/option, 161, 162
  New icon, the Edit/Create New Rule screen, 162–163, 165
  resource section, 162, 164, 165
  Task Change information, 164
Availability of analyst, 126

B

Batched group of updates, 146, 150
Billing Category, timesheet setup, 197
Booking Type, 58
"Building the team." *See* Assigning a resource
Build Team dialog box
  adding a resource, 121–122, 123
  Analyst positions, filtered, 125

Details button/Resource Information, 126, 127
Graphs button, 126, 128
Match button, 125
opening, 122
replacing generic with named resource, 122
Resource Names column, 122, 124
Business process, technology and, 301
Business drivers, 280, 285
Business Intelligence report/link, 267, 275–277
Business Intelligence Center, 275, 276
sample reports/guides, 275, 276
separate web parts, 277, 278
Business Intelligence report type/link, 267, 275–277

C

Calendar. *See* project calendar; resource calendars
Capacity line, 221
Capacity planning
in Microsoft Project Server 2010, 12
standard calendar and, 85, 88
Change approvals, viewing, 158, 159
Change Working Time, no Project Server, 47–49
calendar selection, 49
Change Working Time option, 47
Create New Calendar button, 48
Change Working Time, Project Server and, 40–43
colors, legend for, 37
Details for Default, Work Weeks tab, 41
Exceptions tab, holidays and, 46, 47
instructions, detailed, 37
new Enterprise Calendar and, 44, 45
new title of calendar, entering, 40
nonworking days, gray highlighted, 43
Set days to nonworking time, 42
Work Weeks tab/Default, 40
Change Working Time box, 77, 80–82, 83
Changing time, not days, 83–88
Details button, 84
Exceptions Details box/Working Times, 85
File-Close in Project Professional, 87
highlighted working times, 86
instructions, detailed, 83
saving/closing sheet, 83
Changing working time for one resource
Change Working Time box, 80–82
changing days, details of, 74, 77, 83
changing time, not days, 83–88
description of dates, 81
Enterprise Resource Global file, 75
Enterprise Resource sheet, 78
getting to correct date, 80
"nonworking" days noted, 82
Resource Center on PWA, 75
Resource Information box, 79
resource name, selection of, 76
Christmas Day, 46, 47
Close Tasks to Update option, 207
Committed Booking Type, 58
Confirmation box, update cycle, 153, 156
Contacts section, Task Details, 144
Copy Calendar option, 37
Cost type resources, 51
Create new base calendar option, 49
Create Periods, 205, 206
Custom fields
resource planning and, 307
setting up, 114–116
Custom Fields dialog box
Add Field to Enterprise button, 116–117
Lookup table and, 117, 118
Position values and, 117, 120

D

Daily tracking, timesheet setup, 193
Default Reporting Units, timesheet setup, 193
Default Timesheet Creation Mode, timesheet setup, 193
Defense Contract Audit Agency, 196
Define Batch Naming Convention, 205, 206
Define Bulk Period Parameters, 205, 206
Define Near Future Planning Window, Time and Task Management, 204
Demand, resource capacity and, 18

E

Edit Lookup Table for Position dialog box, 120
Employee. *See* Resource(s)
Enterprise Calendars
existing calendars and, 37
new, after changing working time, 44, 45
for Project Server, 49
selecting, 37, 38
Enterprise Global template, 237–238
Enterprise Resource Global file
generic resource and, 113
selecting more than one resource, 74
Enterprise resource pool, 18
Enterprise Resource sheet, 77, 78, 83
Enterprise Schedule, 35
Excel, 251, 262
Excel Services, 277
Exceptions tab, holidays and, 46, 47
Excess capacity, 221
Exchange Server Integration, 58
Executive, viewpoint of, 6–7

Expediting approvals. *See* Automatic approvals

F
Failed projects, 2
Features, key to, 9, 11
Fiscal Periods screen, 207, 208
Flowchart, permission settings, 33
Forms Authentication, 58
Funeral, 197

G
Generic resource, 51, 122
Globally dispersed teams, 18, 19

H
Holidays, 46, 47
Hourly Reporting Limits, timesheet setup, 195
HR Prioritization analysis, 285
Human resources. *See* Resource(s)

I
Icons, server/local files, 68
Import Timesheet/Current Progress, 189, 190, 191
Information
  generally, 237–238
  Reports in Project Professional, 249–261
  Reports in Project Server, 268–278
  Views in Project Professional, 238–248
  Views in Project Server, 262–267
  Visual Reports, 251–261
Insert Administrative Tasks option, 200

J
Jury duty, 186, 197

K
Key to features, 9, 11

L
Leveling Options icon, 212
Leveling resource assignments. *See* Resource leveling
Level Resource icon, 214, 215
Level Resources box, 214, 216
Line Classifications, timesheet setup and, 191, 197, 198
Local project file icon, 68
Lookup table, building, 114

M
Make a copy of ____ calendar option, 49
Manage Rules icon/option, 161, 162
Manage Timesheets screen, 186, 188, 189
Manage Users setting, 218
Manage Views link, 262
Match function, 113
Material resources, 51
Metadata, standardizing of, 18
Microsoft Project Server 2010
Microsoft SQL Server Reporting Services window, 268
My Tasks page, 169

N
Named resource, 122
Names, reading of, 52–53
New Calendar option, 37, 39
New Year's Day, 46, 47
"Ninety-percent done" approach, 295–296
Non-Billable timesheet types, 192
Non-project file time, 186, 207
Non-project work, 296–297
Non-working days. See also *Change Working Time* box

O
OLAP data, 268
Outlook for task updates
  benefits of, 167
  PWA and, 164
Overallocation. *See also* Resource leveling
  Date Range, 223–224
  generic resources and, 287, 291–292
  graphical, 225, 226
  intuitive management of, 19
  Resource Center and, 226
  stand-alone Resource Pool and, 231
  Team Planner and, 104, 105, 110–113
Overtime timesheet types, 192

P
People, right skills and, 19
Percentage update method, 146, 147
PerformancePoint, 277
Permission templates, 32
Personal time off, 197
Perspectives, resource management, 4–7
  executive, 6–7
  project manager, 6
  resource, 5
  resource manager, 5–6
PivotTable
  data behind, 257, 258
  PivotCharts and, 251
  PivotTable Field List, 251, 257
PMBOK® Guide, 17–18

PMPSpecialists.com, 136–137
Pool takes precedence option, 71
Portfolio analysis, 281
Portfolio management, 301
Portfolio perspective, 279–292
  Build Team icon, 283–284
  business drivers, 280
  business process, 282
  Force in / out column, 286, 288
  high-level tasks assigned, 285
  HR Prioritization analysis, 285
  overallocation, generic resources, 287, 291–292
  portfolio analysis, 281
  Portfolio Server product, 280
  prioritization and, 280–281, 285–286
  Project Center/New icon, 282, 283
  project information page, 282, 283
  proposal, 281
  Resource Constraint, 286, 287
  resource perspective, 286, 287, 289
  resources to select from, 284–285
  security permissions, 282
PPM. *See* Project portfolio management
Prioritization, 280–281, 285–286
Priority levels, project/task, 216, 218
PRO, meaning of, 9, 10
Professional edition, new features/functionality, 7–8
Project 2010. *See also* Project Professional 2010; Project Server 2010
  best practices and, 18–19
  names, reading of, 52–53
  PMBOK® Guide and, 17–18
  setting up, decisions, 25
  standard and professional editions, 7–8
Project 2010 Standard edition, 19
Project calendar, 25–33, 35–50
  Change Working Time box, 37, 40–43
  Copy Calendar option, 37
  defaults, 26
  New Calendar option, 37, 39
  night shift scenario, 26
  security, 31–32
  selecting new calendar, 45
  standard, as basis, 47
  task types, understanding, 28
  time zones scenario, 26–28
Project Center, 282
Project file
  built by project manager, 145
  creation/publication of, 145, 146
  published. *See* Publishing a project file
  saved to Project Server, 135
Project Information Box, 45
Project management
  maturity, 297
  term, 301
Project Management Institute, 280
Project Management Institute's Project Management Body of Knowledge (PMBOK® Guide), 17–18
Project manager
  resource manager and, 145
  viewpoint of, 6
Project portfolio management (PPM), 280–282
Project Professional 2007, 19
Project Professional 2010, 7
  Calendar created for, 49
  compared to Project Standard 2010, 8–9
  connecting to Project Server 2010, steps, 20–22
  PRO, meaning of, 9, 10
  and Project Server, 19
  reports. *See* Reports in Project Professional
  Resource Graph, 234, 235
  in stand-alone mode. *See* Stand-alone Project Professional
  views. *See* Views in Project Server
Project Server 2010. *See also* Automatic approvals; Project Web App (PWA); Reports in Project Server; Update cycle
  Administrator, recommendations, 35
  Assignment Work, 126, 127, 129
  capacity planning, 12
  custom fields, setting up, 114
  functional connection to installed, 19
  Global template for, 238
  improvements/key to changes, 11, 15
  Manage Users section, 218
  Outlook and, 164
  permission templates, 32
  Professional edition and, 7
  project file saved to, 135
  Project Web App (PWA) and, 22
  reports, Assignment Work by Resource, 131, 133
  resource management. *See* Resource management, Project Server
  and stand-alone Project Professional, 19
  Task page in, 131
  time and task management, 14–15, 191
  time entry types in, 169
  Timesheet Manager option, 60
  views. *See* Views in Project Server
Project server administrator. *See also* Time and Task Management
  administrative time/Always Display, 197, 200
  Administrative Time settings/options, 200–201
  business driver priorities, 285

Insert Row icon, Insert Administrative tasks, 200
proposal types and, 282
Publish Project box and, 136
Reporting Services report and, 268
timesheet setup/timesheet periods, 171, 186
Project Standard 2010, 8–9
Project success rates, 19
Project Web App (PWA), 22–23, 25. *See also* Server Settings
Business Intelligence link and, 275
Display, timesheet setup and, 192
newly assigned tasks, 139
Outlook and, 164
permission settings, 33
publishing project files and, 137
Reporting Services Reports link, 268
Resource Center, 74
resource updates and, 145
Server Settings, 35–37
task update/resource and, 150, 152
viewing tasks/security settings, 137
Proposal, 281
Proposed Booking Type, 58
Protect User Updates, Time and Task Management, 204
PTO. *See* Personal time off
Publishing a project file
Target URL line, 136–137
visibility of assignments and, 135
Publishing a project file to Project Server. *See also* Task list for resource
Create a site for this project radio button, 136
File-Publish, 135, 136
Publish button, 137
Publish Project box/SharePoint site, 135, 136
Publish Project box, 135–136
PWA. *See* Project Web App

Q

Questions
and answers, 293–300
to ask, 2–3

R

RBS. *See* Resource Breakdown Structure (RBS) filter
Related Assignments, Task Details, 141, 144
Remaining Availability graph, 131, 134
Remaining Availability option, 131, 133
Replace button, 130–131
Reporting Display, Time and Task Management, 201, 204
Reporting Services report, 267, 268–275
data-centric report, 270–271
delivery methods, 273–274
format selections, 275
icons within report display, 270
KPI report chosen, 269
link to list of available reports, 268, 269
Select All check box, 270
subscriptions option, 271, 273–275
visual items in report, 271, 272
when sent/parameters, 275
Reporting Services report type, 267
Reports in Project Professional, 249–261
Audit Tracking Solutions report, 250
Reports box, 249
Reports icon, 249
Visual Reports, 251–261
Visual Reports icon, 249
Reports in Project Server, 268–278
Business Intelligence report/link, 267, 275–277
Reporting Services report, 267, 268–275
security permissions, 268
two types of, 267
Resource(s). *See also* Assigning a resource
availability, non-project work and, 296–297
perspective of, 5
security and, 31
single source of information, 52–53
types of, 51–52
updates, line of authority and, 297–299
user and, 51–52
utilization, maximization of, 18
Resource Breakdown Structure (RBS) filter, 264
Resource calendars, 35, 73–88. *See also* Changing working time for one resource
generally, 73–74
Resource capacity, 18
Resource Center, 219–225
Assignment Work by Resource view, 221, 222
list of resources/selected resources, 219, 220
overallocations, 226. *See* Trainer example, Resource Center
Resource Availability icon, 219, 221
Units section - options available, 223
View Options - Date Range selected, 221, 223
Resource conflicts, 19
Resource Global file, 237
Resource Information box, 77, 79
Resource leveling, 209–218
box. *See* Resource Leveling box
generally, 209–210

Leveling Options icon, 212
Level Resource icon, 214, 215
Level Resources box, 214, 216
person icon, 210, 211
priority field, 216, 218
Project 3, Resource 1, 210, 211
project file changes, 216
Resource Leveling box, 212–214
system's algorithms and, 209, 216
Resource Leveling box, 212–214
automatically option, 213
check boxes, 213–214
manual option, 213
Priority, Standard option, 213
Resource management
generally, 1–4, 52–53
implementation of, 299–300
information availability and, 4
in Microsoft Project Server 2010, 13–14
perspectives of, 4–7
project management and, 297, 301
as valuable tool, 3
Resource management, Project Server, 13, 313–319
annually—items to check, 317–319
daily—items to check, 313–314
monthly—items to check, 315–317
weekly—items to check, 314–315
Resource manager
home page for, Update Cycle and, 154
project manager and, 145
role of, 5–6
Resource manager guide, 309–319
general philosophy, 309
Project Professional (Stand-alone), 310–319
Resource Names column, Build Team dialog box, 122, 124–125
Resource planning, 303–307
custom fields, 307
general philosophy, 303
setup and planning, 303–305
skill sets, planning, 305–307
Resource Pool
adding standard calendar, 85
Assignment Attributes, New User screen, 60
Booking Type, 58
Build Team dialog box and, 122, 123
Departments, 61
Enterprise Resources, setting up, 53
generic resource and, 113
Manage Users link, 55
New User link, 56
New User screen, 59–60, 63
PWA initial setup, details, 53, 57–58, 62
Resource Custom Fields, 61
Resource Global file and, 237
Security settings, 61, 62
Server Settings, 54
as single source of information, 53
for stand-alone/Server editions, 53
Resource Pool, stand-alone setup, 62–66, 101–104
Custom field for, 114
inserting a column, 65
new Resource Pool, 64
Open Resource Pool option box, 100
Save as option, 65
task assignment, drop-down method, 102
task assignment, recommended method, 103
team details, 63
Resource Pool, using, 66–72
both files open, 69
creating new project, 67
icons, server/local files, 68
instructions, detailed, 66, 71–72
Open Resource Pool pop-up box, 71
Pool takes precedence option, 71
Recently Used project list, 68
Share Resources option, 70
Share Resources pop-up box, 71
Use Resources from another file option, 66
Roles, 287, 290

S

Saving money, 293–294
Screenshots and images, 23
Security settings
Administrator and, 25
flowchart, 33
generally, 31–32
for Project Server views, 262
proposal entry, 282
for Reports in Project Server, 268
for timesheet, 172, 176
views of projects and, 135
Server project file icon, 68
Server Settings
Manage Users setting, 218
Manage Views link, 262
project calendars and, 35–37
PWA initial setup, 53
resource manager and, 309
tasks, timesheets and, 176, 191, 207
Setup and planning, 303–305
SharePoint, 135, 268, 273, 277
Share Resources option, 70
Share Resources pop-up box, 71
Sick time, 186, 197

Single Entry Mode, timesheet setup, 197
Single Entry Mode time entry, 171–186
  accessing, 171
  Add an Existing Task, 173, 176
  administrative time and, 178, 186
  Awaiting Approval status, 178, 185
  date range for timesheet, 172, 173
  dates/hours in 'Actual' row, 178, 182
  Line Classification, 173
  other time entry modes, 169
  project file tasks and, 172, 174
  security permissions, 172, 176
  Select from Existing Assignments section, 173
  Status bar/Pending Send Status, 178, 181
  Submit Timesheet Line pop-up box, 178, 184
  submitting single task, 178, 183
  Task Hierarchy, 173
  Task information, details, 178, 179
  tasks added to Timesheet, 177
  Timesheet entry screen, 178
  updating/saving task information, 178, 180
Skills, diverse set of, 19
Skill set, resource assigned by, 113–134. *See also* Build Team dialog box
  Add Field to Enterprise button, 116–117
  Assignment Work, 126, 129
  Assignment Work by Resource, 126, 127, 129, 131, 133
  Build Team from Enterprise option, 121
  custom fields, 113–115
  department positions and, 117, 120
  generally, 113–114
  Lookup table, building, 114
  Lookup table/*Position* field, 117, 118–119
  Remaining Availability graph, 131, 134
  Remaining Availability option, 131, 133
  replacing generic with named resource, 130–131
  Resource Names column/*Analyst* selection, 122, 124–125
  Text1 custom field, 114, 116
Skill sets
  planning, 305–307
  (Roles), 287, 290
SQL, 268
Stand-alone Project Professional, 19, 101–104, 310–319
  annually—items to check, 312–313
  daily—items to check, 310
  monthly—items to check, 311–312
  timesheets not available in, 169
  Update Cycle on, 164
  weekly—items to check, 310
Stand-alone Resource Pool, 225, 231–235
  free time to allocate, 234
  overallocation, 231
  project tasks and, 231, 233
  Resource Graph, 234, 235
  Resource Pool and, 231
  Resource Usage view, 231–234
Stand-alone schedule, changing working time, 49–50
Standard calendar, Resource Pool and, 85, 88
Standard edition, new features/functionality, 7–8
Starting a project, 3
Status Updates option, 152, 158
Subscriptions screen, Reporting Services report, 271, 273–275

T

Target URL line, 136–137
Task, assigning, 3
Task calendar, 35
Task change approvals, viewing, 158, 159
Task Change information, automatic approvals, 164, 166
Task list for resource
  Contacts section, Task Details, 141, 144
  Filter and Group By options, 141
  newly assigned tasks, 137, 139
  project file Test, 137, 138
  Related Assignments, Task Details, 141, 144
  Task Details/General Details, 141, 142–143
  task/project file correspondence, 139–141
Task page, Project Server, 131
Task Settings and Display, 201, 202
Task types
  examples of, 29–31
  understanding, 28
Task updates. *See* Update cycle
Team building. *See* Build Team dialog box
Team Planner, 104–113
  generally, 104
  overallocations, 104, 105, 110–113
  task details pop-up box, 107
  tasks, assigning, 104, 109
  Unassigned Tasks, 108–109
  Unscheduled Tasks, task in, 106
  View tab/Team Planner view, 104
Teams, globally dispersed, 18, 19
Technology, business processes and, 301
Time, tracking of, 299
Time and Task Management, Project Server, 14–15, 201–208
  Close Tasks to Update option, 207
  Define Near Future Planning Window, 204

Fiscal Periods screen, 207, 208
Protect User Updates, 204
Reporting Display, 201, 204
Time Reporting Periods, 204–208
Timesheet Adjustment screen, 207
Tracking Method, 201, 203
Time reporting, encouraging, 294–295
Time Reporting Periods, 191, 204–208
Create Periods, 205, 206
Define Batch Naming Convention, 205, 206
Define Bulk Period Parameters, 205, 206
Timesheet Adjustment screen, 207
Timesheet entry
importing time updates, 171
by resource, 170, 172
resource manager and, 170, 171, 173
Single Entry Mode, 171–186
by timesheet manager, 170–171, 172
workflow, 172
Timesheet functionality of Project Server, 60
Timesheet Grid Column Units, timesheet setup, 193
Timesheet options, history of updates, 152
Timesheet periods, generating, 186
Timesheet Policies, timesheet setup, 195–196
Timesheets, 169–208
entry. *See* Timesheet entry
generally, 169
Import icon, 189
Import Timesheet/Current Progress, 189, 190, 191
Manage Timesheets screen, 186, 188, 189
miscellaneous items, 186–191
setup. *See* Timesheet setup
Timesheet and Task entry method, 170, 189
Timesheet Settings and Defaults screen, 191, 192
Approval Routing, 196
Auditing, 196
Default Reporting Units, 193
Default Timesheet Creation Mode, 193
Hourly Reporting Limits, 195
Project Web App Display, 192
Single Entry Mode, 197
Timesheet Grid Column Units, 193
Timesheet Policies, 195–196
unverified timesheet lines, 196
Timesheet setup, 171, 186, 191–208
Settings in Project Server, 191
Timesheet Settings and Defaults, 191–192
Time zones, 26–28
Tracking Method in Project Server, 201, 203
Trainer example, Resource Center, 221, 223–225, 226–229
assignment details, 225, 228–229
only trainer selected, 223
overallocation, Date Range, 223–224
overallocation, graphical, 225, 226
project file and, 225
Resource Assignments icon, 225, 227
Types of tasks. *See* Task types

U

Unstructured time, timesheet setup, 196
Update cycle, 145–162
Accept/Reject/Preview updates, 152, 156
Approval Center screen, 152, 155, 157
change approvals, viewing, 159
Comment on Submit option, 150–151
confirmation box, 153, 156
generally, 145
message box, file changes and, 158, 159
percentage complete for tasks, 159, 161–162
percentage update method, 146, 147
Process Status/Awaiting Approval, 152, 153
Process Status/Not Submitted, 149, 150
Process Status/Task screen, 146, 147
Project Server and, 164
Project Web App and, 150, 152
Publish icon, 160
Publish submitted/queued, 159, 160
resource manager home page, 154
Save/Publish file/update, 158, 159, 160
saving task updates, 146, 148
Send Status icon, 150
for Stand-alone Project Professional, 164
Status Updates option, 152, 158
steps for, high-level view, 145–146
Submit Changes comment box, 150, 151
Task Name link/Task Details, 158, 159
Update cycle/approvals, 135–167
User(s)
resource and, 51–52
settings, security and, 31, 32
Utilization of resources, 219–235
Resource Center, 219–225, 226–229
Stand-alone Resource Pool, 225, 230–235
Standard calendar and, 85, 88

V

Vacation time, 186, 197
Versions, 8–9
Views in Project Professional, 238–248
adding column to view, 241–242
editing existing view, 244–248
More Views option, 238, 240
name of view, 238, 240

new view, creating, 242–244
Resource Sheet, 238, 239
Table information - Group and/or Filter, 238, 241
View Group, name of view checked, 238, 240
Views in Project Server, 262–267
drop-down, list of views, 264, 267
Filter section/Custom Filter, 264, 266, 267
Format View, 264, 265
Label fields, modifying, 264
main view, in Resource Center, 262
new columns/new view, 267
printing/exporting views, 262, 264
Sample Resource Data, 262, 264
security permissions, 262, 267
Table and Fields section, 262, 264, 265
Visibility and control, 18
Visio, 251
Visual Reports, 251–261
Create Report box, 251, 253
Excel Pivot Table, data behind, 257, 258
Excel/Visio template, selecting, 251, 254
PivotTable data, generic resources removed, 258, 260
PivotTable Field List, 251, 257
report sample, 251, 255, 256
selecting Create Report Box, 251, 252
updated information, 258, 261

W

WBS. *See* Work breakdown structure
Weekly tracking, timesheet setup, 193
Windows File Share, 273
Work breakdown structure (WBS), 303
Working time, changing. *See also* Changing working time for one resource
with Project Server, 35–45
without project calendar, 49–50
without Project Server, 47–50
Working Times option, 83
Work resources, 51